THE PRAYER OF MY LIFE

HOW GOD CHANGED ME IN SEVEN MONTHS

TONY PORTUGAL

I am deeply committed to reach out to those in need. Whether it be for prayer, biblical information, comments, or well-wishes. I'd love to hear from you! Contact me at: *ThePrayerofMyLife@gmail.com*   God Bless!

Copyright © 2010 by Tony Portugal.

Library of Congress Control Number: 2010902222
ISBN: Hardcover   978-1-4500-4737-1
              Softcover   978-1-4500-4736-4
              Ebook   978-1-4500-4738-8

All rights reserved. No part of this book may be reproduced or transmitted in any form or by any means, electronic or mechanical, including photocopying, recording, or by any information storage and retrieval system, without permission in writing from the copyright owner.

This book was printed in the United States of America.

To order additional copies of this book, contact:
Xlibris Corporation
1-888-795-4274
www.Xlibris.com
Orders@Xlibris.com
75444

Contents

Prologue 13

PART ONE

How It All Began 19
    Entrenched in Darkness 41

PART TWO

Discovering Myself within God 49
    Could It Have Been Jesus? 60
    Searching for God's Touch 66
    My Story of Understanding 92
    My Secret Place 103
    My Character Builder 106
    My Written Will 114
    Unexpected Change of Winds 119
    Empty the Bucket 124
    Through the Storm 131
    Love's Identity 143
    Dying in the Middle of an Inter "sex" tion 151
    Love and Fear 159
    Family United 163
    Beyond Myself 176
    Spiritually Recharged 189
    Receiving It All 194

My Continuing Journey 215
Further Than Expected 221

PART THREE

My First Writings in Prayer with God—The Principles 231
    The Choice of Change 238
    Choice of Influence 256
        The Influence of Christians 264
    Influence of Anger 270
        The Influence of My Love, Not Anger, but Passion 273
    Influence of Worries 281
        I Am Not Worried; I Am Troubled 285
    Influence of Patience 295
        I Am Not Impatient; I Am Eager for People to Understand 300
    Influence of Success 306
        I Am Influenced by Success,
        yet It Has Nothing to Do with Money 313
    Influence of Love 320
        My Story of Understanding 324
        You Are Not Bound in Such Circumstance 326
        God, Send me an Angel 328
    Influence of Children 332
    Influence of the Word 341
    Influence of Witnessing 352
        Evidence for Atheists 352
        Desperate for God 355
        What's Behind My Belief 358
        I Need Evidence 361
        God on My Mind 363
        God is an Illusion 364

God Is a Delusion 365
I Am Saved 370
Influence of the World 375
When the World Says We Can No Longer Speak of God
Confidently 378

CONCLUSION

On My Way Home 387

This book is dedicated to Delano Peña—I've been struggling within my own mind thinking about how we went wrong. It seems like yesterday when we were practicing sports; going through each other's closets, switching our clothes; making jokes and being the life of the party. We have shared in life experiences, many in which no human being should be a part of. I have traveled down a different avenue, on a road that has brought me life. I know that you think I have abandoned you, but honestly, I have been expressing a quiet strength—a strength that has been solely based on leaving everything behind, just so God could have all of me. I love you, my brother, and I die inside every time I hear that you are in jail, high, or hustling. We have been the eyes behind each other's heads our whole life, and the greatest way I could look out for you now is by going to God with the hope that you might follow. I know that you believe the streets are the only thing that you have, but believe me when I tell you the streets will always be the source that takes everything from you. Always remember that I love you, and you will always be in my heart and part of my prayers. I am going to God and will continue to go to God, but when the time is right, I will be coming back for you. This book is dedicated to you to show you that it is possible.

Acknowledgements

My inspiration has been solely based on a desire to know God. Throughout this journey there have been many people who have allowed me to find myself truly in Christ, with support, direction, love, time, and commitment. There are going to be so many people whom I will not acknowledge here, but whom I know beyond doubt have wished nothing but the best for me. My sincere apologies for not recognizing you individually, but always know that I am extremely grateful for your prayers and genuine care for my life. While I lie on the hood of my car and stare at the stars in the sky, I am elated and thankful for these specific people God has brought into my life.

Kathy Morales—my mother, on whom God has painted a picture of heaven for me, before I even knew there was one. Mom, thank you so very much for never giving up on me and continuing to feed my dreams with your devotion. I now realize that without your love I never would have come to know life. The stars remind me of your smile, because even in the midst of my dark reality your smile is what has expressed my only light for so long. Mom, it has been your love that has made me invincible to pain. It is your love that has kept me alive to experience life. Thank you.

Jim and Ada Goodwein—Grandma and Grandpa, you have been the key that has unlocked the prison doors that have kept me bound and broken for twenty-three years. I thank you so very much for being my support system and being the tears and voices that have persistently prayed on my behalf. I thank you for being the angels whispering in my ear, the arms of my comfort, and the shelter from my storm. Most importantly, I express my deepest gratitude to you for positioning the name of Jesus in my life. Thank you.

Charlie B. Sandefur—Granddaddy, I hear you. All night long I can hear you. I hear your voice leading me to a place where no man has been. I hear you all day fighting for me, keeping my adversary from crushing me. Granddaddy, I can hear you. While I sit in my room as if I am alone, I know that you are there—you are my study partner. Some days when I don't feel like reading, I can hear you sliding the Bible across my desk toward me. Granddaddy, I can hear you. Some nights when I am too tired to pray, it is your voice I can hear praying for me. When people claim that I am somebody I am not, I can hear you laughing in my defense—it brings a smile to my face. Whenever I feel like I am alone, Granddaddy, I can hear you. I hope that I am making you proud . . . I know that I am . . . because, Granddaddy, I can hear you.

Chris Kent—My cousin Chris, you are in my heart more than you know. I love you, and I hope you understand that you have changed my life. Without you, I would have never come to know me. I know that at times you may think that you are weak, but that is impossible, because you have made me so strong. Without you I would have never made it through the brokenness to see what God was knitting together in my life. I thank you because I know if it came down to it you would give me your last breath. I cannot wait until you come to the point in your life when you realize that you are more powerful than what the devil is telling you. I am going to be standing on the other side of the bridge waiting for you to cross over, so we can experience heaven together. You can do it. Become what your heart is pleading for you to be. I thank you for being such a major importance in my life, and most all, I love you.

My entire family—I thank each and every one of you for being a great encouragement on my journey. For everyone who has kept me in prayer, know that you have been in mine as well. And it's so true that it's when people don't want to hear what you have to say that God makes what you have to say be heard. I will know when every one of you has found God, because I will see your lives evolving into my prayer requests. Take faith for a ride, because with the right vehicle there is no telling where it may take you. I love you all, and I thank you for keeping me in your prayers.

Chris and Felicia Ganter—Your family has gained my heart. I cannot express in words how grateful I am that you have allowed me to live with you and your family, and for honoring your commitment to me as a friend. You have extended an uncommon generosity, and you have been my guide in a genuine friendship. It has been time that has revealed to me who my true friends really are. Even though we lived in different states for several years, being as close as we are, even miles apart we still managed to stand side by side. Your loyalty has run deeper than I could have ever asked. I owe you more than I could ever possibly give you. Be prepared for what God is about to drop in your life, it is going to change everything, and that is beyond knowing. You are the sort of person who has made my life more fun just by being in your presence. Thank you.

The Birge family—Chuck and Ms. Trina Birge, I am exceedingly grateful for having allowed me to live in your home when I had no place to go. It is difficult for me to find the words that best express my gratitude. You took me in during my times of feeling most empty, my times when nothing seemed comprehensible, and my times of feeling dry simply because I held my own pain aside. During my days of having nothing to eat, no money, and no desire, your family extended to me my greatest blessing in knowing there were actually people who cared for me. My love toward your family is oceans wide. Thank you for accommodating me, not just by making me feel like I was your special guest, but like a person who was part of the family. Thank you for resuscitating the very little hope I had left. I will be forever in your debt.

Monica and Patrick Norman—I cannot express in words how extremely grateful I am for both of you. Thank you for your dedication and commitment and striving past the possibility of the perfect outcome and into perfection. It is priceless to see how amazing God is, seeing firsthand the verification of how incredible and influential the presence of God can be in a single person's life. All of these countless hours have opened a secret wisdom that I never knew I had bound within me. Monica, thank you so very much for your precious time and being patient with me. Patrick, I especially thank you for your commitment and understanding of how important this entire transformation was for me. My experience in North Carolina has enabled me to take with me that there are some absolutely amazing people in this world. You both have been the confirmation that God does indeed send great people and, most importantly, friends into your life to help you on your journey. Thank you.

The Shue family—Thank you for all those great meals, and welcoming me into your home with generosity; the experience of my first country four-wheeling adventure while stalling out after every turn; and the Fourth of July BBQ, and almost lighting myself on fire with a guerrilla rocket. I have especially enjoyed our great Bible studies and deep discussions on the Word of God. You have truly found an everlasting friend in me. Thank you.

Brandon Warren-Gordon and Abel Frederic Jr.—Thank you both for standing up for me in the midst of persecution. Thank you for believing in me. Thank you for watching my back for so many years. Even when we have bumped heads, disagreed with one another, and have said some spiteful things to each other at times, we have always known that our love cuts deeper than those pitiless moments. Thank you both for being the friends who have maintained my hope. We have always said that *"when one of us makes it, we all make it."* I have gained access to something far more profound than anything this world can offer—God's love. I have made it! I am standing at the door, waving you both through. I just hope you will continue to follow me to understand exactly what I feel. Abel, I can remember all of those times sitting in your car, dreaming, reminiscing, and hoping that one day we wouldn't have to live the lives we were living. Brandon, I can remember all of our long trips up north, talking about what we would do if we no longer had to hustle. All of our visions have always been based on providing a way for our mothers to never have to work again. I have found "the way," and the only way. I know that our moms are proud of us all, and I am extremely proud of you both. Thank you for being closer than friends.

Pastor Benjamin and Stephanie May—Restoration Tabernacle, Concord, North Carolina.—*"Loving the hell out of people." www.Restorationtab.com*

Pastor Tom and Mary Ann Peters—Trinity Church International, Lake Worth, Florida.—*"20/20 vision—reaching the next generation." www.tci.org*

Pastor Dr. David and Yvonne Remedios—Trinity Christian Center, Forest Hill, Louisiana.—The Louisiana Outpouring—*"Providing an Environment*

That Is Conducive to the Growth, Development, and Reproduction of the Body of Believers."

www.tccministries.com
www.louisianaoutpouring.com

Bishop Tony Miller—Destiny World Outreach, International Ministry, Oklahoma City, Oklahoma—"*We don't really determine our destiny; we discover it!*" *www.destinywo.com*

Pastor Dale and Jean Gentry—Fort Worth, Texas—"*Let's Pray America!*" *www.letsprayamerica.com*

Pastor Diane Mann—Fourth Avenue International Worship Center, Fort Lauderdale, Florida.—"*Bringing Hope to a Hurting World.*"

Photos, including book cover, taken by Barbara Payne. *www.barbarapaynephoto.com.*

Finally, to everyone who said I would be nothing, you were right . . . forgive me for being the wrong person because the person God exposed I didn't know was in me. Thank you.

Prologue

> *The excitement of any person's future can certainly be measured by what the person has overcome from his or her past; even more fascinating is the belief in the power that promises the overcoming of that past.*

And the unpredicted reality that it can happen *within seven months*. Yes, God turned my world inside out within seven months.

I am twenty-four years old, and for twenty-three years I had no cause in life because I didn't know true life. I had never read a book up until this point, and the Bible would become my first. My terminology was plainly an extraction from the streets, and my conversations were never based on anything intellectual. I say this because what you will read is far from anything I've ever known. I was an unintelligent individual and an unwise decision-maker. I ignored every bit of my family's concern when they tried to spare my life. I put my entire hope in the devil's destruction without hesitation. I've walked down a dark, desolate alley where most will never walk in their entire life.

Do you want to know pain? Do you want to know retribution? Do you want to know about the death sentence of influence that controlled my life? Do you want to know the darkness and rage that took me into a realm of vengeance? Do you want to know about an athlete who at one point was ranked no. 104 in the nation, but destroyed that prospect because of a fight gone wrong at a nightclub? Do you want to know what being involved in over one hundred physical fights in the streets did to me? Do you what to know how the respect of counterfeit friends is established? Do you want to know what it is like to absolutely hate life and hate yourself in the process? I was no longer standing on the edge of defeat and suicide, but I took a nosedive off the highest tower of hopelessness and into a pit of impossible return. I walked directly into a death chamber of complete darkness, witnessing homicide, getting stabbed, and plummeting my way toward self-destruction through the drug movement, robbery, theft, and a mark of death that led me to an awakening of love. I went to kill a man . . . but ***instead Jesus interfered***.

The night I almost killed a man I cried out to Jesus for the very first time in my life, but for two years after that I struggled because I didn't know what Jesus was doing. I would try and do right, and then fall back into the same drug hole. I would try to get away from the bad influences in my life, and then get involved with them again. Yes, for two years I didn't realize what Jesus was doing, until He gave me a proposition that would absolutely change my entire life.

I knew I was down to my last lifeline, and if God was real, I would be the one to find out, because I was going to give Him everything I had and truly seek His face. And if I found no truth, then my life didn't have purpose anyway. I made the decision to give up my life in order to hopefully find where so many people claim life is—in Jesus. Then, something unexpected happened. Jesus brought me out of who I was and made me into who I never thought I could be. The transformation affected me so deeply that I threw over $100,000 in the garbage, because that's what Jesus told me to do.

There is not a person in this world who can tell me God is not real. There is not a person in this world who can tell me God doesn't care about you in spite of what you've done in your past. There is not a person in this world who can tell me that by giving God everything you have, He cannot change your entire life *within* seven months.

My story is a testimony to God's mercy and how He brought me to where I am at this point in my life. One of my main questions for Jesus was, "Where were you?" As God answered, He showed me that He was always in my life's interruptions, and He gave me a deeper knowledge of how He moves and develops transformation. Not only did Jesus take me back, but He also brought various angels and people with Godly insight into my life, at divinely appointed times, to encourage and teach me the Good News. The experience of this book was written with fear and with a page by page certainty of God's grace. The very things that God hates draw us to Him, which ultimately brings us to love Him. I was desperate to follow God's will and learned that we must also have a determined will, with an elevated capacity to know God and to seek what pleases Him. The confirmation of God Almighty in my life was established with conviction and a daily, crying repentance that led me to the Cross and obedience to God's Word, which enabled me to find my way Home. I now welcome the high waters. I welcome the oppression. I welcome the burdens. I welcome the pain. I welcome the suffering. I welcome the high walls. I welcome the mountains. I welcome the fire. I will welcome it all . . . if that is what it takes for me to get to You. Nowadays, you can't convince me that Love doesn't love me. It is the time you spend alone with God that demonstrates that your life is never without God. Giving God every moment of your existence is not sacrificing your life; it is rightfully using it. Allow God to take you beyond the valley through the brushes of the wilderness just to pitch a tent on the far side of the desert, finding yourself in a prayer that builds an everlasting barrier where life's opposition trembles at your voice. While proclaiming the revelation in the city of refuge, mysteries begin to manifest while you speak. The calling of God is not an invitation for contentment; it is a preparation that will prepare you for war! As the world comes tumbling down, you will have an option: either to move forward into the wreckage, screaming for others to run while you risk your life to save those lost, or be part of the people who are running away from the wreckage, while others are risking their lives.

This book is based on the evidence in my life that I have encountered God through His infallible Word. My affirmation—the Word of God—is the greatest implication of truth! I am not the author of my existence; I am the biography to the Author's will. God became my best friend, plainly because I wanted to love everything He loved. Yes, God took me back not to my original condition, but to His original intention. All of this happened simply because I found myself—***in the prayer of my life***.

The arrangement of what is written is not in chronological order. It is written how God has given it to me, bringing me back to certain instances in my life, encouraging me and then changing me. If it seems like a roller coaster of change, good! You can experience what I went through in my seven months with God.

The bold phrases, quotes, poems, free verse and watchwords are my authentic words and are written as given to me by God. They are original and only separated because of their significance and to give clarity and divine motivation.

Throughout the portion of the book that chronicles my life story, you will notice that specific scriptures are referenced in parenthesis. Each reference refers to that particular message of the story. However, the references are left without the verses inserted with hopes that you might find it worthwhile to open the greatest source of power that your life will ever have—the Bible. Find it worthwhile to open your Bible and create a foundation of consistency in which your entire life will be unveiled. There is only one source that can change your natural condition, and that is the Word of God.

If you truly want to change your very nature, your ability "to-do," receive confirmation of God's existence, and obtain a power that only manifests through faith—I dare you to believe!

> My people are destroyed from lack of knowledge . . .
> (Hosea 4:6; KJV)

> Study to show thyself approved unto God, a workman that
> needeth not to be ashamed, rightly dividing the word of truth.
> (2 Tim. 2:15; KJV)

> Jesus answered and said unto them, Ye do err, not knowing
> the scriptures, nor the power of God. (Matt. 22:29; KJV)

> And even as they did not like to retain God in their
> knowledge, God gave them over to a reprobate mind, to do
> those things which are not convenient. (Rom. 1:28; KJV)

Part One

How It All Began

To understand why I am so happy, you must first understand where it is I've come from. I was born into a preprogrammed atmosphere of *"unlikely probability"* in South Florida, in the summer of 1984, and yes, right away it began. By no means could I ever understand what state of mind a man must dwell in to destroy his very own cause for life. Children soak in trails of water left behind by its maker, agreeing with whatever the water may be. ***A flood begins with a single puddle***.

My father was a malicious, intolerable, painful human being who hated the very ground he staggered on. He was a product of criminal dominion whose pursuit in life was not to provide for his family, but to gain respect among his allies. The red that scorched upon his tearless eyes created dry soil for the sprouting of his seeds. My growth was unproductive because my father's idea of raising a kid was not traditional; it was more physical, like *"by your throat."* As a child, I understood, without being taught, that the result of any form of resentment was pain, which ultimately became an awakening for my slumbering hate. The same anger that prowled around in him began to expose itself in me as a youth. You would think this would give reason for discipline, but unfortunately my father praised his baby boy. My oldest sister was unlucky in a good number of my father's feuds; she was his focal point for lashing out. I guess when you're at the bottom of the *"opinion line"* in the streets, you advert your frustration and release it in your own home. Through the darkness of this time lingered not only my siblings, but also my mother, whose inner beauty was deeply coated by violence and confusion. My mother had minimal options, and so she chose to lean on a man who was already in the course of diminishing. My mother has always been the angel wandering in the midst of my eyes.

Moreover, she is a heroic angel, brave in the coming battles, but battles a woman should never partake in.

When I was young, my father continuously and aggressively abused not only my siblings, but his "other half" also. My mother was smothered with unjust words by my father's family as she tried in vain to explain the ordeal she and her kids were enduring day after day. Her in-laws uttered in disgust, "Women serve men. What he is doing is out of love, and you need to shelter it and take it. We all do." My mother is far from inferior; in the disarray of battle, she covered us in the corner of her own home and, indeed, sheltered us, as my father shattered glass over her. Her covering protected us from injury. My mother then stood her ground and demanded he leave. As he turned, he looked over his shoulder with a smirk on his face as if to say, "Ha," but in that very moment joy never felt so good.

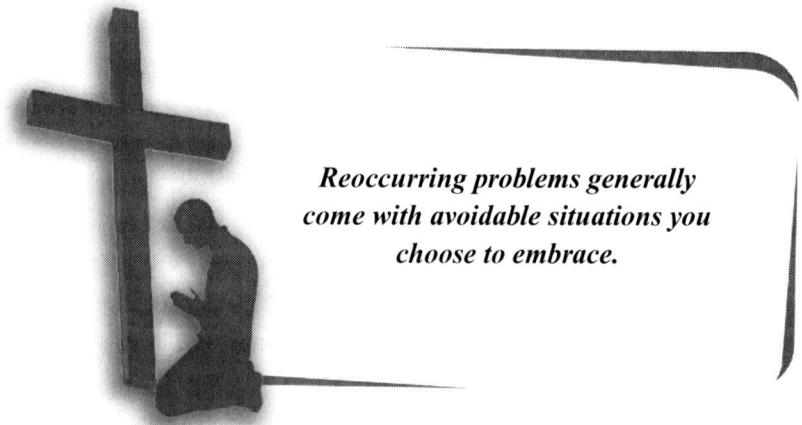

Reoccurring problems generally come with avoidable situations you choose to embrace.

As time went by, my mother married again and found herself enslaved to comparable mishaps, marrying a man who argued with himself over happiness, peace, and enjoyment. As a young boy, I fell in love with my stepfather, whom I considered to be a real father. Was he in reality unsurpassed? Perhaps, I considered him to be so real because he was a better father than the one I knew. Slowly, this man began destroying his family in the process of destroying himself. My stepfather would badger my mother for doing motherly gestures, yet he was very diligent in searching for life's advantages, but advantages that would usually only benefit him. I remember overhearing a conversation with one of his friends about how he was going to purchase a Mercedes one day. I leaned over and jokingly said, "That means I'm going to be able to drive it one day?" His reply was, "Umm, *nope*, what's mine is mine, and you won't be anywhere near my stuff." I don't think he understood, but in that split second he completely trampled on the idea of the father-son connection I thought we had, and that I had always been holding on to.

You know, I am yet to find any suitable reason as to how the devotion of love can be isolated from a parent's natural compassion. My stepfather discontinued the relationship with my sister and restricted all communication with her over a negligible incident, an incident that still burdens my conscience. My stepfather was consumed by the persuasion of people's opinions, and he was easily provoked. Gambling became his fortress until he lost it all, but it was in the abuse of alcohol where he would eventually meet his demise. Given that my stepfather was influenced by his intake, he created a wall between himself and my mother to avoid giving her any sympathy, and this was a wall that enabled him to drown himself in his own pity.

Because of this, my mother was evicted from two homes, had cars repossessed, and became financially unstable. I loved this man from the bottom of my heart, but I never realized how bad it hurt to want a relationship with someone who was unable to see the pain that he was causing. I remember as a kid being on the baseball field on picture day when he lost control of his anger and slammed me on the ground in front of everyone in the recreational area. *It was not discipline; it was more like frustration.* Yet I loved this man too much to hate him. I remember going fishing with my stepfather, and he was consuming alcohol against my mother's approval, and mine at that. At an earlier period he swore to never drink alcohol again because of the effect it had on him. I bit my lip, held my anger within, and never told my mother because *I knew alcohol would destroy my family*. Yet I loved this man too much to hate him. He abandoned my oldest sister just like 95 percent of the men in her life had, and he became another reason for her wavering confidence. *My sister, his daughter, a child, didn't deserve to know the pain of disloyalty.* Yet I loved this man too much to hate him. Before my mother decided to leave him, I waited up all night for him to come home just to ask him, *"Why, why do you not care?"* He said, "I am who I am, and I will not change for your mother." I said, "*She is an amazing woman who doesn't deserve to be treated the way you treat her.*" He gently said, "You're right, but I can't help it, and I don't know why. I am going to die the way I want to, and no one is going to tell me any different." I cried in front of my stepfather because my heart was throbbing. I got up, went into my room, and screamed, "I hate him! I hate him! I hate him!" No . . . I love him to much to hate him. Again, in the same lifetime, my family had to start all over.

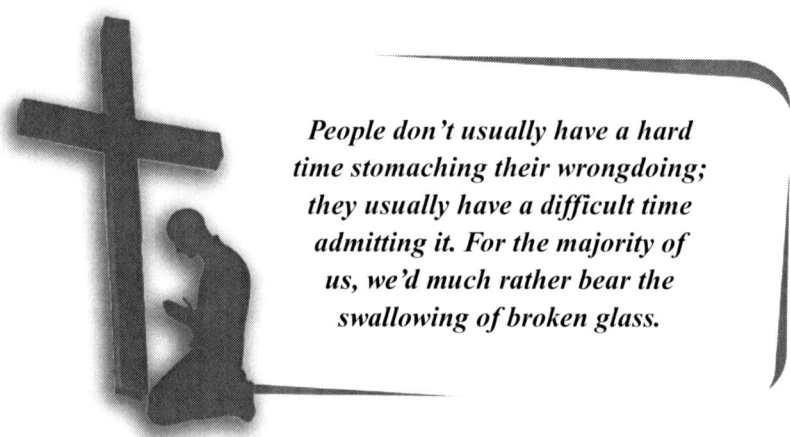

People don't usually have a hard time stomaching their wrongdoing; they usually have a difficult time admitting it. For the majority of us, we'd much rather bear the swallowing of broken glass.

Throughout this period in my life, I developed the very thing that I despised—a force of anger, an anger that affected my way of living (Ps. 37:8). My only solution to have an abundant life was the street mentality, "Get what you want and take what they don't give." I built a group of destructive people around me and withdrew into a tunnel of darkness, assuming it would simplify my life. There was something that always tried to pull me back. I felt as if something or someone had a grip on the back of my shirt trying to drag me out of my despair (Job 33:16-18). Unfortunately, my mind was so full of malice, and I was so self-involved that I was choking myself into believing that the only method for me to breathe was to "*get respect.*" My hands were a tool of development for my fury, and I became accustomed to fighting and the hype that shadowed around it. What initially ignited my fury was a period of time in elementary school when my mother and stepfather separated because of his alcohol problem. That separation also had the effect of crushing my composure. It impacted me immensely, and that week I had a stain of tenderness within my heart. I can remember so clearly, as I was on the handball court after school one day, when this kid walked directly into my bottled emotions . . . I exploded on him like shattered glass! My teacher knew something was wrong with me because it was outside of my normal behavior. What made it even worse was that in the same week I picked up a rock and hit another kid square between the shoulder blades while we were on the blacktop, simply because he was getting on my nerves. I would fight because fighting would empty out everything that had built up inside of me, and it felt good to be noticed (Prov. 7:7). In high school, people would actually pay me to fight for them, dropping a hundred dollars in my face to deal with their problems. I remember walking into a house party and dragging a kid I was paid to handle out to the street and leaving him unconscious. I turned, walking back to my car with new friends and with his raggedy wallet that only had two measly dollars in it. The more I fought, the more free I felt. The baggage of "friends" that I carried with me was more like promoters for my temper. What influenced me was based on my affluence of friends . . . *"the power of the dollar."* As long as we made money together, we loved each other no matter who we had to go through to get it (1 Cor. 15:33). Jail and intervention programs never opened my eyes too much; they only seemed to broaden my ego to continue with the life I was living. I was stimulated by stealing cars and using them as a momentary luxury. My sister's boyfriend secretly told my mom that I was running the streets and stealing cars, but he was no good himself, and his word wasn't honorable against mine. Time didn't make me smarter; it put me more on edge. I was robbing people at times for less than what I had in my own pocket and invading homes in search of material I could pawn. My own family had difficulty understanding how I obtained my money, considering I didn't have a job. I experienced many low times in my life when a burden weighed on my heart because of what I was doing, but the more I tried to stop, the less I felt I had. I gambled for extra cash, which led me into selling dope and the process of breaking it down and doubling my money. My audacity was flirting on the borders of daring and dim-wittedness because of my decision to sell on school grounds. My situations and temper were bringing me down the fast track to nowhere. My only places of peace and collectiveness were being on the baseball diamond and being around my family.

Baseball was my way to compose myself and get away from the streets for periods of time. It was a platform for me to be seen as something worthy of discussion. It took me down an avenue of difference within my own soul. I was nationally ranked every year after my freshman season. I was invited to every major showcase and rated 9.8 out of a possible 10 for professional probability. By my senior year I was nationally ranked no. 104 and ranked no. 20 in the state of Florida. I was rated no. 7 in high school flamethrowers throwing 94 mph in Team One Baseball and rated no. 9 in the Top Prospects Underclassman Showcase. Overall, my projected round in the 2003 draft was 5 through 7.

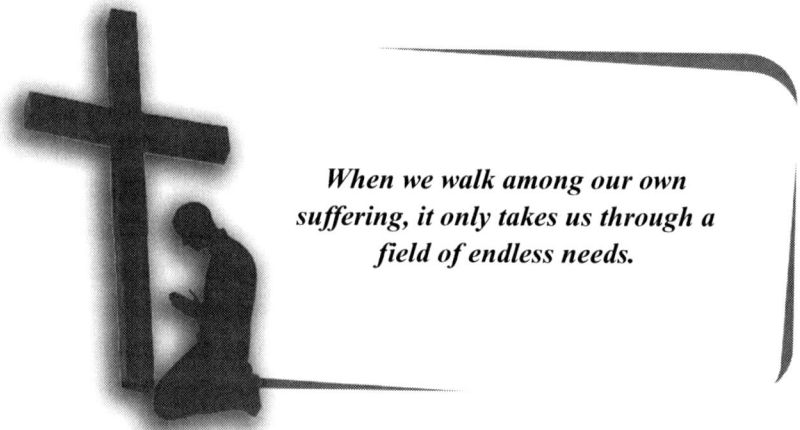

When we walk among our own suffering, it only takes us through a field of endless needs.

I yearned for that Friday night aroma of the freshly cut grass and that lingering smell in the outfield of the grill cooking Ball Park hot dogs. I eagerly awaited the anticipation of the cheers as the bleachers were filled with parents, students, and scouts, forming a confidence of character while hearing my name over the speakers as the announcer gave it life; huddling as a team between innings for support and encouragement, building a chemistry of strength and unity; listening to that perfect sound of the ball dinging off the sweet part of the bat; motivated by the umpires roar pitch after pitch; addicted to the feeling of crossing over the white lines into a battleground of prestige; idolizing myself within some kid's favorite baseball collection; and dreaming of waking up with an entirely different reality. Baseball was my one-way ticket taking me far away from the difficult life I was accustomed to living and experienced off the field. Sadly enough, it was my off-the-field experience that affected that hopeful ticket arrangement. I didn't go in the top seven of the 2003 draft. I was picked up by the Atlanta Braves late in the second day, because apparently I was considered to be an unwanted risk because of my off-the-field reputation. I took the *"draft and follow"* deal, meaning I was still legally part of the Braves program, but I would go to junior college for a year and the numbers I put up would determine how much I would receive in a signing deal. My freshman year in college started to break apart quicker than I could get it back together. Again, I found myself selling drugs while getting into several fights, and in my stupidity, I even tried to go at two of my coaches. My anger was uncontrollable; I couldn't even hold on to who I thought I was as an athlete. I took a cycle of steroids to try and increase my velocity on the mound. All it really did was make me more hotheaded and even more infused with hatred. Steroids became the ruin of the only chance of purpose I ever held onto. I was released from the Braves after that season.

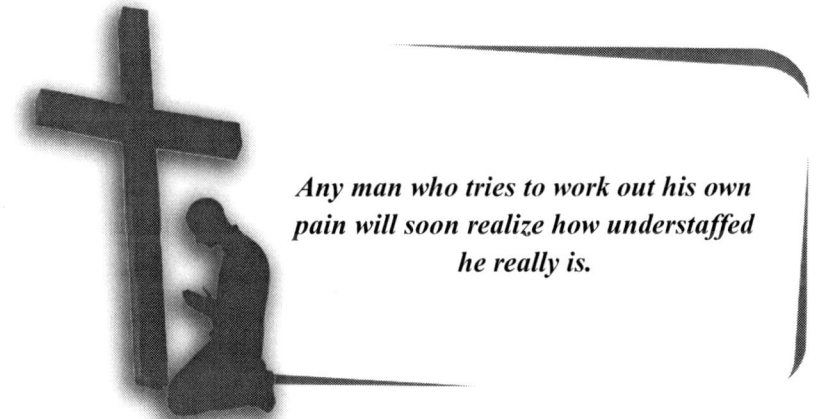

Any man who tries to work out his own pain will soon realize how understaffed he really is.

Now, this is where my future of baseball, in five minutes, became simply a history of worthless expectation. Up until this time I have been misleading people, and even worse my family, into thinking it was a baseball injury that ended my career. I was leaving a nightclub with two of my friends, and as one of my friends fell behind, a guy stuck his head out of his car window and said some ignorant things to him. We ran over to their car as it came to a stop, and they jumped out of the car as quick as we got there. I threw one punch, which evidently did not land in my favor, and I hyperextended my elbow while knocking the guy out. When I got into the car, I knew something wasn't right. The effects of steroids and fighting apparently don't mix too well, and they caused me to tear ligaments and tendons in my elbow (Jer. 44:29). Baseball and my love for the game were now in the shadows behind me. My family didn't know the extent of what I was involved in because I was a completely different individual around them. My family was the opposite side of a mirror that kept me from actually seeing and being me. People could not talk to me because I didn't want to be talked to. I didn't trust many people, and I opened up to a select few. I was involved with some wonderful women at different periods in my life who chose the wrong person to be with at the wrong time. I was a selfish individual who was a prison guard to their own individuality. I harnessed their choice of expression with my persistent requirement of who I wanted them to be. I was the cause of their lockdown, going out night after night while leaving them lifelessly sitting at home. I couldn't be a shoulder to cry on, because I disregarded emotion. My outline of love was not based on communication, because I based everything on my own outlook, and I was the only voice that was relevant. I wasn't the dreamy boyfriend; I was the "learning experience" boyfriend. I used women as a crutch for my own self-pity and began to use them as a buoy while I was taking myself under. There was an assortment of trouble that came with being me. I was ignorant, rude, and stuck in my own ways (James 3:16). The person I thought I loved, I began to hate so much. There were so many times I would sit on the edge of my bed clinching my hair with my hands and just wish I wasn't alive. I would literally yell at myself, grind my teeth, smother my face in my hands, and repeatedly demean myself, telling myself, "*I hate you*." I would cry alone in the dark because no one could see me. I would pace back and forth shadowboxing my pain. The times when I would go out, it seemed like the world didn't even notice me, as if they were able to just walk right through me. What I saw in the mirror made me so angry. My image became a glimpse of a withdrawing hope for my life. Everything about my past started to impact me because I took my frustration out on innocent people who just happened to be at the wrong place at my wounded time. The direction I was going in life started to dissolve any possibility for sanity or reason for me to go on. I balled up my emotion, which absorbed more complexity for life. I did not want to live! The only strand of worthiness I felt for allowing myself to live was my mother. That strand, believe it or not, was built with the toughest substance in life—*love*. "Where do I go and what do I do?" I asked myself that daily as if I was pleading with myself for a solution and direction. Not only was I lost in my own mind, but I was also lost in my own way. It wasn't that I hadn't been searching for a new route; it was more like I always ended up going back to what I knew because searching left me misplaced and confused.

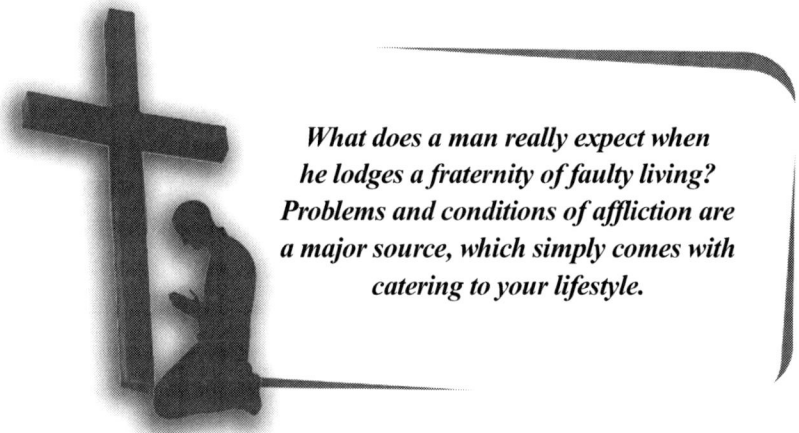

What does a man really expect when he lodges a fraternity of faulty living? Problems and conditions of affliction are a major source, which simply comes with catering to your lifestyle.

As time went on, I secluded myself more and more, and in 2006 my foundation finally started to crack. My mother was struggling with life and with questions that were difficult even for me to understand. "Why does a woman who is so amazing and who would give her last dollar to help someone in need have to endure countless downfalls and hardship?" It was as if my mother, who was like a dove leading many people into their enjoyment, just had her wings clipped. I too disapproved of life, but I held my disapproval within and tried the best I could to give light to my mother throughout this dark time (Job 19:4). I convinced myself to go back to college for one more season of baseball, in spite of not having picked up a ball since my fight injury. The main reason for returning to ball was not for me. If I could have a good season against the odds, maybe, just maybe, I could get a signing bonus, help my mother financially, and let her find some strength within me. During this time I didn't have any place to go, so instead of worrying my mother, I told her I was going to stay with a friend. This friend of mine just happened to be a parking lot close to the baseball complex. Before night would fall and the doors would close at school, I would nonchalantly find my way into the locker room and shower, then head back out to my car and wait for the same day to start over. Sometimes I would go days without eating, or just eat a pack of crackers to get me through the day. Eventually, I did go and stay with a great family who welcomed me in and helped me out generously. Something strange began to occur during the start of fall conditioning. I couldn't keep up, but I figured it had been a while since I ran to this degree, and I assumed I was simply out of shape. Each day, however, that strange feeling developed into a throbbing pain. I could barely finish the conditioning assignments, coming in last every time. Then at one practice, I went to pick up a ball and couldn't bend down to get it. That same day we got word that the college I was attending would be closing down because of Hurricane Katrina. So I decided to head up north to where my mom was living in Palm Beach, Florida, and would wait the storm out there. I didn't tell anyone about the extent of the pain I was feeling in my legs until I got up in the middle of the night and I could barely make it to the bathroom. When I finally made it there, I found myself with an overwhelming surprise . . . my urine was pitch black! Literally pitch black! When my mom got home from work, I explained to her what happened, and she became very worried and immediately took me to our primary doctor. He looked at the urine sample and without delay said, "Go check into the hospital, and I'll be right behind you." At that moment, I knew something was serious. My mother took me over to the hospital and helped me into the waiting area. The doctors began to run some tests, and the pain in my legs was at the point to where I truly felt like a semitruck was parked on them. Yes, very nerve-racking! A few of the hospital's head doctors came in and out looking at my chart, then looking at me, which seemed very odd. One of the doctors said, "*We are admitting you*," and then walked out. My mother and I just kept looking at each other wondering what in the world was going on. A doctor then came in, accompanied by a nurse, and said we can't disclose the problem to you, but your primary doctor is on his way here, and he will explain to you in detail what has happened. Now we were even more worried! Once my primary doctor showed up, he explained that I had what was called rhabdomyolysis and that my creatine phosphokinase (CPK) levels were extremely high. He said, "High enough to where the other doctors don't know how you walked in this building today." He explained to us that based on my muscle mass and age a level of 900 is considered to be high, a level over 8,000 is a case for a heart attack, and anything over 10,000 will cause muscle disease and/or organ failure. He said, "Right now your levels are way beyond 40,000, yes, 40,000." The doctor explained that based on my body type my CPK levels were so high that I was literally "*a dead man walking.*" My levels indicated muscle, liver, kidney, and/or brain damage. Either way rhabdomyolysis was causing my body to start shutting down, a body that, according to the doctors, should have been far worse. Even at the peak of a heart attack CPK levels are reached in about eighteen hours, and then return to normal in twenty-four to thirty-six hours. After two days my CPK levels had not decreased, but had increased. Throughout that first week I literally could not even place a thin sheet over my legs, because it caused me so much agony. The National Hospital reports that there are less than twenty-six thousand cases annually of rhabdomyolysis. It is also found in 24 percent of adult patients who come to emergency departments with cocaine-related conditions. Rhabdomyolysis is believed to be responsible for 25 percent of all adult cases of acute renal failure, and coincidently, one-third of adult patients with rhabdomyolysis develop renal failure. My case of rhabdomyolysis was labeled as "muscular trauma and crush injuries" and less than 15 percent are put strictly under that category. Statistically, I was in a very small category with a high stake for life-threatening potential (Job 5:18). I was kept in the hospital for two weeks, and funny enough in those two weeks only one friend came to visit me during that time.

Around this time is when my mother left my stepfather, which undeniably left her in a broken state. She literally left with nothing to her name and moved in with her parents. My mother being everything to me, her pain naturally caused me pain. In that sense, the lesion of continuous sorrow and dividing loyalty that was happening to my mother within this short span began to reveal to me that this situation was too much for me to hold and bear. If drying my mother's bottle of tears was solely based on someone trying to get my attention, it was working.

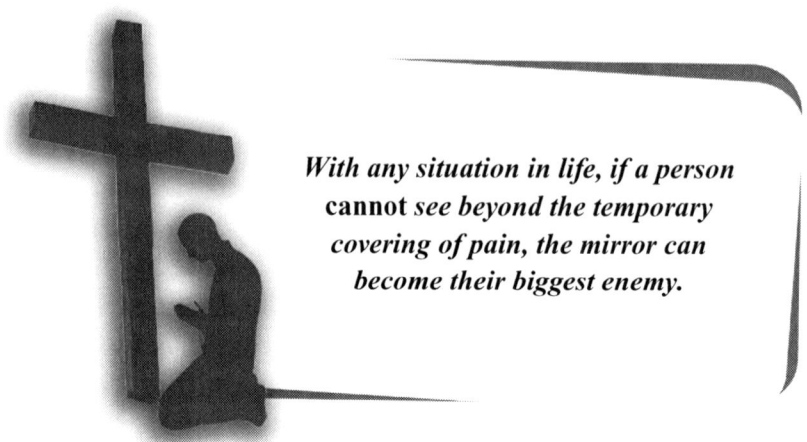

*With any situation in life, if a person **cannot** see beyond the temporary covering of pain, the mirror can become their biggest enemy.*

My entire world would change as I helplessly watched a man hit and drag my mother down the street with his car because she was trying to protect her children. That night I spoke with some friends, who supportively accepted the proposal to go to this man's job and put him into a situation where he would have no choice but to plead for his life. As the hours passed, time began to make the men I was with uncomfortable, and unfortunately I was unable to the see the torture in his expression of misery.

The second night after the incident, sleeping in the spare bedroom at my grandparents' house, I woke up late drowning in my own sweat, hearing something repetitive playing over and over in my head. "Look at your family turning against you! You have to kill this man. Go! Kill this man!" Sometime after midnight I grabbed an old hunting knife, jumped into my car, and drove to a lot that was directly in front of his home. At this point, my feelings were dead and my eyes were bleeding red. I had no conscience, and this man was going to die tonight! As he sat in his car, shuffling through what seemed to be paper, I turned off my car light and silently opened my car door. With his back turned, I planned to grab him and whisper the sweet hate I felt for him into his ear, as I brought his life to an end in the most inhumane way possible. Suddenly, I heard the message tone on my phone go off. I picked up my cell phone to listen to a voice mail and realized that the message had been left for me earlier in the day. I don't know why I just received it, and oddly enough, I can't even explain why I *had* to listen to the message at that moment. My heart stopped as I listened to the only heaven I knew. I heard my mother's voice pleading with me not to do anything stupid. My mother's intuition was an alarm of concerning favor, an intuition I believe all mothers feel. I froze! I sat there on the edge of my seat, watching this man walk into his home as if he had peace, yet I didn't. My eyes started to puddle with tears, and my lips started to quiver. The one woman I would give my life for just told me to hold on to my life and not to lose it. I went back to my grandparents' home and went into the bathroom. I started to cry out to the name my grandparents held as the Savior of their life. I can't tell you half of what I said, but I was crying out, "I'll do anything You want, anything! I'll do whatever, whatever! I cannot do this anymore. Are You real?" (Isa. 45:22).

> *If you were to look into my eyes you would have seen a heart chained to the wall.*
> *Hanging in the same darkness where hope falls.*
> *Bondage!*
> *To explain the pain is beyond this. To be honest, I am in a condition where my belief is godless.*
> *You would have seen faith shackled at the feet.*
> *A face despised and smothered with defeat.*
> *A face confined and a feeling of life without a beat, excuse me, a beat confined only to the sound of where chains cling.*
> *Slowly dying, this is what my days bring.*
> *Dazing, in the dark.*
> *Out of my last breath I plead, Lord, why is it so hard?*
> *A voice speaks, I hear you and I am not that far.*
> *There is pain in love, but I am not that part.*
> *I am pure love, trying to make myself the stain of your heart.*
> *My beloved,*
> *Go,*
> *you are free,*
> *and I will put Myself in place of where you are.*

After crying out to Jesus to save my life, I spent the next two years in a fight with the devil, who undeniably immersed me in every temptation I was vulnerable to. I was a manufactured good for the devil's amusement. He knew my weakest position, along with my most familiar enticement, and apprehended me every time. Between 2006 and 2008, I would pick up the Bible to read it, but it seemed to be written in a completely different language and in a context that was way above my intellect. I struggled to comprehend the Bible and even tossed it on a shelf to collect dust simply because I assumed the Bible didn't make sense to me. I tried to pray often, but my prayers became repetitive and did not really come from my heart. My prayers were not accompanied by faith, but they were enclosed with hope. There was one temptation in my life that I could not shake easily, and that was the means by which I made money. My state of mind was fixed on a *"hustle or be hustled"* perspective. I was taught that *"scared money, don't make money."* You have to give it to get it, and how you get it . . . is nobody's concern. You see, making money became easy because of the young crowd that wanted to be a part of our circle. We called them "birds," because they were the lookouts that easily blended in with the surroundings. Even during police interrogations we weren't held for too long just because of the statement *"I sneezed at the light,"* which means "I didn't see anything." Money constructed a root of bitterness and greed in my life.

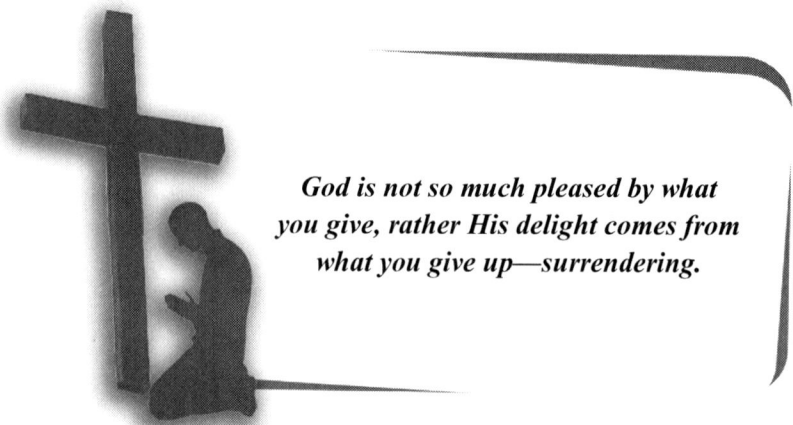

God is not so much pleased by what you give, rather His delight comes from what you give up—surrendering.

I created a business that I personally saw as a potential way to gain financial freedom. In those two years, my business became more of an expense than a successful venture, but I was still going to fight for what I wanted. It was an Internet-based business that took off extremely fast but began to slow down because I didn't have the money to support it, but the problem was that fast cash was my acquaintance. For the majority of us we live our lives in "particulars" having our particular hell, and our particular heaven. I feel as if I am a failure as a parent—my particular hell. So I am going to drink myself into an intoxication—my particular heaven. I cannot stand my job—my particular hell. So I bring my frustration home and release it under my own roof—my particular heaven. I don't have money—my particular hell. But I know how I can get it—my particular heaven. So I got back into selling dope. This business, I would later find out, actually became an awakening for my progress with God. One particular incident I remember that established my view in *"there is only one genuine direction"* was a conversation I had with my granddaddy as he was awaiting his celebration with the Lord. He said, *"Tony, there is a road God is trying to put you on, and you're failing to stay on it. In life you have two roads to choose from, God's road or the devil's road. Both are extremely hard. The devil's road may seem a lot clearer at times and may delude you into thinking there is promise on that road, but when you go far enough, you end up at a dead end with no reward or turning point. The road with God is hard and only seems hard because you're being prepared for what is ahead of you on that road. When you go far enough, you receive purpose. It is a road that never ends, and you'll never want to turn from it because of its reward. You have something in your possession that will keep you from God's road . . . you choose which road you want to be on"* (Matt. 7:13). I admire my granddaddy and value his opinion. My granddaddy saw something in that book he would always read that spoke volumes beyond natural ability. What was in that book? Who was in that book? What is my granddaddy moved by? What has stirred up the passion in his heart? My granddaddy would sit with such intensity reading the same book day after day, year after year, and to him it just never seemed to get old. Why? There was an elegant manner to my granddaddy's life—you serve those who shape your life. My granddaddy's standard for living was hand packaged in letters of red. My granddaddy was different, and if you would have had a chance to ask him why he was so different, he would have said, "because I serve an eternal Word that is changeless." In that book I saw something in red that deeply impacted me. I saw the words of a Man who cared very little about His own well-being, but cared more for the well-being of man. Right in the middle of those letters written in red, a power beyond comprehension is given. Inside my granddaddy's favorite book, I was introduced to a Man who took one look at a low, defiled kid, put His arms around my life, and said *be afraid no more*. In that moment, I saw and felt heroism pull me back into humanity—a truth so unveiled that only the eyes of blind belief could not see. Lord, please, give me what you have given my granddaddy. Let me see what he sees. Let me hear what he hears. Help me to believe! It is time for me to return to my origin, to return to who I was intended to be, who I now desperately want to be! I need the hands of God over my life, why, because you can never destroy anything a man holds as long as what he holds is rooted in faith. My granddaddy was no forged replica of Christianity, but a life lived in the context of true Christianity. I hear the drum line playing in my head while hearing my granddaddy's voice saying, *On Earth you get a one-way pass. What will your time here show? You have one chance in this life to do something worthwhile, and the biggest impact you will make in your own life begins with choice.* Right after that conversation I went outside, opened my trunk, and looked into a cardboard compartment where I had broke down bags of dope waiting to pride the devil's persuasion in distribution. I called a friend and told him I had to get rid of it and that I didn't want to have anything to do with drugs anymore. He said, "Give it to me and go to God." That would be the last time I ever sold drugs.

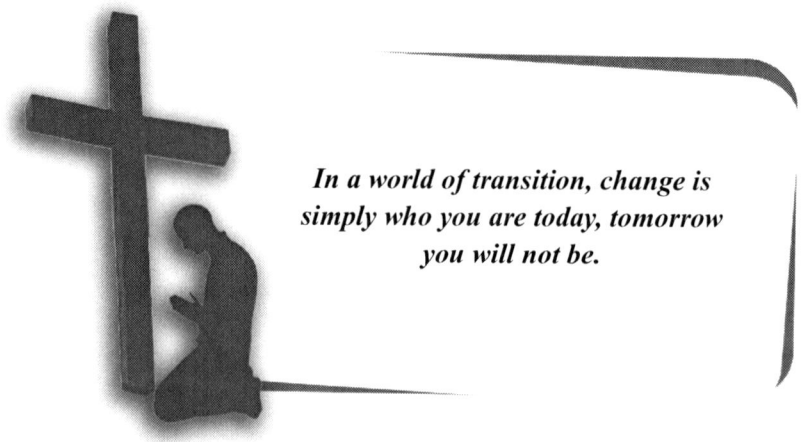

In a world of transition, change is simply who you are today, tomorrow you will not be.

Now, I was thrown into an uncommon position where I wasn't in a physical fight anymore, but clearly a mental and spiritual fight with myself. This fight intensified, the more I desired God's deliverance, and it became more of a battle against the devil's army, only I was standing on my own. Although I had so many faults still in my life, the main source of my destructiveness was slowly being dealt with. I continued to fight for myself in hope that there was a God. My granddaddy's passing led me into a closer relationship with my cousin who began to open a door that had been locked in my mind. Behind that door was the first direction to God. My cousin got me into the 4th Avenue International Church in Fort Lauderdale, Florida, and this is where I started to go to church on a regular basis. This church began to expose the Word of God to me, and the preacher, Pastor Dianne Mann, taught me the importance of a foundation in Jesus. I was now very curious. As I began to read more of my Bible, my ability to understand began to be less problematic. After devoting myself to the church for several months, I was sitting at the foot of my bed, crying a sound that came directly from my heart. Without warning *something* scared the darkness out of me, but instantly brought me to an elevation of peace! A tall, wide image covered in what seemed to be a translucent cloth was standing at the foot of my bed. I could see shadowy silhouettes of angels and doves moving around like a rotating shape display would on a wall. Its face and hands were indiscernible and moved continuously like a following of light. Then, a gracious and gentle voice gave me a proposition that would expose the direction to my divine providence. *Give Me two months of reading the Word and after those two months I will give you a reward that you so desperately desire.* I said, "I am starting to better understand, but collectively it just seems difficult." *If your purpose and character is built directly from the Word, then why wouldn't I allow you to understand it? There is a hole in the Bible, fall deep in it. If you linger around the outer parts of "occasionally reading" for too long, the devil will begin to fill it* (James 1:22). Even at this moment, I cannot specify if this was a physical encounter or if it was Jesus speaking to me through a dream. Nonetheless, it was an encounter that indeed changed my life.

When you take the time to listen to the heart, it will share its opinions about particular issues; your comprehension and execution of what you hear is what assists you in getting out of those issues.

The first week I began to read the Bible it was as if the words were scrambling around on the page, but as I kept reading, everything started to come together and make perfect sense. It was as if the Bible was specifically written and intended for me. I was so intrigued by the reading of God's Word that I didn't even notice that the two months had come and went. I completely zoned out the world, and my mouth was fastened open with amazement. Truth in God's Word may cause you to tremble, but if recognized as liberty, then it shall indeed set you free. My gift from Jesus was something I so desperately needed, and after two months I realized that Jesus just created a habit of Himself within me. My eyes have been opened! We become prisoners of blindness by living our lives based on self-help philosophies instead of divine redemption through the Good News. What is the Good News? Well, in the simplest terms, it is our lives revealed through God. I couldn't put the book of love down, and I was now going into the third month of studying the Word! This small, yet significant conversion with God allowed me to notice that the devil will not offer you something you don't want, but that the devil only takes you to where he can capture you. My seclusion with the Bible was a left hook that the devil never anticipated, because it became a habit in me that was unfamiliar to him. I noticed that our fights to break the chains that hold us captive come with stages of anointing and even though I didn't realize it, scripture began to equip me with that precise anointing. At that moment the devil could not control my mind, because I was continually reading the Bible. The Word of God brings your renewed mind into careful thought and evaluation of false teaching; more importantly, it brings you into truth. So I was actually fighting and defeating the devil by throwing scripture at him (Matt. 4:1-11). Without scripture the devil will knock us out and put us in the dark. I was now within God's light of understanding, and how quick you learn that there is power in understanding! Oh yes, the Bible is not a set of mere words, but a revelation revealing a hand-painted picture that enables understanding with detailed perception. Literally, it's faith with a body beyond words; it is reality with a vision.

> *One of the greatest contributions God has imparted to my life is challenging people on who they initially assumed me to be. It is obvious that I am different than who I appear to be. If you structure your life around knowledge, knowledge can become your lifestyle. In turn, your knowledge can fill ignorant people with proper information.*

I also began to notice that change and progress with God come in levels. He positioned one assignment at a time in my life, and when I completed the reason for that assignment, the next one would be revealed. Jesus has left us a marvelous plan to abide by. So until the Bible is in place of your life, you would never realize that there is no replacement for it. Which simply means it doesn't matter what the Bible says; what matters is, are you *doing* what it says? The initial assignments were so basic, yet so important. God told me to get rid of my unconstructive clothing and throw away all my explicit and meaningless music (Gen. 35:2). Some would ask, "Why would you throw them away? Why didn't you just sell them or give them away?" Well, that's because if God said those things were no good for me because of their negativity, then it was senseless for me to give that negativity to someone else. It is the understanding of difference; it is the dynamic of change, not only for you but for others also. As the beginning of my journey with God started to take route, I felt an overwhelming compassion lift me and a deliverance of peace come over me, because I understood that inside my own worthlessness was and is this improbable reality that God loves me so much to not only give me a portion of His worth through His Son, but actually give me full value by allowing His Son, who lives in me, to be the accountant of my life. I was yearning for more, something to take my faith to the next level. On my birthday, June 12, 2008, I called my mother to see if we were going to do anything special. She said that they were all going to a revival that was taking place in Lake Worth, Florida, at Trinity Church International. God works within his own favorable methods, and my mother basically said that I could sit at home alone or I could come celebrate my birthday with her at church. Trinity Church International was about thirty minutes from where I currently lived. I took the drive up and, wouldn't you know, God again answered my prayers. I suddenly began to establish the prayer of Jabez in my life. My life was a prayer of Jabez. Who? Yes, exactly. Most people will not even know who I am speaking of. That is why my life has been the prayer of Jabez, a prayer which many people will overlook, some won't even care, and most see with no significance . . . my only reply is . . . my prayers were granted (1 Chron. 4:10). Prayer is not only needed for the fulfillment of today, but it touches the architectural work of the future. God answering prayers is not based on your state of emotion, but rather on your state of belief. Without belief you will never meet the conditions of prayer, because it will not win the heart of God nor will it get His attention. We don't obtain results by a prayer, but we obtain results by endlessly praying. If a prayerless person would pray more, it would only bring him to praying often, and eventually often would only be an unattained prayer, because the answering of prayers is understood for those who pray every day. Your delayed prayer today was somebody's answered prayer yesterday. A friend once asked me *how important prayer was*. I said, "Well, it just depends. How important are your needs?" He said, "That's really good, but *I have a hard time praying*." I said, "Me too, until I realized it was the only way to get answers." Prayer is used to establish God's cause, not merely so you can be heard, but effectively so you can learn to hear Him. Our prayers not only allow us to face God, but more importantly, they allow us to embrace God. Power doesn't come from your ability to pray, but from your stability in praying. Prayer has been the central tool in building my faith. I attended that revival some mornings and every evening for the next three months. In those three months, God absolutely changed my entire situation and circumstance, my entire belief system, and my entire life as a whole. Tom Peters, the pastor of Trinity Church International, opened the door that allowed me to fall in love with the formality and stronghold of the church. Pastor Dale Gentry, who was a guest speaker at the revival, gave prophetic words and insight into the possibilities and the outlook of God's work and helped me to understand the gifts and composition of God. Bishop Tony Miller declared and proclaimed the Word of God in such power that it drove a marker of wisdom and knowledge into my mind.

There was one specific service that gave me the "*I know that I know*" and that allowed me to identify that the power of prayer works on my behalf. It also gave me the realization that God wouldn't have kept me if He didn't have something for me. My obedience, persistence, and faith opened up a channel for God's grace to flow through. Many people are one prayer away from a miracle. Many people are one step away from a new way of living. But *too many* will stop at one measure of faith before they get there. God's generosity and devotion were beginning to take me over. God proved to me that any form of kindness makes you feel loved, and good hospitality will never make you want to leave. It all started one night after a revival service as I walked my mother out to her car and started telling her how amazing God is, but that I just wished I knew I was doing everything God wanted me to do. She said, "You're doing awesome, just keep praying." I went home that night and prayed to God about five precise things in my life that I wanted answers for. I tossed and turned; I got up and read scripture after scripture. I would sit staring at the wall, meditating and then petition God some more. My questions were a collection of many things wrapped and condensed into five inquiries I had about my life. I prayed and I prayed and I prayed. The night of July 16, 2008, I prayed all service, but I didn't receive my word.

So I went home and dropped to my knees before my bed and kept praying (Phil. 4:6). The night of July 17, 2008, was my point of no return. Before this point I was a great believer in luck, until I came across divine possibility, which told me that everything I had gone through was all part of my purpose. As my family went into the prayer line, I went with them.

The guest speaker this night was Pastor Dr. David Remedios, a preacher from Louisiana. He was there with his wife, Yvonne Remedios, and their children. Their family was a mighty family of God, a family that I admired. Yvonne Remedios grabbed me first and started praying over me and then she asked me, "Have you ever been filled with the Spirit?" I told her no. Then she said, "Well, there is a gift God wants to give you, and it's a gift of speaking in tongues, which is a one-on-one communication with God Himself that blocks the devil from knowing what you want to tell God . . . you're going to start speaking in tongues, and when it happens, don't get scared, just let it go . . . and it's going to happen now." Off I went, and my tongue started to proclaim the language of God. I felt as if I was free, and when she touched me, I was slain in the Spirit. I experienced something that was completely out of this world. I felt a sensation over my entire body, and I felt like I was the happiest person in the world. Then, Pastor Dr. David Remedios came running over from the other side of the church, got me up off the ground, and said, *"God has told me to tell you this . . .,"* and he repeated the very five things I had been praying so urgently about and gave me the answers to every single one of my questions. *My God, thank you*!

The most supportive and most influential individuals who wind up impacting and leaving a mark on uncharacteristic teenage lives are **not** *those who see teenagers from a perspective of being a problem, but from a perspective of being a person.*

ENTRENCHED IN DARKNESS

I shut myself in darkness and walked down a tunnel of misplacement for so many years. My life was a performance that no eye was meant to see, a place where living was never meant to be adapted to, a circumstance that once you surrendered to would take something beyond human capability to pull you out of. The following are some accounts of my life, shadow by shadow, that Jesus never brought me back to, but that are important to share in order for you to understand just how entrenched in darkness I was, and just how deep Jesus had to reach into my heart to turn my darkness into His light.

> *It was a great model of iniquity; it was the very nature of hopelessness; it was the very center of vanity;*
> *it was a life shadowed with a canopy;*
> *it was a face sheltered with desperation; it was eyes scorched by catastrophe;*
> *it was an image of aversion, a version of broken sanity;*
> *a reflection of profanity, a pro at its prime, a crime written by street parenting;*
> *it was free will that molded this illustration of tragedy;*
> *now is the time to sign this picture by the author;*
> *sincerely,*
> *who could it be but me.*

My living in the streets became a self-mutilation to my own peace. Paranoia was the cause for serenity being absent in my life (1 Sam. 2:9). On several different occasions people who we had prior run-ins with started emptying rounds into our car, trying to end something they evidently didn't like was started. One Halloween night, somebody shot up my house, figuring bullets would send a sign of admiration and fear, but the last thing you ever do to someone who lives as if he has nothing to lose is put his family's life at stake. Being respected was so common in my life that respect became my only source of adrenaline, as if I couldn't be me without it. I was living a life dressed in my own scars. I was a walking target for casualty, a magnet for a mark of death. I have had guns put in my face looking down the barrel at the image of my own death. One evening I pulled into a Miami Subs fast-food restaurant after a night of foolishness, and in less than fifteen minutes of walking on a downtown strip, we were in a three-on-three fight. One person lay lifeless in the crosswalk, and all I can say is that the two people I was with made it back to the car. At the Miami Subs one of my friends went inside to get food while my other friend and I sat in the car discussing our night. As we were talking, we could hear other men's voices but couldn't determine where they were coming from. All of a sudden, five guys jumped over a brick wall in the corner of the lot where we were parked, and started coming at my car on the driver's side. I was looking out the window as they were coming toward us, and instantly they froze. My friend had a 9-mm handgun sticking out of the car window with one in the chamber ready to go . . . *pop*! Throughout this time in my life, my mind's eye employed difference, but my visual eye maintained indifference. I began to have a lack of concern for my own life, because I always thought *this is who I am and will always be*. I got a call from a friend early in the day in the summer of 2000 saying there was a group of guys from the next county over who had some concerns to work out. Obviously, we knew it meant that we had to fight for dominance. We pulled up to a park, and without exchanging words we jumped out of our car, and a brawl of supremacy began. Nearly ten minutes later guys were laid out, some were bleeding and some were untouched. I jumped into the jeep I was riding in, looked down at my jeans, and noticed they were covered in blood. I thought, man, someone got messed up, not realizing that it was my own blood. I lifted up my shirt and shook my head, realizing that I had just gotten stabbed. It was not a direct stabbing, but it was more of a deep incision on the side of my stomach. Instead of going to the hospital, I used some tank tops to clean up the blood and some gauze and duct tape to seal up the incision once I got home.

    I was planting seeds of senselessness in my life and allowed them to multiply, producing a line of continuous misconduct (Job 12:14). I was within my own generation's criminal routine, bearing down on its full use. Oddly enough, I could always sense within that my originality was a game of tug-of-war trying to fight for the correct placement in my life. I started to think to myself, "I don't believe I'm supposed to be who I am," because I began to notice the scattering of leaves that were falling from my tree of originality. I couldn't determine what this could possibly mean, even though I knew deep down inside I was falling apart. But was this reformation? Or was I simply a product of a dying breed?

I would go into a liquor store and steal bottles of the most expensive liquor, even though I didn't drink. I would go into high-end retail stores and take whatever I was capable of walking out with. I would go into a grocery store and fill bags up with meat just to have a cookout. I would get in through a window of someone's home and steal jewelry and anything of monetary value. I was selling my soul, with no form of collateral to show for it. I was burying myself, leaving no way out. I had the mentality that I hated all who opposed me, despised those who judged me, and confronted those who told me so. I would put a gun on someone's face for five dollars. I would sell a bogus bag of dope just to test the bravery of the person whom I sold it to. I would walk into a party and pick the biggest person in the room and put him on the ground just to let the crowd know I was there. If anyone didn't know me . . . they would by the time I left. I and a group of friends had an altercation one night when leaving an all age's nightclub. While we were inside the club, we met a neighborhood friend who was just released from prison, and outside in the midst of an altercation, he walked over and screamed "goodnight" and started spreading bullets at everyone in the crowd. I was a thrill seeker, and just for the fun of it we would take a cab and ditch the cab without paying once we got to where we needed to be. Sometimes, depending on the night, we would rob the cab driver of whatever he had in his possession. When I was younger, it didn't matter if my parents put me under restriction, because when they went to sleep, I was quick to jump out of my window and hit the streets. Nighttime for me became a school of larceny and hustling. Older kids and even grown men would show me the ropes. "Trust no one, not even yourself." I was told that the streets are for those who feel like they've been forgotten. You don't have to be altogether in the streets because the streets are part of a broken system. You're respected in the streets simply by your willingness to do what needs to be done. If you were afraid of death, the streets were the wrong place for you to be.

The uncle of one of my close friends once asked me, "Have you ever killed anyone," and in my uncertainty I quickly replied, "I've never stuck around long enough to find out." The company I was usually with consisted of unhesitant individuals like me. If anyone spoke out of tern or disrespectfully, it was a natural reaction for me to deal with them. I was leaning against my car during a block party when some man decided he could act like we were best friends and talk to me anyway he wanted to. I don't believe he even finished what he was saying before a friend of mine hit him in the back of the head with a baseball bat. Our friendly game of fun growing up explains it all simply by its name, "thug life." A group of us would go into a room with no windows and turn the lights off, and once the entire room went black, we would just start throwing punches, kicking and tossing anything we could pick up. The reason for fighting in the dark was because you couldn't tell who hit you, so there was no retaliation. I remember walking through a parking lot with a group of my friends and one of them saw the same group who jumped him the previous weekend when he was alone. Yes, we didn't let that slide, and we started fighting. When the police pulled up, we all ran in different directions. The police caught six of us and spread us out on the ground. When one of the guys showed up to identify us, his jaw was hanging off the side of his face and his eye appeared to be pushed back into its socket.

My life was a continuous spree of fighting, robbery, death, and just problem after problem. There were so many appalling situations I was involved in, but I have never felt more pain than from the emotions that were tearing me apart inside. I can remember one of the most disrespectful statements I have ever heard: "You are nothing, and you're never going to be anything." That remark instantly penetrated my soul. I grabbed a gun, took the safety off, and cocked one back into the chamber. I walked decisively with anger pouring out of my eyes. I pulled the gun up with my body angled to the side. I was looking into the eyes of someone who appeared to be undisturbed by the face of death. I said, "I'm not scared of you" . . . *then just do it*! I wanted to compress his life. I wanted to blow his face back. I wanted him dead . . . until I realized I was looking at myself in the mirror. I didn't hate the mirror; I hated the person looking back at me. I didn't think I was untouchable; I thought I was irreversible. I figured by splitting the mirror it would allow me to visualize the many sides of me, but in my reality all it would've done is shown my brokenness. I am everything I hate! My insecurity with people was a clash between divine change and loneliness. I hated to be alone, yet I thought I was better off on my own. I would go into my room and lock myself in my own depression, sheltering myself from the world with hopes that I didn't in reality exist. I deserve ruins. So many times I thought like I did as a kid: "I wish I had my pillow, so I could bury and hide my eyes from what I know is coming." I learned to scream without a voice. I was killing myself on the inside, dying just to be heard. Could anyone see my pain? Just because I had no tears, didn't mean I wasn't crying. Could anyone see my agony? Evidently, someone did.

Part Two

DISCOVERING MYSELF WITHIN GOD

June 2008-January 2009

You can never rule out a man who gives everything he has to God, because then he literally has nothing to lose. There is more to the Christian life than just reason, but a reason that guarantees that Christian life is more.

Many people have said that they have dedicated time to God, yet nothing ever happened within that dedicated time. Many people continue to say "there is a reason for everything." Many people also say "I am where I am for a purpose." Well, I'm here to say you're absolutely right. You are where you are for a reason, and everything does have a purpose. If I were to walk into a convenient store and rob someone at gunpoint and an hour later I find myself sitting in jail without bond, I would be there for a reason, but not for God's reason. If I were to consume alcohol or smoke past the point of intoxication, and because of my intake I cause casualty, the consequences will be for a purpose, but not for God's divine purpose (Isa. 1:22). Mainstream society will never see it this way because they have the wrong perspective. What is so different about God's perspective? What exactly is seen through God's eyes? Have you ever sat in a room, turned off all the lights, and just sat in a place of complete darkness? Have you ever noticed that if you sit in the dark long enough the things around you don't necessarily become clear, but they do become vaguely detectable? Unfortunately, the majority of people live their lives moseying on through vagueness and never get to see what their eyes were meant to see. They assume they see great things, but in reality they simply see the shadows of greatness, never the greatness of creation. Well, what is it like seeing through the eyes of God? It is like sitting in that dark room, and all of a sudden the light is turned on.

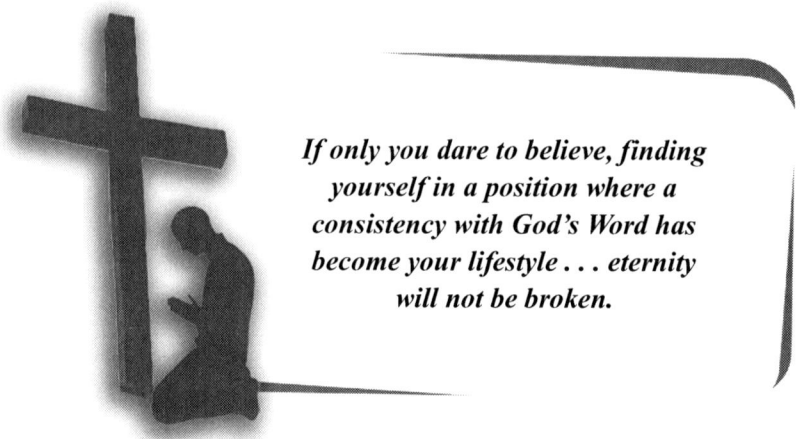

If only you dare to believe, finding yourself in a position where a consistency with God's Word has become your lifestyle . . . eternity will not be broken.

You don't have the option of a test-drive with Jesus; He is your commitment to a journey bringing you to your destination. A time frame for God simply means you're giving Him an examination of His ability, testing what He can do. If there is a time frame that goes along with your dedication to God before you have even begun, you've already created an obstruction to the power of His deliverance. You will understand this the moment your heart pleads for a discovery of truth. If you were to put a time frame on anything with God, you will fail to notice the importance of the first step, which is walking in faith. Faith does not take time, but what we put our faith in does take time. What is faith? It is believing that there is a sun when you live in the darkest part of the night. It is knowing that there is warmth even when your heart cringes in the cold. It is understanding that there is love even when residing under a roof of hate. It is trusting that there is a covering even when having to stand in the rain. It is the certainty of God even in the midst of all your pain. I never told God I would give Him seven months. I just chose to dedicate myself entirely in obedience to Him, and He chose to flip my world inside out within seven months (Ps. 37:5-6). The objective is to plant Jesus right in the center of your problems. The next time you say everything happens for a reason or I am where I am for a purpose, always remember the devil has a purpose for you, and so does God, but only you choose which purpose to live for. The evidence of God's purpose is when you can see everything you've ever hoped for.

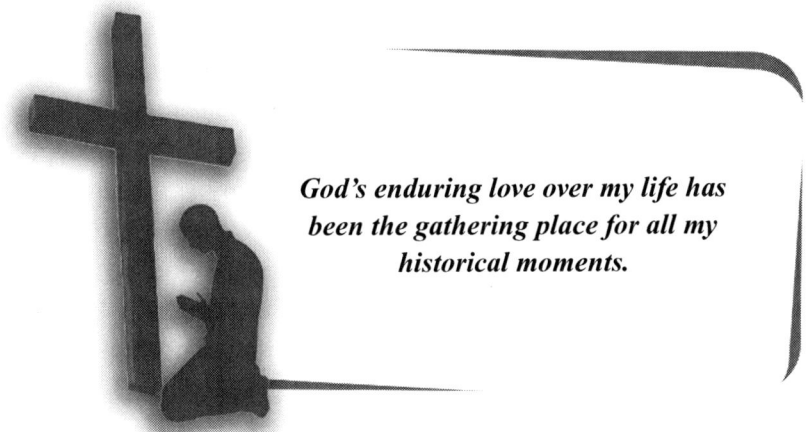

God's enduring love over my life has been the gathering place for all my historical moments.

How did I receive change? *I went to the only place where redemption was offered.*

I was sitting on a mall bench next to a man who was curious about the T-shirt I was wearing, which read *"Under the influence of the Holy Spirit."* He mentioned that his entire life has been devoted to atheism, and it was only a few months ago when statistics began to chip at his concrete mind-set. He said, "In no way do I want to put you on the spot, nor am I trying to dispute your belief system. A lot of people wear Christian T-shirts but can never answer the basic questions." I looked down at my shirt and said, "Symbolism means nothing without spiritual application. What's your question?" He said without hesitation, "Why exactly do you believe in God?" With an assurance I smiled and said, "I literally went to the only place where redemption was offered." With a quick jerk of his head he said, *"What do you mean?"* I explained it to him like this: If I were a friend of yours and came running up to you dwelling in anguish and told you that I hate my life, I wish I were dead, nothing in my life is going right, and I am dying on the inside, what would you say to me? He thought for a second in amazement and said, "Honestly, the first thing that comes to mind is yoga." I explained, "As a person you may be able to change certain aspects of my outer condition, but you can do nothing for my internal condition. So you see, I literally went to the only place where redemption was offered. I believe in God because He is such a key factor in shaping who I am. God did for me what I could not do for myself."

One night during the beginning stages of my biblical stewardship of following the Word of God and mediating on that Word, I was awakened by God's voice. I started writing down every principle I was hearing from God about the center of concern for change and understanding regarding my life (Hab. 2:2). Once I was able to grab hold of the concepts and reasons for each of God's precepts, it elevated my spiritual growth in knowledge regarding a personal objective in my journey. This knowledge is so significant in terms of our reconciliation toward God, because it aids us in continuing His work on earth to now a working of Christ within *us*. It is not merely a change of character, but more importantly a change in curriculum. After learning the principles God gave me, I had a lot of questions relating to my past. Because of God's mercy, He chose to take me back and show me His loyalty and the interest He had in my life. These principles and truths were plainly taking my heart where evidence leads, and putting my mind in a perspective where faith can now see. God has done this, unmistakably, in order for me to clarify my full testimony.

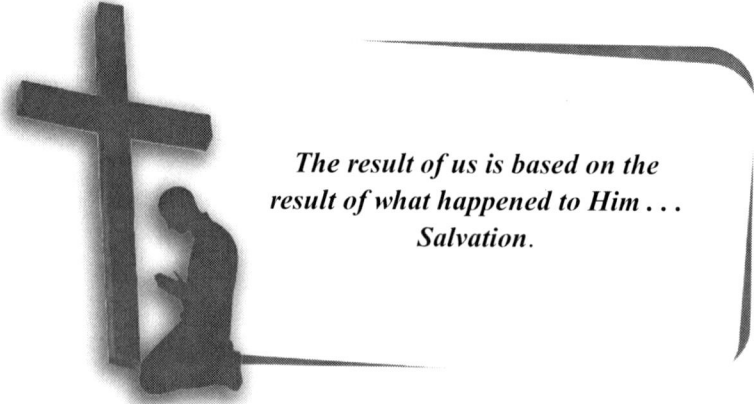

The result of us is based on the result of what happened to Him . . . Salvation.

I realize now that I have been handpicked to be a product of God's grace. My testimony defines God's purpose for my life, and without speaking my testimony I would never conclude the actual reason for the divine change, which is giving God glory through my testimony. We are given light only because it is meant to reflect God's glory. It is God who "changes," but He uses your testimony to draw other people into His change. Your testimony is a solution to other broken hearts. Testimony is more than speaking the Word of God with your mouth; it is speaking the Word of God in visual form with your life. The majority of men will submit not to the Word of God you deliver, but to the surrendering of your life due to the Word of God that you have been delivered as a result of. If you don't speak the change whether by verbalizing or with your life, how can God actually use you? The hardest part for God is not changing you; it's getting you to shut the devil up to allow yourself to speak the significance of your testimony. *What God is saying is as simple as this: who can be a witness?*

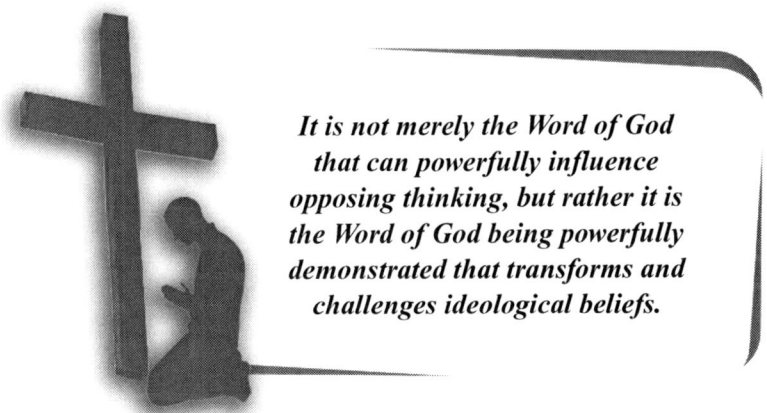

It is not merely the Word of God that can powerfully influence opposing thinking, but rather it is the Word of God being powerfully demonstrated that transforms and challenges ideological beliefs.

God brought me back to the moment in 2006 when I cried out His name in my grandparents bathroom. I didn't realize it then, but He was showing me how worthy His love really is. The moment I went to God, He didn't say, "Here, Tony, now that you've come to Me, you can have all your personal desires." Instead of giving me what I wanted, He gave me what I needed. God said, *Where you are now and what you've become is not what I intended you to be, so in order for Me to bring you back to the intentions I've created you for, I must break you to make you.* I asked Jesus, "Well, why didn't you just start from where I was at?" He said, *Because your foundation wasn't built on rock and when the devil starts positioning the weight of burdens and temptations on your shoulders your foundation will start to crack because it was never strong enough to begin with. In order to build a proper structure you must start from the bottom up.*

When God does something in your life, He does it in such a way that people will know it is God.

Jesus said, *I will break you down, but I will add to your experience. I will break you down so you can break through in order to break out. When I add to your experience I add the glory of My powerful shift from you being lost to you finding life. Adding to your experience gives testimony to how I delivered you from the pits that you fell into* (Ps. 40:2). God allowed me to realize that everything I was going through was simply Him pursuing me, so He could reveal Himself to me.

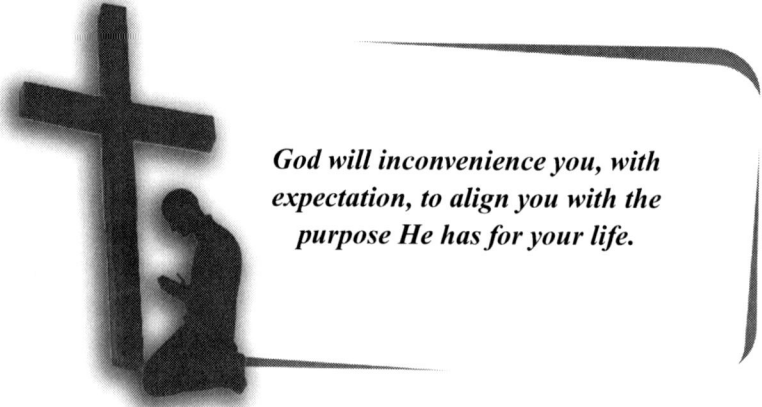

God will inconvenience you, with expectation, to align you with the purpose He has for your life.

Remember, God's purpose and plan for your life never change, but the factor that decides the outcome of your life is the choice and course we decide to take to get there . . . whether we ever get there at all depends on us (Prov. 91:21). "Self" is not the secret of joy, when being selfless finds its true crowing. God's plans and purpose are always bigger than what we can see—faith will stretch your vision. What absolutely drew me to Jesus, undeniably, was the fact that He was the first friend to discover me in the greatest part of my darkness. Quickly I found out that the weaker I am, the more powerful I become. The more broken I am, the more influential I'm made. It is the perfect balance. The presence of God will separate you from where you are and bring you to where you are supposed to be. If you are in a disagreement with your current life situation, it is highly possible that you are not living the life God intended for you. What draws us to God? It is not only His amazing timing, but more enlightening our greatest moment of weakness.

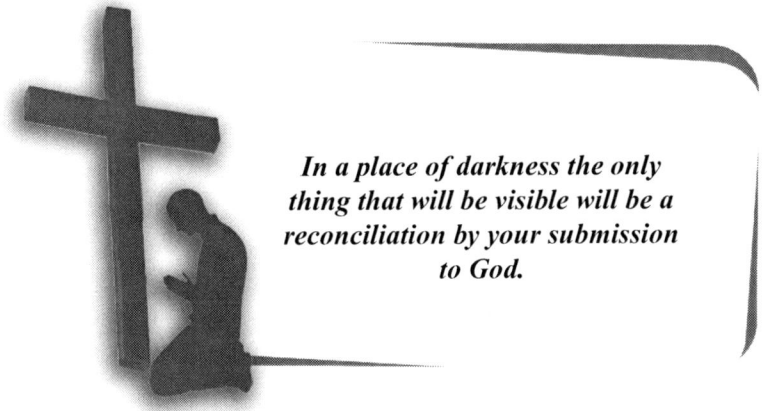

In a place of darkness the only thing that will be visible will be a reconciliation by your submission to God.

To accomplish great things, you must live within your unique creation. I wanted to know who I was meant to be. I knew if the devil were to come after me it would be in the form of some kind of respect like the devil saying, "*Look! All these people know you're someone big . . . come on, let's keep walking.*" Jesus allowed me to see that unworthy respect has the effect of being a source of attraction. Respect has a way of luring weak-minded people into bondage. Timid individuals get drawn into this disarrangement of character because they desire respect, and their friends will follow them, and so on (Isa. 9:16). So what really happens is the devil uses people as a tool to build up a delusion of integrity to allow a collection of individuals to gather in false admiration, but these are people who you don't actually lead. Rather, everyone is following a way of enticement into a cavern of condemnation. This may seem like a bit off subject, but it is extremely important to know that this is why Christians must also be careful when trying to adapt to "culture." Biblically living your life pure and according to God's Word is God's expectation. However, we now are neglecting ourselves and despising God culturally, because culturally we are taught that living our lives somewhat close to God's morals and principles is okay because we are simply flesh. Christians should be different from our culture because nothing significant happens when you develop the very idolatry the Bible opposes, nothing significant occurs when you adapt to a culture that idolizes self-interest and self-power. What is culture? *Getting familiar with worldly things.* Culture has become the result of a deluded church. The problem now is not so much with the persecuted church, as it is a major problem with the deluded church. The persecuted church is full of martyrs who are willing to die for the cause of discipleship and exposing truth to a fraudulent world. However, a deluded church which has become contagious with lukewarmness is spreading news that is not so much Good News anymore as it is appealing and cultural news—worldly combined, not heavenly divine. People are not affected by being cultural-like, nor do they respond to religion, but something that sits in the middle and is elevated above the two, called creativity. One of the very first things a pastor ever told me about being effective with power is when you can make everyone in your congregation stand up, just to lead them to the Cross, and fall.

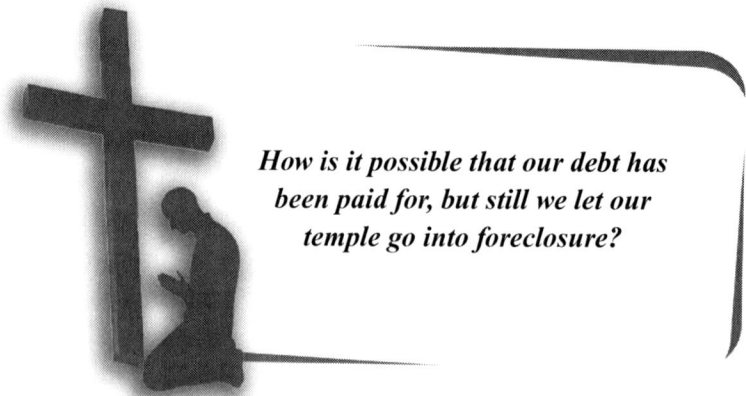

How is it possible that our debt has been paid for, but still we let our temple go into foreclosure?

We were intentionally created by God to be a household for His purpose and glory. I asked Jesus, "As a child of God if I have become lost due to my sinful nature, how then can I ever find my way Home?" (1 Cor. 10:13). When you walk into sin and follow its path, you walk into dismay, anger, worry, temptation, deceit, hostility, and a continuing list of wrongdoing. The moment you decide to turn around into *"change,"* the road gets difficult. When you turn around, you will go back through hostility, deceit, temptation, worry, anger, and dismay, and this is why it is difficult and the point in which most people give up. These are symptoms of a breakthrough, not a breakdown! The devil will use what you are accustomed to in order to draw you back toward him; he will use what you are enticed by or where your heart tends to worry to accomplish his goals. Jesus said, *Do not look at the hard road of change. The reason why the road is hard is because of its reward when changed. It's going to be difficult; but imagine the reward. Yes, the sin you put yourself in, I will reward you for having to go back through, just to get to Me.*

We know we are not perfect people. God knows we are not perfect people. Just don't let your imperfections become habits.

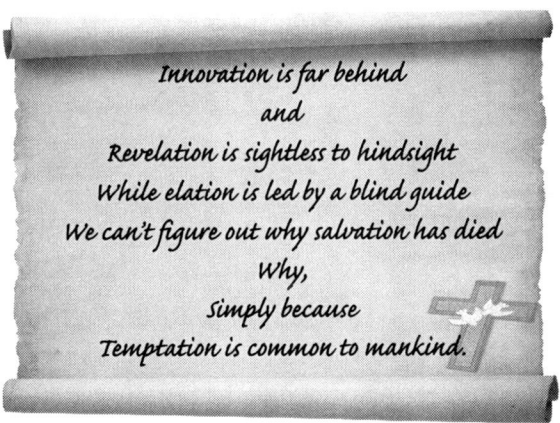

*Innovation is far behind
and
Revelation is sightless to hindsight
While elation is led by a blind guide
We can't figure out why salvation has died
Why,
Simply because
Temptation is common to mankind.*

The first time I went to jail I was in middle school and I had been arrested for theft. I was put in a juvenile intervention facility (JIF), and as I sat in the cell, I looked over at the corner of the wall and saw a unique scripture that read as follows:

***Stay in here long enough and these walls will close you in,
There is only one way out,
Hopefully you find out before then.
Jesus***

You see, the scripture said, "Stay in here long enough and these walls will close you in." As the walls close in on you in jail, there is a small keyword under the writing: "There is only one way out, hopefully you find out before then" . . . and it noticeably reads . . . *Jesus*.

There is a choice we must make before the devil closes us into his disarrangement of living, and sometimes you must go through difficulty in order to get to where you want to go, and if you aren't going through anything, you probably aren't going anywhere. Now, a lot of people in return will say, *well we all have to go through problems*. My reply is this: Know the difference between God's will and free will because there is no reward with problems that you choose to live in.

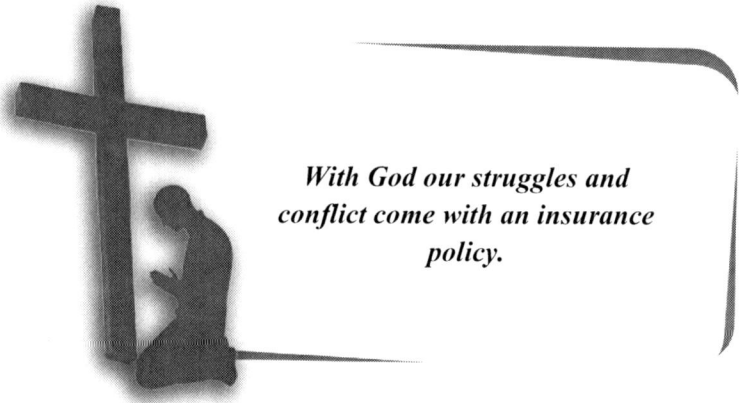

With God our struggles and conflict come with an insurance policy.

Always remember that even if you are going through *something* in your life by reason of God's will, you can be sure there is a reward standing behind your difficulty, because it would be pointless to fight for or invest your time in something that has no return. In my times of affliction, Satan actually comforts me, knowing his persecution against me only ensures me that my day of good inheritance draweth near. The extent of the reward that we receive is based on the glory we give to God. I always stop to think about whenever I was self-absorbed with victory that I was neglecting the One who gave me the victory. Remember the time when you spent those countless hours doing all that work, then someone else came along and got the credit for the labor you just put in. Now just think of all of the accomplishments and progress you've made throughout your life, and while God's hands have been blistered for your advancement, you were self-indulged. Imagine God's heart when He invests His time in your life just for you to claim it for your own glory; so always keep in mind Who must be glorified (Rom. 11:18). There are so many materialistic ideas and objects that people put their belief in, and that's probably why God doesn't say just to believe, but to have belief in Him. Did you know that there are no limits when you're driven by the proper belief? The principles you live by determine what manifests in your life.

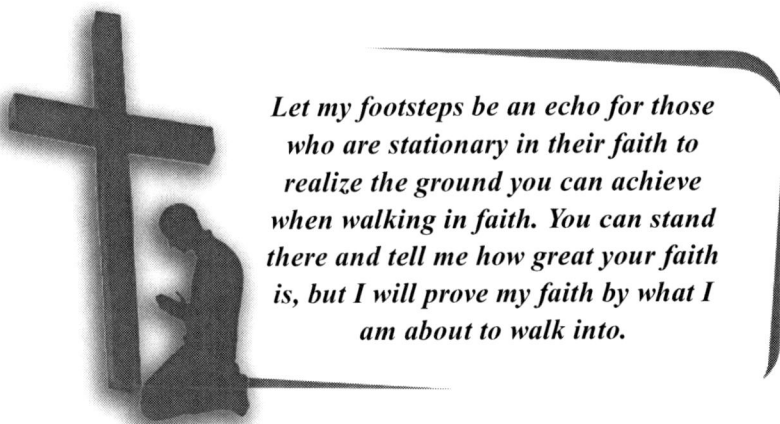

Let my footsteps be an echo for those who are stationary in their faith to realize the ground you can achieve when walking in faith. You can stand there and tell me how great your faith is, but I will prove my faith by what I am about to walk into.

Jesus has been taking me on a journey of growth and understanding. He doesn't allow me to live in my past, but to live away from it. The only way my mind would process this is if God took me back in feature form showing me situations from my past to give me the realization that He was always there. God didn't take me back to relive my past, but to understand what is current from the progress of my past.

I have picked up tomorrow and placed it in my hands today; with no regrets I have left behind yesterday, and am looking forward to this life I can enjoy for always.

Could It Have Been Jesus?

As a child, I would sit in front of my bathroom on the corner of a small hallway adjacent to my bedroom and listen not to the tone of my father's voice but to the content involved. The majority of the time I would fall into a daze, which took me away from the conversation. *Could it have been Jesus* who took my focus off the conversation and into His attention? *Could it have been Jesus* sitting with me, putting His arm around my shoulders, and saying, "Close your eyes and ears, and let's go elsewhere. You are not to become what you hear. This is a character barrier, not a quality builder".

One night as I was standing at the entrance of a dense alley, an oblivious man put the barrel of a pistol on the back of my neck and said, *"Tonight, either your date expires or learn what it's like not to walk . . . I ain't even gotta tell you what I want, just give it to me!"* I took a deep breath, looked up to the sky, formed a sarcastic smirk on my face, and shook my head as it went down. No more than eight seconds had gone by when I slowly looked over my right shoulder, and this man, with a hoodie over his head, was casually skipping across the street. I literally said, "What in the world just happened?" Maybe it wasn't actually something in this world, but outside this world. *Could it have been Jesus?*

During my early teen years, I was sitting in a Walgreens parking lot at about four in the morning, holding a switch blade so firmly against my throat that it began to leave an indention. With tears running profusely down my cheek, I began to reflect on the day and why my mind was so irrational. I felt as if the world and certain people I loved were coming against me. The animosity I had for myself had been building since the previous night and it brought me to a breaking point. Everything I thought I had control of started to hit the fan, and I could see the world pointing amusingly at me as the pieces of my life were starting to fall over me. I absolutely hated that I had no love for people. I detested my own being because I thought the people I loved were completely against me. However, that night sitting in that Chevy, I began to think about a family member who said to me earlier that day, *"You'll be as big as me one day."* I smiled . . . and smiled . . . thinking about what this person said because he was everything I wanted to be. I just smiled . . . and ended up falling asleep in my car. His statement was so small, yet so significant. *Could it have been Jesus?*

One Halloween night, I was caught in a moment that could have cost me a lifetime and very well should have. My sister was humiliated and beaten, and I chose to take vengeance on a grown man who felt he had the authority to place his hands on a teenaged girl. While my sister was heading to the hospital, I was heading to this man's house. Without getting into descriptive detail, here is what happened. In Florida it is a fifteen-year sentence to a PBL (punishable by life) for a home invasion, without including forceful entry, carrying and firing a loaded firearm as a minor, and excessive damage to property. There are certain aspects of this situation that this man's family chose not to disclose. As I sat in the courtroom awaiting my interrogation, I wondered why the entire story was never told. I guess during the whole ordeal, God placed a silence over my curiosity that came along with a *"one day you will thank Me sign."* How could anyone look into someone's eyes, screaming, crying, and horrified while having your home invaded and say, *"He doesn't live here,"* and only disclose excessive damage to property? *Could it have been Jesus?*

A fight broke out with me and a couple of guys in front of a house where a party was taking place. The altercation came to a quick halt when the police showed up. We relocated the fight, and this time it was a fifteen-on-fifteen uprising. The fight went on for about five more minutes, then everyone scattered as my friend's arm was smashed with a crowbar and shots were fired in the air. Later on that night a couple of friends and I were leaving my girlfriend's house when we noticed something odd happening down the street as a crowd of people was walking toward us. We got into the car, not thinking too much about it, and drove off. Fifteen seconds later two cars pulled up on the side off us with guns and bats and started emptying rounds and swinging for the fences. We hit 90 mph down a small 30 mph road, running through every red light, barely missing cars until we lost them. Something got us through those intersections and cars . . . *could it have been Jesus?* The full extent of who we were dealing with and what we were involved in was made apparent because one month later they ended up killing each other because of a dishonest gang affiliation. It was undeniable that we were lucky to still be alive . . . or was it favor. *Could it have been Jesus?*

I got a call around eleven at night to go to a party. I got dressed, then sat down to wait for a call back and decided not to go. At this party was the best friend of one of my really good friends, but more of an acquaintance to me. He got into a dispute with another guy at the party and got jumped by several other men. I have no doubt I would have gotten involved in the dispute trying to help a friend of a friend; it's kind of a homeboy and street code responsibility. On that night, he was stabbed and killed. I didn't go because the call I got was fifteen minutes too late, and I had already gotten comfortable enough not to get back up. *Could it have been Jesus?*

Around the time I was ten years old, one of my best friends kept me on edge. He was addicted to trouble and drew it in wherever he went. Yes, even at the age of ten. As we got older, all eyes were on us because of the fights we were in as kids. At the ages of twelve and thirteen we were fighting fifteen- and sixteen-year-olds. I got drawn away from him at different periods throughout high school, but we would always be drawn back together again, and I never understood the shifting. We were so close growing up, yet his rep at that time was way beyond mine, but our association gave us the same credibility. In one of the periods in which we were apart, he was arrested for strong-armed robbery and was sentenced to six years—a four-year prison term with two years on "paper" or probation. Yes, it was at that period when we were drawn apart. *Could it have been Jesus?*

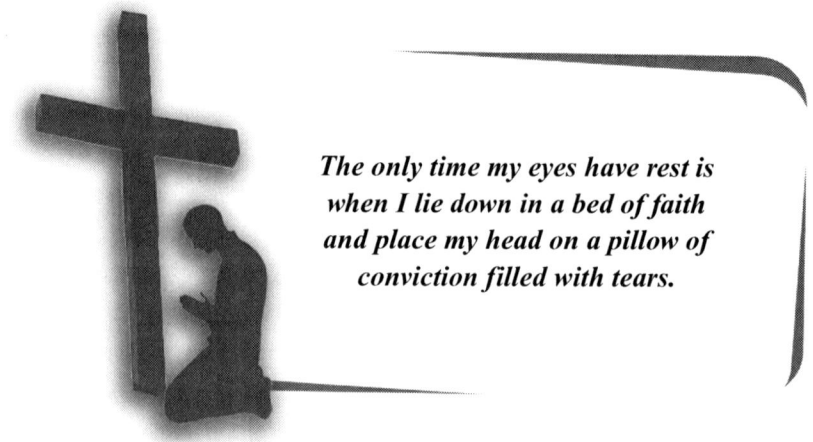

The only time my eyes have rest is when I lie down in a bed of faith and place my head on a pillow of conviction filled with tears.

People have asked me *why Jesus saved me from death but not them. Why did Jesus save me from prison terms and not them?* My only answer is that *I don't know. I can only dictate my life, and so I can't answer for theirs.*

If it wasn't Jesus then it wouldn't have been done!

As Jesus brought me back through the interruptions of my life, He first brought me to the bizarre feeling of having rhabdomyolysis and being overwhelmed with worry. During those two weeks sitting in the hospital, my mom and I would ask the doctor every time he came in the room, "*Do you know what you're doing and are you sure you have this under control?*" He would confidently say, "Yes, *no worries*. It will be fine. It just needs some time."

Worries are the departure from our trust in God.

Yes, no worries, and exactly what I needed was just a little bit of time. I walked out of that hospital without any side effects or problems (Ps. 41:2-3). Thankfully, Someone whom I didn't even know too well stood in that room with me for two weeks, and I didn't even get a chance to thank Him until years later. Thank the Lord! In this particular moment, giving thanks to God was quite different than what I had always perceived. I then realized that you have two types of men: one who thanks God sitting at a table, and the other one who thanks God on his knees before the Cross.

I said, "But Lord, I didn't really have a relationship with You for You to restore my health, and You said not to have worries because it disrupts progress with You. I wasn't making any progress with You." Then God said, "*Son, somebody prayed you back to health and because they trusted in Me they didn't worry whether I would show up or not, because like you said 'Someone who I didn't even know too well stood in that room with me for two weeks.' You may not have made progress in that time, but somebody else did and because you are learning it now . . . well, now you're making progress.*" This made me realize that not only is God amazing, but He also has a sense of humor.

One night in particular, I woke up at about four in the morning with God clarifying questions that were brought up to me in high school. I grabbed a pen and started writing.

A friend, who believed in Jesus in high school, brought up a question and a reason why he now didn't believe there was a Higher Power anymore. It made no logical sense to him that "*if Jesus is so faithful, why did my family member just receive a life-threatening diagnosis?*"

Jesus reminded me and then said:

I am faithful to everyone who trusts in Me, and if I am Jehovah Ropheka, your healer, what would be the reason for My name if there were no times of illness. Why is it that when your faith is tested, I find out how weak your reliance and trust in Me really is? (Acts 28:27).

Belief and deliverance, trust and healing, are all strung together by one thread—faith.

When a person questions his appearance and asks, "Why did God make me like this?"

Jesus said, *How can you question something that was made identical to perfection? You are made from the image of perfection regardless of what angle you are looking from. It's what people don't see that appears to be without perfection, until they come to Me. Let your heart be reconciled to that perfect image* (Ps. 51:10).

We are made in His likeness, yet uniquely and distinctively different, because it is the detail in God's beauty.

Why do we have to lose our loved ones? Why do you take people we love before their time?

Jesus said: *I don't want you to know why . . . because then you wouldn't be walking in faith.* (Heb. 11:1)

When we fall into misunderstanding or unreasonable grief, we must find ourselves in God's love. His love is immeasurable, which means it is impossible to fall beyond it.

There is so much controversy and debate about God and His Word.

Jesus said, *Choose not to spend your time debating, but rather glorifying. Debate only adds uncertainty. If you're certain about Me, there is no reason for debate. You will spend your entire life debating and still never receive certain answers, because they were never meant for you to know. Some things are kept for you until you get to Heaven, for greater is your reward when you get there.* (Prov. 25:9)

The Bible is God's greatest choice for man; what God reveals in His own Word is His greatest choice for you.

One of my favorite accounts came when a woman tried to explain to me why she doesn't read the Bible. Her reason was because she thought there was so much contradiction in God's Word. I said that it's not contradictory, it's extraordinary. I run to God, just so I can rest. I call out in prayer, just so I can be still and silent. I praise God, just to be criticized by men. I am comforted with peace, just to find myself in God's battle. How marvelous!

Searching for God's Touch

If ever a kid could place his mind into solitude and completely lose touch of his emotions that would have been me. I was probably the biggest burden to my mother's heart, not because of what I was getting into, but because of the root of what led me into what I was involved in. My hate put me above the *"ordinary"* teen scale. *I guess you could say my standard way of living wasn't a normal child's way of living.* I linked my character to the depths of the avenue, depths meaning the darkest parts of the streets, which was living with an "I am invincible" mind-set—*"a live by, die by"* mentality. "Corner boys" and "Block Burna'z" are other names we would call our state of hustle showing one face with no love. It is said that on the streets, *showing love will get you killed*, but how can you be killed when having no love makes you dead already? I was living what I knew, but something just wasn't right. My stubborn ways overpowered my common sense trying to tell me *if the shoe doesn't fit, then it's not for you.*

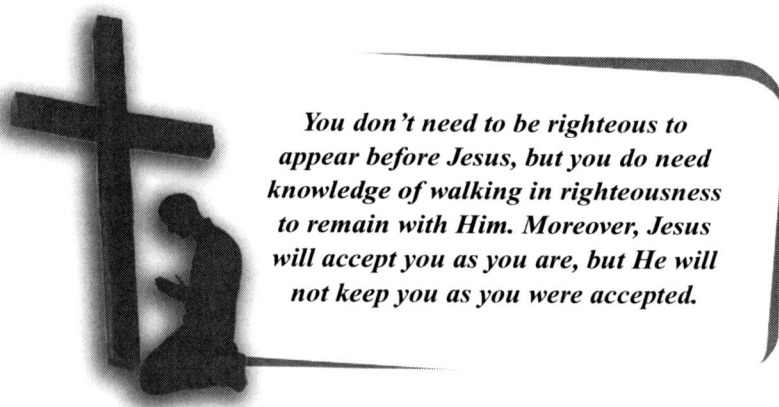

You don't need to be righteous to appear before Jesus, but you do need knowledge of walking in righteousness to remain with Him. Moreover, Jesus will accept you as you are, but He will not keep you as you were accepted.

I was dead emotionally and alive with hate, and with no exaggeration, by the time I graduated high school, I had been in over one hundred fights . . . physical fights. I broke my wrist by hitting a guy while he was sitting in the back of a Ford Mustang convertible, because his girlfriend thought it was humorous to almost hit me with her car, so I let him know I didn't think it was that funny. In another incident, I was with my usual group at a club when a fight broke out, and some guy picked up a metal chair to smash it over my friend's back. I took the brunt of force from the chair by jumping in front of it, busting the back of my head open. I've sprained my wrist numerous times, and my fighting ordeals had gotten so serious that we would preplan fights with people we didn't like from other locations. I would tape up my wrists, tighten up my belt, tighten my shoe laces, and jump in my Chevy to earn my keep. Hatred made me unafraid to run up on a crowd of people.

Yes, you can only live out your persuasion.

I was only able to acknowledge the small amount of respect I got from my forged friends and overlooked everything fighting was taking from me. I was not an emotional person, and the only time I ever expressed sensitivity was when my family had to endure pain. I didn't care about anything because I had no regard or sense of repentance for what I was doing, simply because I blocked out my own feelings. The majority of people are not afraid of their emotions; they just have a hard time dealing with them. However, through all of this, I could feel my heart being penetrated, and I wanted to expose the light within me that would bring out my care and concern for life.

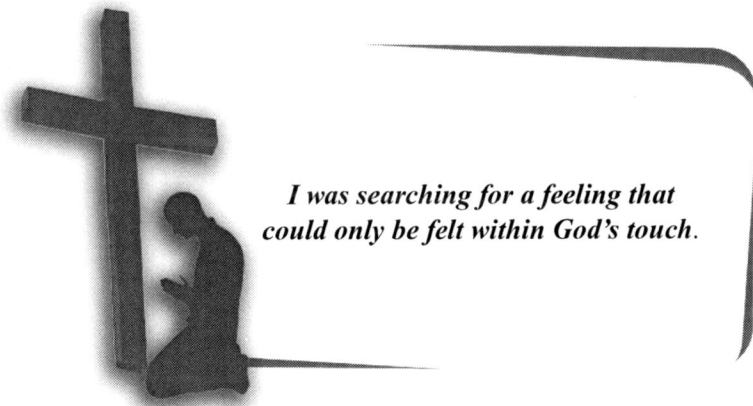

I was searching for a feeling that could only be felt within God's touch.

I love this question: Do you feel God? Absolutely, because I have allowed my heart to be filled with everything God feels. You can also easily feel God's touch through His words of assurance. I never realized that your voice can reach far beyond what your hand can extend. Sometimes just by speaking truth love is revealed: love for people and most importantly love for yourself. I wanted to be known as something other than what I was known for. It's amazing how walking as if nothing in this world matters attracts deadened individuals to you. You become familiar to the eye of the common outcast, clearly because you are suffering in silence and these deadened individuals assume you have slid into a related medication of theirs. All of this occurs because the devil has succeeded in enclosing your emotions.

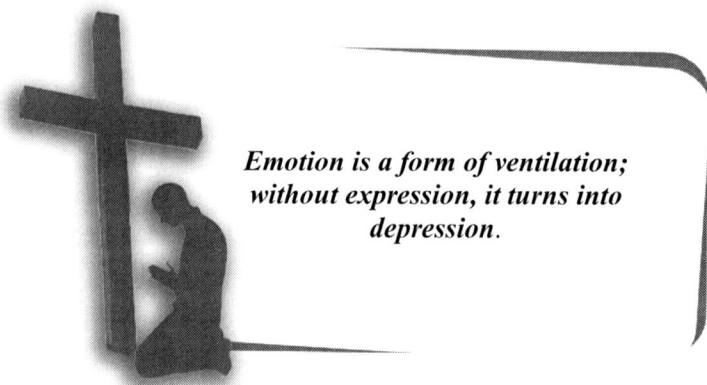

Emotion is a form of ventilation; without expression, it turns into depression.

By letting your sensitivity emerge, it will reveal that you have soft spots or compassion for what has been concealed in your life.

When the light is turned on is when you get a glimpse of some sense.

I found myself locked in between four walls, and my freedom of expression lingered on the outside. The cause for holding in my tears became the captivity of any sympathy or goodwill I had within. I pleaded for a desperate release of any type of passion.

Then Jesus said the following: *Anything I ever give you should never be held within. Emotion is the effect of the heart in a state of simplicity, a realization of being set free, divine liberty presenting a new form of love . . . this is the result of being in My presence and the expression of My grace.*

What a feeling far from "my" ordinary! I felt the release I needed when I allowed myself to fall into the atmosphere of faith that surrounded the church. I would go to church and cry; I would open my Bible and cry; I would hear a message and cry, hear a testimony and cry, shout in worship and cry . . . cry, cry, and cry (Ps. 18:6). It is easy to praise God when praising becomes a fashion, but when there becomes a remnant of non-worshipping people an undertow of backsliding begins. This is when you find out that it is difficult to stay above water with hardened or heavy hearts. Worship is more than just a praise gathering; rather it is an individual gathering of praise. Losing intimacy with God is most often established when leaving holes in worship. How you worship demonstrates your current approach to God. Remember, before the first amen or even before the preacher takes the pulpit, every person's relationship with God can be determined—in worship. It was a new way of expression for me that I was definitely not afraid to address anymore. Being able to show my love for God through my tender emotion was an indescribable sensation. I now let the overflowing of my love for God that comes from my heart and soul pour out in carefree tears.

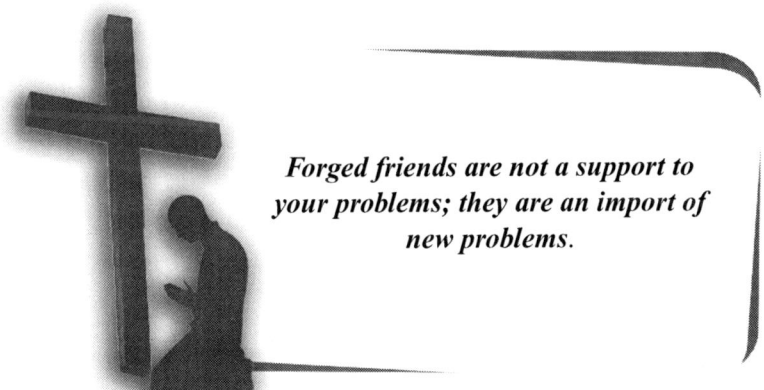

Forged friends are not a support to your problems; they are an import of new problems.

My hate came from a misconception of people. I thought everyone was judging me because of the way I looked, but never realized they were just speaking honestly about the way I was. So I figured I had to completely change the way I dressed.

Jesus then brought me back to my appearance. Jesus said, *I am not telling you to change your clothes; I'm trying to tell you to change your makeup. Quit thinking people are judging you. You are not being judged when you make stupidity and ignorance evident. It's truth, not judgment!*

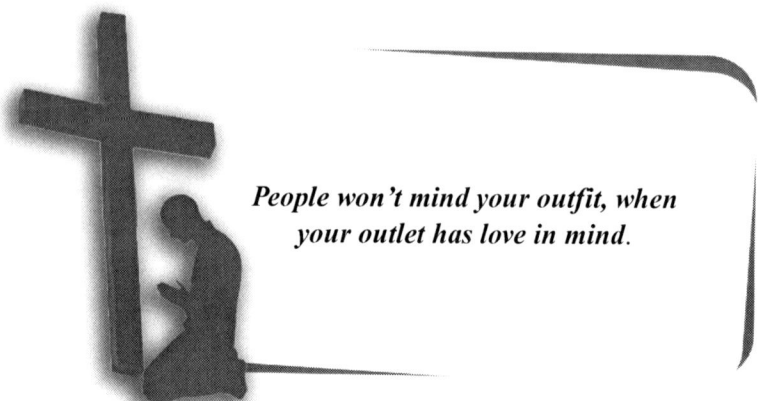

People won't mind your outfit, when your outlet has love in mind.

At another incident in a juvenile detention center, a correctional officer said to me as he was walking me out of process, "*Are you as dumb as you look or just as stupid as your decisions . . . you'll be back here.*"

Jesus said, *You read into destructiveness and that's what you will become. Think money and your heart will turn green. Live a lie and you'll never know truth.*

I thank God for the brutal honesty given to me by certain people throughout my life. It allowed me to understand that if I am a flat tire, it means nothing for someone to come by and fill me up with air, "halfway truth," to feel elated and travel a short distance just to find myself curbside again. If I am a flat tire seeking for difference, the only way I can truly experience change and enjoy the journey is if I am made a new tire—a new creature.

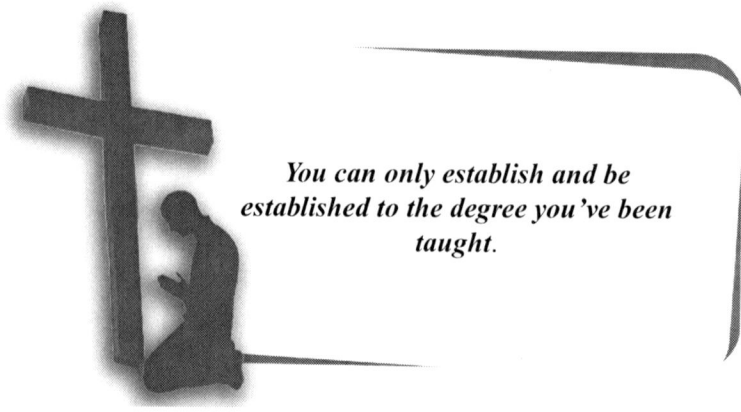

You can only establish and be established to the degree you've been taught.

Our intentions are motivated by our thinking. You can tell what a man is thinking by what he says, and you can tell who he is by how he acts. Jesus said to me, *Without Me you thought your way of living was understandable, but it was the outside of that understanding that gave you reason for living, which actually is the inside of understanding . . . Me!* (2 Cor. 3:14).

I sat in the living room of a friend's house enjoying him and his family's company. Everything changed the moment a commercial about a new Christian movie came on television. The uncle of my friend started his taunt of Christianity and his evidence in atheism and that the logic behind belief in God is a weak fairy tale meant to deceive. I fought within myself as he was speaking. Should I say something? To me he appeared to be an intellectual man. What could I possibly say? Then he looked over at me and said, "Atheism is evidence in which I know." As tears slowly dropped down my face one by one, he asked me very confidently, "Are you crying because of what I know?" I said with my heart aching, "No, I am crying because of what you don't know."

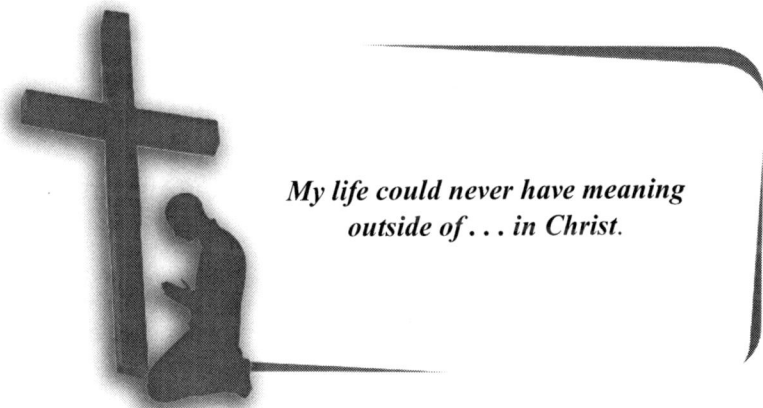

My life could never have meaning outside of . . . in Christ.

The understanding is that the word in the Bible is the proper teaching to the essential being of Christ within you—a Christian, being Christlike. The understanding is if your words do not pass the love of God, then don't say it. If your actions don't pass the character of God, then don't do it. When you walk out of a room, people will think one of two things: I'm glad he left, or I wonder when is the next time he's coming back.

There is a secret place that God has taken me to, and this place is where I have learned and have been instructed by God. Because of sin we naturally segregate ourselves from truth.

The secret place of God is a realm of spiritual discernment.

We keep no secrets from God. So when you go to your secret place, it is not about what you tell Him, it's about what He is going to tell you. There is power in the Holy Spirit. Being in the secret place of God is a spiritual experience and allows you to understand and comprehend what you would reject in the natural world. I have always been told to forget my past, but in this secret place, God has told me to remember it. There were so many devious situations I was involved in and only by the grace of God was I saved from them. I had to accept the consequences for everything I went through or participated in, whether it was jail, broken bones from fighting, or people turning their back on me. You need to understand that God saved me from death, but because I didn't have Him personally in my life, I had to endure what came along with living away from God—the consequences (Ps. 107:17). The majority of men in the Bible who turn against God do not die in an instant, but in degrees. I was slowly dying. Even though I wasn't buried, I was still a dead man walking because I had no life without Christ. People ask me how God handled my situation, and my reply is as easy as this . . . He put Himself in it! God's grace is His empowerment to draw us in; we cannot achieve anything divine based on our own strength because we have been rightfully created with this incapability. The Word of God and His amazing grace are everything but natural ability.

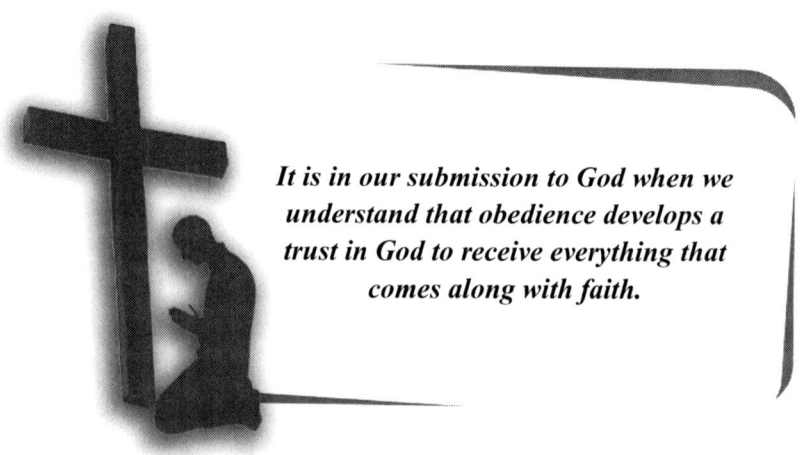

It is in our submission to God when we understand that obedience develops a trust in God to receive everything that comes along with faith.

You are not struggling with your thoughts. You are not struggling with your influence. You are not struggling with your everyday temptations. You are not struggling with your situation. You are not struggling with idols. You are not even struggling because of Satan. You are struggling because of your lack of faith which has caused you to have a lack of God! Thinking back on my actions, I would have to question my own stupidity. I wonder why I was stupid enough to risk my life in order to have a fashionable living. In high school, I didn't sell drugs to get rich. I sold drugs for rims, clothes, and attention . . . a fast living, *real fast*. I put my future freedom in jeopardy because I wanted to look "trendy" and have "the look." The police officer at the high school I attended would call my stepfather and let him know I was selling drugs and up to no good, even though the officer could never prove it. He would tell my stepfather about my watches, jewelry, gold teeth, rims, and the rumors that were going on in the school hallways. The officer and the school guidance counselors made it a routine of theirs to pull me out of class and search me every Tuesday or Friday around one in the afternoon, just to make a point.

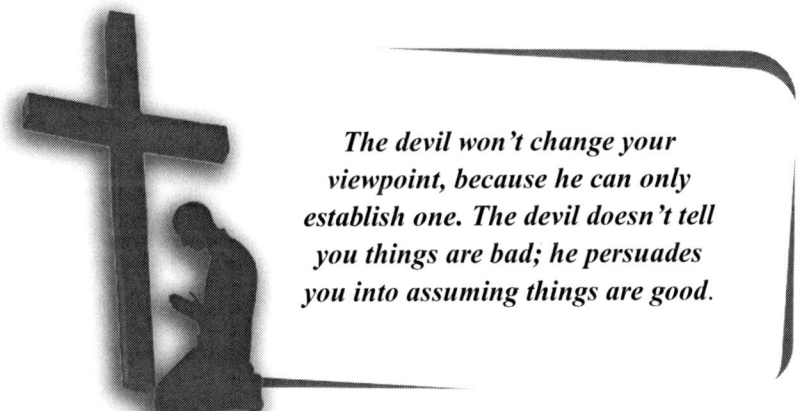

The devil won't change your viewpoint, because he can only establish one. The devil doesn't tell you things are bad; he persuades you into assuming things are good.

In college, I was stimulated by neighborhood enticement, "the rags to riches" dream. I started making a substantial amount of money in a short period of time by changing my approach in the drug game. I always stayed aware of my surroundings and walked within shadows to keep myself from being exposed. The hate I had for myself was stronger than the concern I had for myself, causing me not to care anymore. I stopped selling drugs in college only because life started moving too fast, so fast I couldn't keep up. Ironically enough, as much as I've been around drugs, I've always stood firm enough to veer away from using any substances. I smoked and drank a few times, but I never let anything consume or take control of me. Sober life is pure living that demonstrates an unspeakable advantage.

God began to make me realize that drugs as a whole are a product of the devil, regardless of whether they are being consumed or being sold (Ps. 143:3). The problem was that I was employed by the devil himself, and even though I wasn't doing drugs, I really was. God allowed me to realize that I was as much at fault as the users were, and probably even worse, because without dealers there would be no users. God then sent an angel into my life, and this is what happened.

I received a verbal declaration from an ex-drug dealer who pleaded for me to recognize the value of what it is Jesus does and can do for His people. I sat on a stool in front of a barbershop in a local neighborhood known as "The Gove," and got into a discussion about the life of a drug dealer and where God has His role. He first stated this: *"Do you know why the owner of Target can never work for Kmart . . . because it would be a conflict of interest and they are competitors who have the same intentions, but who have two different plans. So why is it that dealers choose to believe in God, but yet work at the devil's expense? Conflict of interest destroys the alternative for growth. Drugs are an inferior product that the devil fabricated and swayed man into distributing, which then becomes a primary source for unaware desolation. Did you know that in their ignorance drug dealers believe in God and pray to God and then turn around and thank God for the money they just made? The majority of drug dealers are unaware that Jesus is in the salvage business trying to protect and save the lost, producing a testimony after His arrangement of saving even the worst of lost lives. He doesn't help drug dealers make money, but what God does do is protect the worst of people who still have the slightest hope in Him. Drug money will never last long, and over 90 percent of dealers will end up dead or incarcerated. It will not be that God put them there, but that the devil succeeded in overtaking their mind and convincing them that this particular lifestyle is tolerable. The devil has succeeded in allowing a dealer to distribute death into a city, which will eventually cause them to arrive at their own death. God didn't give up on them, but they continually went against what the Bible commands, and because of the constant dispense of a product that ruins lives, God allowed them to face their own conforming ways because He is a fair God."* The ex-drug dealer ended by saying, *"Son, go to Jesus and get away from this **'death style'**, so He can take you to your purpose, a real **'lifestyle.'"***

I asked Jesus, *"Why not just tell people their purpose so they know why they are here?"*

Like me, people have the tendency to be narrow-minded by wondering why God doesn't just expose their purpose the moment they turn to Him. Understand that our God is a working God, and He is continually working for our benefit. God will meet you through *your* imperfect matters. If God were to reveal your purpose, you'd never see what was directly in front of you. You would miss the message and the growing process, and you would never know what to do with your purpose (1 Cor. 3:7). The best place to experience "difference" is right in the center of God's will. It is the development and growing in the Word that gives you a platform to face the future of your life and to work and grow in the process of change. Pay attention to the small things, and collectively they will bring out your purpose. The first question is, would you receive the gift of God, as if there is nothing in this world comparable? Jesus's death is not a response to how much we are worth; it is a clarification to how unworthy we really are.

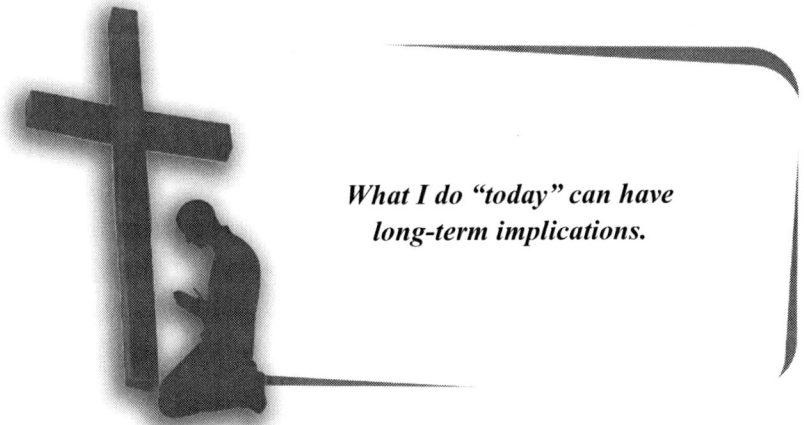

What I do "today" can have long-term implications.

One of the most profound yet obvious ways God works in our lives is that He works out a way for people to make a way in their lives for

Him, whether it is through a good or a bad situation. God will not allow you to understand your purpose until you understand Him. Perfect! How great it is that God works everything out.

"I don't really read the Bible, but I believe in God."

You cannot understand God without knowing the Word, and you cannot understand the Word without knowing Him. Why, because they are one. He is the Word and the Word is Him (John 1:1). As a Christian, we have the privilege of experiencing not only a great life, but every aspect in life's experience. Whether it is friendship, marriage, parenting, working ... etc., without having a biblical understanding in *every* aspect of your life, portions of your great life experiences may very well be temporary. That's why the totality of the Bible must be implemented and understood in our daily lives, which can teach us obedience, patience, trust, faithfulness, bravery, and a continued list, which ultimately affects our marriage, parenting, and lifestyle. It might sound confusing, but Jesus was telling me that anything you need answers for, if you want to come to know Me, and if you want to find yourself ... the answers can all be found in the Bible. The Word of God not only elevates you, but it renovates you! The Word will pave a way for you to walk in righteousness, everything that will bring you to the Cross and everything that will draw you away from it. It is vital that we realize that death on a Cross put Christ in our history and the Resurrection from the grave put Christ in our present. What does that mean? It means if I have laid down my life to pick up the Cross, everything that I do, I do it *to* the Cross; also, everything is done *from* the Cross. It will show you not only how to gain life, but how to gain life for others; not only to be prosperous for yourself, but how to make others prosperous through God (Josh. 1:8). The Word of God is all around you, but it is literally impossible for anyone to advance in faith and toward the will of God without an open Bible before them.

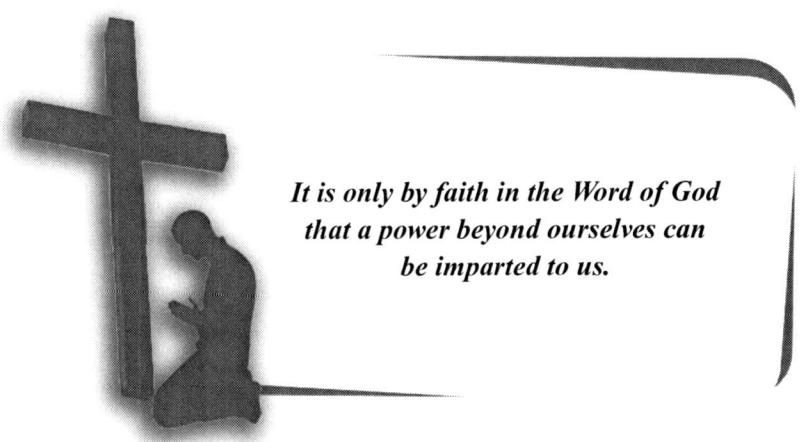

It is only by faith in the Word of God that a power beyond ourselves can be imparted to us.

Becoming familiar with God's Word makes you become familiar with everything He did for you (Mark 8:35). It makes you live for the sake of Jesus's death. Yes, Jesus has forgiven you, but you will not receive forgiveness until you face the Forgiver. Yes, Jesus has paid for you in full, but without any interest in Him, you're just a debtor whose interest is due.

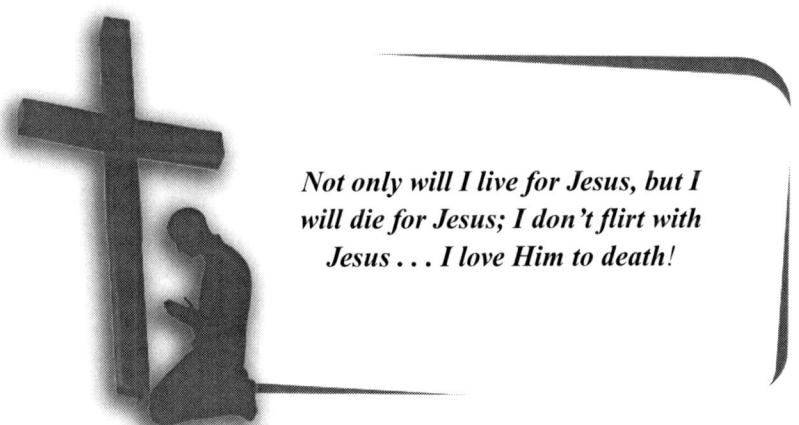

Not only will I live for Jesus, but I will die for Jesus; I don't flirt with Jesus . . . I love Him to death!

If people believe they know everything, they will stop trying "*to know.*" How can you possibly know everything about Someone who is limitless? You do not need to know everything, but you must maintain understanding! Remember, the Bible is what brings you into a relationship with Christ, so it's not actually what you know, but Who you know. If you maintain understanding, you will never want to stop knowing more.

I don't know everything, but I do have revelation, but more important than revelation, I have relation.

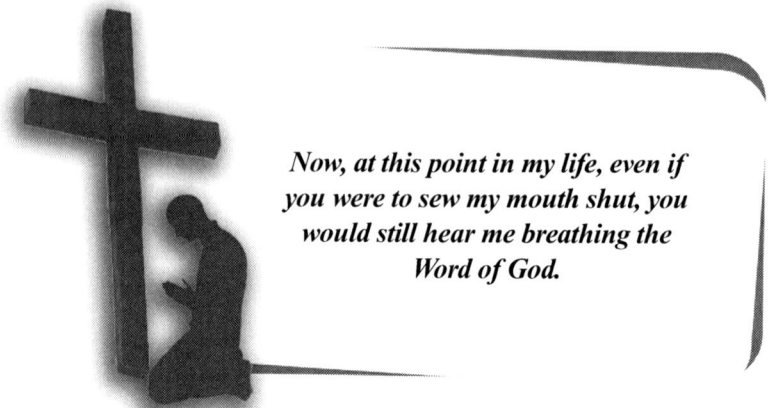

Now, at this point in my life, even if you were to sew my mouth shut, you would still hear me breathing the Word of God.

I was having a conversation with a woman at a jobsite I was working at, and I began to explain the move Jesus was making in my life and the excitement it has given me. She proceeded to tell me details about how she gave herself to whatever Jesus wanted from her several years back. She said three years later she found herself far away from the commitment she made to Him. She said at the time all she was focused on was filling the void of love she had in her life. Within those three years she never received what she asked Jesus for. After sitting in her room one night almost six months after slipping away from God, she asked Jesus why He didn't come through. She said it was then that she realized that throughout those three years Jesus was using her as "love" in the lives of others and was using her life for His purpose to ultimately give her a gift of love before filling her own personal desire for love. She said her problem wasn't that Jesus didn't commit to his Word, but the problem was she didn't commit to her own word. She told God to do whatever He wanted with her life, and He did just that. God was filling her life with what she asked, but was using it for His benefit and purpose. She said that she gave up because she was missing what God was putting right in front of her face and that she grew impatient. Her biggest regret wasn't giving Jesus three years; it was giving up just before receiving what He wanted so much to give her. She told me to enjoy the entire transformation of change and to keep my eyes "limitless" and open. Receive everything

Jesus promises just by following the Word and being patient for your purpose. Three years is so insignificant, considering the *entire* span of life you can have (James 1:12).

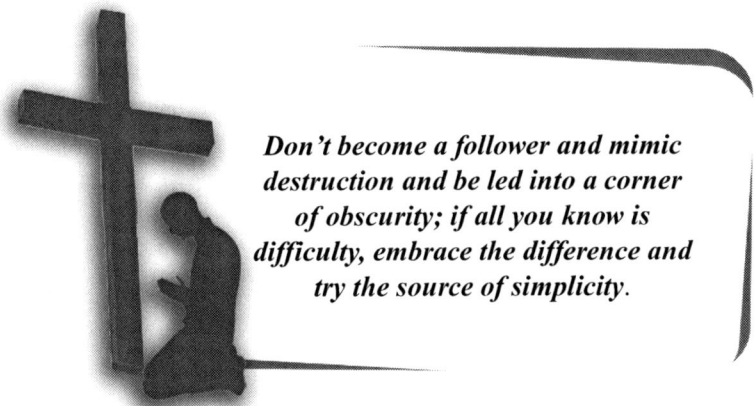

Don't become a follower and mimic destruction and be led into a corner of obscurity; if all you know is difficulty, embrace the difference and try the source of simplicity.

A teenage mind is centered within the motive of "*what's cool!*" When other problematic middle school kids were stealing bikes, I was stealing cars. When other middle school kids were sleeping, I was driving a stolen car and sneaking into girls' windows. I started stealing cars only because of certain influences I was around. Since my influence was getting a lot of "c*ool points*" from kids at school, I wanted to become part of that chart, so I started stealing cars as well.

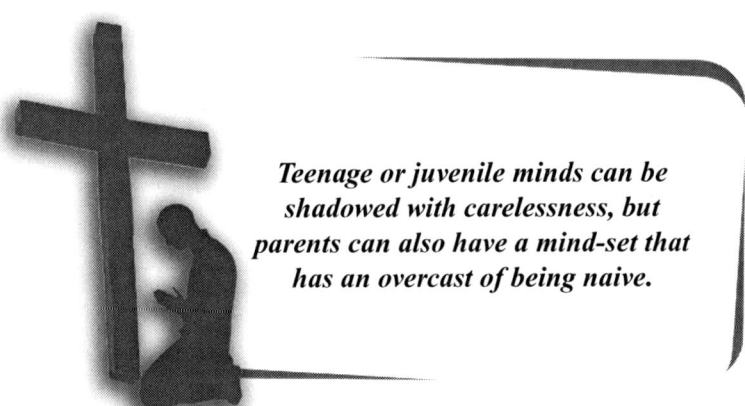

Teenage or juvenile minds can be shadowed with carelessness, but parents can also have a mind-set that has an overcast of being naive.

At thirteen, a friend of mine stole a car and unintentionally pulled up on the side of my parents' car one night. When my mom got home, she asked me about it. I smirked and said, *"Crazy kid."* When you get away with trouble, you always go back to it. Unfortunately, we never realize that what we are building is a stack of blocks that keep getting higher and higher, and one day eventually everything will come crashing down.

Jesus said, "*You would never know how to build a machine without instruction. If you are around people who build trouble, you will become troubled. If you are around people who build trust, you will become trustworthy. If you want to know Me, then start surrounding yourself with people who have been built up by Me.*"

Before your walk with Christ understand this:

> **Jesus doesn't overload, He overflows.**
> **If you fail to remember what you have received,**
> **you will never again receive.**
> **Because**
> **We look for the blessings ahead of us, but forget all the blessings behind us.**
> **You are called to remember.**

You don't need to walk into an opportunity with God, because His opportunities are all around you. If you've asked God for an opportunity and you're still waiting for an answer, I would make some serious adjustments, one of which would be turning around and noticing all the ones you've missed. Even without having Jesus in your life, He still presents the opportunity to fill that important void. The beauty of what God does is when you decide to go to Him; He will always meet you more than halfway. The exciting part about the promises of God is that He always gives you more than you expect (Ps. 78:29). The reward of adding Christ to your life is that he multiplies everything He guarantees. The hard part is not receiving *all* things that come with Christ; the hard part is truly finding yourself in Christ that you would be able to receive all things (Rom. 8:32). God's determination to preserve you is for the purpose that He wants to fulfill through you. While I am here on earth, my ultimate purpose is not to know about heaven. My ultimate purpose is to know about God—God *is* my beautiful place. God's plan is a done deal in heaven, but *if only* He could make it a done deal in you. However, after finding myself in Christ, *my* desire shouldn't instantly be to radically jump out and change the world, but to complete what I lack in my likeness to Him. This will allow me to establish His perfection in me, with the results of delivering His perfection to the world. Some people choose not to believe in God and that's why God says what you believe is what you will receive. Perfect, because the teaching of the Bible allows you to understand that without Christ you have nothing (John 14:6). Belief will be based on the fruit of your works. The fruit of your works can be distinguished with your perspective, which should not be "I will do this," but "I want to do this"—serve. The scope of Christianity takes a national voyage for an individual acceptance. However, this is not merely an acceptance that Jesus is in fact Lord of our lives, but more important, an acceptance to follow His Word and characterize our lives as "a fruit-bearing lifestyle."

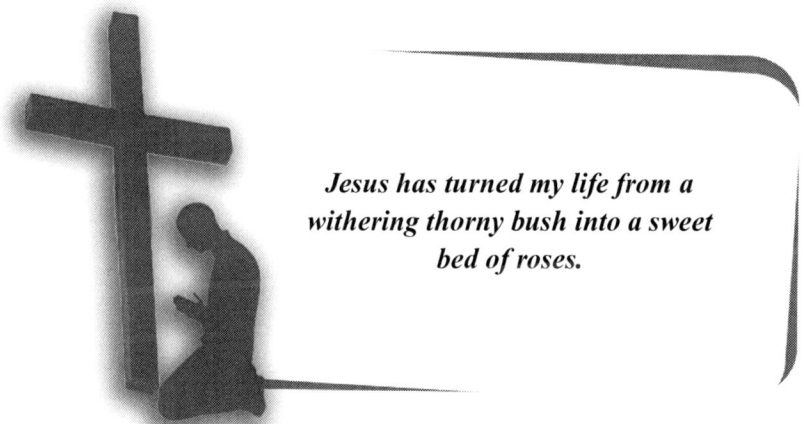

Jesus has turned my life from a withering thorny bush into a sweet bed of roses.

The dominion and outreach of God to His people of faith are that He will do something so impossible for you that it will be impossible for people to say that it wasn't God who did it to you. If God didn't do it, then it wouldn't have been done. Acknowledging faith when you've never had any allows you to become a danger to darkness. It allows you to become a lamp in a dark room that turns on and shines with an intense light, a light powerful enough to still give light to everything around it. Light was created to cover the darkness (Gen. 1:16). Always keep in mind though that sometimes God has to put the light in your eyes to blind you from what you've always seen, to allow you to see what you've been missing. One of the greatest accomplishments is becoming part of God's light. You will know when you are God's true light when you find yourself in the snapshot of other peoples' lives, and in the instant *you* have become the light in their life's portrait—you are empowered to impact.

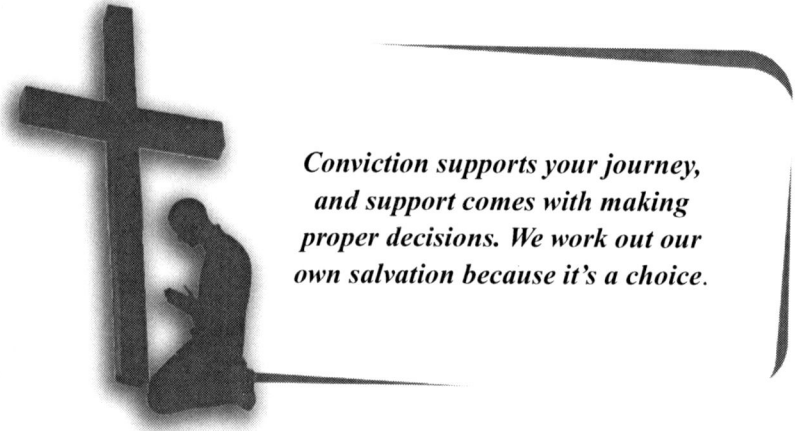

Conviction supports your journey, and support comes with making proper decisions. We work out our own salvation because it's a choice.

It took me falling into a pit of destructiveness to know I was in deep need. It was my need that drove me to Jesus.

> *My wings have been cut short and I'm blind to anything that's out of sight,*
> *Will I continue to live dark under this rock simply because I'm afraid of any heights?*
>
> *I approved myself at one point . . . but that was only for a moment,*
> *Where I thought I got a hold of hope but my heart just condoned it;*
>
> *The same heart that constantly bleeds won't allow me to be accepted,*
> *I tried to throw life away, but something out of the dust intercepted;*
>
> *There's a passage to my mind that allows the devil to go inside,*
> *But a hidden secret now developing that won't let it coincide;*
>
> *There is something screaming in me that's pleading to be alive,*
> *And if I didn't listen to this voice*
> *If my pen could bleed it would only leave*
> *. . . A trail of my written suicide.*

I did not want people to fall into the pits that I fell into because they decided to follow me. I didn't want to focus "change" on my circle of influence, meaning I don't want to change those who look like me, but those who look at me . . . everyone! And *character changes choices*!

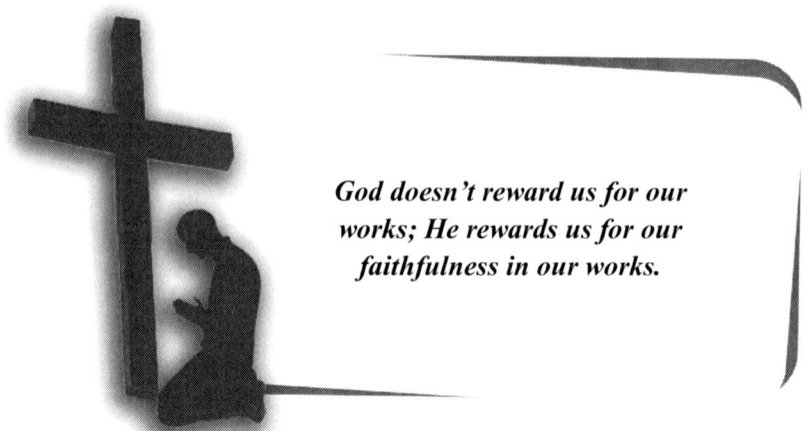

God doesn't reward us for our works; He rewards us for our faithfulness in our works.

God has to teach you and clean you, so you don't bring your lack of knowledge and problems into His purpose. Dishonest behavior that negative people put themselves in is like a dirty substance of sin. When we touch dirty things and are not cleansed, we pass it on to others. Sin can become a domino effect. God said, "Allow me to cleanse you, and as an alternative to the dark I want you to allow Me to be your light that shines when all else fails. Instead of people falling into a hole of darkness, I want you to lead them into a light where truth is exposed" (John 3:21).

I believe that when I used to say I can't do it, it was Jesus saying "don't say you can't do it, if you've never done it."

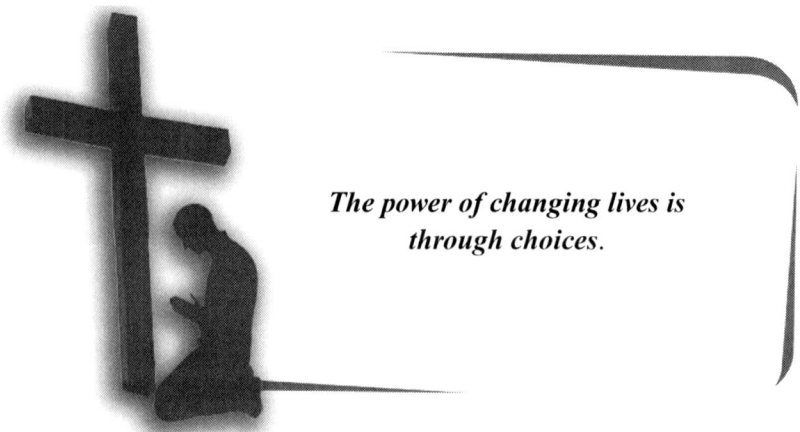

The power of changing lives is through choices.

The Lord directed me to call a friend whom I had been out of contact with for several months. I had not spoken with him for so long only because I was secluding myself completely in the Word and focusing on God. When I heard what he had to say, I knew right away why Jesus wanted me to speak to him. He spoke about a loss of hope, depression, and running off course. At the time, he didn't know the impact and transformation God was having on my life, because at one point I was leaning on him for support and at other times he was my sidekick who I was in the streets fighting with. I understood that this person was stronger than what he was telling me, and I loved him too much to let him fall. So I just started speaking the Word and power of God over him and declaring a clear road for direction in his life. He has a major gift, but no gift is unveiled if it isn't for the glory of God. I just allowed God to have His way through me to minister to him that night over the phone (Mark 16:15).

Then in time I got a text from him. *I know it's early, but ever since you spoke to me things have become clearer. I have not been able to get our conversation out of my head. I've prayed for direction, strength, humility, and the strength to keep my faith. I want to live, Tony. I felt dead inside. It is no longer I who liveth, but Christ who liveth in me. I can't escape this feeling, and it feels good. He gave me the ability to reach people through my music with my voice. I intend on telling my story, the truth, and the whole truth. I don't care about the fortune and fame it may bring me. I want the comfort it gives me. I want to make real music. Not the music I made previously. I want to tell people my story over music. I want to build them up, encourage them, and show them Jesus moves! I want to show them that God can breathe life into anything. I was dead inside, T. I didn't feel dead, I was dead. Thank you for being my brother in life and in Christ. I love you and God Bless!*

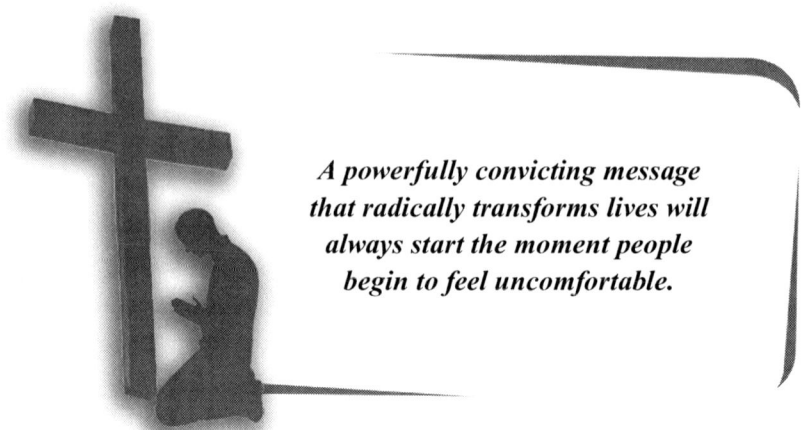

A powerfully convicting message that radically transforms lives will always start the moment people begin to feel uncomfortable.

There are specific people God will position in your life. Sometimes their position is only momentary, and other times an everlasting bond is created that helps drive you to your purpose. The right individuals the Lord positions in our life are given to us as support and strength. The wrong people in your life will make your journey and process with God an unbalanced reach for success. Just when you feel like you're getting somewhere, those people don't become a crutch, but they become the reason you need a crutch. Believe it or not, every divine purpose is accompanied with assistance and comfort.

With God you will stand out, but never stand alone.

The attainment of your purpose opens an envelope full of gifts for every individual God has appointed to help you grasp your purpose. Imagine this: God is hanging your purpose from a string in the middle of a high ceiling and the only way to get to your purpose is by using a ladder God has left for you. However, this ladder has no support, it is only one-sided, and there are no walls to lay it against. The only way to reach your purpose is with the right, trustworthy people God has positioned in your life to hold the ladder stationary while you are increasing level by level to the top. These people are your support, strength, and comfort when the climbing becomes uneasy. Without these divinely appointed people in your life, the climb to your purpose would clearly be more difficult.

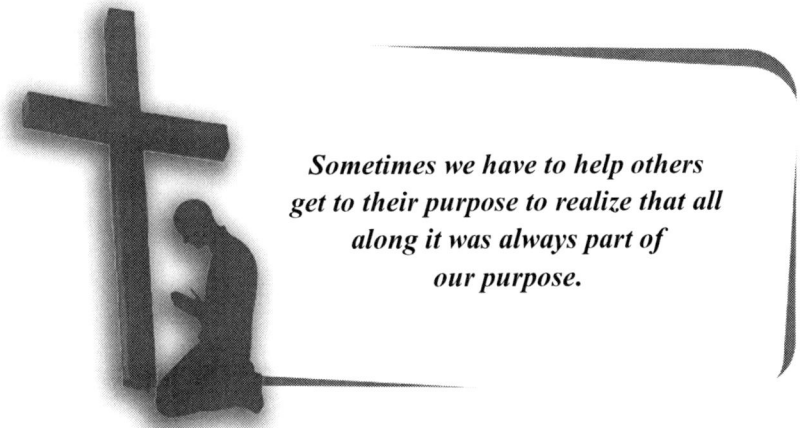

Sometimes we have to help others get to their purpose to realize that all along it was always part of our purpose.

One of my athletic coaches always gave an effective description of how a team becomes a success. In order to be a successful team, you don't need the best players; you just need the right players. It only takes one wrong player for the entire team to fall. You cannot build a team on a bent nickel.

Sometimes it is hard to understand, but there is a good reason for the intention God has for your life. Unlike your choice of the company you keep, your family is God's best choice for you. God doesn't make mistakes, and you were specifically placed into the family you were born into. That means there is a justifiable reason why you inherited the misfortunes or blessings that are occurring and will occur while your life is in bloom. Remember that not everyone is born into wealth or into a clear direction, but for those who were, it had to start from somewhere.

Imagine if you are the chosen one to change your family's course of direction (Gen. 9:9). What if the seed you plant will change the root problem of your family's finances? What if you being born into a family of wealth was precisely designed to change the views on how the money is spent and the foundation on which that money is built on? But I am in a foster family. God doesn't make mistakes. Just because there was a separation doesn't mean there was a separation from Him. You see the situation of my environment made me assume that if you climb out of a dark hole, you'll just fall into a deeper one. So while those of us in the street continued to reside in the same hole, it swayed our minds into thinking we were living with "no way out." I always said that I was a product of my environment, but it took the realization of the mind of God that I wasn't a product of my environment, but a victim of my own preventable circumstances. You cannot help the family you were born into or the neighborhood you live in, but what you can help is what you do when you leave your front porch and who you hang out with. Again, there is a choice that is made that can change the responsibility of your family's overall outreach.

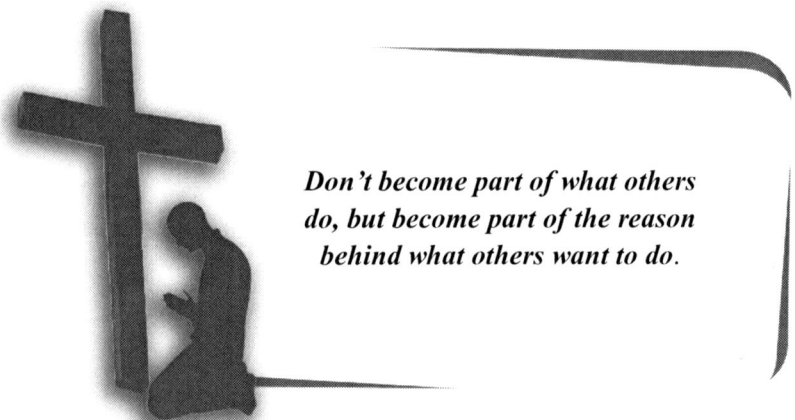

Don't become part of what others do, but become part of the reason behind what others want to do.

Even if you feel like you are at a vulnerable level, just remember in order to work your way up, you had to start somewhere below. I'm not just invested in God, but most importantly, I am "faith" fully invested in God! Allow faith to catch fire in your life, and light a path that allows you to walk directly in the steps of God. Ask yourself a life-changing question:

Is your faith based on the complaining people of Israel who never got to see the promised land, or the small group of two in Joshua and Caleb who knew they could conquer? (Num. 13). "My faith tells me that *I am bigger than where I am!*" I have bought with my life not only a front row observance of miracles, but a part in the main event to demonstrate the power of faith. We must take systematic action, a working we call faith, only because we know that in order for God to be fully expressed in our lives, it comes with a process. Not so much because of God's will, but more due to our impatient human desires. Faith can take you somewhere you have never been, but you have to attempt something big enough, and then triumph, just for faith to turn and tell you, it still wasn't big enough! We enlarge territory by eliminating boundaries. God will never give life or direction where faith isn't necessary, and without faith we sustain ourselves below a counterfeit line of potential.

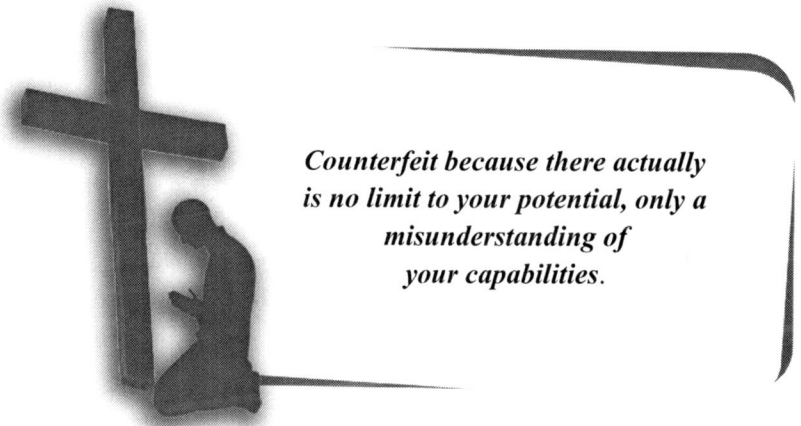

Counterfeit because there actually is no limit to your potential, only a misunderstanding of your capabilities.

We limit ourselves by using this simple statement. I can't do this! Yes, you are right you cannot do this. This is why you must have "Jesus Faith" that will renew your mind into a way of thinking that everything is believable and achievable *with* Christ. I want to get past statistics and into God's evidence, where it plainly proves that statistics are simply man's limitations.

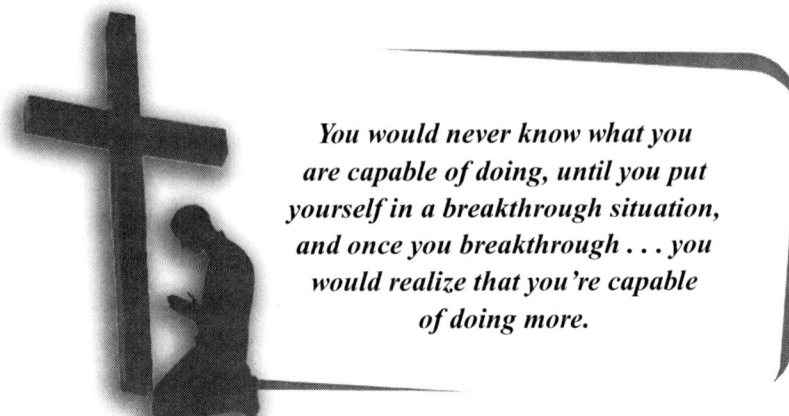

You would never know what you are capable of doing, until you put yourself in a breakthrough situation, and once you breakthrough . . . you would realize that you're capable of doing more.

I had a friend who I got into a number of discussions with about his curiosity on the topic of God. He was explaining to me how his family is good people, but financially they struggle day in and day out. He said his family honestly didn't really mind: "*My father is fortunate and content with where he is at.*" That night I asked Jesus, "Why do people become content with where their life is, if they are living in a rotation of hardship . . . especially if you guarantee more?" Jesus told me that "*even when you reach your purpose there is always more. You do not become content with where you are; you just gave up and settled for where you're at*" (2 Chron. 15:7).

If Jesus has a plan for you that will encompass the means for giving, you better trust He is going to give you more than enough. In Christ we establish a full pattern of restoration and redemption; if we are truly in Christ, we would undoubtedly receive it all. Jesus Christ is an extraordinary facility. There is a method of trust when it comes to God's generosity, and it doesn't have to do with our arms being extended, but rather the direction our wrists are turned. The individual who holds his wrists to the sky is always expecting something from somebody, and the individual who holds his wrists to the ground is always willing to drop something into somebody's life (Prov. 18:16). Our bodily expressions can determine and become a factor for the position in which God's wrists are turned in our life. A good reference would be to picture a tape measure. A tape measure gets more capacity by what is put out, and by not locking in on its purpose, it winds back up, and the tape measure loses its expansion. Success is a tape measure of life and is measured by what is put out, and will only lose what is taken in. Remember, becoming a blessing in the lives of others doesn't necessarily mean you have to give money.

God will not check your bank account before He asks you to do something or be a giver to others.

Just by giving to others you will notice how much more you have before your desire for it. Greed has a way of building you out of reward, because self-indulgence assembles four concrete walls that enclose possibility into solitude; and with no window . . . how will you ever grasp the opportunity?

My Story of Understanding

Concrete: Concrete is the opposite of abstract, and refers to a thing that actually exists or a description that allows the reader to experience an object or concept with the senses.

My Concrete Jesus

A nineteen-year-old young man had been struggling with finding direction and purpose for his life. The young man was attending school in another state, and because of a family reunion he decided to take a trip back home. Amongst the group who he hadn't seen in a few years was his grandfather. He sat with his grandfather, who asked, "How is life going?" The young man put his hands over his head and said, "S*ometimes I wonder where I'm going to be a few years down the road, how do I make it easy, and who do I have to push out of the way to get there?*" His grandfather gently asked, "What do you want to be?" The young man replied, "*Anything, as long as I'm rich and telling people what to do*!" "Well, who do you trust for that?" His grandson laughed and said, "Me!" His grandfather smiled and said, "In the morning, you're going with me."

The next morning the young man was awakened by his grandfather, who told him to get his boots on because they were going hiking. As they set out, his grandfather pointed out a patch of flowers and stated how remarkable it is that these flowers bloom into something so extravagant. The young man looked out of the corner of his eye, as if he was thinking "*huh*." The young man asked what his grandfather meant. His grandfather went on to say that in order for these flowers to bloom they must take root in good soil, and for the flowers to bloom into their full potential, they must be constantly nourished. The flowers do not need to be in full bloom to be noticed; however, they must be positioned properly in order to take bloom.

They continued walking, and his grandfather asked his grandson if he would like an orange from an orange tree. The young man said, "O*h yeah, I love oranges*." His grandfather began to explain to his grandson the beauty of the fruit. He said, "The beauty is not actually the fruit, but how the fruit is established. It takes time for production because production takes time. Everyone enjoys the fruit, but many overlook the years it took to develop something so sweet. Significantly, before the tree can produce anything, it must have years of daily maintenance. It is a miracle of nature, how over time and with proper development, a small seed can have a reward of a bountiful supply. Always remember, a tree cannot grow where it wants to; it can only grow where it was intended to."

His grandfather turned and said, "Your life is like the flower and the fruit. It is essential for you to realize that growth starts with groundwork. God is your foundation, and without Him you are not properly positioned, which means you will never grow into your full potential. Your life must have daily maintenance to make known its true beauty. Yesterday, you said that you want to push and walk over people to get to where you are going, but wouldn't it be more gratifying if you were the one picking up the people who were getting pushed, and carrying those who've been walked on? You said you wanted to be rich and tell people what to do, but how about being blessed abundantly and becoming the example of how others want to live their lives? Son, it isn't you who makes things possible. It's the Lord who makes everything possible for you" (1 Cor. 3:6). Without Jesus you will never be noticed.

> I am a flower still trying to prove, I am what I am even
> if I haven't bloomed;
> I am a tree still trying to show, I am what I am even
> if I haven't grown;
> I hear a gentle voice that says ... I agree
> You were meant to be something other than what
> people see, The problem is,
> nobody knows who you are because you never reached
> your full ability.
> We could try to prove who we really are,
> yet nobody would ever believe us;
> We could attempt something so incredible;
> still nobody would ever see us;
> But if God were to plant a seed and it grew under solid rock,
> You would hear the people screaming ... My Concrete Jesus!

Growing up, I was never fond of church. Like the majority of families, we would attend church on holidays. As I got older, and given the situation and the people I accompanied myself with, I began to disagree with church completely (2 Cor. 11:3). It was as if the only way you could get through the doors was by following "the formal code:" wear a suit and shiny shoes, no earrings, cover your tattoos, make sure you're cleanly shaven, no babies in the congregation, and you must have a Bible in hand. It was never God saying this, but mainly people who never attended church.

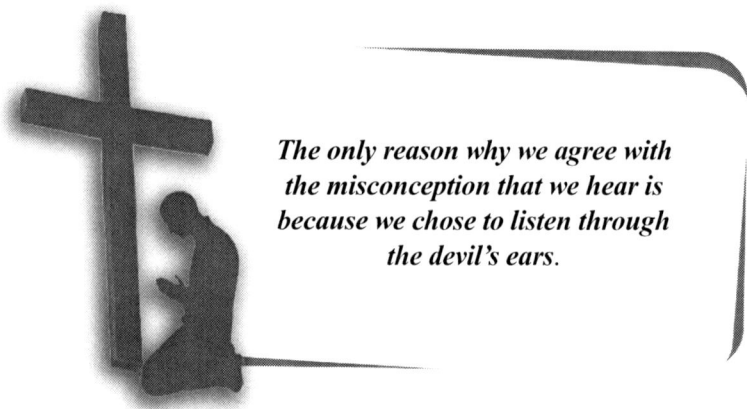

The only reason why we agree with the misconception that we hear is because we chose to listen through the devil's ears.

My hesitation with going to church was more of me being afraid of the possibilities the church would provide and the effect it would have on me. Sure enough though, when I found myself going to church, I was given "suggestions" on how not to wear my earrings, not to show my new tattoos, and even a warning about my cell phone. Yes, my cell phone of all things. My phone accidentally went off during a worship video, and I didn't even realize it was my phone. A female greeter came over to me and said, *"Turn your phone off, and if it's not Jesus music, you need to throw it away."* Just the way she said it made me want to see myself back out the door she just greeted me through. I think the complication with members who regularly attend church is that they foolishly are so quick to try and change new people instead of giving a thoughtful and warm greeting. People of faith have a responsibility to get individuals who are off course and without God into church. Once they have done this, it's time to step aside and let God do His thing. Those who grew up in the church must understand that the mind-set of any person who first comes to church or sits on "the fence" of wondering how church is inadvertently does not focus on God, but the assumption *"you can only look a certain way and be a certain person to go to church."* The only way you can change someone *"new"* in church is by changing how they assume church and church people really are. Before any new person in church realizes that church is not a social hour, but rather a place of restoration or establishment for spiritual power, he or she usually comes having a different objective. Believe it or not, the people who first come to church don't initially go for the entirety of God and His blessings, but they go for the chance to meet some good people who can possibly take them away from the crowd that has kept them a lost person.

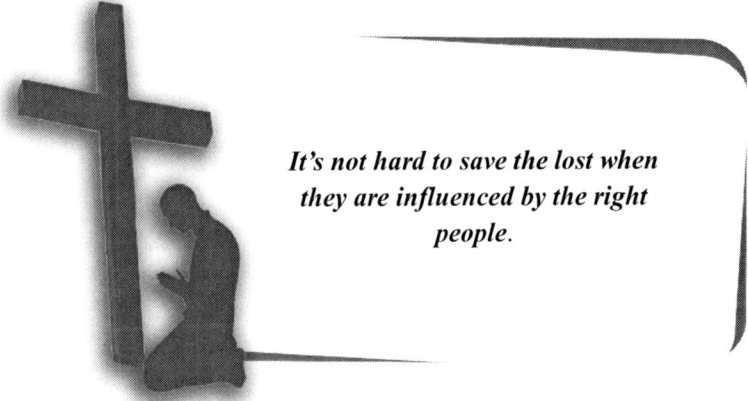

It's not hard to save the lost when they are influenced by the right people.

Again, thankfully, God jumped in the middle of my cluttered state of mind and made me stay in church to realize there are some absolutely amazing people of faith and mighty people of God in between the church walls.

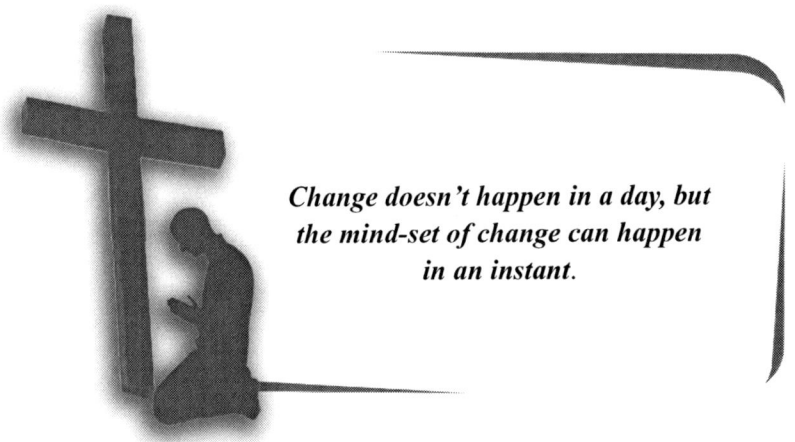

Change doesn't happen in a day, but the mind-set of change can happen in an instant.

My small-mindedness only allowed me to focus on what was bad and not the numerous, boundless, powerful things in the church. Really, when understanding is developed, the people who we tend to focus on are still in the midst of their change.

I let people who didn't believe in church persuade me into not going to church: *they take your money*; *church is only for good people*; *there is no reason for church*!

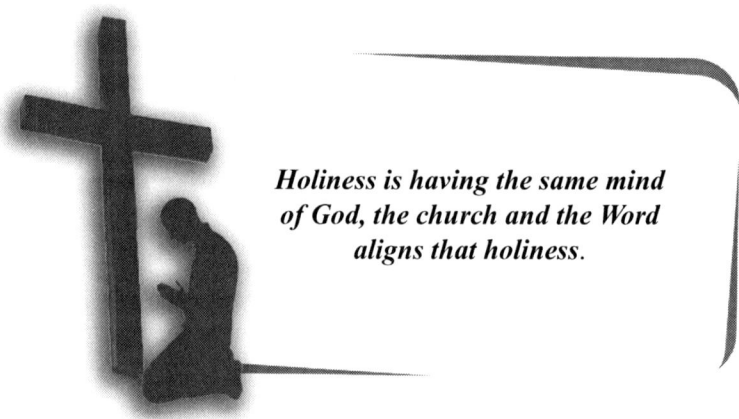

Holiness is having the same mind of God, the church and the Word aligns that holiness.

During my alternation of mind, God attuned my viewpoint on others' opinions about church and the statement, *"All they want is money!"* In reality, if that were the case, why wouldn't the church charge a door fee? *"That was part of the Old Testament. It doesn't clarify that we need to pay tithes in the New Testament!"* Well, show me where in the New Testament it says that we are exempt from tithing. I can afford to pay tithes, but I can't afford to be wrong.

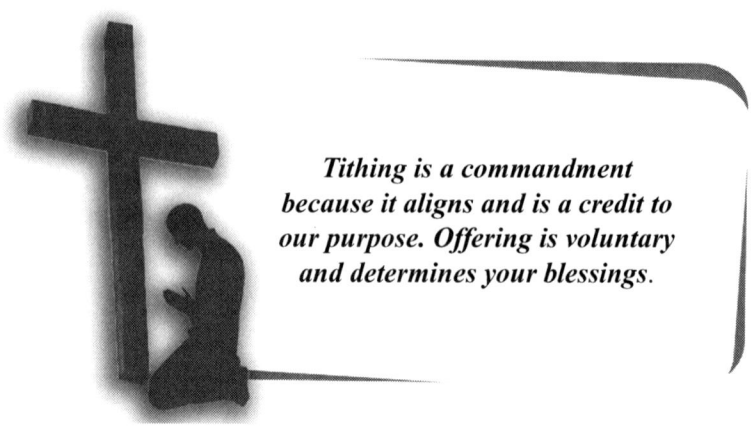

Tithing is a commandment because it aligns and is a credit to our purpose. Offering is voluntary and determines your blessings.

I like to think this way: Tithing and offering is not only a worldly blessing, but it is a heavenly investment into our home in the kingdom of God.

No one says you have to give when the tithe and offering plate comes around, only God! No one says you have to listen when tithe and offering is discussed, only God! No one says you don't have to be in church, except the devil (Eph. 6:10-11). The church is the atmosphere of faith. The church is the greatest institution. The church assists in accessing God's inside information. The church reveals the lenses for you to get a glimpse into your life. The church exposes your weakness so you can grow in strength. The church is the restoration gateway to the restoration God. The church is the deposit box for your blessings. The church is where God's thoughts are revealed. The church exposes the word, behind the Word. The church is the birth place of difference. Oh, and most importantly, the church is the last stop before heaven or hell! But let's go beyond that to the individuals who are in unison with God, realize that as God's people . . . we are the church!

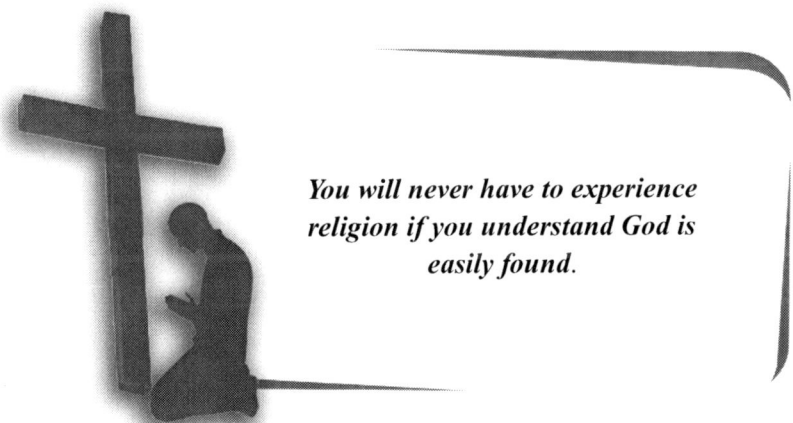

You will never have to experience religion if you understand God is easily found.

Many people have asked me how I got so deep into religion; they have tried to experience it as well. My only response is that I never knew religion. It all began with a relationship between me and God that grew to a level of intimacy that allowed me to become familiar with and confident in God. Religion is man's attempt to get to God or, as others like to say, "failed attempt," and a relationship is when you have found God. Intimacy is the confidence and familiarity of God. I initiated my relationship with

God by surrendering myself to Him. God then tested my heart and led me to a door that I never knew was there. I gained intimacy with God when I went through that door, shut it, and locked it, completely closing myself in with Him. Jesus arranged me in a place of seclusion where He could establish a strong base of the Word in my life. How do you know where your life is? Just ask yourself, *"How does my life stand in front of the Word of God?"*

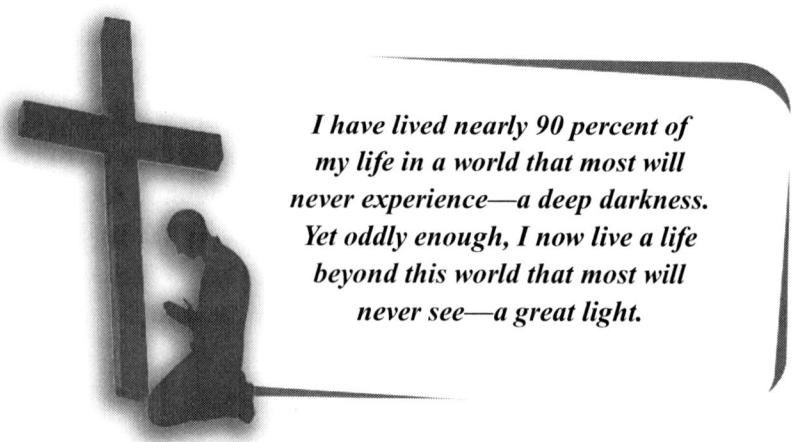

I have lived nearly 90 percent of my life in a world that most will never experience—a deep darkness. Yet oddly enough, I now live a life beyond this world that most will never see—a great light.

How is it possible that we impregnate our hearts with truth, but still give birth to lies with our mouths? The answer is a lack of devotional life! Many still ask me, how did God become such a passion in your life? How did God become absolutely everything you do, speak about, and see? A great analogy would be to picture an image from a distance. No matter how big the image is, as long as it stays at a distance, you'll never experience its vast magnitude. The majority of people of faith have this problem, when not realizing how big our God actually is. The moment you drop everything in your life and truly go running to God, the closer you get, you would realize how big He really is. When you get close enough, God then becomes the only thing you see. The greatest thing I've done for myself is establishing the significance of Gethsemane in my life: a new fear of being separated from God.

The problem with believers today is that the Bible has become the greatest Word unspoken.

Jesus then told me this: *The world will second-rate your mind, and even before you've started man has already counted you out. When you are already expected not to win, what do you have to lose? Stay within the Word because the Word is light.* If I have read God's Word to become part of what it promises me to be, and what it promises for me to have, if I don't have its power, its spirit, its wisdom, its sovereignty, I will not only stand before men, but before God feeling naked. Lord, help me to become as powerful as the Word that I read! The light plainly makes clear to every man that what has been done to you has been done because of God. The Bible will only change you and lead you to light with understanding and application. Stay within the Word and don't take shortcuts around the Word, because shortcuts are filled with shadows and you will never experience the light if you stand in the dark. Always remember the only way the devil has power in our lives is if we give attention to what he is offering (Matt. 4:3-4). The devil does not grab us and pull us in; he attracts us, and we end up going to him. So it is important to know that the devil doesn't choose to walk with us; we choose to walk with the devil. The light is a support of God's grace which allows you to conquer the devil's pitiless attempts to trouble your life. Man's turning to God has a reserved attachment set apart strictly for a deep satisfying experience that can only be experienced while in His will over your life. Nobody can create the response of God in your life, your only cause of God being evident is very simple, your belief must exceed your disbelief. When you have a lack of faith it means you have lack of God. When you are lacking God your own logically acceptance is skepticism. Without any demonstration of God in our lives we are simply living within a practical atheism without even knowing it. I believe in God's Word "The Light" and believe the Spirit of God's greatest impartation in our lives are the capabilities of signs, miracles, and wonders.

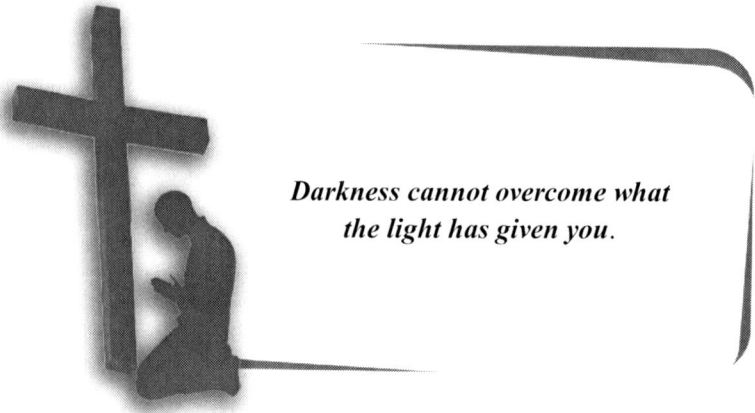

Darkness cannot overcome what the light has given you.

Jesus gave me an abundance of grace and light, which started to reign in my life. The opportunity that drew me closer to Jesus was an encounter with the devil that I overcame.

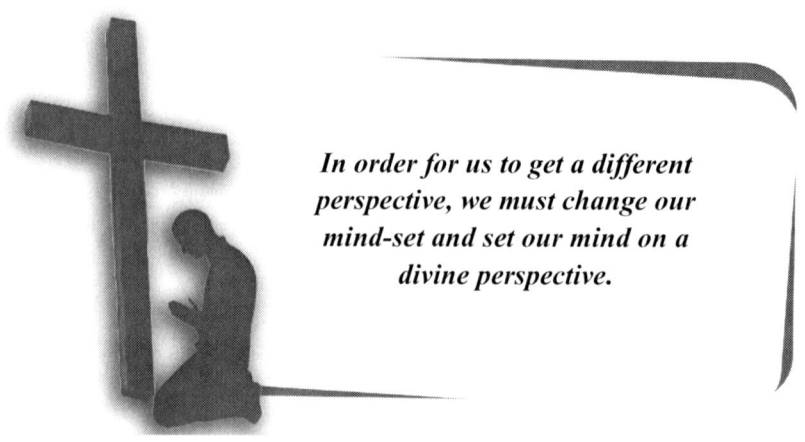

In order for us to get a different perspective, we must change our mind-set and set our mind on a divine perspective.

I personally got closer to Jesus by allowing myself to become absentminded of the conflicts the devil put in my life. You see, one of my biggest faults was my anger; so God being the loving God that He is, made that His main point of deliverance in my life. While Jesus was in the midst of cleansing me and setting me free from the bondage that kept me from Him, He explained this to me: *Anything that I deliver you from I completely cleanse and empty out from your spirit, which means I evict the devil from what holds you captive, but I warn you whatever I empty out will always leave a large vacant space, and if you don't fill that space of deliverance with the Word and the trust and love of God, the devil will come and seize the opportunity to fill that space with not only anger, but with rage and hate: the sister and brother of your biggest faults. Yes, it will leave you worse off than before. I will deliver you, but you must fill in that space with trust in Me* (Matt. 12:43-45). This prepared me for the devil's attack. The devil knew that my weakness was my anger and desire for respect. I woke up one morning with God heavily on my mind and His voice declaring this: *Today is the day, get ready . . . today is the day, get ready.* I knew that morning was the day the devil was going to test me. Man, was God right, and I didn't even have to wait long. That morning about an hour after the Lord prepared me for what was about to come, I let my dogs out in the backyard through the side of my house. The backyard of the house I was renting was shared with another tenant whose house was on the same fenced-in property. I always let my dogs out whenever I knew that she was gone so my dogs could run freely in the yard. Not even five minutes after I let them out, I heard a loud scream of profanity. I went out in a hurry and saw the devil coming out of this woman. She was screaming that she was going to kill me and my dogs. The whole time I tried to reassure her that it was not intentional, and I apologized for having them out in the yard, but she never let me speak. So I just began to pray the Word of God over myself, and I asked God to help me keep my composure. She threw her hands up and said she was going to call the landlord and went into her home. In that instant I thought, "Man, that was easy, thank the Lord." Not quite. About ten minutes later I heard the same screaming in the backyard, so again I went outside to tell her that, if she would listen to me, it was an accident and it won't happen again. But before I could say anything she walked up to my face and spat! This woman just had the audacity to spit on my face. She turned quickly and headed to her door. All I could say was, "*You just spat on my face,*" and she said, "*Prove it!*" I went into my house, and for the next twenty minutes I kept praying for God to calm my nerves and situate his peace in my heart. The Lord helped me keep my composure during this mess, but all I was thinking was that I would have rather had her punch me in the face than to leave me feeling degraded. Just then, I realized I had a light embracing me and a space that was now being filled with the trust that I now had for God. This was a trust solely based on the belief that with God I can overcome my greatest weakness. Close to an hour after this situation, I saw her in the front of my house, so I opened the door and told her that if there was anything she was going through I was willing to listen, and that I forgave her for what just happened, and no matter what I still had love for her (2 Cor. 2:10-11). In that moment, I could literally see the obstacles that kept me from the road of God completely fall before me.

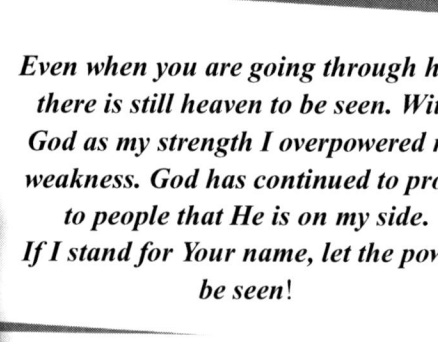

Even when you are going through hell, there is still heaven to be seen. With God as my strength I overpowered my weakness. God has continued to prove to people that He is on my side. If I stand for Your name, let the power be seen!

MY SECRET PLACE

In my mind's eye, the probability of an actual God throughout high school was minimal, simply because I figured that the painting of my life was hate engraved and destined for the grave. I would cry myself to sleep knowing that the world didn't want me. The spaces in between my heartbeat let me know how close I was to actually giving up. From the crying of my heart I wanted something different, but nothing happened. I was internally drowning myself with sorrow. *If there was a God, why would He allow me to live outside of me?* Soon, I found out that mysteries in the Bible or even in life are not something that needs to be answered, but understood that in a place greater they have already been answered. In high school, I wrote a short abstraction of my life.

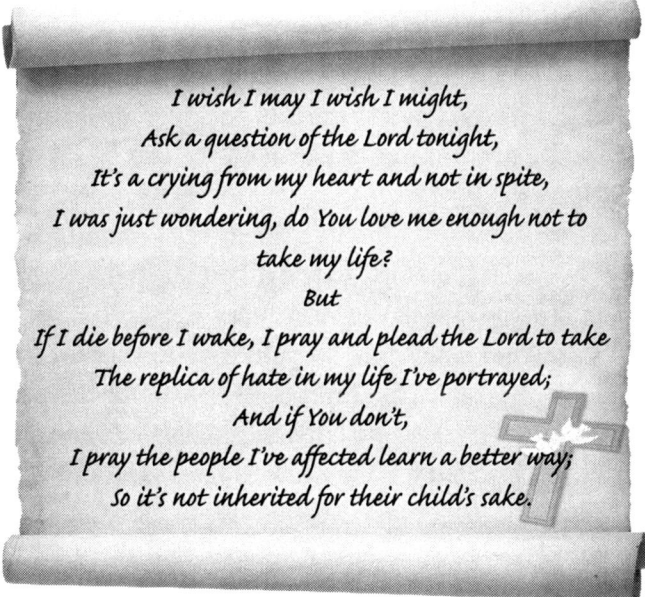

I wish I may I wish I might,
Ask a question of the Lord tonight,
It's a crying from my heart and not in spite,
I was just wondering, do You love me enough not to take my life?
But
If I die before I wake, I pray and plead the Lord to take
The replica of hate in my life I've portrayed;
And if You don't,
I pray the people I've affected learn a better way;
So it's not inherited for their child's sake.

God quickly brought attention to that pain and framed its displeasure. God was showing me that in that frame was an upside-down picture and it was up to me to turn it back around, by choice. My life is a demonstration of one thing—a God answering prayer. Praying is not about getting all the right answers; it's about finding all the right questions. This has allowed me to appreciate what *our* prayers can establish for others. We are in a time where we are completely lost as children of God. Selfishly, we are pleased because *we* are in good health. *We* are financially secure. *We* have a job. *We* have a roof over our head. *We* have food to eat. That's great, but *we* are missing the very center of discipleship, impacting and transforming individual lives. Do we not realize that we can actually pray power into being? That we can pray the transition of lives into being? That we can pray the glory of God's cause into being? We have not, because we ask not! When God stands before His congregation, silent, He is not thinking where are the men of honor; He is thinking where are the men of prayer. One of the most fascinating changes God made in me during my transformation was taking a place of paranoia and turning it into a place that became my main prayer corner. You see, when you become the reason for affecting other's lives, it actually affects yours . . . either good or bad, but for me it was bad. There was something about my bathroom that gave me a mistrusting fear. I could not go into my bathroom without looking behind the shower curtain. I would open one side, then the other, and even look between the shower curtain and the shower liner. Even as I was leaving, I would have to quickly look again. It was not just my house, but literally any bathroom I walked in. The bathroom made me nervous!

The outlets on the walls were like the eyes of iniquity staring at me. I would have to look in the outlet to see if I could find a camera and then turn off the bathroom light to confirm there was no red recording light on, weird! If I used the bathroom, I would have to shut the lights off just to make myself comfortable. As God would have it, the bathroom became my secret place with Him. I would have extremely deep conversations and visual experiences with God in the shower. The bathroom was a place of uneasiness; it was the first place I called out to God, and it became my secret place with Him. I would take a notepad and sit against the wall in the bathroom and just pray (Matt. 9:29). Obviously, the bathroom does not concern me now; I actually like taking shower after shower just to continue my conversation with God. There is a place where we can all meet God spiritually; the question is, have you gotten there yet?

The one place I was paranoid about is where God brought my prayer about.

**If you look into anything I've overcome
It was with the help of being under One
Who guarantees the possibility of it being done.**

My Character Builder

Why would God place so such pain upon me? I thought that He was a loving God. Imagine the influences in your life to be like small pebbles, and *you* are the marvelous opportunity hiding behind the tinted window. When something around the house is cracked but not completely broken, the majority of us find something to support its brokenness. The small pebbles being thrown your way chip, crack, and splinter your life, but are never enough to allow you to see the pebbles or the bad influence for what it actually is—damage. God's love becomes quite visible in times of our brokenness, because the only way for the *window* to see the need to be replaced is when it is completely broken.

There is a secret dominance that captures our overall aptitude for intellect in our lives. The only way this mental power becomes confined is by covering it or filling it with the influence of the devil's substandard traditions. The way the devil can capture us is by making it personal, by arranging who we are not meant to be through the influence of the wrong people. Our character determines the quality of our nature, meaning our surroundings will establish what we learn and who we become as a person. We must realize that whoever or whatever we allow to build our character will establish what we obtain and retain in our existing lives. Do not allow your character to be equipped by the opinions of your inner circle. Why would you try to change your life without removing your influence? Meaning, what would be the point in pulling up a thorny bush from its root, if you were just to plant a seed that never grew?

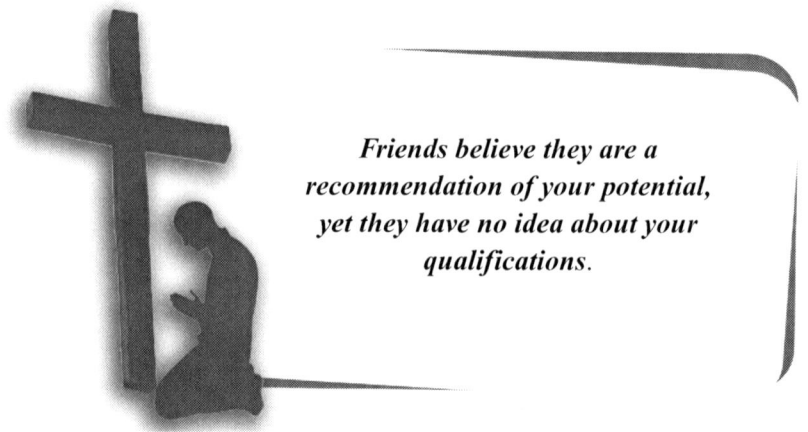

Friends believe they are a recommendation of your potential, yet they have no idea about your qualifications.

It was vital that I understood this because the Lord told me that He had to separate me from the motive that has built my character: "*I have to separate you from your character builder*" (Jer. 9:5). In order for God to make a move in your life, sometimes you have to move people out of your life. This puts you in a perfect position for God to use *you*. The Bible is not based on logical thinking, but illogical people. That's what makes you so important to God; you are perfect for Him. You don't lack knowledge because of who you are, but you lack knowledge because of who you are with. If you were to put two inferior individuals together, you would realize that their intellect is based on what they are accustomed to. *They never exit their comfort zone*. Now, if you were to separate these two inferior individuals and position them in the presence of people whose life objective is based on wisdom planted in fertile ground, they will adapt to that style and become accustomed to that increase of knowledge.

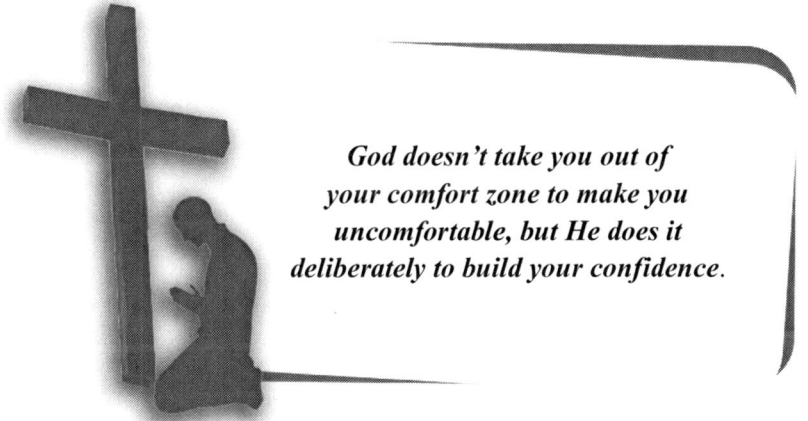

God doesn't take you out of your comfort zone to make you uncomfortable, but He does it deliberately to build your confidence.

Your immediate friends dictate what expands your heart and mind, which will in turn develop your overall character. Always remember though that not all friends build up confidence, because not all encouragement builds up courage. Our life can turn on a "*drop of a dime*," but only you choose as the dime turns if you will be lying face up or face down. Our character has everything to do with the position God has in our life. Our character determines how God will use our life as a demonstration for others. With a bad character God demonstrates what it is like to be without Him, and a Godly character will demonstrate what it is like to be with

Him. Start making adjustments with the company you keep. God is not telling you to push people out of your life, but instead push them into life. You're not pushing people out of your life; you're just making room for what is coming in your life. I say all this because it was something I had to do, and now this is something that I have to continue to do. It's a way of showing people that I am no longer scared of information; I am no longer scared to feel as if I am alone without anyone's approval. For me, it has now become the only way to show the source of intelligence and more importantly deliverance in Jesus Christ.

I was at a recreational park, leaning up against a fence one night, watching a ball game during my teens. A parent of one of my friends heard about some of the things that were going on in my life, and he said, "Tony, you are better than what is around you." I replied with, "You don't understand." He said again, "I understand that you are better than what is around you." I looked over at him and said, "You have no idea what I have been through in my past." He said, "You are right. I don't know about your past. But if you continue to hang around the people you are hanging out with . . . I can tell you all about your future."

I am amazed when hearing God speak, because just by hearing what He had to say to me, even in rebuke, it allowed me to be reintroduced to myself. It changed me. When Jesus speaks, you can hear behind His every word . . . these are My words of opportunity. I realized that the right company will completely change the way you think, which determines how you find your way out of obstacles.

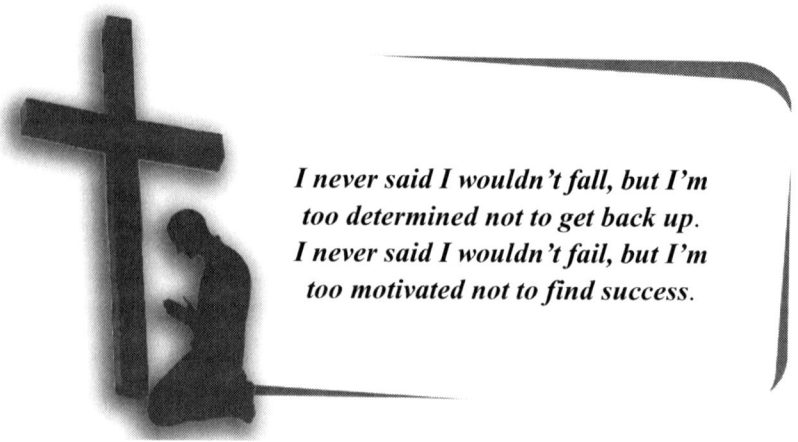

I never said I wouldn't fall, but I'm too determined not to get back up.
I never said I wouldn't fail, but I'm too motivated not to find success.

My friends' opinions used to influence me until I started thinking with this mind-set: *My friends' opinions of "who I am" no longer interest me because they don't dictate who I'm meant to be. You see, certain friends said I would stumble and fall, but God said I would be far from the ground. Now my question to them is, what hurts more? To see yourself in the same position you're in, or seeing me out of the position I was once in?*

Many people now ask me how I got to where I am today, and all I say is, *I started walking for a cause that was greater than my own interest.*

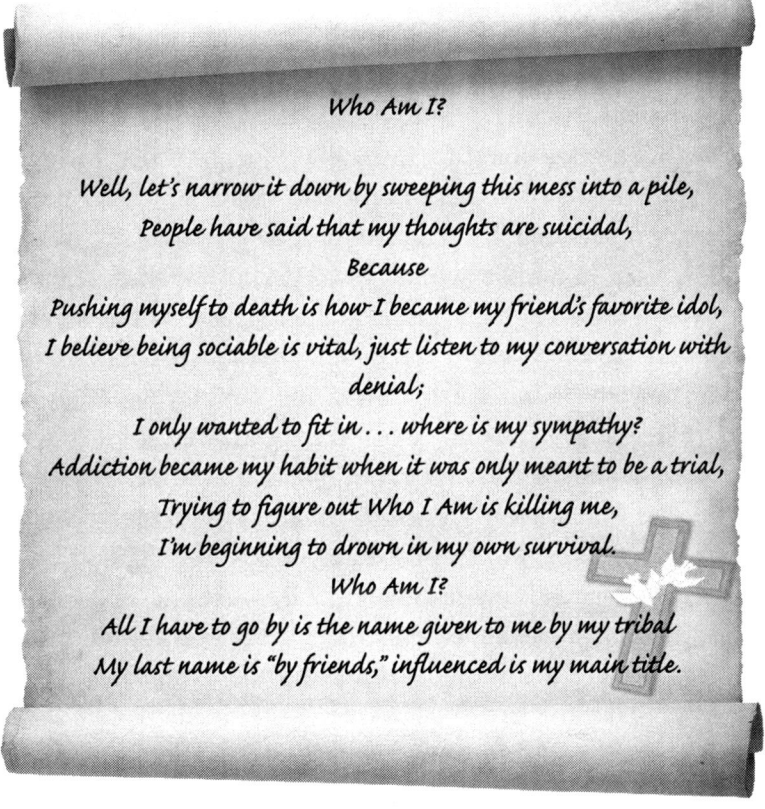

Who Am I?

Well, let's narrow it down by sweeping this mess into a pile,
People have said that my thoughts are suicidal,
Because
Pushing myself to death is how I became my friend's favorite idol,
I believe being sociable is vital, just listen to my conversation with denial;
I only wanted to fit in . . . where is my sympathy?
Addiction became my habit when it was only meant to be a trial,
Trying to figure out Who I Am is killing me,
I'm beginning to drown in my own survival.
Who Am I?
All I have to go by is the name given to me by my tribal
My last name is "by friends," influenced is my main title.

Why does God keep you in a progressive mode? Being connected to the wrong company makes your movement routine. If your movement is routine or dwells inside a comfort zone, it simply means that the devil knows who you are, where you are, and the next move you will make. In other words, the devil has you right where he wants you! We are obtained by the blood to do God's will, not maintained in the blood to do as we will. God's plan is always prepared and established for advancement. It's not just moving; it's progressing (Deut. 1:6-8). The devil's hate of progression is his disadvantage, because growth and increase cause irregularity. Irregularity creates a game of hide-and-go-seek for the devil, but now you have the advantage.

> ***Remember, just because you are moving does not mean you are progressing.***

When Jesus said that He had to separate me from my character builder, instantly, one person in particular came to mind. There was a certain individual whom I could perhaps trust my life with and could unquestionably always count on to be there for me when I needed him most. This person's involvement in my life was a bonus for me simply because we were undeniably connected. On two separate occasions I was jumped as a teen. In middle school, I was part of the track squad. I was heading over to the local high school at the location where we practiced as a team. This particular day I and another teammate headed over there early because we were in the same event and were trying to get finished ahead of time. All of a sudden we heard a shout from some high school dropouts who demanded that we get off *"their sidewalk."* My teammate moved; I didn't. There were five of them, and I never said a word, but I also didn't budge . . . until one of the guys stuck his finger in my face.

At first, I had the advantage in the fight because I never gave the kid a chance to swing back, but about ten swings in my foot got caught in a gap between the fence and the sidewalk. Before I could reach down and pull my foot out from under the fence four of the five kids jumped in. Witnesses said that it seemed as if they were trying to stab me but instead smacked me in the back of the head with a fence post; yes, a fence post (Lam. 3:2). The friend whom I had such a deep relationship with saw the ordeal from a distance and ran up with a few other friends of ours and scared the group off. He was also part of the assembly in those days who took serious the phrase *"If you hurt him, you hurt me. If you mess with him, then you mess with me."* And yes, we got our retaliation. The second incident was in high school, and we were going to a New Year's Eve party arranged by a group of football players from another school who graduated a few years before.

We headed over to this party with a group of five that got cut down to four because one of our friends got arrested for a narcotic possession. He got arrested as we were on our way to the party because we decided to steal boxes of chicken from a grocery store. He was actually arrested and charged with narcotics and not for the petty theft. Well, needless to say, we crashed the party because one of the football players pushed a friend I brought, and we started fighting. At that particular moment it was my friend and me against about ten people, so he ran out the front door and I ran out the back door. It was a smart move on my part because I went out the door where everyone but my own friends were. I was now being stomped on by about fifteen people, who were all about fifty pounds heavier than me and about five years older than me. Nobody would jump in to help me out except this individual who was not only my friend, but one of my very best friends. Being as close as we were, instead of me continuing to get trampled on, he smashed a guy in the face with a bottle and intentionally shifted the entire group on to him.

It is kind of an eccentric story considering we had become "partners in crime." My first encounter with him was in sixth grade. I took his chain, and shortly after it turned green I gave it back to him. Somehow out of that situation we became inseparable. Now, where our account of inseparability is summoned apart is when God didn't tell me to make the right decision, but instead he put the right decision in front of me. One night my friend went out with a group of other kids, and in about five minutes he became involved in a drug deal gone wrong. In five minutes, trying to make some fast cash, he found himself taking a plea bargain for an attempted murder charge and was sentenced on a first offense to serve three years mandatory. I stood by him as a "friend" when no one else did. For three years I sent him pictures and commissary/canteen, and I visited him many times in different state prisons. I didn't know God at the time, but while he was in prison, he sure sent a lot of truth in the scripture he would mail me. The day he was released it was a pleasant feeling, but that feeling didn't last long. I question what makes a man turn back to the same people who never did anything for him in life or while he was incarcerated. Why would you go back to the same hole with the same substances that were trying to bury you in the first place? Some people are too weak to realize the formula of the street (Ps. 55:11). The "street law" state of mind is where ignorance makes you want to be the man in your own limelight. You do meaningless things in the streets so people you admire can cosign for your respect, giving you "street credibility." In the streets you are given two options: become a "jackboy" or learn to spot a "jackboy," meaning to stay on the move before somebody moves on you. The only way you can become street certified is if people fear you, basically where pain is your vision. You'd think you would have some common sense to realize what the street routine provides when you've got half of your influence in the courtroom fighting for their lives. Until you face your life, you will never understand what time means. When you lose your life, the only thing you find yourself fighting for is an appeal. What is even more ridiculous is when you are locked up; that's when God becomes everyone's best friend. The best way to explain a street person's relationship with God is that when you're face-first on the ground you can't stop calling out to Him, but the moment you're comfortable it's like God no longer exists. Three months after he was released he was issued an active warrant. He was later taken into custody and on his way to trial, facing consecutive life sentences. While he was awaiting trial, I alone, again, stood by his side. The third day of trial the verdict read *not guilty*, and he was free once again. Not even an hour after he was released he was sucked back into the undertow of the street routine. This time around God was filling my life with His good grace and had reinforced a bolder of truth as a backbone in my life. The problem was that I had stood by this person for so long, yet somehow he didn't recognize me anymore. My question was, "why?" During the last months approaching his trial date something started happening to me. I had been having intense dreams. I dreamt dreams of peace, difference, and a change in me. I also dreamt about a young woman crying on my shoulder as we were standing on a hill overlooking what seemed to be a large city. All she could say was "*Thank you . . . thank you . . . thank you, Jesus*!" I woke up in tears. The person who I thought was me wasn't me at all. It was a totally different person that I couldn't even recognize, but nonetheless . . . *it was me*! It was through this particular dream that I fell into a circle of understanding. I started thumbing through the Bible and came to Genesis 1:26: "Let us make man in our image . . ." I also found Hebrews 13:5: " . . . Never will I leave you; never will I forsake you . . .," and Hebrews 13:14: "For here we do not have an enduring city, but we are looking for the city to come."

Jesus had been trying to demonstrate a new life to me for so long, and He didn't want to lose me. He showed me that the man in my dream is the "God in me." And although the city is not completed, He was showing me the city to come.

You see, during this trial I crossed paths with an old lost friend, and not too far into our conversation he said, "Let's get into something tonight." I said, "I think I will. The Bible is calling my name." He laughed and quickly said, "Man, you really ain't the same." I anxiously replied, "*I have no problem reintroducing myself.*"

After speaking with this other person, I realized that my best friend could potentially keep me from getting closer to the Cross. God wasn't telling me that I couldn't be there for this person, but what He was saying is that I couldn't be with this person. You can't be with this person not because you don't love him, but the problem is that you love him to much. His trouble might get you into trouble. Before I last spoke to him, I planted a seed of hopeful transformation in him and let him know that I am no longer a part of death, but a part of a life that is predicated on living. Jesus is the only One who can bring restoration, not back to your original condition, but God's original intention. You can't possibly love Jesus to the highest degree until you know how much He loves you. God let me realize that I can't change anyone unless the person has the desire to change. The only way you might be able to make an impact on his way of life is by completely changing yours and letting him see that the God who is in you wants to be in him. The God that is abundantly providing for your needs will do the same for him. Some people have to witness miracles before they become a miracle themselves.

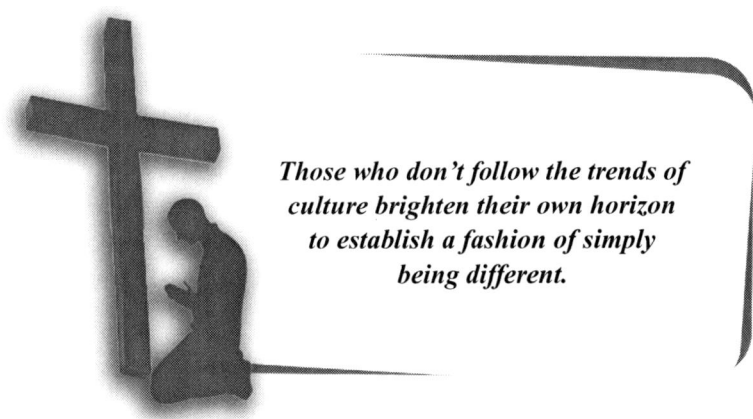

Those who don't follow the trends of culture brighten their own horizon to establish a fashion of simply being different.

MY WRITTEN WILL

I faithfully took a walk toward obedience and learned not to settle for anything less than scripture. You don't develop the Gospel in your life; you understand the Gospel, and it begins to develop you. So I resisted all social aspects and pressures that could have hindered my direction toward God. I knew with all my heart that Jesus had a message He wanted so desperately for me to know. My question was, *"how could I hear God?"* Then it came to me.

Sometimes before we hear God, we see His written will.

My faithful walk led me to a mailbox with my written will from God in it. You have absolutely no understanding of Christ without having gone through the Gospel to get it. There is always a message from God waiting to be disclosed that reveals His will. It is imperative to understand that we are not waiting on God to give us the message, but God is waiting on us to open the message. In this message it doesn't tell you how, where, or when, but it simply gives you awareness of the importance of your purpose. I can remember so well what led me to the mailbox. It began at work while I was installing carpet on a staircase. For the next hour, without even realizing it, I was repeating "Deuteronomy" over and over in my head. At that moment, I was literally at the mailbox, but didn't recognize the significance of what I was saying. I completely disregarded it. Then about three days later I woke up in the middle of the night saying "Deuteronomy" again! I looked up and said, "I don't understand what that means. *Are You wanting me to read Deuteronomy?"* In my foolishness, I didn't pay much mind to it after that. More than two weeks later I woke up again, now for the third time, with "Deuteronomy" on my mind. I told my cousin, *"I think God wants me to read Deuteronomy*." That night I sat down and read the thirty-four chapters of the Book of Deuteronomy. I didn't initially have the mind-set to read it to actually understand anything. I didn't even overemphasize going back to comprehend what the meaning was for each chapter. I read the complete Book of Deuteronomy without stopping or letting it sink in. When I was finished, the Holy Spirit sent a roller coaster of scripture throughout my mind. I could literally see everything I just read in a secluded form. I went out to the living room, paused, and told my cousin, "*I think God is telling me something now*." That is really all I could explain. I went back into my room, picked up a pen and paper, and just started writing what I could see in my head. I wasn't reading as I was writing because it was all coming and going so fast. I was just writing. After that last word, I went back and started reading. Now, everything that was written was not written for comprehension or in any chronological order. I was just writing as I could see it in my head. I kid you not, about a quarter of the way into my reading I dropped my pen and a tear trickled down my cheek. It was as if God Himself wrote a letter for me, sealed it, put it into an envelope, and said, "Here, Tony, this is what you need to prepare for." I could not believe what I was reading and how it came out. Now remember, I read the entire Book of Deuteronomy without putting anything in perspective. I wrote only what I saw in my head and never stopped to read it. The outcome is exactly what you are about to read without editing or putting it in sequential form. You will read it as written and exactly how God gave it to me.

Deuteronomy
August 31, 2008

You have stayed at these mountains long enough. I have given you new land and opportunity; go and take possession of it that I swore would be given. You are able to increase one thousand times and be blessed as I have promised. Your numbers will increase today as many as there are stars in the sky. Go hear the disputes amongst the world, but *do not show partiality in judging; hear both small and great alike*. Do not be afraid of any man because judgment belongs to me. Bring me any case too hard for you, and I will hear it and at that time I will tell you what to do. Where can you go when your fellow man has lost heart, "The people are stronger and taller, the cities are larger, with walls up to the sky!"

Show them that it is I who said do not be terrified; do not be afraid; I am here and will fight for you before your very eyes. You are never alone, and when you are weary, it is then when you will see I will carry you until we reach this destined place. It is by my Word which you will not be lost. Trust in me because I am ahead of your journey, in fire by night and in cloud by day, to search out places for you to rest and to show you the way you should go. Follow me wholeheartedly, and I will give you the very land you set your feet on. If you choose not to follow me, turn around and set out toward the desert along the route to the Red Sea. You must do as I command. *You must fight when I say fight, not as you wish, because I will not be with you, and you will be defeated by your enemies.* I have been with you throughout your journey, and you have not lacked anything. Listen to my commands. You will come across men who will be afraid. Do not provoke them into war. Greet them with hospitality, and I will bless you in all the work of your hands. With patience and direction I will deliver what has been promised. I am about to teach you more, but do not add to what I command you and do not subtract from it. You have seen with your own eyes I have *taken and destroyed everyone who was wrong for you* and all who held fast to me are still alive today. You must choose wise and respected men to follow. *Do not follow followers; you must follow leaders in order to lead.* Observe them carefully, for this will show your wisdom and understanding to the nations *who will hear about the decrees I have told you.* Be careful, and watch yourself so you do not forget the things your eyes have seen or let them slip from your heart as long as you live. You will also teach this to your children and the children after them and remember the day *you stood before me and asked me for "more" and the deliverance of your well-being.* You are very near and standing at the foot of the mountain as it blazes with fire to the very heavens with black clouds and deep darkness. You have heard the sound of the words but have seen no form. Be careful of the mountain you stand on and the corrupt fire that lurks. *I was once angry with you because of your betrayal, but because of your turnaround faithfulness you will take possession of good.* Do not make yourself an idol in the form of anything I have forbidden, for I am a consuming fire, a jealous God. *Do not become a part of evil because it provokes me into anger.* Instead *depart evil from evil*; demanding "If you seek the Lord your God, *you will find him if you look for him with all your heart and with all your soul.*

When you are in distress and consumed with bad you will not return to those latter days, but to the Lord your God and obey him, for our God is a merciful God; *he will not abandon or destroy you!" You have seen my miraculous signs and wonders that I am God and there is none like Me. I have brought you out of turmoil by my presence and great strength.* These are the commandments I have proclaimed in a stern voice on the mountain from out of the fire, the clouds, and the deep darkness. Today you will learn that *a man can live even if God speaks to him,* so walk in all the way I have commanded you, so that you may live and prosper and prolong your days. *You will increase greatly in a land filled with milk and honey.* I will provide you cities filled with all kinds of good things already there. Continue to do right and what is good in my sight and watch as I thrust out the enemies before you. *As a testament you will tell others that you have been saved by my mighty hand and have witnessed miraculous signs and wonders. I have brought you out from your troubles and brought you into what I have promised.* You are to speak the truth of Me and by this it will drive out the wicked and nonbelievers, you will not be able to eliminate them all at once or they will multiply like wild animals, but one by one the images of their false gods are to burn in fire. *I have led you through the desert to humble you and test you in order to know what was in your heart. I have humbled you which has caused you to hunger, which made you learn that man does not live on bread alone but on every word that comes from my mouth.* Continue to walk in my ways and *I will bring you into a good land*—a land with streams and pools of water with springs flowing in the valleys and hills. Do not say to yourself, *"My power and the strength of my hands have provided wealth for me"* because *it is I who gives the ability to produce wealth,* and if you don't believe, it is you who will be destroyed in time. You may think, why do they have and I do not? Then I say to you I have seen these people, and they are stiff-necked people indeed. Do not worry; let me alone destroy them and blow out their name from under heaven and I will make you stronger than they. Remember today that your future generations were not the ones who saw and experienced my mighty hand and outreached arm, the signs I have preformed, and the things I have done. *It is I who has given you possession of mountains* and valleys that drink rain from heaven. *If you choose to love and obey and serve me with all your heart and soul, I will send the rain in its season.* See, *I am setting before you today a blessing and a curse—the blessing, if you obey the commands I have given you, a curse if you disobey and turn away from the commands I have given you.* You must also go to the one place of worship and *bring your tithes and offerings,* and *then your family shall eat and shall rejoice in everything because I have blessed you.* But do not give offerings anywhere you choose, but only as I command, and I will again enlarge your territory. My year for canceling debts has been proclaimed. There shall be no poor among you for I am giving you possession in the inheritance. *I will richly bless you if only you fully obey.* You will lend to many but borrow from none. You will rule over many, but none will rule over you. You will be openhearted and freely lend a poor man whatever he needs, but be careful not to harbor his wicked thoughts. I will bless you and everything you put your hands to. *The year for canceling debt is near. Be sure to take care of the hand which has served you; supply him liberally from your flock.* Give to him as I have given to you because his service has been twice as much as a hired hand and I will bless you in return. In the coming battles do not be afraid, do not be terrified or give way to panic, for I am one who goes with you to fight for you against your enemies to give you victory. *Follow my commands and you will be blessed in the city and in the country.* Those who rise up against you will be defeated before you. They will come at you from one direction but flee from you in seven. As I am now, I will make you the head and not the tail; you will always be at the top and not at the bottom. *If you walk in my ways I will bless you as a holy man and the people on Earth will know you are called by my name . . . the name of the Lord.*

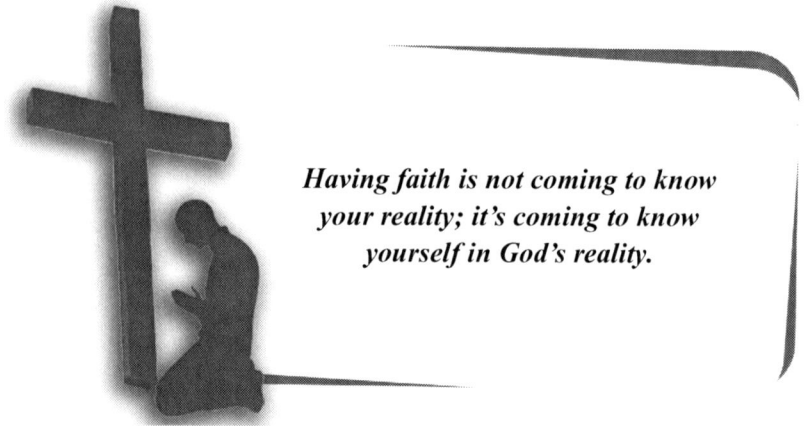

Having faith is not coming to know your reality; it's coming to know yourself in God's reality.

Unexpected Change of Winds

It's unbelievable how believable God really is. The moment I started progressing toward His will for me and left the world behind, He put me into His presence where I could be situated outside the world we see. I cannot put into words how incredible the simple presence of God creates a surreal experience. The only way I can explain it is by saying *I know a man who is blind, yet he sees the world ahead of him.* People now see me as different, but to God I am no longer different. I am normal to God. My hunger is normal to God. My work ethic is normal to God. The fire in my heart, my hunger and understanding for the Word of life is normal to God. When ordinary people see my simple desire and my principled obligation to work as a unique calling from God, it shows the world is spiritually in a poor condition. I didn't let *"A"* word affect me; I let *"The"* Word affect me. You work for the benefit of God by finding yourself preoccupied by God. Acquire a deep thought of responsibility to work in an unfailing source of faith, because faith and work will never fail (2 Cor. 1:24). You must give yourself a chance to work and be effective for Jesus, not idling and waiting for Him to show up. Whenever we are idling, the motor is on but the body is inactive. Consider an automotive engine when it is idling. It is extremely dangerous for a vehicle to idle because the engine is not working at its peak operating temperature. This will lead to deterioration of its exhaust system and reduce the life of the engine. In life, when you idle you can completely burn yourself out. Idling will burn gas and still get you nowhere. Have you ever gotten tired of going nowhere? We all have. So obviously we know the most common reason for idling . . . is waiting (2 Thess. 3:7). It is important not to idle, because waiting and working contradict one another, and we serve a working God who expects for us to work as well. But wait, I thought we cannot be saved by works? I am not talking about being "saved." We are not saved *by* works, but *for* works. If our sins could be removed by our own efforts, what need was there for the Son of God to be given for them? *However*, after redemption if there were nothing that *we must work and abide by*, then what was the need for Jesus's teaching and the glorious New Testament? To truly serve is an opportunity that presents a changing of life toward the greatest quality of life. A service in Christ is what keeps righteousness imputed to us. Sin is atoned for, not tolerated for. Actions that have no spiritual life will breed hopelessness of defiled flesh. Again, we are not saved *by* works, but *for* works.

We work based on visions having faith on the results.

Idling in life can also demonstrate a state of confusion where we overthink and underact. We, as people, have the tendency to question a condition or direction we are afraid of, not because it is forbidding, but more because of its possibilities. We don't question to actually get an answer, but we question simply to talk ourselves out of any outcome. We need to step outside of our understanding, get away from our sense of risk, and work beyond our steady level of performance. To God we are not objects of pity, but we are hope in a prearranged possibility. How did I find this road of continual opportunity? I decided *not* to take my own journey; I decided to take the one which was already prearranged for me.

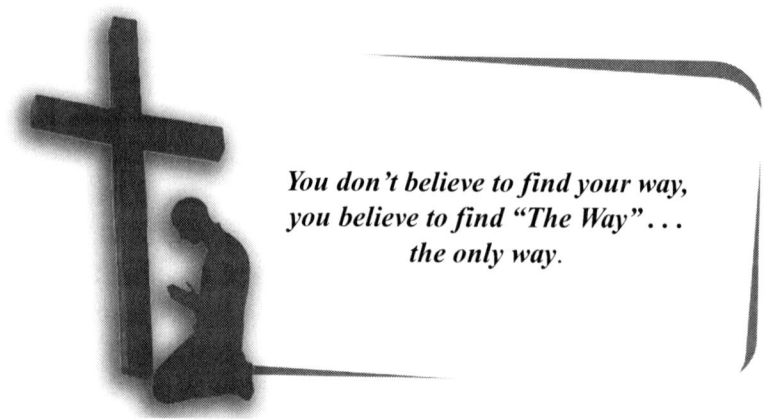

You don't believe to find your way, you believe to find "The Way"... the only way.

Even if I didn't hear God, I would still have to believe . . . because how do you explain the unexpected change of winds that are now suddenly against my back? There is only one explanation. Even on God's road there is difficulty that is hard to understand. It is that of faith which gives enlightenment that clarifies setbacks are a setup for the devil's upset. Make sure your thinking is aligned with your faith, strong and unbreakable. Yes, I have come up short, again and again, but if you were to add it all up, you would find me at a place called purpose, where every day the celebration is *"never gave up"* (Gen. 48:11). I don't need to understand God's plan. I just need to understand that I am working within the plan because of Him. Difficulty and lack of understanding is a process of healing, because understanding is curative to the spirit. God's way of healing you is by making you better off than you were before. His direction for you is medicine to you, so when you arrive at your destiny . . . you arrive equipped and in good mental shape.

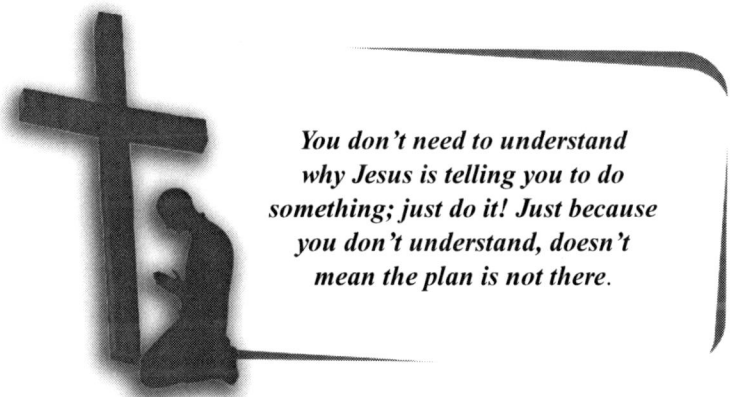

You don't need to understand why Jesus is telling you to do something; just do it! Just because you don't understand, doesn't mean the plan is not there.

Jesus will never tell you to do something without already knowing the outcome. The outcome is where most receive their understanding. *"Oh, now I understand why He told me to do that."* Believe it or not, the only reason why people become confused is because they aren't trusting in the formation or layout that Jesus gave them because it didn't make sense to them. You don't have to have an answer to go with God's instruction. The only thing that needs to be understood is that God won't send you anywhere where He hasn't already packed His bags to go as well. There is no *"what if"* with God because the world has no detour for

God's plans ... *He makes the way.* Why did I choose God? In all honesty, I believe He looked upon an unmerited, angry delinquent, and for that reason, He chose me. Why do I read the Bible? Because not only has it changed my course, but more importantly, I believe what it says. *I will make you greater than you have ever been*—and I believe that. *I will take you to a place you have never dreamt of*—and I believe that. *I will show you a power that you never thought possible*—and I believe that. Thus far, everything the Bible has told me that I can obtain I have received, so who am I to not believe.

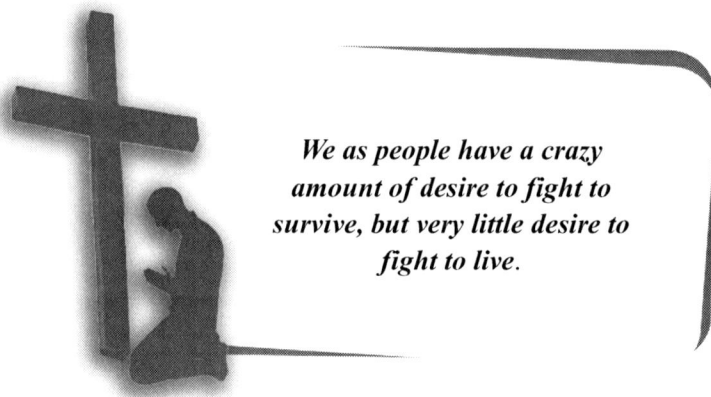

We as people have a crazy amount of desire to fight to survive, but very little desire to fight to live.

I will fight my way through life. I will push trouble out of the way. I will fall face-first in conflict. I will get spit on just to overcome my struggle. I will cry through every second of the battle. I will bleed while scraping my pride because of a slight margin of error. I will tear myself to pieces just to get through a "small gate." I will fight for everything ... just so I can surrender to God!

I am willing to die for what I am willing to live for. Because when it comes down to it, what I am willing to do for Him, He has already done for me. Everything that I need to know about myself was revealed the night I decided to fight for something greater than myself.

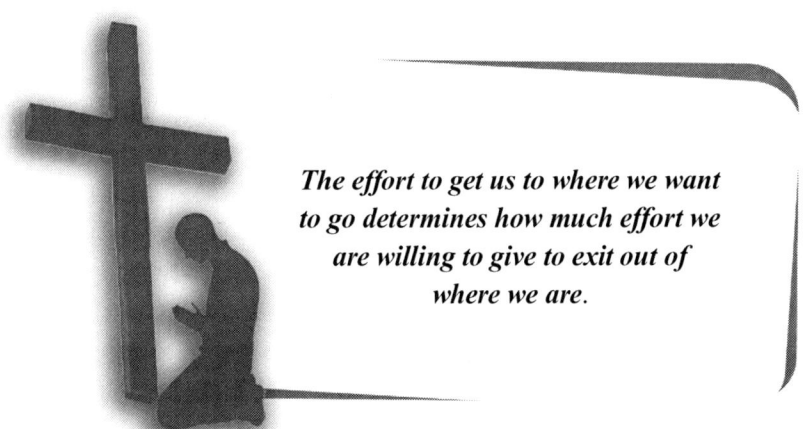

The effort to get us to where we want to go determines how much effort we are willing to give to exit out of where we are.

God will never leave you in the dark about what the light has for you. The more you can trust God, the more you will discover about yourself. The sad part about all of this is without "Jesus faith" most of us will never experience our life's possibilities, because people have a tendency to handicap their own potential with doubt and believing there is impractical thinking.

Anxiety will keep you in the secondary; being noble will keep you in the primary, but faith makes it capable for man to hold more than what he was meant to carry.

EMPTY THE BUCKET

I can remember sitting in my room preparing myself for God as if I were getting ready for a garage sale. I started reflecting on the "complete me" and literally began separating what I didn't like about myself and what I did like about myself. As aggravating as that week was, I noticed that the more I did this, the less I had. I gave Jesus what I didn't like about myself, and all it was doing was leaving me with an empty space that was not being filled. I actually got frustrated enough to toss my Bible to the side of my bed one night, but that lasted less than twenty minutes. As I was sitting on my bed watching TBN, a strong word from God provided me with an edifying perspective on my "Garage Sale" for Jesus assumption. The word was *"How do we know what we hand over to God is right? When we look back in our hands and they are empty!"* The submission factor.

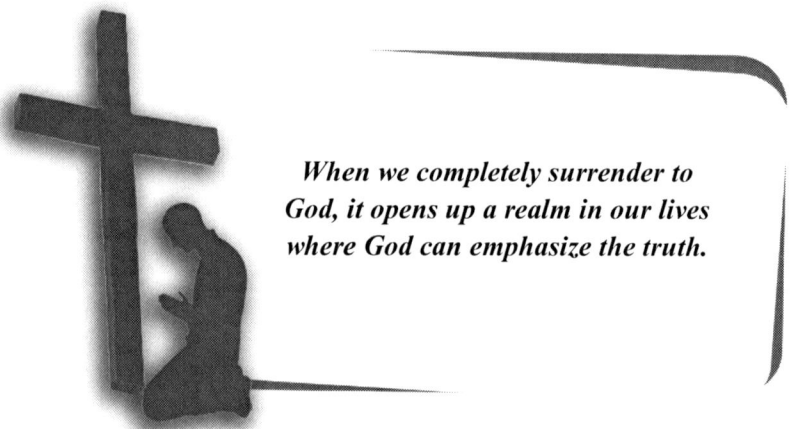

When we completely surrender to God, it opens up a realm in our lives where God can emphasize the truth.

We can be doing something for God, yet He has absolutely no interest in it because it involves our self-interest. We have to make sure that selfishness is not mixed in with our desires. Yes, there is a disconnection from yourself that comes with God's affection. My mind was so attentive to God's distribution of advantages that I overlooked the significance of the initial disconnection from the "selfish me." Not only is there a major distribution with God, but there is also an important disconnection by God.

We don't give God what we don't want, and we don't give God what we do want, but instead we must give him *everything we have* (Luke 14:33).

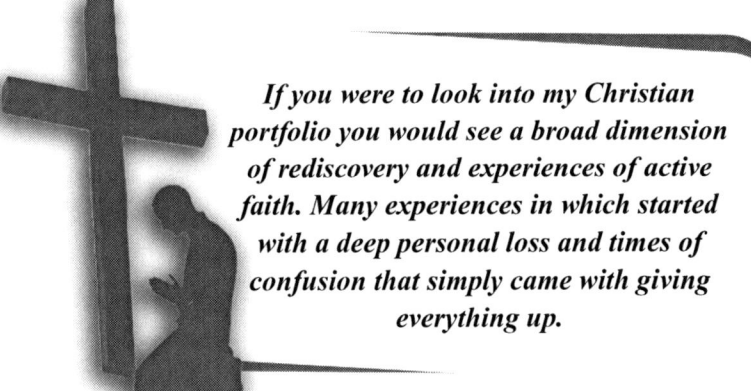

If you were to look into my Christian portfolio you would see a broad dimension of rediscovery and experiences of active faith. Many experiences in which started with a deep personal loss and times of confusion that simply came with giving everything up.

An old baseball coach used to tell me to *empty the bucket*! *Huh, what does that mean*? It means that it doesn't matter the day or the game you are in because you never know who is watching, what is at stake, and the progress that can potentially be derived from that opportunity. There is a bucket that you put everything you are and everything you have into . . . everything! Then, when you get to the field, you empty the bucket! If you leave everything you have on the field you will have no regrets no matter the outcome.

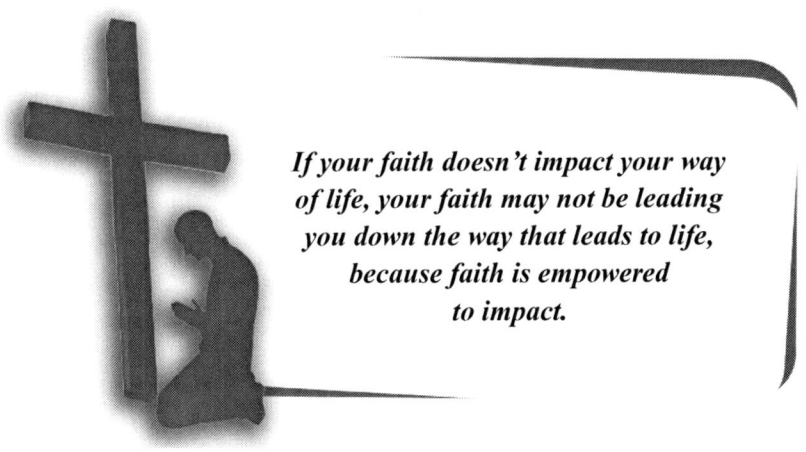

If your faith doesn't impact your way of life, your faith may not be leading you down the way that leads to life, because faith is empowered to impact.

Imagine Jesus's hands as that bucket. Give Him everything you have, both the good and the bad, and allow Him to balance you, accumulating the necessary tools so when the bucket is emptied the person that may be watching is witnessing the probability and credit of God. Now the wager becomes higher, yet less complex . . . you're now the closing pitcher trying to save the "*lost*," and the result of God's progress in your life has the effect of eternity for others, simply by emptying the bucket after giving God everything you have. Always remember, you can be a mighty person of God, but doing things out of sequence will make it seem like you are without God. You should fill the bucket every day, and in return God will empty or drop something important in your presence. We have many gifts from God, and just because you don't see a particular gift one day does not mean that God threw it away. Or just because you think you don't have a gift, does not mean it won't come (Isa. 45:9). God is always equipping you for the day or opportunity at hand.

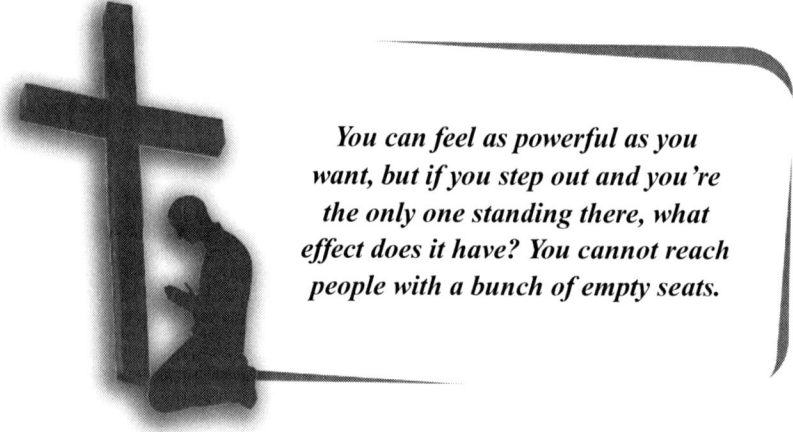

You can feel as powerful as you want, but if you step out and you're the only one standing there, what effect does it have? You cannot reach people with a bunch of empty seats.

> *It's not complicated; it's unusual. It's not difficult; it's perfect.*
>
> *God's purpose and promise are perfect for you.*
> *How do you get to the perfect you?*
> *By separating yourself from the usual you.*
> *How do you get to your purpose too?*
> *By separating yourself from what you usually do.*
> *It is a promise that is unusual too.*
> *Because it is a separation from the usual you.*
> *A separation of two, the usual you and the perfect you.*
> *Now get the perfect you and go back to the beginning of the unusual separation where it's not complicated, it's unusual, it's not difficult, it's perfect;*
> *It's where God's purpose and promise are perfect for you.*

Regardless of where you're at in your life, you were designed for greatness. Sometimes all it takes is going back to view the original plans for your life, and who better to give you advisability than the Originator of those plans. Remember, God's plan never changes. What changes is our choice to be changed. There is only one way that leads to light; all other routes are highways of darkness. This simply means that God's plan still stands, but sometimes He has to change *our* course to align it with His prearranged plan. Here is a hint for those who have said they have lost their way . . . Jesus is the way (John 14:6). If Jesus is "the way" and if you have "the way," how can you possibly be "lost?" As long as you are walking on God's road, you don't have to worry about the plans, because you know regardless you are heading toward a "purpose." Remember, where excellence is developing the splintering of persuasion will arise. Why, because excellence makes people nervous. Excellence is a wrinkle in the devil's perfect disaster.

How devoted you are to following God's road is dependent upon the measuring of your steps. We don't stand in faith; we walk in faith. We don't take a step in faith; we take steps of faith.

We have in our possession who we are, but God has possession of who we are counted on being. Everything we give God has an effect. We must allow our hearts to display an entrance of truth that sends out an invitation to God, who has already reserved Himself a place of acceptance (Acts 15:8). The invitation is the realization that our lives are anything but perfect and we need guidance down an abnormal road where luxury and serenity await. The road rarely taken is called change. Although this road will have its stumbling blocks from time to time, the great concept of stumbling blocks is that they were not designed for you to fall. Imagine now if you were to give God everything, what it could do for "change" in your life. Don't go through the motions of God but become part of His motion, so when He moves you move. The ideal reason for having a Savior is so when a storm hits we are never damaged, when troubles are pushed against us we are never broken, and when we fall . . . we do it knee-first as we yield to Him. Why would you ever choose to be without the means that allows you to reach new levels? Jesus is like the elevator of thankfulness because when we hit the wrong button in life and find ourselves going down, Jesus has the ability to reset our choice and get us going in the right direction.

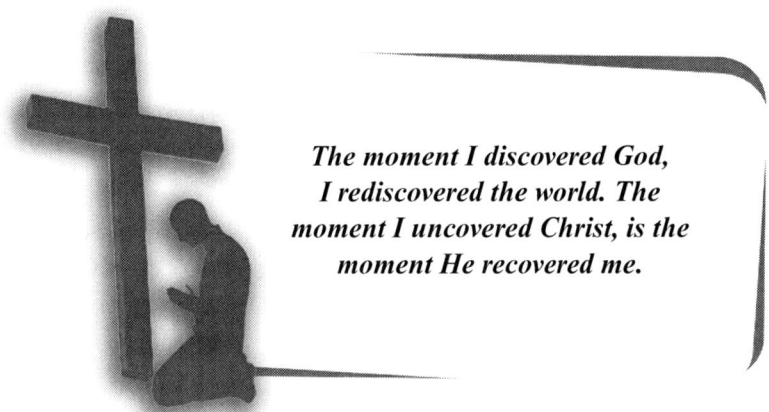

The moment I discovered God, I rediscovered the world. The moment I uncovered Christ, is the moment He recovered me.

Jesus allowed me to realize what it is like to be without Him through this analogy. If you place a ball on top of a high hill, it's able to roll down to the bottom all by itself, but once that ball is at the bottom how will it ever find its way back up? Prosperity is never alone, but you are able to destroy yourself . . . all by yourself.

**If you don't reach out for Me, you will stay in the hole
that you're in;
and
if you don't live for Me, then you will die in your sin**.

We get closer to our purpose with every choice we make, and with every right choice, it makes clear that what has been done has been done with "divine purpose." The reason why we empty the bucket is to show the demonstration of God's power (2 Thess. 1:11). Be patient and allow God to thoroughly equip you. Just because you have filled the bucket does not mean it will be emptied that day. No worries, it just gives you the opportunity to keep on filling it! Every bucket has a time and purpose, just like every season has a time and purpose. When someone asks you what are you doing, tell them *I'm waiting on God's time and place for me and my purpose to show up.* While you are giving God everything you have, the empty bucket that He holds in His hands will in return be filled with what you lacked, missinterpreted, or never developed throughout the course of your life. You will see what has been in the heart and mind of God all along. There are some things God will never take from you because it can be a service for His unique deeds. It takes God refilling the bucket to redefine your ability and personality for you to apprehend the true meaning of "you." Because God is the best for you, He will always bring out the best in you. God will allow you to keep the abilities He has placed in you because they can be used for a higher purpose. When the bucket is not filled, your ability that is being misused becomes a vulnerability to God's kingdom. When the bucket is filled, your true intentions will always reveal why God has given you what He has given you.

I could identify very well with giving God everything. My problem was I didn't realize what He was trying to give back to me. I completely disregarded my personality and began sheltering myself from my unique qualities. Then Jesus told me, *Your ways to make people smile will show them that I have a sense of humor; don't lose that.* It was actually very reassuring, because I know the ability I have to make people smile is a very important part of being who I am.

Always remember not to let people's opinions alter who you are and change your personality, because it may not mean much to one person, but it can mean the world to somebody else.

Give God everything you have and then empty the bucket!

Through the Storm

Truth is what will provide you an open doorway into a dark culture.

There was a feeling of hopelessness in my life that took control of all my passion and love for simply waking up. The basics of just being alive were so numb to me. Each day, day after day, I had the urge for more. What made me want to live was the dying feeling I had on the inside. I would toss and turn at night, knowing *"This cannot be life!"* (Ps. 116:3). It's the little lies that keep you awake at night. My lie was based on the fact that the life I was living was never intended to be my life. What kept me awake at night was one horrific experience in particular that didn't become so painful until a burden to make a difference lay on my heart. I ran into a house about ten at night on a Saturday with a couple friends. We knew that in the back bedroom of this house was a substantial amount of money that was hidden in an empty computer modem. We planned to take this money at a specific time based on a hunch, not particulars. We thought that there would only be two men in the house and they would be easy to get through. So we ran into this house, and the two men were not in it, but there was an elderly lady sitting in a lounge chair with her hand over her heart. She said, "Take what you want," and just then her left hand slid over *my guilt* . . . the Bible. To this day it tears me apart to know I let the worst parts of my life become somebody else's. I cried out to Jesus and let the pain of my past ungodly ways pour out. When I cried out to Him, He reached out His hands and took a hold of all my tears and being the amazing God that He is, He gave it back to me as a symbol of comfort. Jesus showed me that this woman was living out her intent in His divine way of life by her existence in persuading the infidelity in me to realize a truth in dependability in Him. Many people would question God because this woman prays and gives complete priority to Him, but yet God couldn't stop some hoodlums from breaking into her home. Sometimes God allows the weak to meet up with His strong, righteous people. Given the situation and the mind frame of God, it shows that it is not always how much you say, but what you say. This woman said . . . *take what you want* . . . and now out of that I have a heartfelt responsibility to be better than what I was. Jesus prepared this woman and gave her strength for this precise encounter to show me how weak I really was. If God didn't allow this encounter or this woman to endure that time of unpleasantness or if Jesus would have changed that situation . . . it might not have changed me.

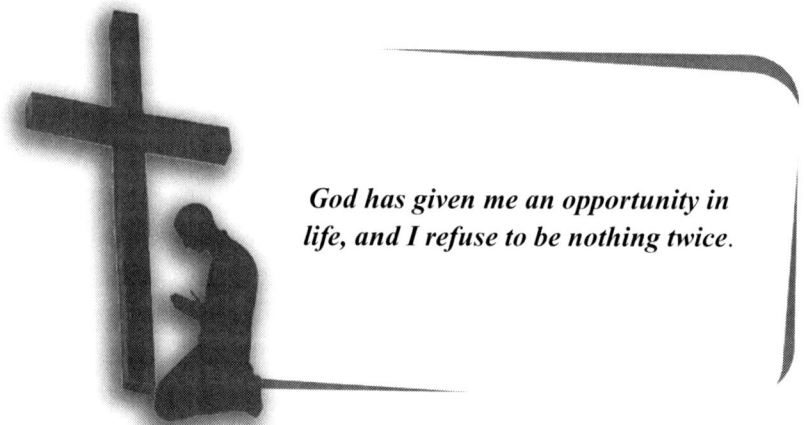

God has given me an opportunity in life, and I refuse to be nothing twice.

This incident gave me a change of heart to better myself and to notice what I was missing in my life . . . a Savior. God said, *Once you realize that your lack of comfort at night was purely Me trying to wake you up, I will give you an idea about the definition of prosperity. This is for the eyes that are still waiting to see possibility. This is for the mind that cannot visualize the vision. I am the victory for your life. You will accomplish things that will collectively make you a success. Allowing others to be a part of your success will make you successful, and then I will open a whole new revelation past success where you can go from glory to glory* (2 Cor. 3:18).

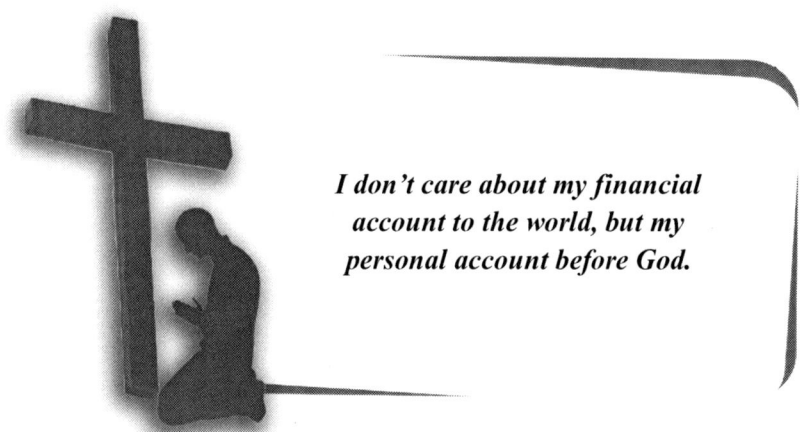

I don't care about my financial account to the world, but my personal account before God.

    I got this wake up call in the middle of the day. God didn't say, "Wake up, and when you do you'll have success," but God said, "Wake up because you're not giving me your best. You'll never have success unless you give me your best. Wake up, give your best, and then we'll start traveling the road to success." The first thing I learned was to leave all my excuses and doubt with its contractor. Don't buy into excuses because they will only leave you in debt. Your debt has already been paid for, so what it actually leaves you with . . . is wasted time . . . and God said that we are now on His time, so we have none to waste. The second thing God told me was that the weather may change but our mission, plans, and purpose never do. Just because you are experiencing a storm doesn't mean you are not in season. God will situate His canopy of devotion over your life during a storm so it doesn't cause a rain delay or a settling in your mind to wait the storm out, but a desire to get through the storm.

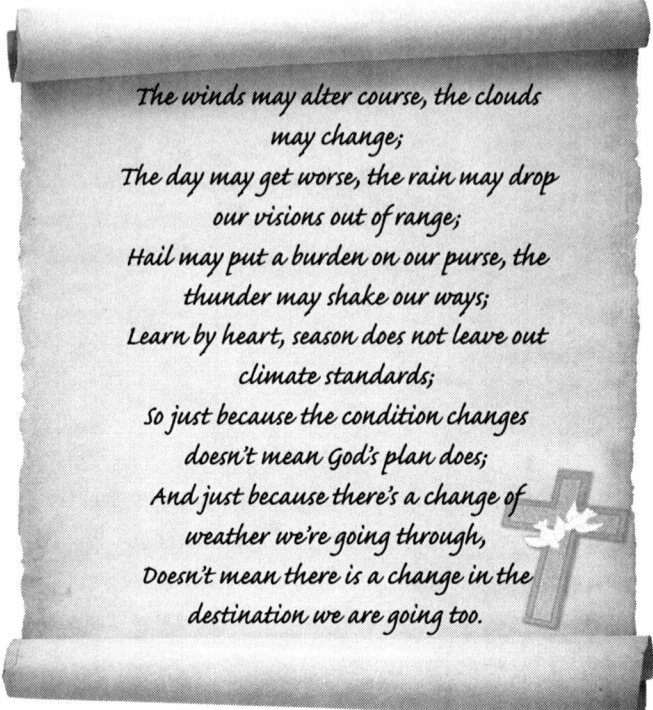

The winds may alter course, the clouds may change;
The day may get worse, the rain may drop our visions out of range;
Hail may put a burden on our purse, the thunder may shake our ways;
Learn by heart, season does not leave out climate standards;
So just because the condition changes doesn't mean God's plan does;
And just because there's a change of weather we're going through,
Doesn't mean there is a change in the destination we are going too.

    The unfolding of "*your*" word gives way for "*The Word.*" We don't make oaths to God, but we make choices in favor of God. The power to change your life is in choice. The power of changing lives is through choice. The influence of sin in our lives has made God in our minds as the alternative. We usually go to God not when we are going somewhere, but rather when we have no place to go. A lack of a clear conscience or coming up on a dead-end road will drive us to the "alternative." The significance in choice is that it has the effect of breaking grounds past our alternative in realizing that God has always been "the way," not a way (Rom. 8:1). There is a blissful revelation that is disclosed by acknowledging the true way and simply receiving the Word. We know the way to stay healthy and strong is by eating what is right. Allow God's Word to be your daily diet. The Word has given me a vision. It is amazing how when you read page by page you can literally see your purpose being laid out.

Don't just read the Word, but receive the Word;
Don't just see the Word, but be the Word;
Don't just need the Word, but find the "Me" in the Word.

This means, in order to build a connection with your purpose, you must first build a relationship with "the way." Jesus is the way. *How can you be Christlike?* Just by reading the Word that Jesus Himself spoke will bring you closer to knowing His character (2 Thess. 2:14). Our heart, which is a house for God means nothing if we can't furnish it with understanding. You will come to know His importance, and you will come to know His morals. By reading the Word you will come to *see* yourself revealed. There is a mystery in the Word of God. This mystery, however, must not be confused with "the unknown." The mystery in the Word of God is not hidden from us; it's hidden *for us.* The moment we start peeling back the layers of the commands of God, the principles, the righteousness, the truth, the certainty, the visions, and the character, the mystery then becomes a precision in purpose, direction, promise, and salvation.

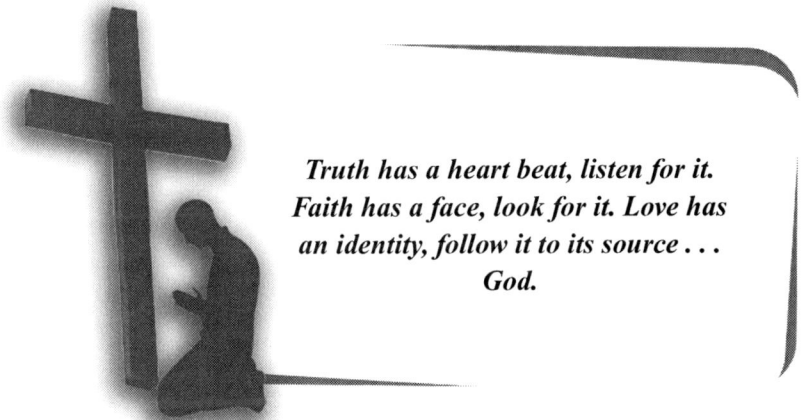

Truth has a heart beat, listen for it. Faith has a face, look for it. Love has an identity, follow it to its source . . .
God.

The Word of God is in my heart, and it is something my heart refuses to be silent about. I am no longer scared of information! When we start receiving the Word, there is a releasing of wisdom and knowledge not only for the way of Jesus, but the way of life under heaven. This releasing makes everything seem less complex, and instruction for the smallest to largest things in life seems so effortless. When I found myself deep in the Word of God, my entire stance of education, instruction, learning, perceiving, and understanding fell into a state of simplicity. Everything began to be so straightforward. Things I disregarded in school because of their difficulty became like tying my shoes. I got into several conversations with people during Jesus's perfect transformation in my life about falling into the Word of God and finding yourself on His road of the perfect will for your life. They would always look at me as if to say, *"You seem so smart,"* and in a conversation with an old friend, she said, *"Tony, not to say that we use to be dumb, but you just seem so intelligent to me now."* It made absolute sense because without knowing God you can't know your direction, purpose, or will for your life. Without knowing God how can you ever really know yourself? So in the same sense, without God you appear dumb, mainly because you are lost (Rom. 11:33). Receiving the Word of God is like eating a sweet, delicious pie. There are four types of people concerning this pie—the person who will never taste the pie in his entire life, the person who will only get one piece of the pie, the person who gets the whole pie, and the last person who serves the pie and gets pie whenever he likes. Remember, it all begins with choice and ends with the alternative, which is actually the only way . . . Jesus.

The choice of change is a changing choice.

The days I contemplated suicide before I took up the Cross in recognition of what Jesus did for me, I had to understand my life wasn't mine to take (Matt. 16:25). That gentle sound in my ear gave me hope to recognize that my best days will be appreciated from my worst days. The gentle sound went a little something like this: *How can you take a life that's not yours to take? How can you end a life that hasn't yet had a chance to live? How can you say you've lost hope, if you haven't yet found it? How can you say you're worthless, if I paid the price for you to live?* There are always people who are going through something similar to what you are going through. The majority, however, assume they are not strong enough to get through the difficulty, so they become engulfed with hopelessness. The lack of hope is based on believing their situation is impossible to get out of, which brings out the thought of suicide. How does hope appear? Hope becomes existent when witnessing another person's testimony of prevailing, which simply tells you this: *You have the world waiting on you to know that it is possible.*

Truth is often heard through the whispers of the wind; love is often captured in the glistening off the oceans tide; wisdom is often found in the array that shines through the clouds; and desire is often burning when fire sees no sunset.

My suicidal thought came before I had no choice but to deal with the "base" of myself. Contrary to popular opinion, getting down to the root of your problem doesn't necessarily bring light. I had to trust God to add light to the truth, to understand everything I believed to be right . . . I was simply lying to myself about.

*Try and convince yourself you're going somewhere you're not going,
You claim you're treated unfairly but forget that you reap what
you're sowing;
You choose to walk through the wrong door, because you don't
have the key to the right door.
You don't have the key to the right door, because you chose to walk
on the wrong floor. What's all the hype for?
The reason why you broaden your eyes for?
You're walking the streets on a stereotyped tour.
You say you're willing to fight for your respect, but really that's not
what you're fighting for.
Convince yourself that you were born to be . . .
A product of the street . . . Producing the vision you see,
Selling a dream that you can't even afford to be;
Unfortunately,
For you, if you don't grab a hold of the truth,
Your life will be a demonstration of what lies do.*

Always be aware that when you go to God, He will completely put your mind on restriction, but it is for your benefit. Think about growing up and the point of being "grounded" or placed on restriction. It was to keep you from doing what you wanted to do, so you could learn what it was that had to be done. The most powerful way to change yourself is to change the way you think. If you can change what you normally think of, you may perhaps find an explanation for why you are where you are. That's why Jesus is so essential, because He challenges preconditioned thinking.

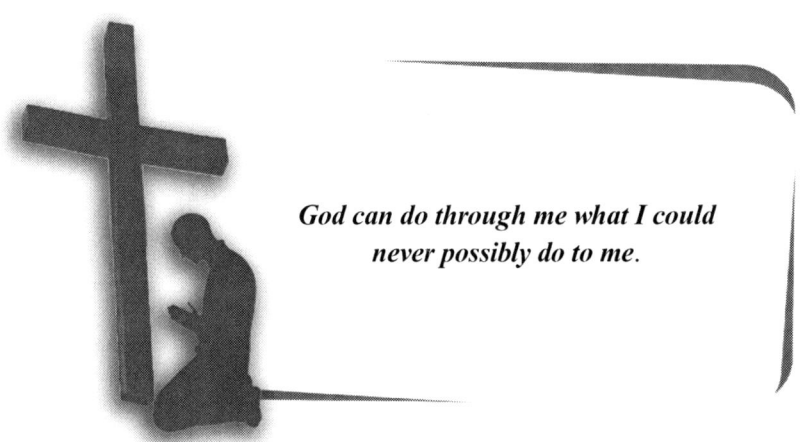

God can do through me what I could never possibly do to me.

Whether good or bad, dreams and visions are simply a reflection of the future *you*. I found myself within two places of obscurity during my teenage years. These two places became a visualization of consequences for all the pain I brought others. I was thinking myself into a hallucination (Dan. 4:5). I saw certain aspects of my life as if they were painted on my bedroom wall. I could see the side of a kid's head getting shot off in the back alley of an all age's nightclub after a dispute with one of my friends. I could see a kid getting stabbed in the side of his chest by my friend while trying to stand up for his friends. I hear an echo residing in my consciousness of screams and pleading while pistol whipping people over respect. I would sit in my room wondering when this payback would set in. I would sit there in the dark seeing the walls paint my demise, as if these pictures were displaying prior transgressions of mine for a future deserving consequence. I would also sit in my car and take a drive into a mental picture of stealing credit cards and using them for my own luxury, walking into homes and robbing people of their possessions and sense of safety, and stealing cars and using them as a momentary freedom. I was driving myself into a place of regret. This is how great our God is, which many people tend not to understand. Why would God have compassion on me? If you are to turn your life over to God and live according to His plans for your life, He will allow you to live abundantly because He has mercy on you, and He will do it in spite of you not deserving it, because you have restoration through His grace.

God's mercy gives us what we deserve. God's grace gives us what we don't deserve.

We all have to deal with the consequences of our sins. Those who are without God are constantly in a cycle of consequences because they are outside of God's grace. Those who are with God will know their consequence because it is God's way to demonstrate His kindness, which is meant to bring us toward repentance. After repentance is when God gives us solutions for our problems. My room was a place of darkness, but God said all I had to do was turn on the light to get a completely different visual of pictures. My car was a vehicle I used to dwell in my past, but God said that all you have to do is look at your offenses in the rearview, and they will become your past as you begin to progress. Before I knew of any change, all I knew was deterioration . . . a *life that's falling apart*. All of this led me to a cavity of change, not only a filling for my life, but the opportunity to fill the grace of God in others' lives. God easily made me understand that I will know my weaknesses before I can be a strength for others. Yes, because when you accept your weakness is when you are able to begin your own change. You cannot give somebody strength in any area you are weak in, but vice versa. You cannot change an individual without being the example of change. The wonderful substance of change, when we put it into God's hands, becomes so much more. Sometimes the perfect change in you isn't so perfect for other people, but nonetheless, it is a change that guarantees that it will change them. I had a very close friend tell me, "I think you forgot where you came from. I miss the old Tony." I said with a smile, "I haven't forgotten where I came from. I just can't remember why I enjoyed being there" (1 Cor. 16:9). Change will impact everyone around you. If you can walk away and nobody misses you, then you didn't have an impact.

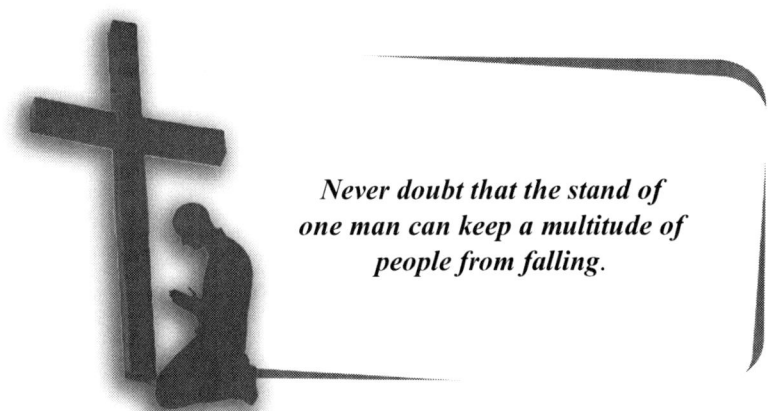

Never doubt that the stand of one man can keep a multitude of people from falling.

I had been traveling half an hour for church every Sunday to Trinity Church International because of the powerful presence of God that moved there. One Sunday after spending the day with my grandparents, I stopped at a gas station off my exit in Fort Lauderdale, and an angel of God broadened my perception on change.

A man approached me at a gas station, who I assumed to be homeless, and while I was pumping gas, he asked me if I had any extra change. Before I had a chance to reach into my pocket, he asked me a significant, yet rhetorical question, "Why is it that every time I ask for change people always ask what I need it for? Then, when I mention I have lost my way in life, they say God will show me the way. But when they see me at the same gas station week after week, they never stop to think that if I am still here asking for change . . . maybe I haven't received it . . . and maybe I haven't lost my way, but maybe I never found it. Why do Christians pray for the moments that will revolutionize the world, but they don't stop and think that it begins with a single person, and maybe it's not that my footsteps should be directed but maybe my footsteps need clarification on how to be directed?" This man turned around and walked away and sat on a bucket near a brick wall with his head down. I finished pumping my gas, stunned at what I had just heard. I walked over to him and said, "Sir, if I had money I would give it to you." He said, "I never asked a single person for money, I was literally asking for change" (Acts 3:3-6).

What was so significant wasn't what he said at the end, but it was what he said at the beginning. He asked if I had any "extra change," meaning the value of this encounter was plainly God allowing me to realize that what He is doing in me is more than enough for others as well. He is not only doing a change in me, but a change through me. The greatest thing I could ever tell you about God is the smallest thing He has ever done for me . . . promised there would be change.

LOVE'S IDENTITY

Now, you don't change for love, because love never actually changes you, it's the addition to you. If you change for love, you take away the wonder of being "you." You don't have to change for love if you've experienced the right conditions, because then you'll be able to experience the response of unconditional love. True love molds your heart into completion, finding the me in you, keeping all your uniqueness and not changing you, but completing you.

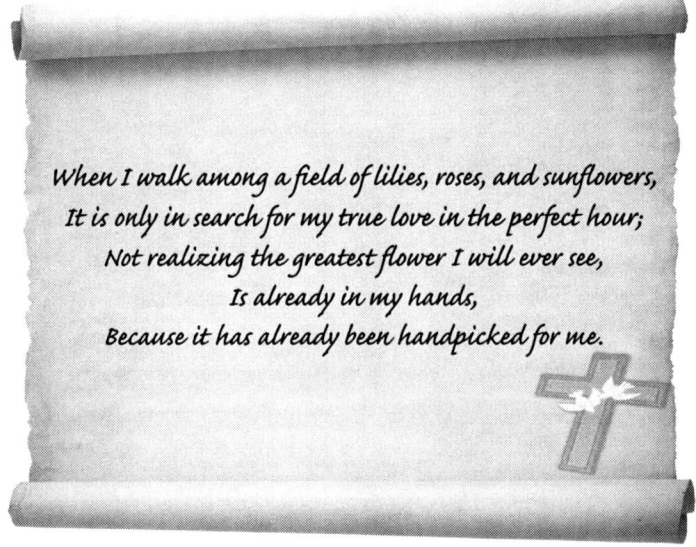

*When I walk among a field of lilies, roses, and sunflowers,
It is only in search for my true love in the perfect hour;
Not realizing the greatest flower I will ever see,
Is already in my hands,
Because it has already been handpicked for me.*

I've had some great and amazing women be part of my life. The problem I had facing them at the time was that I had my back toward God. Without the perfect love of God I didn't know communication, loyalty, openness, compassion, and sacrifice. My verbal abuse was like throwing a rock into the glasshouse of a woman's confidence. I became a muzzle to their opinions. A woman shouldn't smile because she has to, she should smile because she deserves to. These wonderful women would hand over their heart to me, but my immaturity and ignorance would set it aside until I found use for it. A great man is one you could hand your heart over to and trust him to handle it with care. At the time, I wasn't that man, until I questioned myself about love and God poured out some answers. How you find yourself into a woman's heart is by showing her that she is in yours (Ps. 36:10). Women are an amazing gift from God who deserve divine attention, a sense of being required, and a noted appreciation for everything they do (Gen. 2:21-22). A man is only a man, if he can be a real man to his woman.

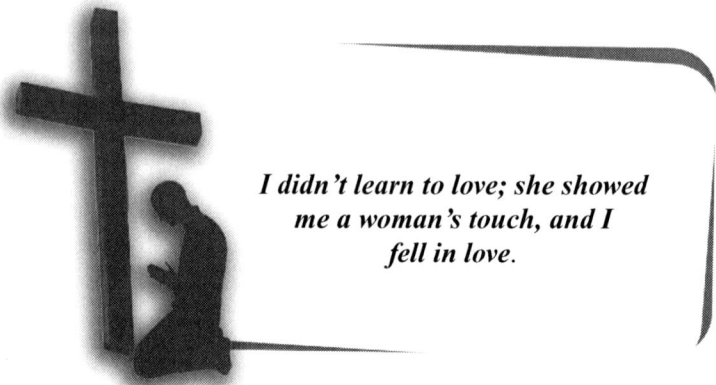

I didn't learn to love; she showed me a woman's touch, and I fell in love.

Each day you are able to spend with your significant other don't let appreciation take a vacation; let them know you care. Every aspect of your love will teach a woman something about her placement in your heart. Loving each other is your lifestyle. A woman shouldn't have to earn a position to be first in your life, because when you put a woman first, you acknowledge the importance of her worth. Women have the power to become the wealth of your heart, so never underestimate your hidden value. Don't let time make you feel relaxed and content. You will always appreciate love as long as you understand that you may have a hold on love, but you're also a fingertip away from losing it.

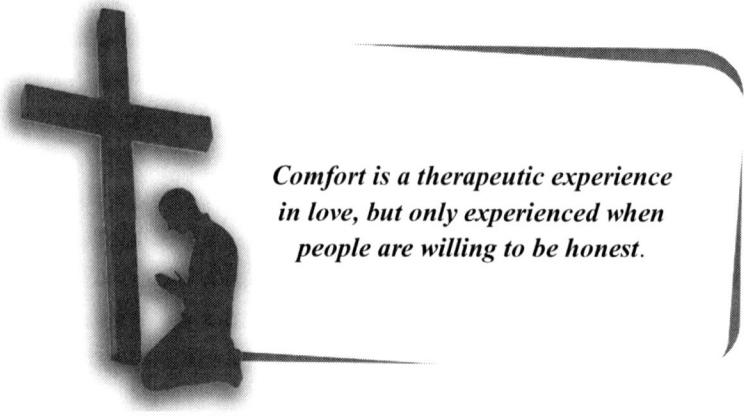

Comfort is a therapeutic experience in love, but only experienced when people are willing to be honest.

Whenever a situation occurs where you bump heads remember that the only way to put a problem out of work is to work the problem out. You cannot just talk; you need to communicate. Talking makes words fall on deaf ears. Communication opens a doorway for trust and devotion to enter and grow in your life. Devotion is a communication that speaks for itself . . . I will join you in the middle of your problems, until we find a way out together. In a relationship you are still responsible for your part. The most powerful interaction a man can have with a woman is with the most powerful expression in our existence—communication.

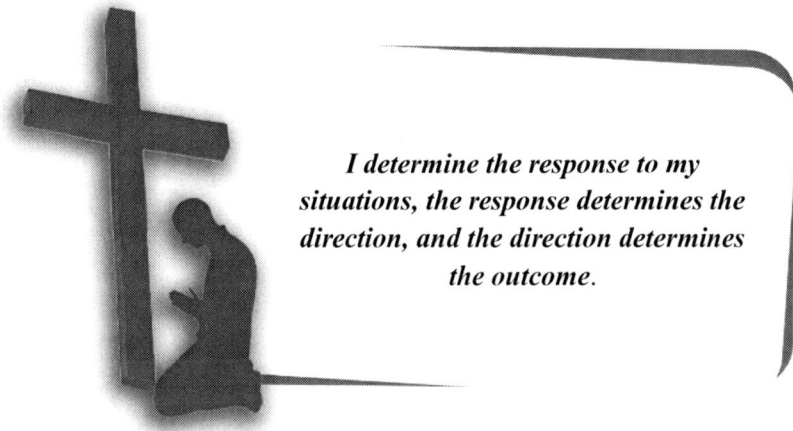

I determine the response to my situations, the response determines the direction, and the direction determines the outcome.

The connection in your relationship should be so essential that you feel empty when you are separated. *I'm gone for the same amount of time every day, yet every day it seems like it is the longest time I've spent without you.* Love doesn't drain you; it empties you, an empting that allows you to give all that you are. A women's heart typically starves for genuine affection and a deep desiring interest. Just as your significant other is uniquely fitted just for you, it is your duty to clothe her with effective words that uniquely fit her, and, in return, genuine passion will become your nature. So you must learn to enrich your words with creative language, and creative language will do its part in creating a richness of lasting benefits. Passion for your significant other is not just stating the typical "you look pretty today," but it is the describing factor, "How amazing you look dressed in heaven." Cheesy? Maybe. Effective? Absolutely.

Perfect love will make you want to fill in the space between you. Believe it or not, that separation is not a lacking of affectionate love, but the God of Love. I heard a valuable story about a woman and her husband who were in dire need of a revival in their marriage. They got married without the placement and constant union of God in their relationship. Instead of jumping into a divorce, they decided to separate for several months to gather a hopeful resolution for their marriage. The husband spent his days reading books of love and asking friends for advice. The wife found herself in the embrace of Jesus and God's true place of restoration in the church. After several months the husband had only a few methods and quotes to go by, but the wife, however, not only found love, but the perfect love. The moment they came back together the husband knew something was entirely different about his wife and all he could say was, "*I don't think we were reading the same book.*" She placed the Bible over her heart and said, "I have found all the answers." The husband told his wife that he didn't need God, but he needed her. She said, "*I have fallen so deep into God, that the only way to get to me is to go through Him.*"

Divorce is a death sentence, because you don't get out of love alive. Why is the Christian divorce rate the same as the atheists' divorce rate? Easy. Christians have fallen into a pit where we are serving ourselves. Many Christians have forgotten that " . . . *as for me and my house we will serve the Lord*" (Josh. 24:15). There is nothing that love can't work out, because love stands tall. It's done on purpose, so if you were to ever fall, you'd have plenty of time to work things out before you hit the ground. It's not that we need new love, we just need to renew the love we already have . . . the perfect love in God. It isn't enough to say "I love you," considering most of us don't say "I love you" enough. Obviousness is crucial in a marriage. It is obvious that you love her more than the first time you told her. Jesus paid the price even for marriage that gives a value of hope that your journey and life together will be worth it. Yes, the church is the bride of Christ, and the church doesn't lead Christ; Christ leads the church. Here it is, but they *love each other* all in the same. You don't lead your wife; you let your love lead your wife. If I tell you forever, not only does it mean a lifetime, but the time of our life. If you want to know your wife and love your wife with a deeper affection—study her! The things we study, we begin to learn from, and what we learn from always leaves us wanting to know more, simply because as people we love and yearn for knowledge and understanding. Learn to be a student of your wife. Forever is a promise you keep. I refuse to let you down, because I refuse to let you go . . . if you fall, then we'll fall together.

The promise of love is a hopeful feeling. The model of love in a relationship should be the love we have and expect with Christ . . . a committed love.

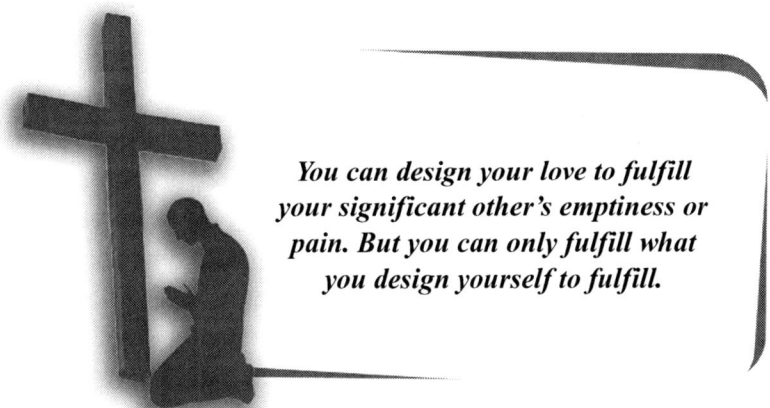

You can design your love to fulfill your significant other's emptiness or pain. But you can only fulfill what you design yourself to fulfill.

Now, did you know that the simple effort of listening illustrates more of a consideration than even the most thoughtful gift? It is important to listen to a woman because her words reveal her heart, and if you are familiar with her heart, you will know how to mend it when it begins to get tattered. Listening also has the potential to unlock a place of security into an individual's dependence in secrecy. Exposing this secrecy simply by listening allows the other person to become "*part*" of their partner. Did you know that the main factor in understanding is not established by inquiry, but by listening? Even if you can't hear my voice, my actions will still say I love you.

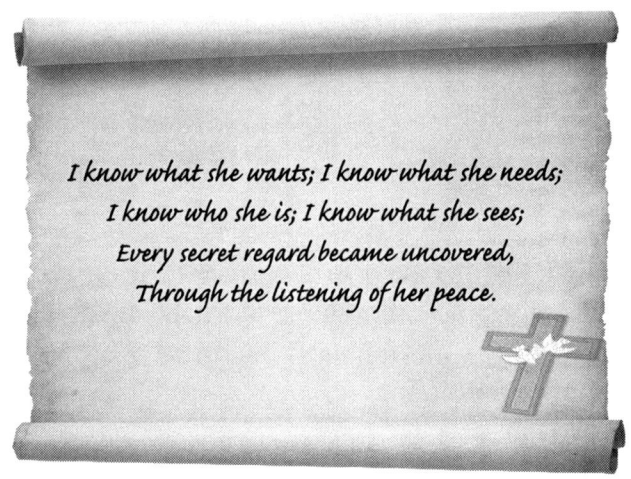

*I know what she wants; I know what she needs;
I know who she is; I know what she sees;
Every secret regard became uncovered,
Through the listening of her peace.*

The words of love are trusting information.

There is a difference between listening to your significant other's peace and constant words of love. Not just words of love, but constant words of love. These constant words *of love* can take a relationship into a vicinity that is above the world's opinions, worries, and burdens, because love passes pain (1 Cor. 16:14). Have you ever noticed that the messages that have such a major importance to us in this world whether to children, work-related presentations, or inspiring messages are *always* expressed with passion, originality, and creativity? Now, have you ever noticed that the women in our lives who should mean the world to us never get the same messages, communication, and expression with time and creativity? Rather, most often, they are simply routine, short, and typical gestures, not well thought, kindling, and poetic. The only way the devil can split the assurance of love is by silencing it. This silence manifests as one of two things: love with a one-sided personality, or a betrayal of communication that leads to seclusion. Love isn't a place where the usual is suitable. Imagine now if you were to "Love" listen your partner into peace, and speak love into their "Love" confidence.

Daily love creates new grounds. New grounds allow new development, and new development creates divine revelation in compassion.

Yes, we know that the devil is the prince of darkness. The hardest part of recognizing why a relationship is at a standstill or withering away is by recognizing how is it being unproductive? Love goes wrong when there is a lack of responsibility; we are responsible in assisting the sun to rise and not to fall.

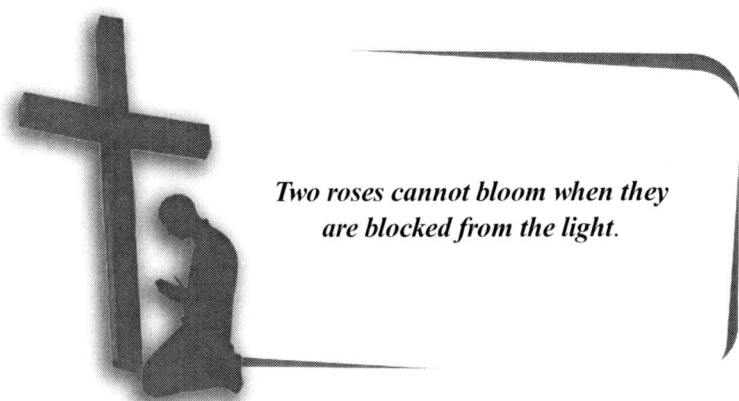

Two roses cannot bloom when they are blocked from the light.

Remember that the devil does not give problems, but persuade incidents that usually always turn into problems. The easiest solution to living in the light which is typically persuaded elsewhere, is purely loving your way through the persuasion.

Love in a relationship is always worth chasing. The biggest persuasion that turns into pointless problems is pride (1 Cor. 13:4). The most challenging area is not running after something that's worth chasing because of pride, but learn to move your feet. Walk past your pride, walk past the problem, and walk into the light, because love deserves good things.

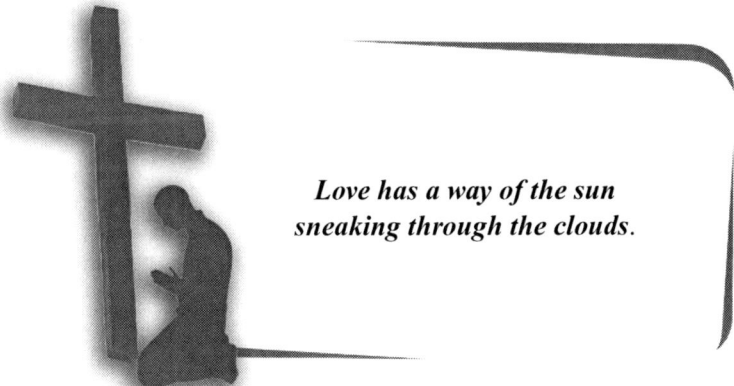

Love has a way of the sun sneaking through the clouds.

The expression of love has a way of carrying a relationship through its gloomy days. The embrace of love has a technique of comforting when our narrow road becomes widened. The smile of love has a manner of spreading its luxury. The communication of love has an approach of planting a seed for growth. The trust of love has a respect that a relationship moves in one motion. The outreach of love has the effect of bringing your partner back into the sphere of hope when the world comes against them. The attention of love has a desire to simply be the ear. The conception of love has a process of disclosing its original identity. The molding of love has a way of revealing God's hands at work. The binding of love has the purpose of exposing God who facilitates the source of togetherness.

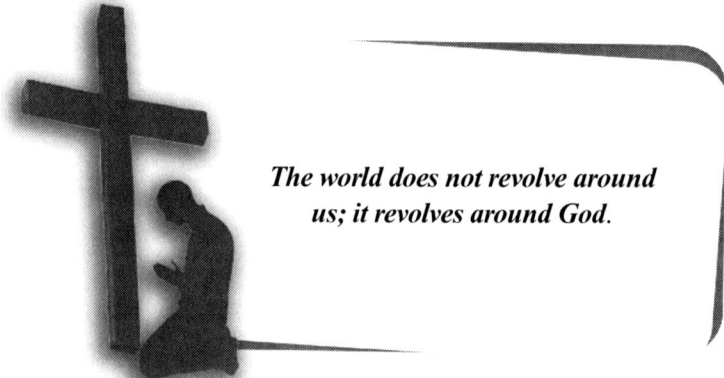

The world does not revolve around us; it revolves around God.

The definition of forged love has a way of dragging lust behind it, but the definition of perfect love is a strength that carries completion with it. The perfect love distinguishes plainly that complete love is all you need. I am only half of me without you, because the other half of me is in you.

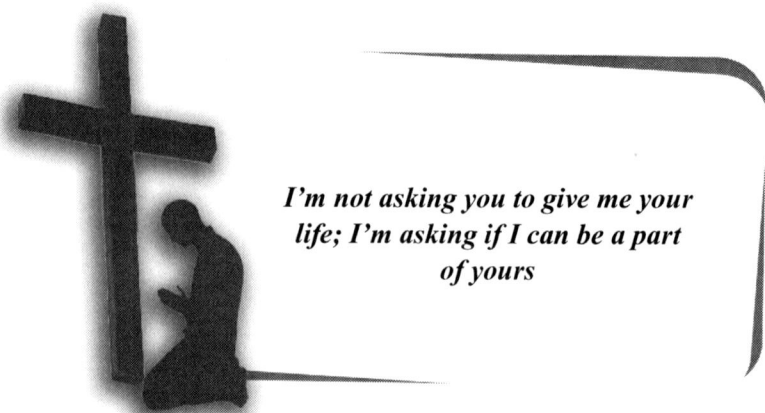

I'm not asking you to give me your life; I'm asking if I can be a part of yours

Someone asked me if I ever dreamt of what my wife would be like, and I answered, *"I couldn't compare my wife to the woman in my dreams, because I couldn't make up a woman as amazing as she'll be."*

DYING IN THE MIDDLE OF AN INTER *"SEX"* TION

I only know what the future holds, when your hand is upon mine—marriage.

It was brought to my attention how important women are to God, and also how important they are for the indulgence of a man. As basic as it can be said, sex outside of marriage ruins your progress and clarity with God, and receiving God's perfect love for you. I lost my virginity when I was twelve years old, and the majority of the women that I have been with based having sex not on satisfying their desire, but satisfying mine. I know the mind of a man who does not have a Godly perspective, and now that I have fallen into the love of a God-honoring truth, it is my duty to let my heart speak (Jer. 20:9). I have come to inform women that they actually determine the course that can keep not only themselves, but also men from *"dying in the middle of an inter "sex" tion."*

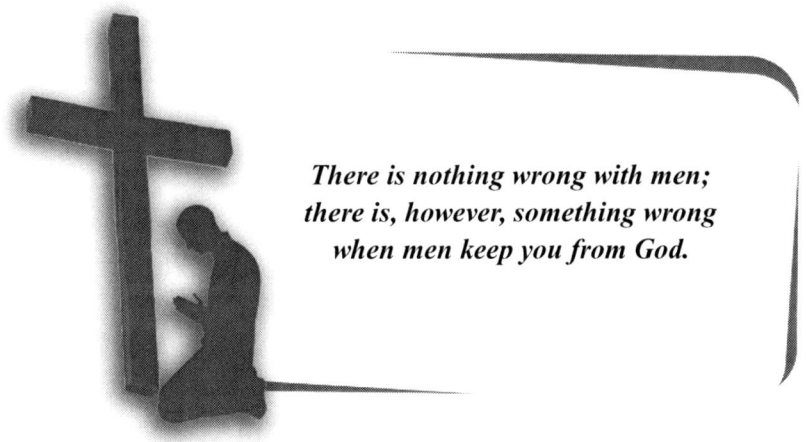

There is nothing wrong with men; there is, however, something wrong when men keep you from God.

Women have what I like to call a *"Notebook"* from God. Your Notebook from God is a love letter from Him to you connecting all the characteristics in which a true love will follow and meet the requirements of your desires. It is a code that has been written in your childhood diary that reveals your Prince Charming. The purpose of this Notebook is for you to identify the man who pursues and accomplishes the mysteries of your heart, being everything you want and need. Hold on to your Notebook and do not settle for anything less. When you settle for less, you're disagreeing with the person God has specifically planned for you. For a woman, this Notebook will guide you to your perfect love (Prov. 11:4).

Here is a glimpse into this divine arrangement. The title of your Notebook is "No." The secrecy of standards, the integrity of morals, the poetry of Prince Charming, the written will of marriage, the combination to the entrance of your heart, the key to your purity, the value of your peace, the understanding of your choices, the commitment to your obligations, and the appreciation of that responsibility are all found within its pages. The conclusion to your Notebook should be this: True love is never rushed into deception, only trusted with agreement.

The majority of the love that we will receive in our lives will be placed in a shoebox full of photos and flattering letters.

Even if you are currently in a relationship that is being pushed for "more," you must stand firm on the meaning of "No," even if he leaves. You must trust God when nothing makes sense. Sex outside of marriage detaches your relationship with God, and that relationship simply becomes a withered branch that has been disconnected from its vine, and the flower that fell before its peaking. Not only is your choice of "No" important to you, but it's important to God. Just by saying no, a blessing from God transpires. If you think that's something, wait for marriage and a completely different cycle of blessings will be opened up by the hand of God within the dynamics of a marital relationship. Let me tell you, God has a way of giving blessings, and when God blesses you, He will tear down some walls to do so, breaking down your burdens in order for you to stand taller.

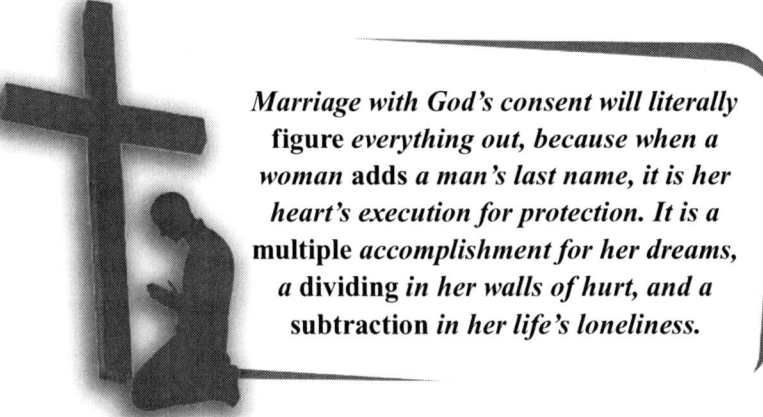

Marriage with God's consent will literally **figure** *everything out, because when a* **woman** *adds a man's last name, it is her heart's execution for protection. It is a* **multiple** *accomplishment for her dreams, a* **dividing** *in her walls of hurt, and a* **subtraction** *in her life's loneliness.*

I think people have become confused about dating. *Well, what is dating?* Dating is a comparison of your interests and morals. It is a social activity, not a physical activity, and just because you are compatible doesn't mean you are meant for each other. Don't put a time frame on "dating" and classify a man as "the one," because it leads to the destruction of your purity, and puts you into a man's book as *used*!

Why would he do this to me, "love me and leave me?" It was never about you; it was about the accomplishment of obtaining you. A man who isn't after love has tunnel vision, goes in for one thing, and finds his way right back out (Prov. 14:5). You wonder why the fading interest . . . because *you're blowing out a candle that should have never been lit.* Love is based within favoritism, and when it's not your favorite food, you can't eat it for too long. Women, don't be naive and mistake the difference between a sweet gentleman with a man's approach to get what he wants. How do you know what he really wants? By plainly telling him what he can't have!

Women, please understand this: Men shouldn't be an interference to the things you are trying to achieve, nor should men alter or change your dreams. The perfect man will help build your dream, because it is a dream meant to be bigger with you, than what it would be separately.

Ladies, be careful who you sell your dream to. A dream can easily be ruined if you're awakened before it's over. A woman who knows her morals is not self-conscious; she's self-confident. The easiest way to prevent someone from knocking on the door of your dreams is this:

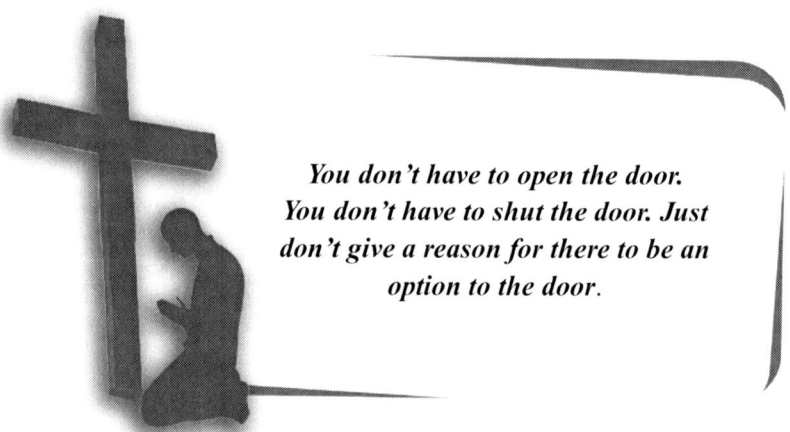

You don't have to open the door. You don't have to shut the door. Just don't give a reason for there to be an option to the door.

If you ever encounter a real good man, his power is based on what he is willing to wait for. A real man is someone who can condition your smile and build tolerance in your belly after continuous laughter. True love is inspired by the willingness to respect your choices. Love is not pressured or persuaded; it's an egg in a hand that's dealt with care and understanding because of its fragile importance.

Yes, love is considered to be a passion and an elevation to happiness and honesty, but it's having the license of marriage that enables exploration. Marriage does not ruin purity; it's the essential attachment to its purification. Ladies, it is supposed to be difficult and challenging because for a man, his wife is the one he has to chase. Don't give in; *keep him running*! It's actually part of our process of elimination, or "E*women*ation." A man who acknowledges your desires of wholesomeness will concentrate on the pinnacle of its fulfillment. This means he is standing by his word of accepting your requests while encouraging your trust. Purity is what allows a man to give trust. If you can trust someone, you can certainly form a foundation in "what men really want," while still holding on to your Notebook.

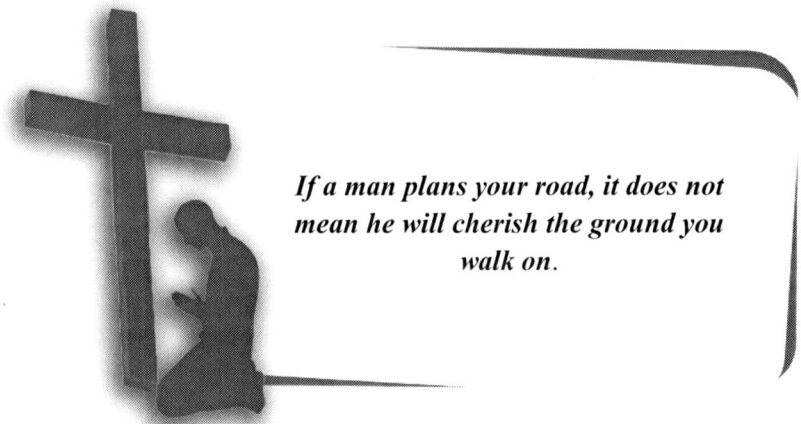

If a man plans your road, it does not mean he will cherish the ground you walk on.

Don't change or redefine yourself because of what a man says he wants. Rather be yourself and wait patiently for the man God gives you to where you are *"everything he needs."* Men pleasure women by respecting their wishes; women pleasure men by staying true to their word. A woman's direction inspires a man's direction; stay on the right path and he will follow. I'm not talking about leading him to a destination of purpose, but an understanding of what's important to you. Put your priorities in the front seat and let him sit in the back for a while, until his respect earns his keep. If he truly loves you, he shouldn't mind sitting behind your priorities and obligations, because as long as he stays in your vehicle at the proper speed limit, he's still going to the same place as you are anyway (Prov. 13:15).

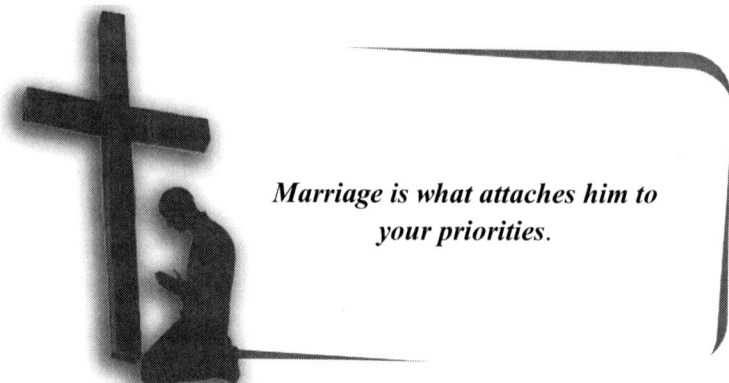

Marriage is what attaches him to your priorities.

Ladies, be independent and make perfectly clear that you don't need a man. Ladies, here is a small tip: *men need women*. We have difficulty being alone. If a man knows you don't really need him, he will go out of his way to make himself be noticed. Hold your ground, and a man will submit to your demands. The fundamental traits and qualities of a woman are based on the essence of her standing her ground.

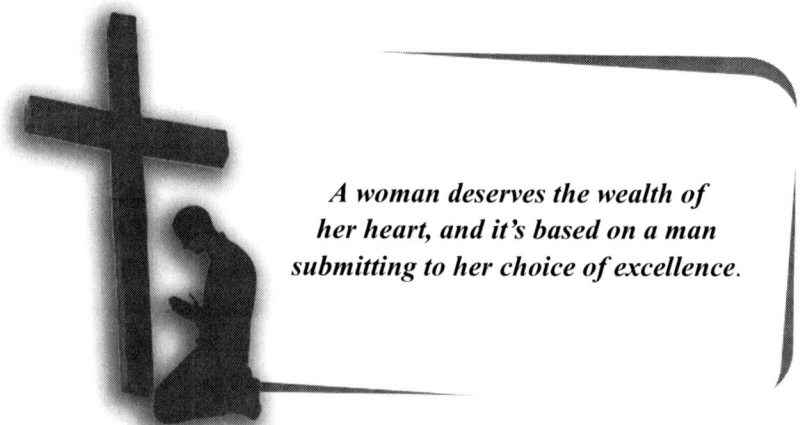

A woman deserves the wealth of her heart, and it's based on a man submitting to her choice of excellence.

A woman deserves choice and free will, not decisions and options; dreams and visions, not plans and ultimatums. Men are specialists in manipulation, sweet talk, and playing the role of Mr. Wonderful. How do you really find out how wonderful he is? Try asking him what *your* interests are. If you've never told him your interests, it simply means you have your guard up and there is a reason for it. But if you have told him your interests and he doesn't know what they are, then I can plainly say . . . *he has no interest*!

Women have the tendency to say, "I can go without sex, but I do it because I love him." Well, how about testing how deep his affection is for you by telling him to put you first, without sex, and see if he can do what you want because he loves you.

Men, it is about time to put your cape on and throw that "S" on your chest and start being a man. Stop being a nuisance to a woman's vulnerability. Stand by her decisions and stop being a burden by leaving her with choices. A real man is defined by what he is willing to do for his woman, not what she is willing to do for him. Her willingness was when she decided to give you a chance to be a man.

God has done wonders of greatness within me, and I never realized how much a woman's smile can make you live again. Without sex as a mainframe, you really start to acknowledge the beauty of a woman (Prov. 15:30). When sex is far away, you can actually place your hands on a woman's comfort and security. Without sex being involved, true love emerges to a realization that your sun doesn't shine without her. There is no substitute to develop new love before marriage; it's either love or it's not. A man's persistence will never amount to your awaited satisfaction on your wedding night. Heaven knows when you cry for a man out of love, it's because he had the decency and "loving" obligation to let you fulfill your Notebook . . . tears of joy, not tears of regret. Being in love is good for your health, but it should never have you questioning yourself. A man should be compelled to effortlessly but effectively please a woman through laughter, communication, and patience. Why, because a woman is the outer layer of a man—she is his makeup. A man who doesn't appreciate a woman's moral obligations won't ever be rightly connected to her because sex is a hindrance to a man giving everything he is. Sex before marriage is not a deeper connection; it is a mounting for interference. If you want to know the deepest feeling of a man, keep your secret, a secret. A man will attach his heart and soul for the pursuit of your happiness. Without sex you receive your most desirable necessity; a man who loves you for you. If a man could gratify a woman's requirements of her Notebook and surrender his solicitation, it would effectively leave a trail of rose pedals that lead to her dreams. A man should know what you need, simply by reading the story in your eyes. When you look into loves eyes the feeling will always meet you halfway.

    Ladies, sex appeal for a man has nothing to do with what you expose, but more of the curiosity of that hidden value. Let your beauty be the cover to a magazine, but never uncover the secret to that magazine. The worst times in your life are meant to build up your spirituality, and for women the majority of your worst times are based within compassion and affection. Don't let a man push you or pressure you into problems. *How does God develop a strong, powerful woman?* God will attach the problem to you, so you can learn how to persevere, and then you can say *"Look what I have that no longer has me!"* (Gen. 50:20). Stop looking for fulfillment when the sanctuary of love has been abiding with you the whole time. Enter into the providence in which God has for you, and listen as He speaks to your needs. Draw yourself into the unconditional embrace of a loving God, because He is the only one who truly knows the desires of your heart.

True love is an exchange of words of commitment. Love is
for life.
Stay pure and true to yourself, and avoid

Dying in the middle of an inter "sex" tion.

Love and Fear

How Does Love and Fear Conciliate for Deliverance in Your Life?

With God, Love is consistent
Missing no pieces, together the pieces are persistent,
There is a knocking to my soul
and opened only for a moment, a moment for
opportunity to make whole.
With God, Love is pleasurable
Immeasurable,
immense and in a sense that sorrow falls in one tear;
Love is the completion, knowing completion is near,
Where affection is near, apprehension veers,
because perfect love drives out that particular fear.
But there is now a different fear,
because fear of the perfect love is the driver that steers
He is the God to fear; He is the God of love
Fearing this love will add Life to your years.

Growing up, I always lived with a mind-set of being "the giant" of bravery among people of undersized timidity. My bravery was more about humiliating individuals' morals and character rather than about actually being brave. I wasn't in reality the bigger person, but more of the bigger example of who not to be around, who not to be like, and who not to be led by (Eph. 5:11). Right before I decided to embrace Jesus, a sense of fear came over me regarding some of the situations I encountered at parties and nightclubs. My sense of fear never lasted long, and the majority of the time it would end in fighting. But the closer I came to surrendering to and accepting the ultimatum God was giving me, fear started to seize me.

Jesus began to open up with answers that would support my uncertainty about fear because of my willingness to listen and understand. One of my questions was, *"Why did I begin to have a fear of people?"* Jesus said, *I was preparing you. You didn't have fear for people, but a fear of what you were doing to people because of the fear you began to have of Me. If you fear Me, you will never want to do all things you did.*

Fearing God strictly keeps a person from condemnation, misconduct of character, deceitfulness, and the entirety of the life I was living. Jesus was revealing so much to me that it would have been extremely stupid for me to backslide into my old habits. I was afraid that if I did what I was used to, God would stop the transformation He was doing in my life. I didn't want to test God because I knew there was no possible way I could win.

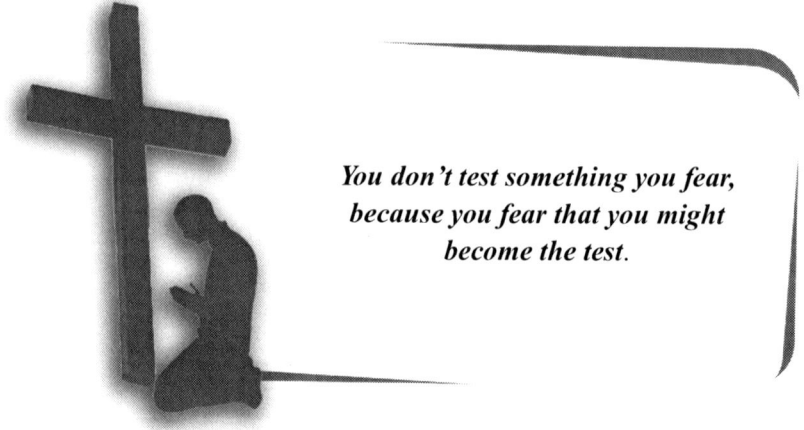

You don't test something you fear, because you fear that you might become the test.

The fear of God is an influence of love. The fear of God works on your behalf. This particular fear keeps you from all the bad and allows you to receive nothing but the good. This is a fear that is justifiably productive, where the birth of character evolves, the arising of ethics is established, the formation of trust is produced, and the proper meaning of bravery is defined. Ironically enough, Pastor Dr. David Remedios put a smile over the fear of God and essence of love in my heart when he looked at me and shouted, *"You are a mighty man of valor. You are a mighty man of valor!"* (Josh. 6:2). Yes, the fear and love of God has a unique system of "real" defining, not redefining the actual meaning of personal traits like valor.

Valor: Elevated bravery, strength of mind braving danger, and a warrior in the coming battles.

I got into a conversation with a friend about the love and fear of God. My friend said he had to experience the love and fear of God through a situation his family went through, so he understood why it was so vital. His story was very intriguing about those who lack the fear of God and decide to test His love, which made me understand more in depth that—

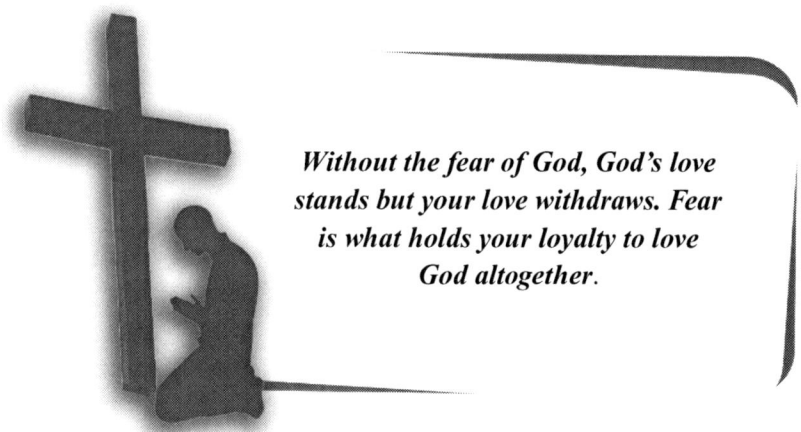

Without the fear of God, God's love stands but your love withdraws. Fear is what holds your loyalty to love God altogether.

He explained his story like this: Not too long ago, I visited my distant family, and while we were all sitting in the living room discussing one of my incarcerated cousins, his cousin from the other side of the family began telling me an ingenuous detail most people never come to understand about the vows we make with God. He never knew of the troubles that his incarcerated cousin was involved in growing up. His parents kept this information from him because of his age at the time. When he grew older and more curious, his family thought it would be best for him to take a trip to northern Georgia to visit his incarcerated cousin. He began to explain that when he arrived and sat down to talk with him, his cousin began to clarify something about God. "I sat in the county jail for over eight months awaiting trial, pleading to God on everything I believed He was, knew He could do, and that He would sit in the courtroom on verdict day and whisper "*innocent*" into the jury's ears. While I sat there awaiting the verdict, all I could do was cry out to God and quote scripture after scripture so God would have mercy on me. If He could just give me a chance I would do right by Him." He put his head down in silence, and all I could say after that was, *"Just believe in God and realize that there is a purpose for everything and there is a reason why the verdict came back guilty."*

He then looked up at me and said, "When I didn't believe in God, He still believed in me. I betrayed the vow I made with Him." I said, *"I don't understand."* He calmly stated, "The verdict on that day came back innocent on all counts." "I betrayed everything I promised God I would do if He would set me free. When I turned my back on Him, God allowed me just to keep walking. When I sat once again in that courtroom all alone it just showed that when you go against God you will never win, and now I spend my time realizing how much I really need Him" (Jer. 23:12).

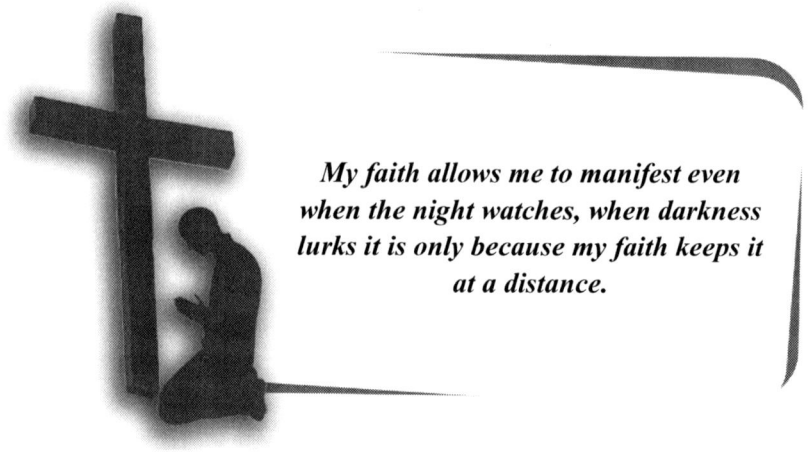

My faith allows me to manifest even when the night watches, when darkness lurks it is only because my faith keeps it at a distance.

FAMILY UNITED

I began to pick up the pieces of my life. As I was doing this, a sense of regret came over me because I noticed that the majority of the pieces were lying within shadowy moments, and these dark moments seemed to be so consistent.

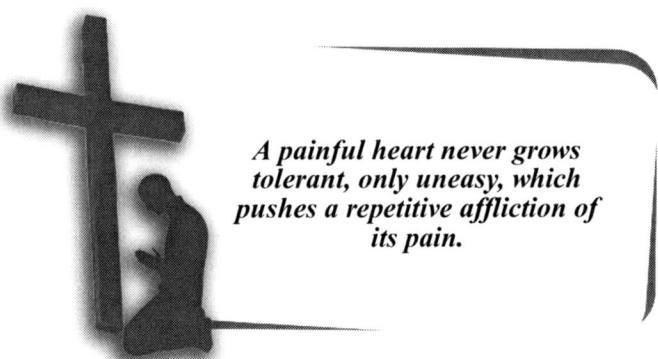

A painful heart never grows tolerant, only uneasy, which pushes a repetitive affliction of its pain.

Everything that pushed against me caused me to react and push my pain out as problems for others. An individual's response to pain has the process of the devil's undertaking . . . taking everything in life's response under. Anyone who cared anything for me responded by trying to alter my withering lifestyle, but somehow being consistent with the devil's pain has a way of deluding the mind into thinking your only response is, *"You just don't understand!"* (Ps. 73:22). This was the response that I gave to everyone. In fact, the devil does this purposely to stop the exchange of any good wisdom that would counteract his plans for misery. My most sincere regret is that my family had to deal with my rejection and affliction.

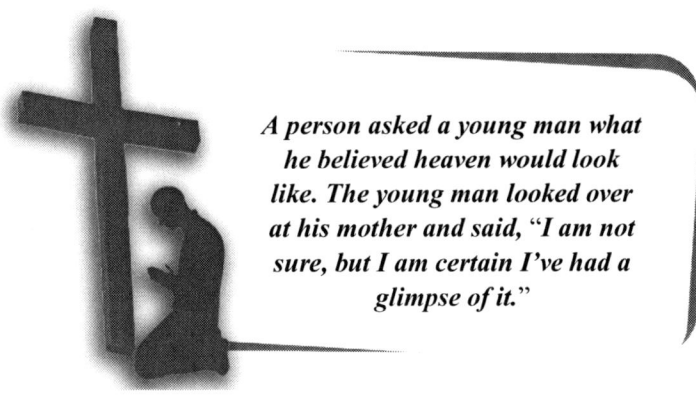

A person asked a young man what he believed heaven would look like. The young man looked over at his mother and said, "I am not sure, but I am certain I've had a glimpse of it."

I look back to the brightest parts of my life and what I see is pure bliss; what I see are my mother's eyes. I thank God for saving me, but I also thank my mother for unconditionally preserving me so I could be saved by God.

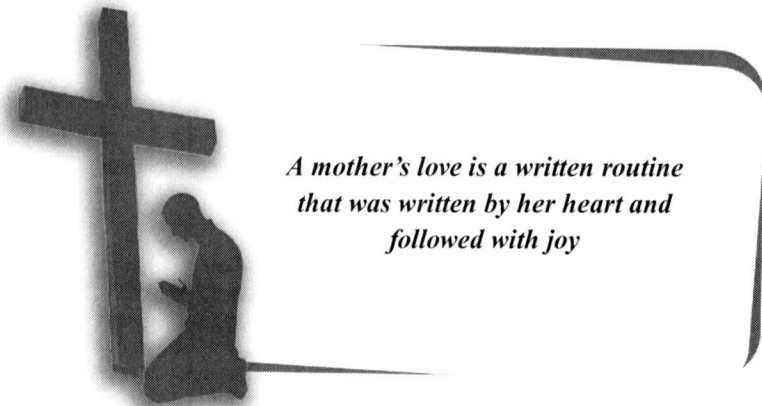

A mother's love is a written routine that was written by her heart and followed with joy

My mother stood by me when I couldn't even stand myself. My mother gave me hope when I didn't even know there was a meaning of hope. My mother not only believed in me, but believed in the *possibility* of me coming to know the real me. My mother never shut me out even when I became consumed with anger, but rather she shut me in with her love. My mother is the secret to a growing heart. My mother's life kept me from ending my life. My mother's love kept me from taking the love of her son away.

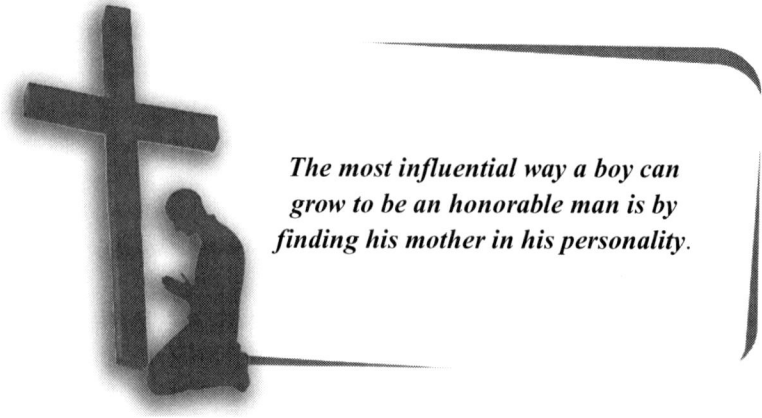

The most influential way a boy can grow to be an honorable man is by finding his mother in his personality.

My mother is a strong woman who has endured individually more than what any collection of people have had to endure in their lifetime. My mother did everything she could to protect her kids and give us a sense of hope in life—giving us quarters to get candy so we wouldn't see her using food stamps at the grocery store; having not a dollar in her pocket at times to still finding a way to get us whatever we wanted; taking her friend into a drug hole unaware and bearing down on her because of the possible repercussions of losing her kids to years in prison because of a single moment; standing up to anybody who talked down to her children; being the shelter for us against a broken husband's rage; picking me up from jail without saying a word, but letting me see the puddle of tears that showed the piercing of her heart; and walking me out of court after my trial and placing a passion of hate upon a man for demeaning her child. My mother's fight for life has caused me to fight for life because of witnessing the battles she has overcome. I thank my mother for providing the foundation for me to be a man. I thank my mother for supporting the smallest of my dreams to the impossibilities of all my hopes. My mother is the greatest woman to ever come my way. Mom, you are my model of prevailing. I thank you for your loving voice and singing my problems to sleep. I thank you for being the patch to all my healings. For all those times I was lost, it was your footprints that brought me back home. I thank you for choosing not to go to sleep, just to be sure I was the one seeking my dreams. You are not only a mother of strength, but even more a woman of grace. Thank you for being the extension of my happiness. Thank you for being a full-time mother. I express my deepest gratitude for my mother allowing my sisters and me to speak to her about anything, enabling us to be open enough not to hide our problems, situations, and burdens. I thank my mother for making promises and commitments, and always seeing them come to past. I'm relieved and at peace knowing my mother is my best friend.

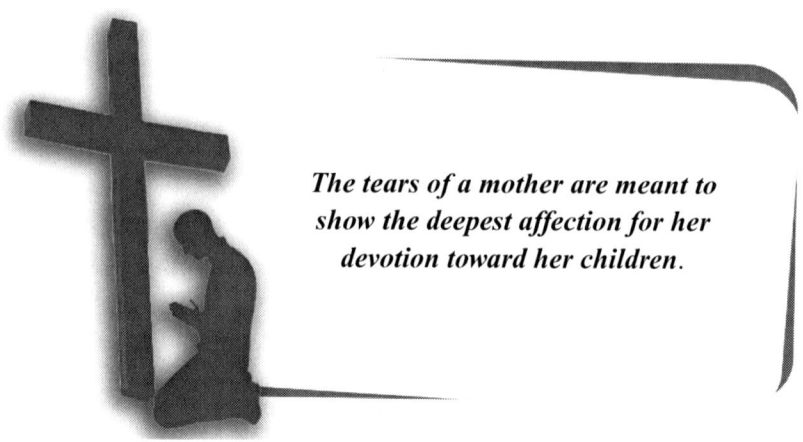

The tears of a mother are meant to show the deepest affection for her devotion toward her children.

My admission of guilt toward my mother's heart cuts deep because of the people around the neighborhood saying that I was no good, because I was stealing cars, sneaking out of my window at night and running the streets, and fighting and creating my own deathbed. I commend my mother for waiting up most nights just to see her baby come home safe, and I give my mother my deepest apology for leaving her with the concern, *"Please don't let that phone ring."* I entrust my mother with everything I am, because she has a major affect on who I am. I could live my entire life for her, just to see her smile of peace.

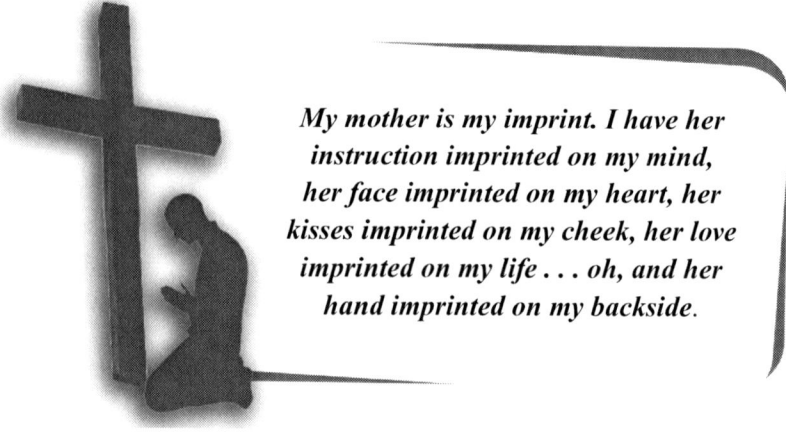

My mother is my imprint. I have her instruction imprinted on my mind, her face imprinted on my heart, her kisses imprinted on my cheek, her love imprinted on my life . . . oh, and her hand imprinted on my backside.

My mother gave me a small Jesus promise book when I was sixteen, and I never even opened it until my conversion with Jesus. In this book my mother wrote the following:

> ***Tony, keep this always and remember I love you! Life sometimes is very difficult and a lot of times it's hard to know what decision to make and you feel confused and wonder what to do or need answers, this book will be your guide. Tony, be smart and look out for yourself. You can be anything you put your mind to. Be the best! You are a masterpiece of God! Hold your head up high and soar to the top and when you get there, let it never be enough . . . Go Higher!***

It has been my mother who has been the keeper of my life for so long, because I didn't want life. My mother has made me want to live, and with everything she has done for my well-being, she still gives credit to God, knowing that only God can bring me to my true intentions. "I preserved you, now let God save you." Mom, thank you for bringing me into this world and leading me into life (1 Kings 17:23).

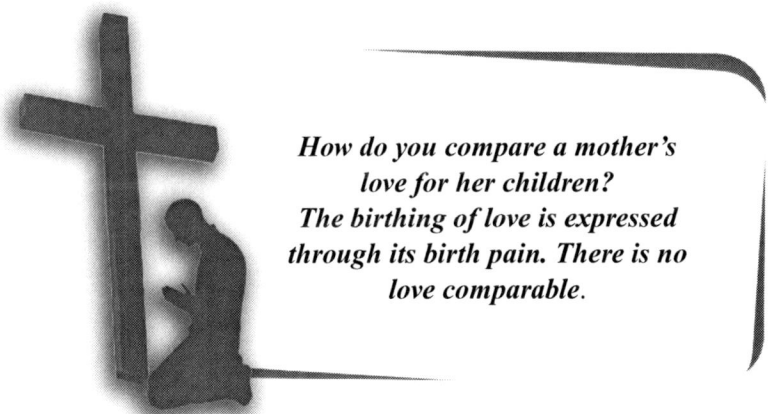

How do you compare a mother's love for her children? The birthing of love is expressed through its birth pain. There is no love comparable.

My entire family has played a crucial role in collecting the pieces of me as they began to fall. I love my family from the depths of my soul to the beat of my heart. My family has given me experience, expression, example, and direction. Jesus has allowed me to learn from mistakes and incidents that bundles of love and growth were developed out of those interruptions.

When I was in high school, right before I was about to get into a fight outside of a house party, my oldest sister jumped in front of me and began grabbing my shirt and pleading for me to stop. With force, I pushed her out of the way and proceeded to fight. When my emotions subsided and the fight was over, I realized I had just pushed my sister. I walked over to her and kissed her, but never realized the meaning of what she did. You see, until God's interruption in my life it took me until then to realize He was using my sister in that situation for an awakening, and to know there was and is a multifaceted root of her love for me and my security. In another incident with my other sister, I took an over eight-hour drive to Tallahassee to express my love and need to keep her secure. Once I got there, I threw her boyfriend into a shelf and made him lie on the ground and feel as undignified as any man should feel who puts his hands on a woman. At that time I didn't have God, only a desire for Him. God didn't show me retribution in that interruption, but appreciation. There were many other situations, and it may seem odd to most people how my physical confrontations became lessons in the development of God's purity. I've asked Jesus why He used discomforting moments involving my sisters as an approach of remembrance. Jesus keenly said, *There is an infusion that escorts unconditional love that makes a person more aware of what happened or is occurring in moments of transgression, which actually gives light to Me. This mixture of love connects awareness, appreciation, understanding, and obligation, which all has the possibility for my main purpose . . . change. I don't work in process unless the outcome is contagious. I often used both of your sisters' love for an opening of understanding and a breakage in your tendencies. Now the change that I am creating in you will play the role in illuminating their understanding. Watch, the change in you will mark an entrance for them to come to Me and make the desperate change I want in them.*

My grandparents would be the ones to show me a world completely different from the one most people live in. My grandparents' lives have been the evidence of God for me. If there is a possible reproduction that embraces both the grace of God and the kindheartedness of love, it would be my grandparents' blessed marriage. Their loyal marriage and connection are what I aspire to have in mine. My grandparents have paved the road of God that comes with an abundance of provisions that have set an example, showing me that Jesus is exactly who He says He is, "The Provider," to anyone who keeps His commands and obeys them. God answers when people cry, even if the request comes from those who don't trust in Him. I didn't make it here on my own . . . *I know now that my grandparents prayed me here.*

In speaking with God, many of my questions to Him were answered by using the example of my grandparents' marriage. One of the most influential responses Jesus gave me and that I hold dear to my heart is this: *"I have taken you back to find Me in your moments, but I have shown you your grandparents to show Myself in their life."*

My grandmother enthusiastically emphasized my role in *"purpose"* for me being in this life, that we are not here by accident, but for divine incident . . . God's incident. I have gathered strong morals and a fruitful character from my grandmother's branch of life. My grandmother never pushed Jesus on me; she just positioned His name in me. During my long-awaited transformation with Jesus, my grandmother excitingly gave me a very useful word of wisdom. I keep it as a reminder and a symbol of what tomorrow holds: "God is preparing you for what He has already prepared for you." I've learned in my preparation that the more you give God, the more you will get from Him. *Expand your fields and I will fill the land.* My grandmother has given me a delightful insight and the understanding of how to see the work of God in my life, but first it was an understanding that made me realize why I couldn't see God working in my life.

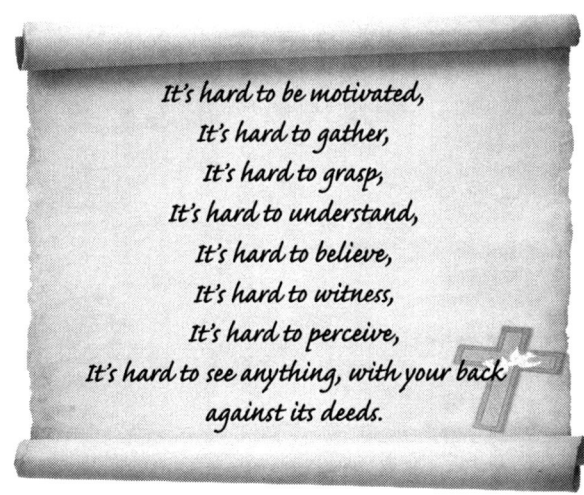

It's hard to be motivated,
It's hard to gather,
It's hard to grasp,
It's hard to understand,
It's hard to believe,
It's hard to witness,
It's hard to perceive,
It's hard to see anything, with your back against its deeds.

My grandmother would write scripture on a notepad and give it to me as a hopeful change of attitude. It's bizarre in a sense how the Word of God written on a notepad can bring awareness to how a person presents himself. I may not have realized its importance then, but show a child the way of God and he will never fall far from it (Prov. 22:6). When we make that necessary life-changing choice, my grandmother would say, *"God will meet you more than halfway."* I would have to say thanks to God, because in my life He has met me along the lines of more than three-quarters. My grandmother is the manifestation of the influence character has on the ability to impact not only your life, but everyone around you. There is something about my grandmother's arms that ensure safety, and there is something about my grandmother's presence that claims the source of peace. I can remember a *"if by choice forgettable"* incident at my grandmother's home where I was internally enraged and choked with misery. I took my pain out on one of her doors by punching a hole through it, and she calmly came to me and said, *"I'd rather you do it to my door, than to somebody else."* It was as if she was saying "I love you and I am part of your pain . . . take the time to find your peace . . . destroy anything you want in here, **because it can be replaced** . . . so you don't destroy yourself out there, **because you can't be replaced**."

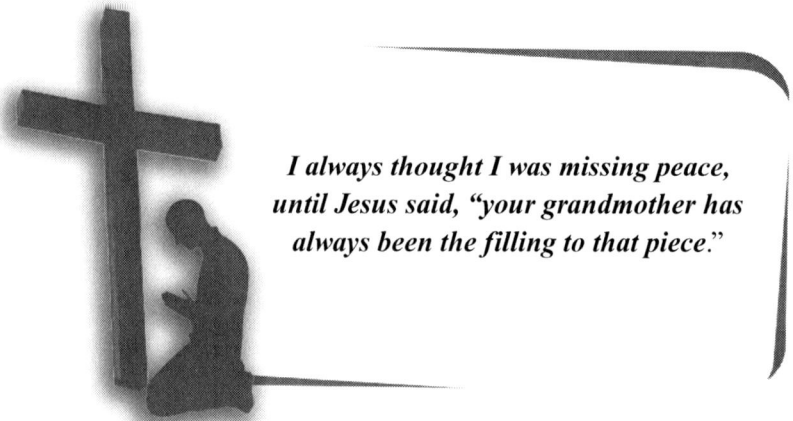

I always thought I was missing peace, until Jesus said, "your grandmother has always been the filling to that piece."

Grandma, thank you for being the candy hands, the sad lip before my punishments, and my "give him one more chance" good fortune.

I appreciate you, Grandma, for spoiling me even after being as bad as I could be. No worries though, just think like I used to, it's fine because bad and spoil go together.

A short conversation with my grandma will have you assuming doubt is a foreign word. My grandma has not only shaped my imagination, but to me, she is the visibility that God is with us. Thank you, Grandma, for working all these years on my behalf, planting my seeds for me when I didn't know there was a harvest to reap. My heart wouldn't have been built if I didn't have you in it.

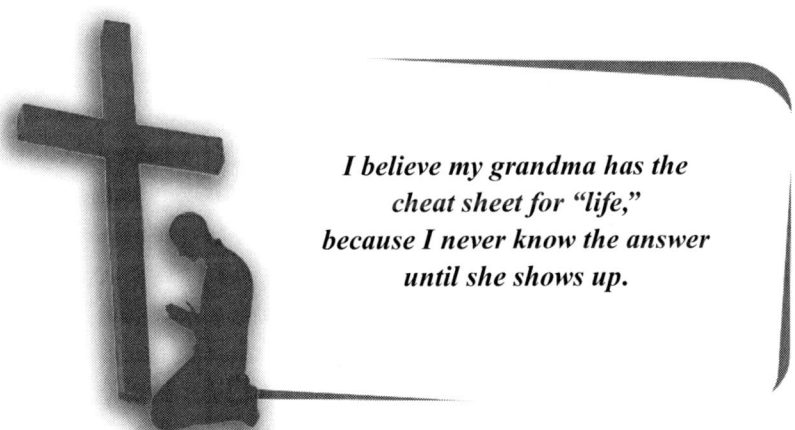

I believe my grandma has the cheat sheet for "life," because I never know the answer until she shows up.

My grandfather is the demonstration of how a man can single-handedly lead a family into security and toward a prosperous direction. Besides the adoration of my God, the man figure I aspire to be just half of is my grandfather. No one can compare to the role model my grandfather has been in my life. There is no person who comes close to the effect he has on me. There is something about my grandfather's compassion for his family that reveals richness in his heart that's derived from love. Many times my grandfather has spoken to me out of tough love, in a changing dynamic, and a sense of urgency coming from his heart. Those times he has spoken to me out of his "gut" feeling, or "God" feeling, I should say. Ninety-nine percent of the time his Godly intuition held accurate. I never let him know how right he actually was, but I would always wonder how he knew so much about the little I spoke.

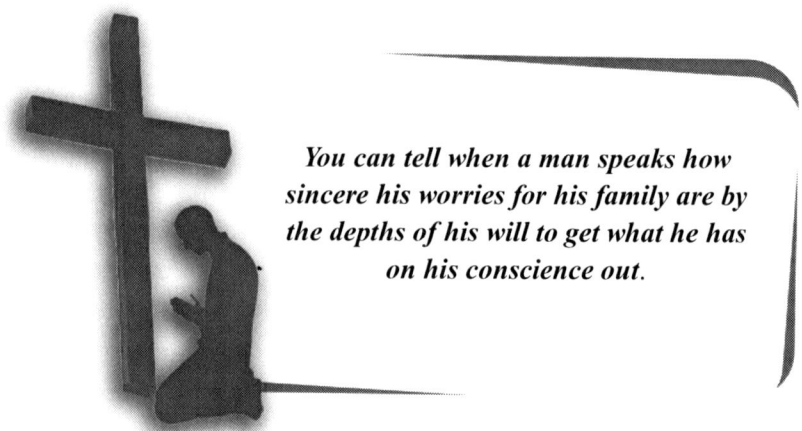

You can tell when a man speaks how sincere his worries for his family are by the depths of his will to get what he has on his conscience out.

With all that my grandfather brought to my attention, I knew that my anger was a main concern of his and that he feared it would affect my life. This is one of the things Jesus didn't have to tell me, because I already knew ... my grandfather is the man I want to be. My grandfather allowed me to realize that no matter what mess you're in or what you are going through that your attitude dictates the outcome of a situation and the day you are in. Your attitude is not the end of a matter; it's your approach into the matter, and how you approach the matter will determine the end.

Thank you, Grandpa, for coming down to where I am just to walk on my common grounds. Thank you for taking disciplinary measures to build my character with lessons in life. Thank you for being my branch of knowledge that helped me understand the importance of self-control and the ability to gain control. Thank you for continuing to bear with me in spite of my anger, stupidity, and repeat occurrences of rebellion.

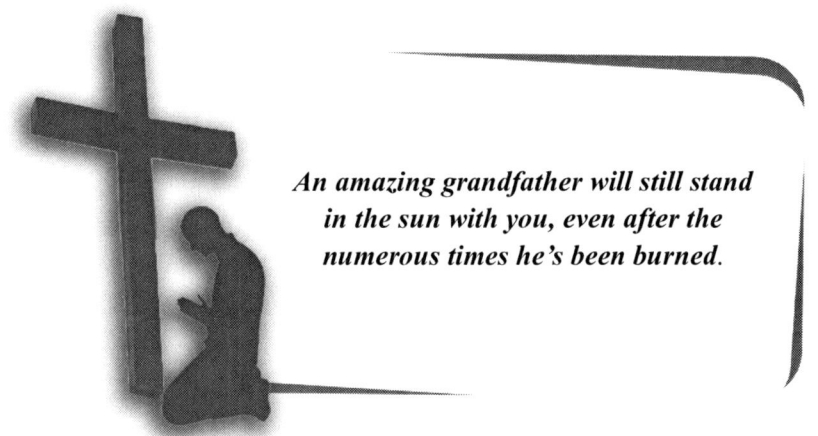

An amazing grandfather will still stand in the sun with you, even after the numerous times he's been burned.

Thank you for being the demonstration of a man's compassion and for showing me the quality of a *"man."* The terms of endearment, intentions, and strong affection you have had for your family have played the essential role for me to continue carrying them out. Thank you for brining a smile to my life throughout all these years . . . you have been my facial expression. You have a special worth that I not only want to embrace, but also want to imitate. Thank you for being devoted to my ability. Thank you for bringing out my possibility . . . and I thank you for being my number one fan.

You may never know it, Grandpa . . . but you have saved my life.

It would be an injustice for me not to recognize my stepfather, who I've always considered to be a real father. It has eaten me alive, because I feel like you have abandoned me. Whatever happened to our visions, our long talks, and "I'll be here for you no matter what"? I've been waiting for you to show up for so long. I've been waiting for you to apologize for so long, and for so long . . . I'm still waiting. There are many things I don't understand and may never understand, but at this point in my life it's almost irrelevant. I love you, and I choose to forgive you outside of my own comprehension, because I could never neglect the time and effort you put into raising me as your own son. My eyes are crying love, Dad. I plead to God on your behalf that you may come to know the God that I know. Even if you feel you have done nothing wrong, it doesn't mean you are right with God. I am not praying for a relationship between me and you, but a relationship between you and God, which will inevitably build our relationship. Dad, try not to hear me with your ears, but try and hear me with your heart. I have hated the world, until I put the mirror on myself. I took a hold of my own expression and gave it to God. In His hands you learn that pride is not worth chasing if you are losing the most important things in life. You learn that even if you feel you are not wrong, you plead for forgiveness so your heart is right. You learn that instead of waiting to see if your children care, you fight to be part of their lives so they know you care. Dad, I love you.

I'm Still Waiting

Dad,
If you ever think of me and wonder where I went,
My heart would leave a path to all the time **I wish** we spent,
I'm still sitting in the backyard with your tools
waiting to start that tree house you promised me as a kid,
Still waiting to play that video game you promised me after my game winning hit,
I'm still sitting at the corner of my bed crying waiting for you to come in,
To put your arm around my shoulder and tell me that you love me even after what I did,
I'm still waiting to hear that you're proud of me so I no longer have to wonder **IF**,
I'm still alone in the backyard tossing up the ball, waiting for you to grab your mitt,
I'm still sitting at the baseball game with these other dads waiting with an open seat for you to sit,
Mom is out of town and I'm still lying in my bed waiting for you to take her position and be the one to tuck me in,
If you're wondering where I am,
I'm still sitting in the same spot I've always been,
But what's important now is that you know…
I'm still waiting on that call to catch up on all the time we've ever missed.

While gathering the strands from my "genes" and loving the outfit I am in, I thank God for my family!

BEYOND MYSELF

You must know that God did not rewrite my life; He brought me to "the" writing of my life (Heb. 12:2).

Before you even open up the Bible there must only be one perspective—God's perspective. The Bible is not a catalogue for personal goods where your first thought is "let's see what I want." Rather, it is a plan that is prearranged where your only thought should be "Okay, what do you want for me, God." This is a perspective that will affect you personally because it establishes Christ's identity in your life, and as you correctly navigate through the Bible, it will bring you to truly discovering yourself.

There is something I've learned from the streets and the Word of God. In the streets there is this motto: "*You can't tell someone to stop selling dope unless you're going to be the one to take care of them.*" You can't tell someone to change unless you're the example and directive source of change. In that regard, I've quickly learned that one word from God has not only the result of change, but the means of providing what you never thought was possible. *The Word of God is like salt. Salt affects everything, and nothing affects it.* So when Jesus said, *Stop what you're doing*, I didn't see change, but I could honestly feel it. God was, is, and will always be my provision for change, and this is what led me to my profession of faith.

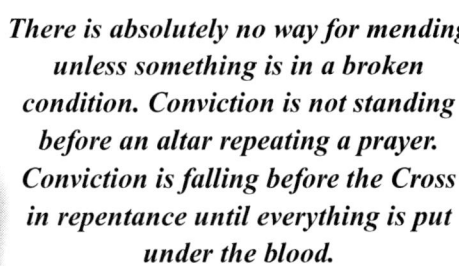

There is absolutely no way for mending unless something is in a broken condition. Conviction is not standing before an altar repeating a prayer. Conviction is falling before the Cross in repentance until everything is put under the blood.

I understood immediately that my profession of faith was not saying a simple repetitive prayer. It actually has nothing to do with a repetitive prayer people like to call the "sinners' prayer." It is impossible for the human heart to be sincere by repeating an unexpected sequence of words. It should be a pleading cry from a dying heart to *live*! How can you completely be in right standing with God as a new creature if you have lingering in the back of your mind the question of what it takes to serve God (1 John 1:6-2:25)? Jesus allowed me to understand what it would take to serve and be in right standing before Him, by saying this: *You must acknowledge that you are a sinner who has sinned without excuse, and for the remainder of your life have fellowship with the King of Glory who does not wander in the midst of darkness; by keeping the commands of God as the core of your life; by loving others as yourself; and to love nothing of the world, and the Father will remain in you and grant you eternal life.* By acknowledging this, the greater work of Christ will begin. Then by continuing in repentance for a constant cleansing for the necessity of righteousness, it will allow you to walk in the light of truth for the rest of your life, which permits Christ to finish the work He has started. *This is your profession of faith!*

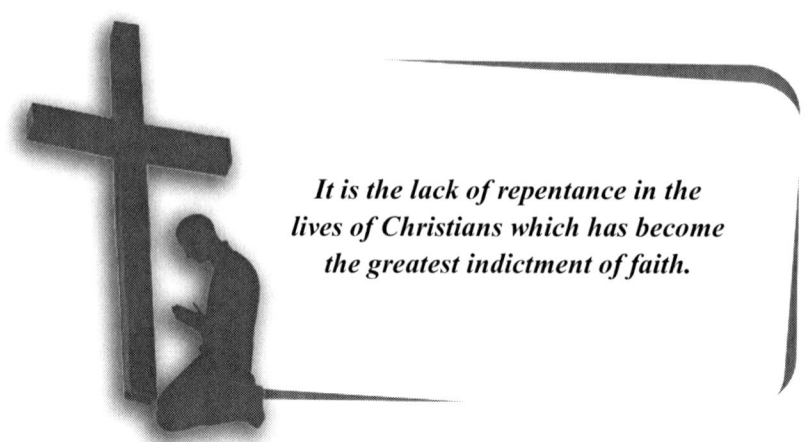

It is the lack of repentance in the lives of Christians which has become the greatest indictment of faith.

Then Jesus said this: *Your faith can never grow without you putting trust in Me. Now do you trust Me enough to give up everything? I am not telling you to get rid of your dreams and your greatest desires. What I am saying is to lay them on the altar and put them in good hands. I am telling you to trust in Me and put everything that you have ever wanted in your life—every vision that has ever come to mind—put it down and take a walk with Me. I say this because unless you deny your life and everything in it . . . you cannot be My disciple. I am not saying that your life will never have anything. I am saying that until you deny yourself and everything in your life, you cannot possibly have anything you've ever dreamed of, and it will ultimately cost you everything* (Luke 9:23).

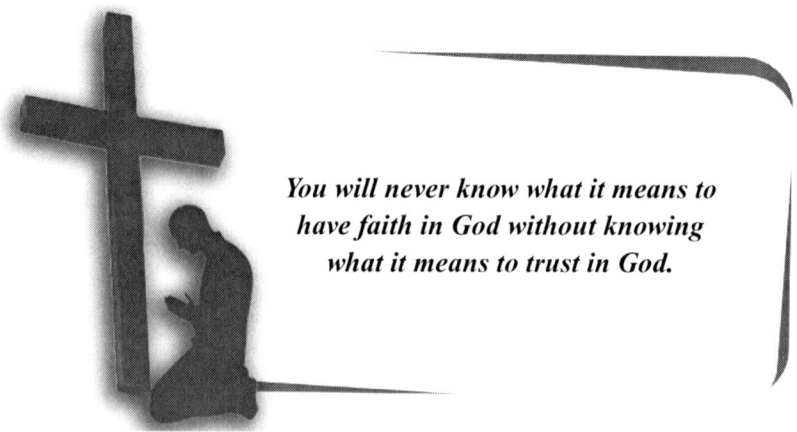

You will never know what it means to have faith in God without knowing what it means to trust in God.

So what is faith? Faith is committing yourself to a road that no one else is willing to travel. Faith is a personal matter; it is something between you and God. Your will to serve Christ is determined by your faith, and your faith will determine what you will do in the name of Jesus, and by using the name of Jesus it will ultimately cause God to demonstrate Himself in your life. Most importantly, the most profound expression of God's hands at work in our life is in the upsurge of your faith.

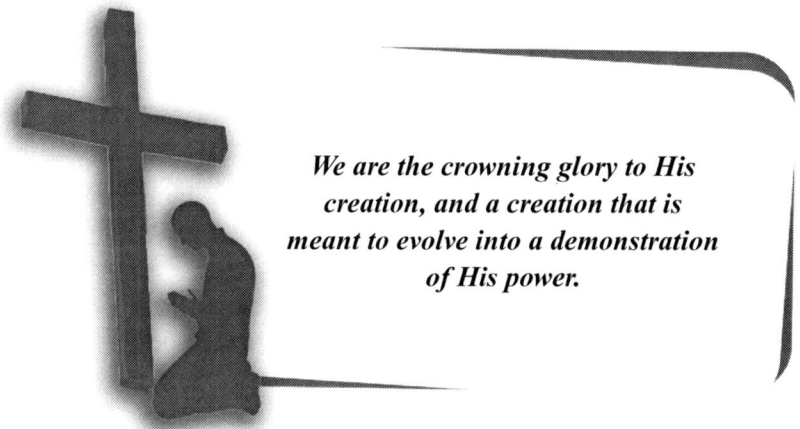

We are the crowning glory to His creation, and a creation that is meant to evolve into a demonstration of His power.

All of this brought me to one of the most important reasons and incentives people put their hope in God—possibilities. I got into a conversation with a visually impaired man. I started the conversation with God, and he started his with faith. He said that you can talk about God all you want, but if you don't surround God with faith you will be speaking about a god that no one will see, including yourself. I said, "I don't really understand." He said, "*I am a blind man, and the sad part is that without faith in God we all see the same thing.* Understand that my faith in God has allowed me to see what people assume I don't. I am a blind man and I work harder than anyone else." I said, "Wait! What do you mean?" He replied, "Did you know that God's way of building us with strength is by faith and not by physical works?"

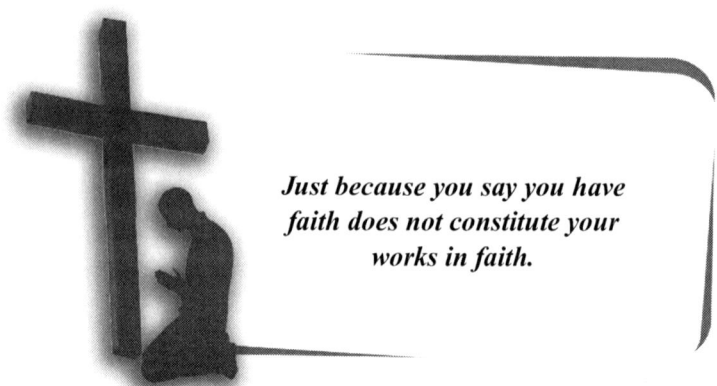

Just because you say you have faith does not constitute your works in faith.

He had a story and it went like this: A young man called out to God and asked, "Why am I so weak, and day after day people are telling me it is impossible and You have said that anything is possible with You." God asked the young man, *"How mighty are you and where does your strength rest? Here I have placed this massive rock on the ground. Now move it!"* The young man tried and could not make it budge for the life of him. "You see, Lord, I cannot." *"My son, you cannot move mountains by pursuing them as if it were work. You don't move mountains by strength but by the power in faith that gives you strength. You see this rock has made you fall, but it has allowed you to trust in Me. Now, how mighty are you and where does your strength rest?"* The young man enthusiastically replied, "I am mighty by the hand that brings me out, and my strength is everlasting because by faith nothing is impossible for me."

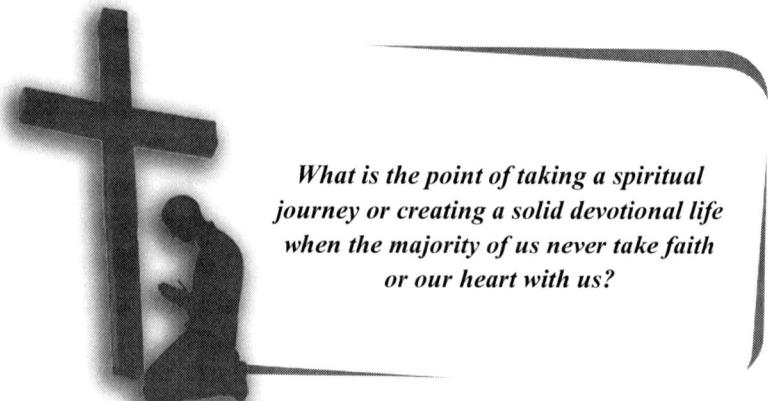

What is the point of taking a spiritual journey or creating a solid devotional life when the majority of us never take faith or our heart with us?

He told me to read Romans 9:30 when I got home. I smiled, and he asked me why I was smiling. I said, *"Huh?"* He responded by saying, "I told you I see what most people assume I don't see, and yes, I can read the Bible. God is about possibilities, not impossibilities."

Romans 9:30 explains that on a daily basis trying rocks and mountains will appear in our lives, but do not pursue the overcoming of our troubles as if it is work. Do not work on dead deeds because they will come against you, but on deeds that are built on faith. If you feel you are weak, increase your faith and allow it to work for you. Our faith allows everything to work.

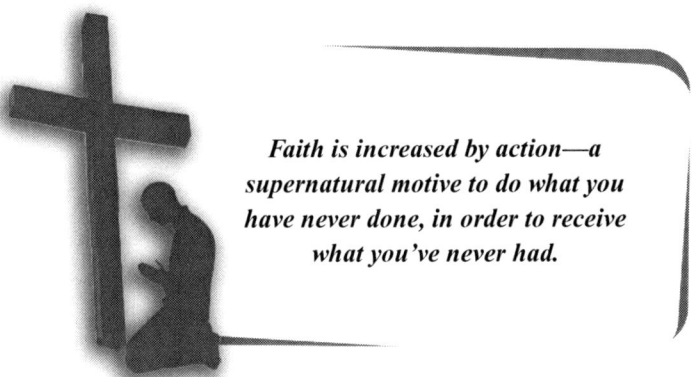

Faith is increased by action—a supernatural motive to do what you have never done, in order to receive what you've never had.

God gives precise descriptions on how people without God and people who think they are right by God view their life objectives, goals, and dreams. I became very attentive after God brought it to my attention, because I asked, *"How do people push impossibilities upon themselves?"*

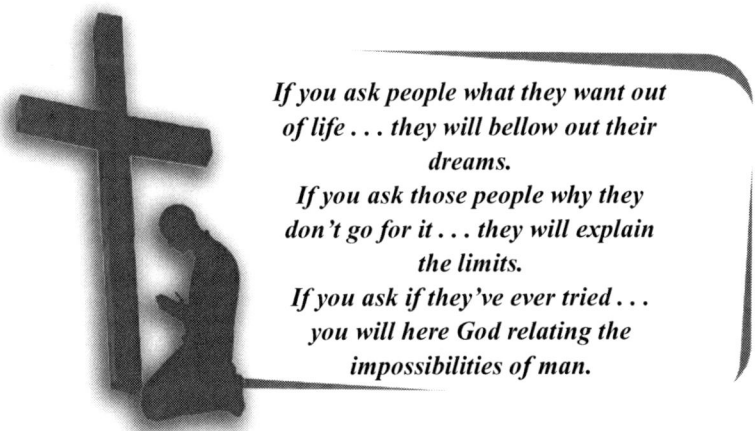

If you ask people what they want out of life . . . they will bellow out their dreams.
If you ask those people why they don't go for it . . . they will explain the limits.
If you ask if they've ever tried . . . you will here God relating the impossibilities of man.

What is impossible with man is possible with God.

This conversation allowed me to realize that faith must not have association with compromise, because compromise will make you settle for the minimum of what you need to do, and where it is you need to go. Compromise will put you in a position where it is still possible to lose all desire and find yourself regressing in faith. Faith must be accompanied by a desperation for God, a desire for His presence, and a plead for His understanding and compassion. You will know when you are walking in faith when your heart begins to agree with what your mouth says. I can do it!

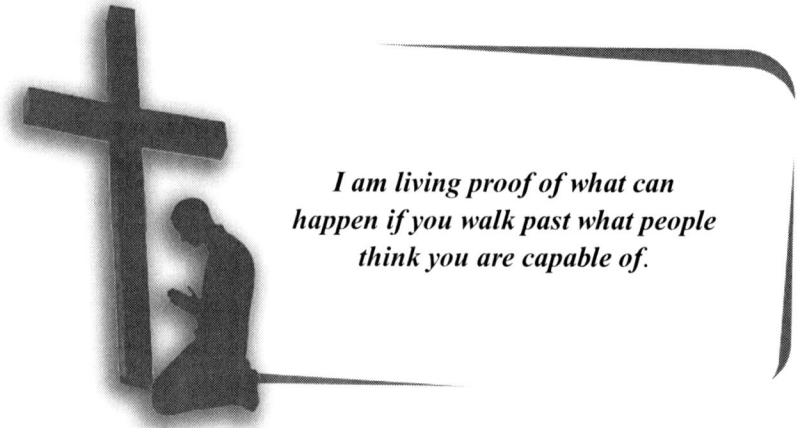

I am living proof of what can happen if you walk past what people think you are capable of.

Faith gives you an opportunity to change your life. It is meant to make you a completely different person, because faith is about putting yourself in a position where your biblical thoughts can now become a reality. It is not going to church and opening your Bible to get peace of mind, just to turn around and do the same things you've always done. It is going to church and it's opening your Bible and preparing yourself for war, to fight through everything you've always done, to end up where you've never been. It is not about waiting to see what God is going to do; it is about believing it is already happening. Have you found yourself sitting, staring out of the window of your car, looking up to the clouds, wondering . . . *is there more*? Yes, there is more! But it is going to take more faith than you've ever had in order to receive more than you've ever gotten (Rom. 14:2). Faith can shatter preconditioned thinking and eliminate curiosity in the common person's mind. Yet there is nothing in this world more acquainted with the heights and depths in the human will, than that of faith. Tell me what God has done in your life, and I will tell you about your faith. Tell me what occupies your life, and I will tell you about your faith. Tell me what it is you do when you are alone, and I will tell you about your faith. Tell me about your burdens and what all of your problems are, and I will tell you about your faith. Tell me everything that weighs you down and holds you back, and I will tell you about your faith. How can you expect God to show His power in your life when you live your life with a faith that is punctuated with a period? If only each person could understand that tomorrow's faith must have more faith than yesterday's faith, they would then come to a point in their life where their faith in God has become the reality of God.

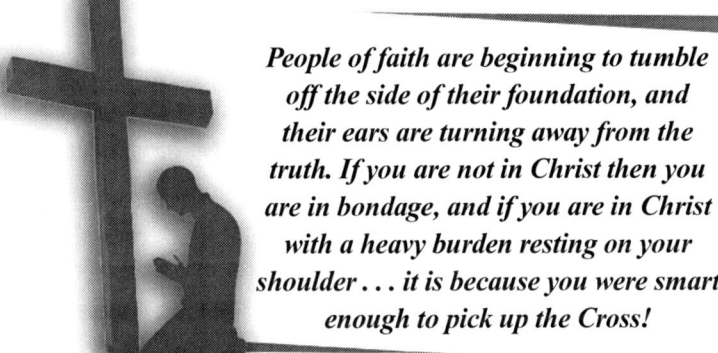

People of faith are beginning to tumble off the side of their foundation, and their ears are turning away from the truth. If you are not in Christ then you are in bondage, and if you are in Christ with a heavy burden resting on your shoulder ... it is because you were smart enough to pick up the Cross!

Jesus said, *I am the greatest desire in your life, but you would have never known it, until I brought you to your greatest weakness. Your greatest weakness will break grounds into your greatest desire, you may not know your greatest desire, but you will know your greatest weakness. So you say you've got mountains?* Faith is when you are being pushed by opposition, engaged with difficulty, overwhelmed by your adversary, exhausted while having to endure pain, and in the midst of all this ... you keep pressing toward God. Many people find themselves far away from their purpose because their determination has lost the consciousness of faith (1 Cor. 16:13). Faith is not for the weakhearted; it is for the desperate-hearted. When you are desperate, you will always find a way to prevail, and when you are desperate, all of a sudden your faith is awakened. Being hungry for God is a form of desperation, and you sustain, not satisfy, that hunger with faith.

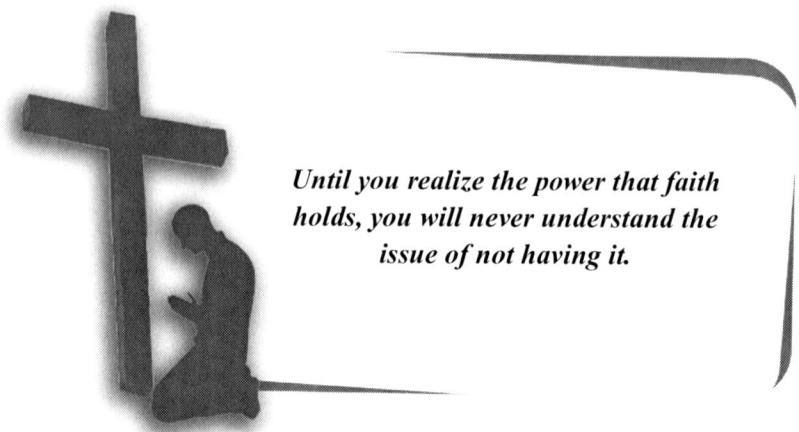

Until you realize the power that faith holds, you will never understand the issue of not having it.

Faith is knowing God is more real than what you can see, more real than what you can feel, and more real than what you have heard. Faith is knowing God is "more," until your faith allows you to see, feel, and hear God *for yourself*! Faith must contain a keen eye to be able to discover what many people will overlook, and it is a keen eye that allows you to see what God is knitting together. Let a passion for God's touch burn like fire within your heart to ignite faith to rise within you. Faith is meant to be the destroyer of impossibilities, but unfortunately, because of lack of faith, people are letting their faith destroy themselves.

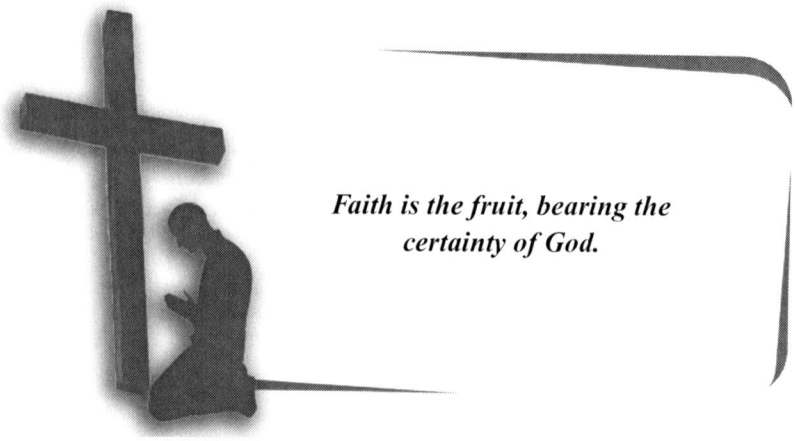

Faith is the fruit, bearing the certainty of God.

So how do you build faith? Faith is built in your devotional life and strengthened during your worship. When hell puts a muzzle over your prayer or faith, it is only in worship where the chains of silence are broken. Worship is what uncovered a compilation of hymns that brought my heart around to notice the need I had for Jesus. You will know this sweet symphony when your heart beats songs of redemption. We go to God individually, we are raised up by God individually, and God will work in individuals simply to reach the collective. Faith and faith alone is the next evolution to understanding the deity of Christ—a faith that is strictly developed and pursued by burying your mind in God's Holy Word (Rom. 1:17)! Faith has surrounded my life with the doctrine of Christ, and has written on my heart the will to seek the glory of God, and a responsibility to spread the Good News. I live in a Gospel that demands power. I live for a Christ that demands authority. I live for a God that demands me to know Him. Those who are called to know God are called to know the deepest parts of Him. In return, the power of God working through you will place wings on your words to reach the hidden depths of the human heart. The best way to know the mind and thoughts of God is for your "self" to become thoughtless, where your opinion does not override the truth in God's Word, because God's Word is the only Word that is relevant. Faith comes by hearing, and if you can hear God's Word, it will certainly build a body of believers who understand Jesus is more than just "belief." This enabled me to understand that my walk has no certainty apart from faith. My mind has no understanding apart from God's Holy Word. My filth has no purity apart from Jesus's blood. My tears have no distinctiveness apart from repentance. My life has no meaning apart from Jesus Christ. *What are you saying about faith?* It will allow my life to be a demonstration of who He is.

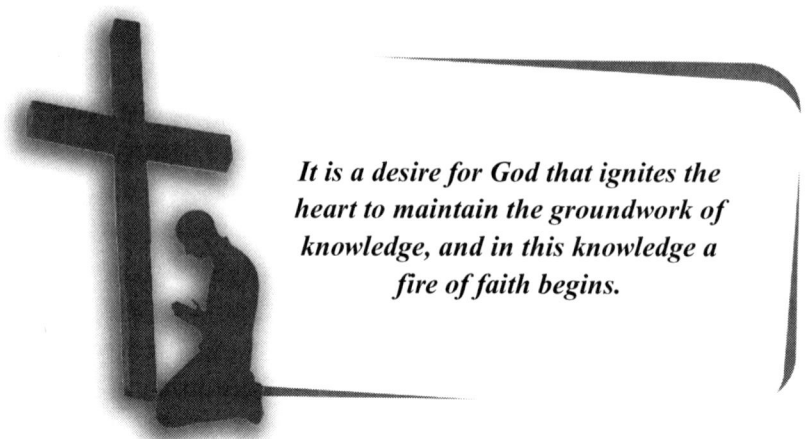

It is a desire for God that ignites the heart to maintain the groundwork of knowledge, and in this knowledge a fire of faith begins.

With every Word of God and every time God speaks there is possibility (Col. 1:5). So we must understand the possibilities and then send faith to accomplish it. Anything that has ever been accomplished in man has been accompanied by faith. Remember that the devil wants your faith, not your flesh. So when the devil comes knocking at your door, send faith to answer it. When you start walking in faith, don't let faint make you take a break; give possibility a chance to accomplish. Faith will present a different approach than the ordinary. The approach of faith is—

In order to experience the uncommon way, you must first exit the commonplace. By staying faithfully in the Word of God you stay daily in the workstation of God.

Faith is meant to establish a belief that is beyond doubt. Always remember that Christianity is not bad, it is just at times misused by ignorant people. When you are approached by someone who is trying to convince you there is no God, allow your approach in faith to convince them otherwise.

A cheerful heart is good medicine (Prov. 17:22).

A strong Christian man was sitting on a bench at a mall, waiting for his wife to finish up in the store she was in. As he was sitting there the man to the right of him noticed his shirt which said, "Jesus is the reason why I smile," and impolitely started mocking the Christian life:

You realize Christian life is declining?

— Christians have the tendency to go back down, to find those who may be lost.

Christians think that they are better than everyone else.
— No, we're just happier than everyone else.

I know Christians who sometimes sin.
— I know bad men who sometimes do good.

Not everyone follows the Word!
— Then not everyone will lead as a result of the Word.

The Christian man's wife walked out of the store, and he began to sit up when the impolite man said, *"Wait!"*

What about the Church?
— Nobody goes there anymore . . . it's too *crowded*!

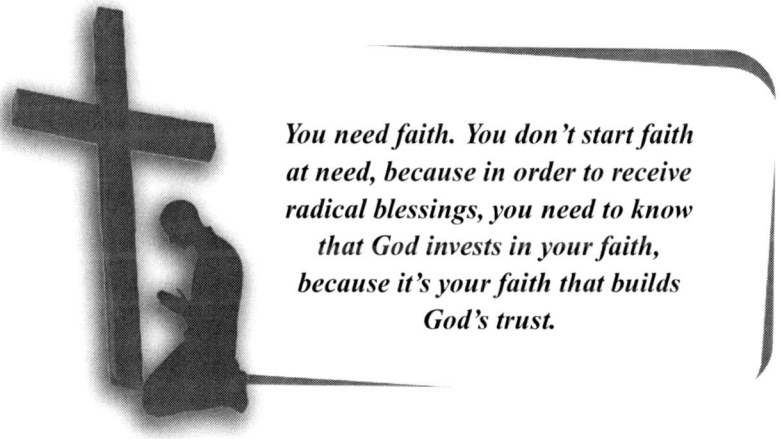

You need faith. You don't start faith at need, because in order to receive radical blessings, you need to know that God invests in your faith, because it's your faith that builds God's trust.

My faith has allowed me to stand. Faith has been the distinction in building who I am, which acknowledges that I have never done anything on my own. Faith has been the canvas that has enabled God to paint the subject of my life. We must understand what faith actually does. Well, what it does not do is what you are already capable of doing; faith enables you to do what is beyond impossible.

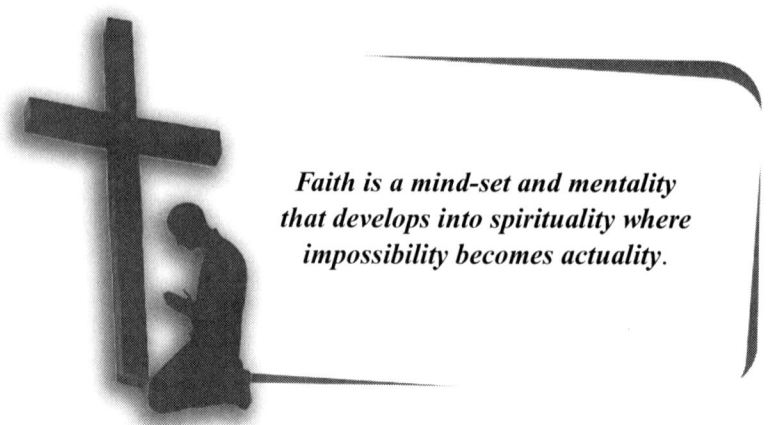

Faith is a mind-set and mentality that develops into spirituality where impossibility becomes actuality.

My understanding of God has given me a reason beyond doubt. There is a whole land of possibility that faith makes possible. I thank God for how relevant faith is, because no matter the situation, faith will put me in a position where I can still smile. We can be on what seems to be a dead-end road in the middle of nowhere, with nothing in sight, standing in the worst storm of our lives, and even then somehow, given the situation, God still makes a way for the asphalt to glisten. Faith is your system of discovery, because faith pulls out what you didn't know was in you. What's even more enlightening is that your faith has a way of leaving a trail of hope, so even when a fragment of that faith is picked up . . . it will begin someone else's possibility of change, breakthrough, and deliverance (1 Thess. 3:7). I was speaking to a friend on the phone and he could literally hear the promise in what God was giving me. He said, "You have something unique in you." I said, "No, it's actually not exclusive. It's the same thing that wants desperately to be in you. It's consistent yesterday, today, and always." The uniqueness is the journey He takes you on. At an earlier period in my life I had another conversation with a classmate who asked me, "Why is it that I try so hard to blend in and still I'm never noticed?" I said, *"Maybe you're creating a mistaken solution."* I ran into this woman several years after graduation; she smiled and said, "I didn't have to create! I was given an accurate resolution . . . a powerful voice in my ear told me that in order to be noticed you don't stand in, you stand out. Not only do you listen, but allow yourself to be heard. There is something very distinctive about being different, because nothing special ever occurs when you blend in. It's better to be the peach amongst a patch of lemons."

SPIRITUALLY RECHARGED

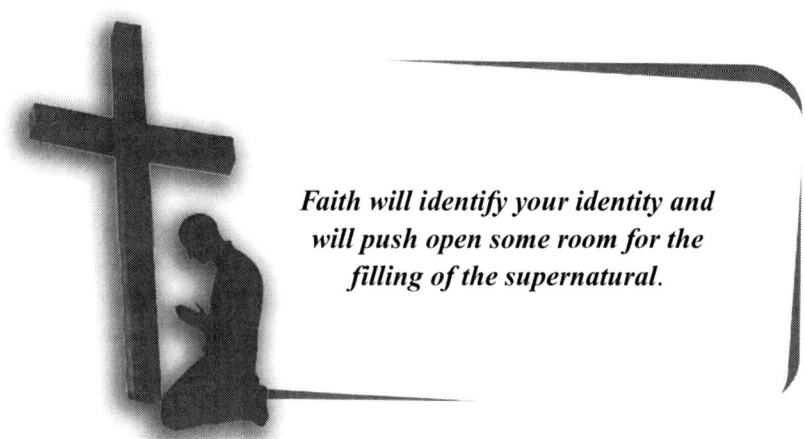

Faith will identify your identity and will push open some room for the filling of the supernatural.

What motivates men? It is disbelief destroyed in its greatest moment. It is impossibility proven to be realism. It is doubt shown to prevail. The motivation of men is found when the Spirit of God shows no limits. The Spirit of God is a crucial and vital element to receiving the Living Word. It is the answer to receiving various living things and fundamental emotions sent by God Himself. The Spirit is a revealer of God's thoughts because He searches the deepest part of God to find every certainty, path, and purpose He has for your life. The Spirit is love that transpires from God's secret wisdom for a more perceptible direction to your purpose. The same Spirit who knows God's purpose for your life in return speaks through you in your own prayer by searching and filling the confusion in your thoughts, because the Holy Spirit interprets our need for God's divine purpose—God's thoughts and plans (Rom. 8:26-27). The Spirit takes us out of control and into God's control . . . that's why it becomes so personal, because now it is the God in us who is able to work through us. The Spirit's only means of power is when He is in control—not just being filled with the Spirit, but being led by the Spirit. Being led by the Spirit paves a way for you to take a private walk with God. If the Spirit is not in control, you might be missing out on a crucial walk that will lead you to your purpose. The Spirit can make a nonbeliever believe and make a believer be amazed at what he has been missing.

If I am going to form my life according to God's Word I want my life to be everything except what the world sees everyday. Why do I want supernatural power? Why do I want to witness a crazy manifestation of miracles? Because, this is a Gospel that I know. This is a God that I know. This, is all that I know.

The Spirit of God is what makes the invisible, visible; and the denial, justifiable. The Spirit has extracted the remaining *what ifs*, *disbeliefs*, *same old days*, and *I can'ts* out of my Christian intensification. The Spirit has turned my *what ifs* from supposing to composing, my *disbeliefs* into certainties, my *same old days* into inventive days of development with God, and my *I cant's* into groundbreaking possibilities. It's eccentric in a wonderful sense that without the Spirit all I had was questions of doubt, but when the Spirit was deposited in my life, it was as if I was being dragged into my understanding and answers (Rom. 5:5). The Spirit has been my physical partner in development and my physical contact with Jesus. Without having the Spirit as a filler and leader in my life, I could honestly say I would either be wrapped in a bundle of confusion, still having the main question of whether God was real or not, or be far away from where the Spirit has dragged me and led me to where I am today. Yes, the Spirit has given me an understanding beyond my own possible understanding.

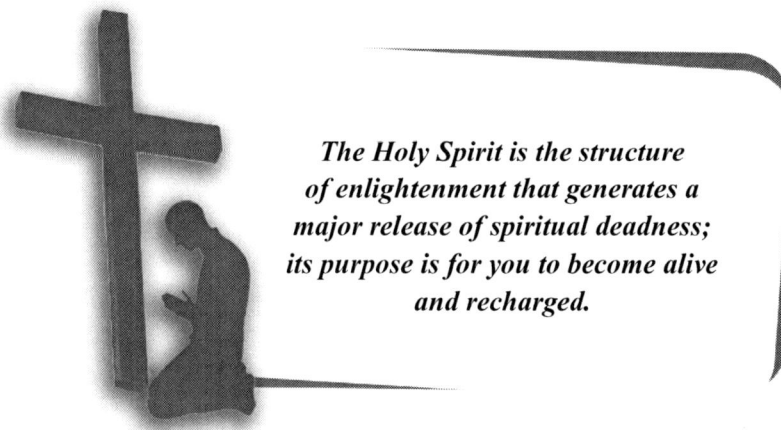

The Holy Spirit is the structure of enlightenment that generates a major release of spiritual deadness; its purpose is for you to become alive and recharged.

The Father is the Creator and Commander. Jesus is the Savior and Instructor of the creation and commands. The Spirit is the Comforter and Distributor when we follow those commands. It's the Spirit's duty to help us conform to the likeness and purity of God, and most importantly to receive the gifts that enable God to not only work in us, but work through us. It is great to be a Christian when we can have the same mind of Jesus. His thoughts and approach to men are as follows: *I am not only One who teaches the law, but I come as One who has authority in the law* (Matt. 7:29.)

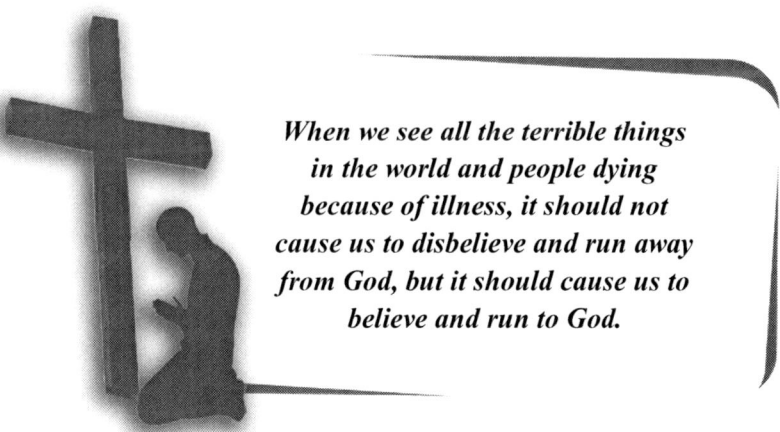

When we see all the terrible things in the world and people dying because of illness, it should not cause us to disbelieve and run away from God, but it should cause us to believe and run to God.

There is a spiritual power that we are lacking because of our deficiency of faith, which has made us powerless to command the power of healing in

Jesus's name. Unfortunately, in Western Christianity we lack the witnessing of the Spirit's power to heal, the Spirit's power to deliver signs, and the Spirit's power to orchestrate miracles because of our deficiency in faith (1 Cor. 12:7-11). For example, when is the last time you witnessed something absolutely unbelievable happen before your own eyes in the streets by one person who demanded it be done in Jesus's name? When is the last time something unbelievable became a believable thing? The problem is that it is not impossible for it to be done; the problem is that people of faith don't have the faith it takes to walk up to someone with a disability and instantly demand healing in Jesus's name. The problem is that Christians are too timid in their faith to walk in faith and command miracles to be done in Jesus's name. Why do I need faith? Why do I need God? Because, so unworthy I am that only God can make it possible. So lost I am that only God can lead me through it. So undeserving I am that only God can make it happen. So weak I am that only God can give me strength. So unintelligent I am that only God can speak me through it. So incredible, so indescribable, so unimaginable that my faith alone will make people know that only God has done it. Miracles are not impossible, it is just impossible for miracles to happen without an assurance of faith. *What if they don't believe? It is your faith that is meant to make them believe*! Additionally, you have pastors in church who believe they have the Spirit's power to heal and perform miracles, but never will you witness it being done outside of their own congregation. *But I see people getting healed all the time at my church.* The majority of the time it is not because of the pastor, but because the person who was healed had the faith it took to be healed. This is what I mean: Do you have enough faith to demand healing for someone who does not believe in God's power, to make the healing happen so they are astounded, leaving them with no doubt that God exists? Faith and the Spirit of God are meant to do more than just heal your broken heart. This is not a church issue; this is a kingdom issue. I am searching beyond morality where my tongue has an authority to command in Jesus's name. I want the Spirit of God to fall on a place where one man raises his hand amongst thousands and commands the barriers of darkness to flee. Then from the aftermath of his authority it will make everyone who surrounds his faith to fall out in amazement of a living God who reigns with power. What if your faith was dependent upon the experience of your own imparted miracles, how much faith would you really have? But wait! Is not faith without works dead (James 2:14)?

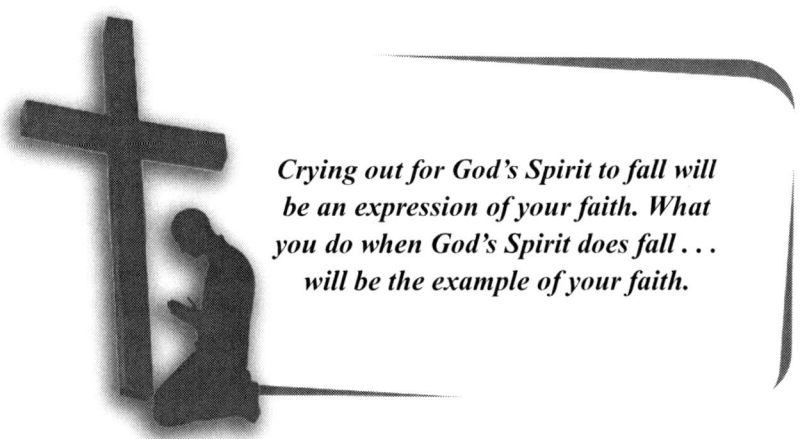

Crying out for God's Spirit to fall will be an expression of your faith. What you do when God's Spirit does fall . . . will be the example of your faith.

Let me ask you some questions. Is it God's will for a person to have cancer? Is it God's will for a person to have a disease? Is it God's will for a person to be mute, lame, or blind? Or is it God's will for that person to be healed—a healing where His Spirit can fall, because it was called by His person of faith for others to witness a transcending power of Jesus's name? Did you know that you are not suffering because of your disability or sickness? The Bible clearly tells you that there *will* be suffering as a Christian, but there does not have to be illness. *How is that so?* That is God's Word, but furthermore, have you ever noticed that Jesus was never sick, but He did indeed suffer? Did you ever notice that Jesus wasn't the one being healed, but was the One giving the healing? Not only that, but what does Jesus tell you to be?—Christlike. My question is . . . does your life and faith tend to touch other people?

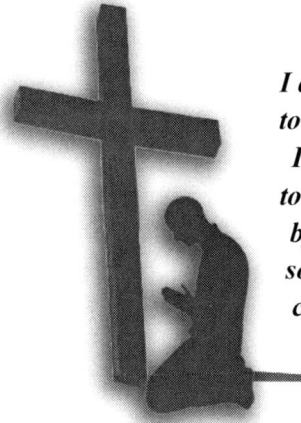

I don't want to open doors for people to ask me about God, merely because I am talking about God, but I want to be the vessel of God's given power, by His Holy Spirit, to do something so incredible before people that they come up to me and ask me . . . how in the world did you do that?

Receiving It All

My own understanding regarding success has always been based on *how far you've gone in life*, and not *how far life has taken you*. You see, now that I know Jesus is my life and my life is Jesus, my success will be certain because I am being fulfilled wherever *life* takes me. I have gained a deeper understanding of success that has allowed me to appreciate its whole meaning. Success is more than being financially blessed. When people say "success is having money," the statement is not inaccurate; it's just incomplete. Money is easily recognized as a subtotal—a partial set of figures. I don't understand when people say that one day I will be successful, because Jesus has been my success and my every possibility. So every day, I believe I am accompanied by the source of success, because success is merely a word to coach you or encourage you into what victory actually is, and in the midst of Jesus I don't know how to think otherwise (1 Pet. 1:7). How big we think about our God will determine how big our future is. God is our greatness and as long as you have "greatness" in you, it can also be brought out of you.

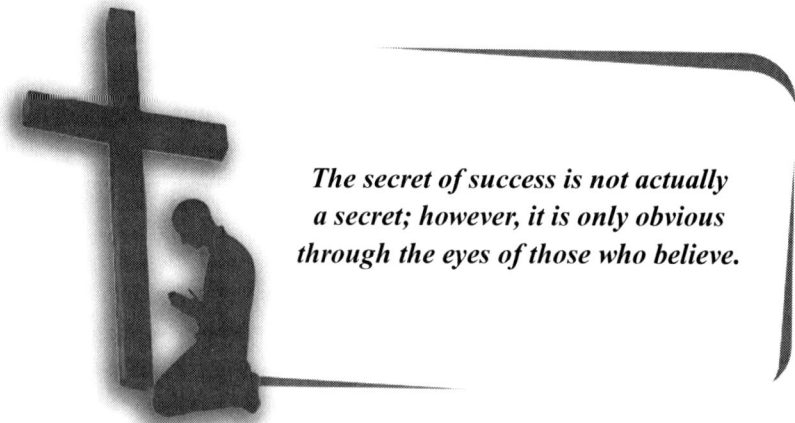

The secret of success is not actually a secret; however, it is only obvious through the eyes of those who believe.

I have learned a lot from my time being on the baseball diamond. I asked a coach what he loved so much about his captain. He told me it was "*the fact that he never finishes first.*" A team will never be a success if only one man finishes the game. Sometimes you have to drop back to push each other not to give up, so the team can finish together. In another discussion with a baseball coach he explained to me that you cannot carry a team by trying to place it on your shoulders. It is how you carry yourself that enables the team to learn to carry each other.

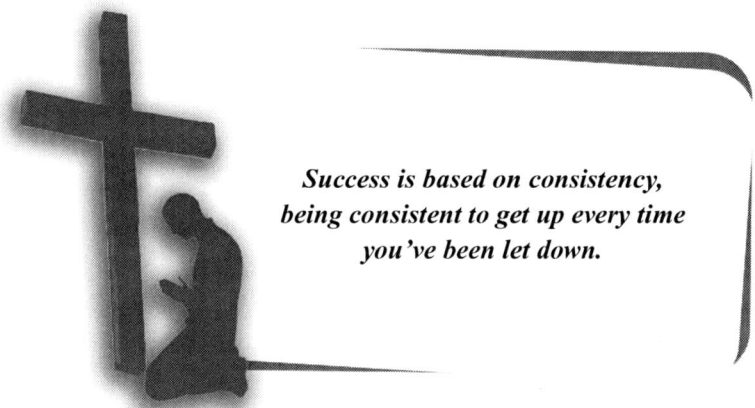

Success is based on consistency, being consistent to get up every time you've been let down.

Finally, in one of my favorite talks about possibilities with an assistant coach, he explained to me that potential doesn't make you a professional; it's potential that gives you the ability to become a professional. If you don't exercise that ability, it will never become a strength. Whenever there is potential with the reward of professionalism, it must be applied with patience. Patience will teach you that failures are not actually failures, but that they are answers for improvement. Patience will reward you as a professional. You cannot be hard on yourself, because the journey is hard all by itself. In your life, use the game of baseball as inspiration; a batter can fail seven out of ten times and still be named a Hall of Famer.

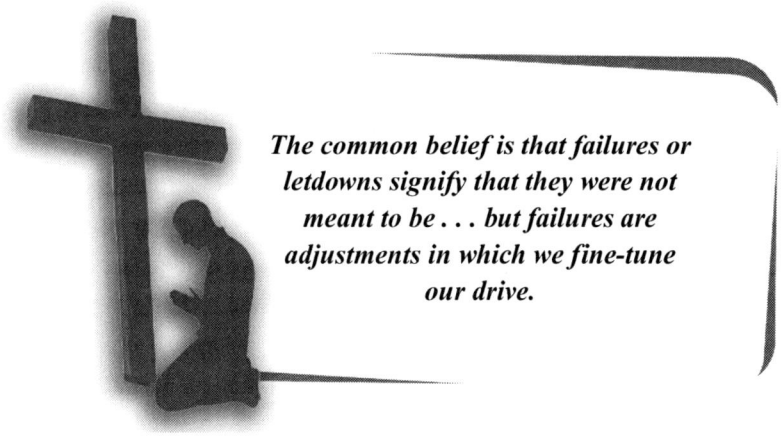

The common belief is that failures or letdowns signify that they were not meant to be . . . but failures are adjustments in which we fine-tune our drive.

If you keep with you the certain principles of God, humility will guide you to a place where possibility has become your favor. I have lived my whole life searching for ways to be financially secure. I have lived my whole life telling people that I am going to be rich. I have lived my whole life dreaming of what money could do for me (1 Tim. 6:10). But now, as I lay myself down to sleep I cannot stop thinking about Jesus. I cannot stop dreaming of His presence. I cannot help but believe that now that I have Jesus . . . I have received it all. I am saddened by people who go to Christ and believe, just so they can get a return—so their bills can be paid, and so their bank statement will bring a smile. Is Christ not enough? *So you're saying that when I go to Christ I will get nothing?* No, I am saying that when you truly go to Christ . . . you will understand that you've just received it all.

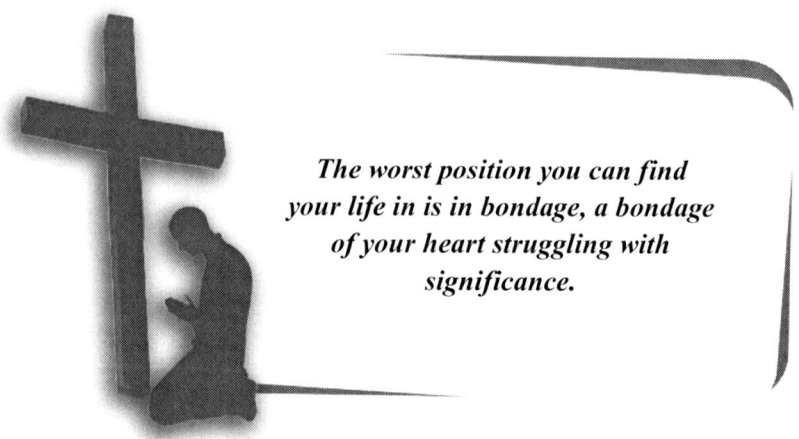

The worst position you can find your life in is in bondage, a bondage of your heart struggling with significance.

God will always give us visions, so we can prepare for what is coming. God will give us visions simply so we can be part of them. However, you must understand that God's vision is not in money (Eccles. 1:7). Why, because there is no vision in money. Until your very nature has been changed, money will be deposited in a box with your unredeemed flesh. Without a full redemption, money will always have the attachment of greed. Greed will leave you with a mind-set that you need to spend money to have a sense of life, but humbleness will lead you to a clarification that states, *What a wasted life it would be if we spent it on money!* If gaining money is your objective, you are building a structure that will soon come tumbling upon you because the Spirit of God is not measured by our abundance; rather its outpouring is increased by our obedience to the will of God. So it is not what I will get out of it, but it is what He will get out of it. God will *not* take me to the Cross so I can see pain, but He will take me there so I can feel pain. God will take me to the blood of Jesus *not* so I can understand glory, but He will take me to the blood so I can stand in glory. God will *not* pour the Holy Spirit on me because I am being rewarded, but He will pour the Holy Spirit on me so He can get the full reward of glory through my life. When you have truly found yourself in Christ, you will also find that nothing else in this world matters or will satisfy. You want to know where your life is. It is attached to the Cross. You want to know where your answers are. They are attached to the Cross. You want to know where your freedom is. It is attached to the Cross. You want to know where your purpose is. It is attached to the Cross. And you will notice when you get there that money will not be there.

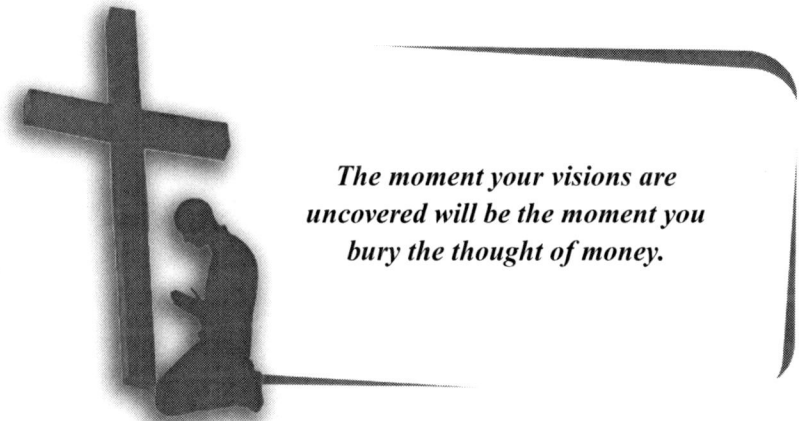

The moment your visions are uncovered will be the moment you bury the thought of money.

I asked Jesus at one point why I have so many innovative ideas if I can't do anything with them. There were so many times I've tried to run with creative concepts, but the running always met fatigue before a breakthrough. Once again, God informatively intervened with perfect reason. *I give you ideas, I give you visions, and I give you promises to hold on to. They are simply for you to know they are there, to let you know success and variation of dreams and visions are accomplishable in your life. In order to see that these ideas and visions come to pass, you will still hold on to them, but you're going to put them to the side for now.* And *first seek the kingdom and His righteousness, and the rest shall be given to you* (Matt. 6:33.) This enabled me to learn something very important when it comes to our ideas and intentions, and that is to always consult God before we do anything, because the devil will allow us to establish a business, simply to destroy our faith. Some of the things the devil gives us seem like a bright picture. The importance of having Jesus is that He will separate the bright things from the right things.

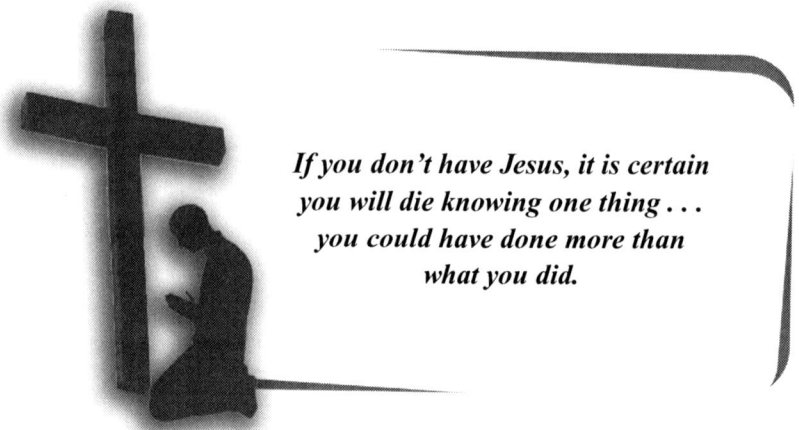

If you don't have Jesus, it is certain you will die knowing one thing . . . you could have done more than what you did.

To identify with creditable success, you must first know what God accepts as creditable and glorifying. Every business that I ever established was always with my benefit in mind. This business in particular enabled me to walk into an entirely different experience, not because of the business itself but because of my obedience and trust in Jesus. I created an Internet-based business at the end of 2006, before Jesus drew me to the Cross. I fought for this business and put every dime I earned into it because I could see my own desires being distinguished through it (Prov. 17:16). I didn't have the luxury of the million-dollar budget it would take to make this Web site an overnight success, so I spread its progress out over the next two years. I brought a high school acquaintance into the picture because of his hustling savvy and his way of promoting businesses and events. Little did I know at the time that our working together would create a bond of friendship and brotherhood that I will be forever thankful for. I obtained a true friendship that I had been deficient in for so many years. It built a foundation of accountability, dependence, and honesty. This friendship has both challenged me and allowed me to take some risks by giving trust. I was able to release the empty bondage in my life by realizing that "friendship is God given."

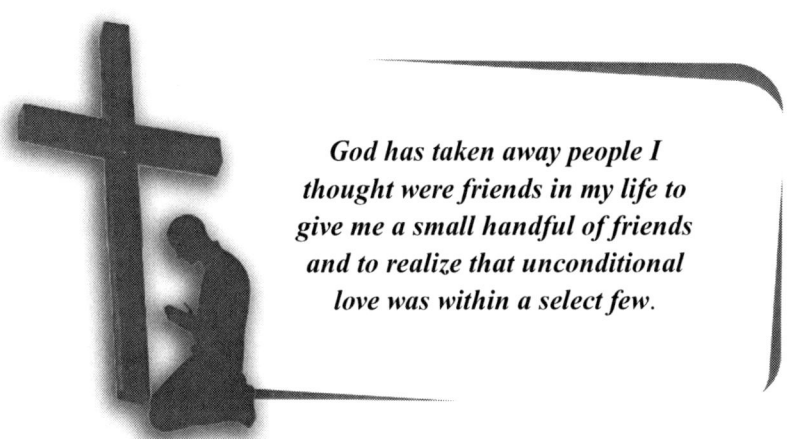

God has taken away people I thought were friends in my life to give me a small handful of friends and to realize that unconditional love was within a select few.

Genuine friendship consists of always "being available," having discussions of life, and demonstrating the deepest concern for each other's well-being (Prov. 18:24). Whenever I wanted to walk into a financial mess he would always be the one to turn me from it. We both struggled in our own ways, but I came to understand the concept of a true friend. We all are people who have faults because of sin and temptation, but true friends, even though they have faults of their own, will always push you away from yours, and vice versa. Ironically, we both had time in the drug movement, and whenever I wanted to get back into the drug game he wouldn't let me. Every time he wanted to get back into the drug game, I wouldn't let him. So basically we were two true friends not pushing each other into the drug game, but "drug" each other from it. However, we both made dense decisions throughout the development of this business by using the streets as a way to get by and get ahead financially. In June 2008, when I completely committed my life to Jesus, I already had over $100,000 invested in this business, and it was near completion.

You cannot experience God's glory unless you are revealed through His glory.

Jesus allowed me to grow into many right decisions before leaving me with a "choice" of allowing divine intervention. Around December 2008, as I was taking a shower, I kept hearing *"Go to the mountains, go to the mountains"* like a whisper in my ear. When I got out of the shower, I had North Carolina on my mind. I went into my bedroom, lay on my bed, opened my Bible to the Book of Genesis and to the arrangement and story of Abraham's life, and began to read. As I came to the story of Lot, Abraham's nephew, I focused in on the part where the angels told Lot to *hurry . . . Flee for your lives! Don't look back . . . Flee to the mountains* (Gen. 19:14-17)! Just as I finished reading that section of scripture, I got a text message from an unknown number, and it simply said "Hurry!" Amazed, I went outside to the living room and showed it to my cousin. Right away we started preparing for North Carolina. I prayed heavily that night. The next evening as I was reading my Bible, I had Trinity Broadcasting Network (TBN) on in the background. I heard a pastor speaking about God's opportunity for us and taking advantage of your opportunity. Hearing the message, I leaned up and slid to the corner of my bed, and as I did so, a piece of paper fell out of my Bible. I didn't pay attention to what was on the paper; I just leaned over and simply picked it up and held it in my hand while still watching and listening to the television. After the message concluded, I nonchalantly looked down at the paper, opened the fold, and read: *Your dreams are buried in the middle of the* **Lot**, *but you have to purchase the Lot to obtain the dream. You must draw attention to your opportunity, and God will prove the impossible!* I looked down at my Bible, stunned at God's approach and the way He reveals messages.

While I was watching TBN, I began to move around, and the pages of the Bible fluttered and just so happened to fall open to the scripture about Abraham, and my eyes instantly centered in on the following passage: "*. . . On the mountain of the Lord it will be provided*" (Gen. 22:14.) The scripture expresses *to trust in God and not to withhold anything*. The very next thing I did was look up the definition of the word *Lot*.

Lot: A station or condition determined by chance or destiny or a means of deciding something by chance. A great many; a great deal.

> "*Better is a man who enjoys his work, because that is his lot*" (Eccles. 3:22).

My cousin and I decided we were going to North Carolina within the next couple weeks with field, land, lot, and purchase on our mind. I was checking in constantly with God and praying for my business greatly, because it was just about to be completed and I was excited about that, and I continued praying about going to North Carolina to be sure that was where God wanted me to go. Oddly enough, all I was getting was silence from God. That following Saturday I woke up with the word "*release*" on my mind. I asked God what this was, *release what?* During the next couple of days I focused on my business, but realized that I had not made God a priority in my business. I began to pray and apologize to God about not making Him the head of my business and not going to Him for my main source of direction. I said, "Lord, the business is yours. Do what you want with it. It is in your hands." Without hesitation I got my response . . . "*Get rid of it*." I said, "Huh, *get rid of it*? You mean like put it aside for a little bit?" "*Get rid of it*." "Are youuu surrre?" "*Get rid of it*." So I called my partner and true friend and told him I needed to meet with him. I met with him and told him I believe God is telling us to get rid of the Web site. He said he would call the programming company and see if we can work something out more suitable for us in terms of money. I agreed. He called me back the next day and said the programming company said it was no problem to work out a payment plan. I said, "Okay great, let's do it!"

That night God dropped something heavy on my heart while I was in prayer, and then He responded by saying, "*I didn't tell you to make a more reasonable arrangement, but to get rid of it.*" Ironically, the next day I had an investor wanting to give me $30,000 to invest in the final programming fees of the Web site. Out of love and fear for God, I told him no, I couldn't do it! He looked at me as though I was crazy, and I got up and walked out.

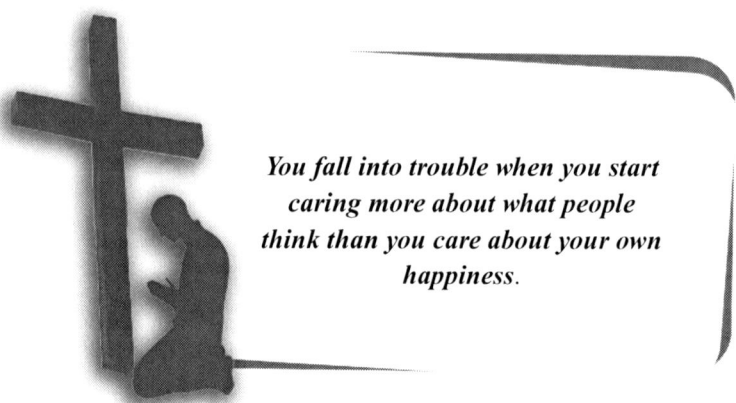

You fall into trouble when you start caring more about what people think than you care about your own happiness.

There were two other individuals involved in this business with me. I had many questions about their involvement and questions about the success of my business in general. I opened up to God that night for a desperate understanding, and the following is what He allowed me to understand. Every time God speaks, whether in rebuke or in compassion, it is in a vocabulary of love. Now, this understanding from God may seem like a cyclone of bewilderment, but it was precisely given to me as a perfect understanding for why my business, or any business at that, cannot and will not be a success.

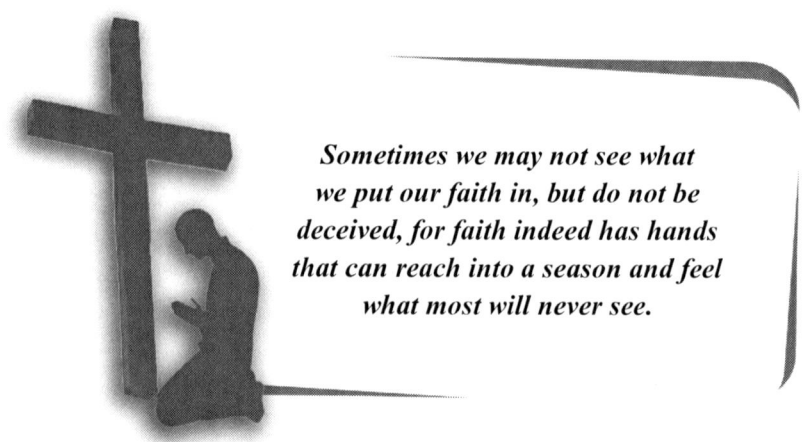

Sometimes we may not see what we put our faith in, but do not be deceived, for faith indeed has hands that can reach into a season and feel what most will never see.

The initial question I addressed was actually a question that I had to ask myself. Can my business become a success if I am the head of the establishment righteously pursing God, yet the herd that follows is lost in its own way?

> *"A man's steps are directed by the Lord. How then can anyone understand his own way?"* (Prov. 20:24)

Why would my business not be prosperous if I have given it all to You?

You must keep your eyes and ears attentive to God's plans and direction for your life and business. Everything that you do must be biblically and spiritually backed up. If your company does not bear good fruit, then it may spoil the whole tree, and whatever is spoiled will impact what is distributed. God will not allow the product of your business to be distributed because of its unfruitfulness. God will keep corrupt branches and corrupt fruit from being affluent. God has given us all these great things to enjoy: real estate, businesses, and happiness, but we have turned good pleasure into self-absorbed, greedy desires.

An obscurity or problem within a business does not have to be a development error or an underestimated specification on budget or cost, but the realization of who is part of the business. Who would eat from a tree if only one branch bears good fruit? People will assume the tree is dying out and will not eat from it. God said for the sake of one righteous person He would not destroy a city. However, God never said the city would prosper because of that one righteous person, but rather the Lord will have compassion and give wisdom that will teach him *to go where he is instructed*. God giving me instruction was simply a testing and a perfect building of faith. I realized that it is only through your trials of faith when you learn how strong your testimony of faith really is, and remember, every trial of faith will always contain a verdict.

> *"You did not choose me, but I chose you and appointed you to go and bear good fruit—fruit that will last . . ."* (John 15:16).

One of the partners of this company had been investing portions of his money into life's obscurity and the devil's destruction. He was living the "great" worldly life, but me, having a servant's mind, I already knew that when the world is at its best the world is at its worst, and when the world is at its worst it shows how deprived we really are. I could have sold this business and made a decent amount of money on it, but that was never the point. If I had sold the business for a profit, this partner would have been entitled to his share. Without him knowing God, he would have simply invested more money into transgression. So instead of him investing into the devil's purpose, I decided not to make any money myself for the sake of righteousness. I actually didn't want the money. I was already telling myself that when I find myself in Christ not only I will go on to greater things, but most importantly, if I am truly in Christ, I am found in the greatest thing.

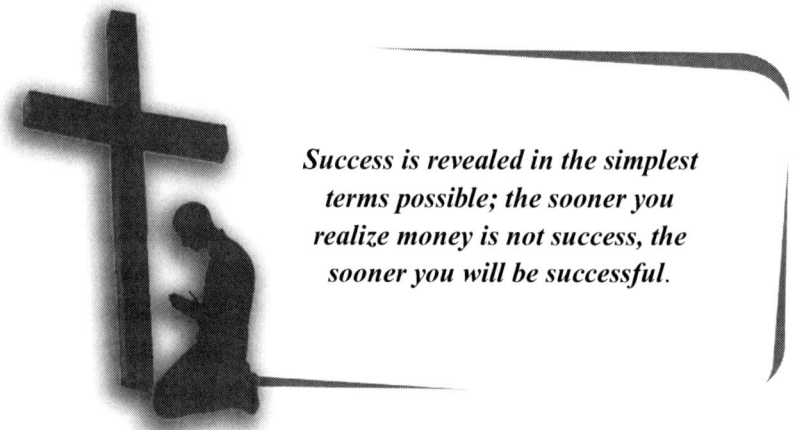

Success is revealed in the simplest terms possible; the sooner you realize money is not success, the sooner you will be successful.

You can explain to a man "it's no good" and still he goes off and boasts about his own worth and success. You can enlighten him about God's demands backed by His promises, yet he still buries his hand into the dish.

"*Many are the plans in a man's heart, but it is the Lord's purpose that prevails*" (Prov. 19:21).

If there are two partners in a business, one righteous in the Lord and the other disoriented and living away from the truth, ask yourself if God would bless your company with a reward of crowned finances and success if one man claims God did it and the other claims he did it himself.

If one man brings his portion of income into the storehouse and does what is obligated, and the other partner boasts and invests his portion into transgression, it goes as said:

No success comes at the expense of denying the truth.

"Do not let this Book of the Law depart from your mouth; meditate on it day and night, so that you may be careful to do everything written in it. Then you will be prosperous and successful" (Josh. 1:8).

A man who does not acquire Godly intentions will pursue selfish ends while defying all sound judgment. How can one man say God has done this for me and the other say, *"Look,* I do not live according to all of God's Word, yet I still have."

You may say to yourself, "my power and the strength of my hands have produced this wealth for me." But remember the Lord your God, for it is he who gives you the ability to produce wealth . . . (Deut. 8:17-19).

If your partner does not listen, then you alone must obey God's instructions, because His intentions are for the virtuous to prosper. I don't expect to do wrong; I expect to do right, so if I am wrong, I'll know and repent. God will then guide you into a position where your ability and earnestness will provide you success for the absolute glory of God, which can then leave a possibility for others to change, because of the favor that was provided due to an adequate following of divine expectation.

I wrote this small footnote to myself, and it has allowed me to remember how important exalting and giving God full glory amongst others is to Him. *Lord, please allow me to understand what my relationship with You has been. I may not acknowledge You like I should, but You are always on my mind. I may not read the Bible as much I should, but I try to go to church as often as I can. I may not stand up for Your name at work, but I do kneel when I am at home alone. I may not pray every day, but every day I see my favorite scripture on the wall. I have given money, with nothing in return. I have given out, with no gratitude given back. Lord, I don't understand. I have given, given, and given, yet I have gotten nothing in return! And the Lord's reply—"Yes, I agree."*

No success will come to your company if the foundation is built on sand. The glory of God stands firm and builds upon a rock. Go where God instructs you, and do what He tells you to do . . . then receive full success and glory in Jesus's name! I have been born into God's thoughts since the beginning, but it was following His instructions and then uniting with Christ's heart that has allowed me to live in the end.

As obedient children, do not conform to the evil desires you had when you lived in ignorance (1 Pet. 1:14).

The second person involved in this business is my true and honest friend. Even though he believes without a doubt there is a living God, he still lacks the intimacy and familiarity of God's understanding, customs, and decrees. He is currently in the midst of his divine change, and he is walking into the light that will expose his purpose and give him a full understanding of who he actually is. I know that without him giving everything he has to God and seeking his purpose, he will never grab a hold of the true meaning of the journey. It is in the journey where you are prepared and instructed for your purpose. If God were to drop a million dollars in his lap right now, he would unintentionally veer from the journey, as anybody would, and never know what to divinely do with that money. Yes, a person who believes in God will give 10 percent to the church and give other portions to charity, but if you can't hear God and understand His process, you will never know where that money was specifically intended to go. We can only provide as God guides and enables us. Remember, God works through people, and the blessings He gives you are specifically intended to be planted in the progress of someone else's destiny.

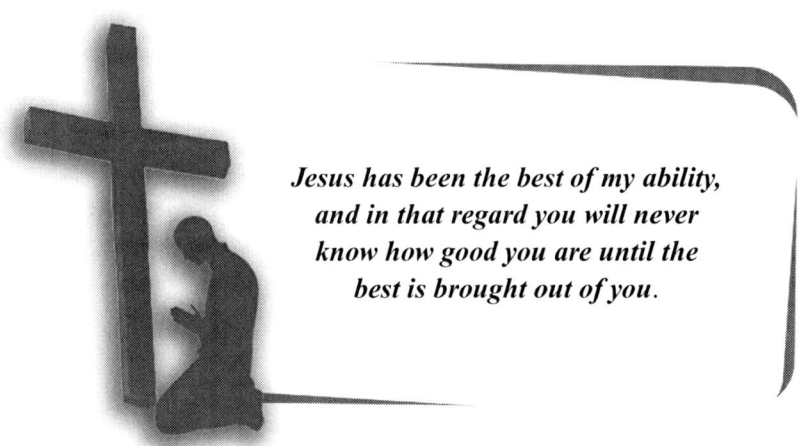

Jesus has been the best of my ability, and in that regard you will never know how good you are until the best is brought out of you.

A partner of a company who desires the change within so he never lives without must do so in the presence of the Lord, because Christians are accountable to God individually.

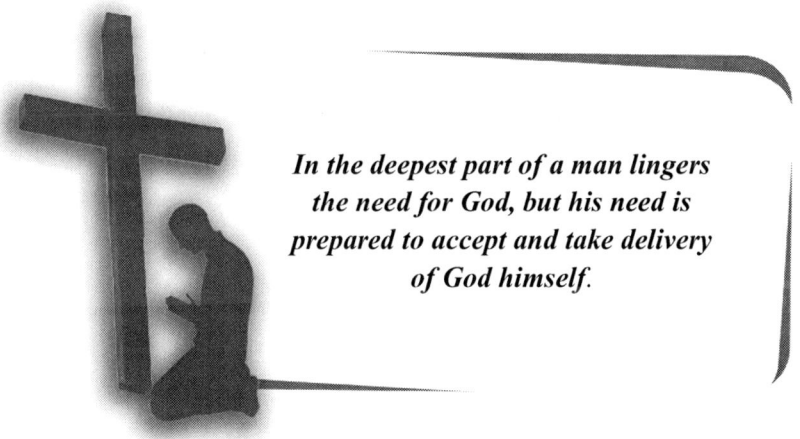

In the deepest part of a man lingers the need for God, but his need is prepared to accept and take delivery of God himself.

With anything in life there is a process for growth. A person who seeks God earnestly must grow in dependence on God before receiving independence. Faith develops wisdom and knowledge, and change leads to revealing the details gained from obedience.

Don't let the journey of success allow you to lose your identity. It is not the journey that makes you who you are; it's Who made the journey which enables you to be who you are.

The Lord was telling me that *"He must come to Me himself, and I will properly prepare him for his destiny and bring out his rightful intentions."*

The final person involved in this business was my cousin—the same cousin who got me into church; the same cousin who would give me his last two dollars if I needed it; the same cousin that I lived with for two years. My cousin is a warmhearted, God-informed individual who constantly stays in prayer. His problem is that he is easily tempted and completely misses the God that is right in front of him, waving him down, directing him, loving him, and trying desperately to have him progress in assignment, levels, and trust.

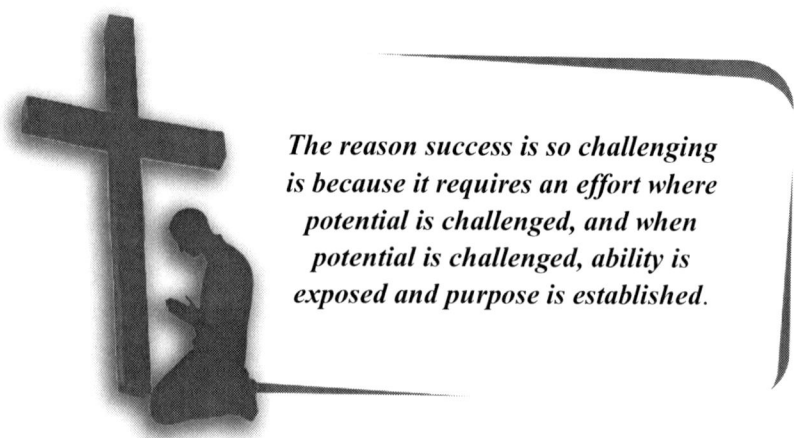

The reason success is so challenging is because it requires an effort where potential is challenged, and when potential is challenged, ability is exposed and purpose is established.

God understands we are not perfect, but if you have read the Word, which is perfect, and are still disobedient to what pleases Him, then it is your actions and mouth that lead you into sin. It is better to not know the Word and sin, than it is to know the Word and sin, because those who know the Word are without excuse (1 Pet. 2:21). Jesus not only saves us from Satan, but more importantly, He saves us from God—the wrath of God. If your company has Godly intentions but exposes deceitful acts, it will become far worse for you.

A man who strays from the path of understanding comes to rest in the company of the dead (Prov. 21:16).

If you have told the partners of your company that they need a divine change for the business to be a success and they haven't listened:

The Bible teaches us that if a word from God was spoken as a plan for your life or business and you are disobedient to the message, then the message will build like a high wall which will crack, shatter, and scatter so that not a single piece of that message can be found again (Isa. 30:12-14.) What is worse on the heart? To never know God while He's standing right before you, or to think you know God and you have Him standing behind you?

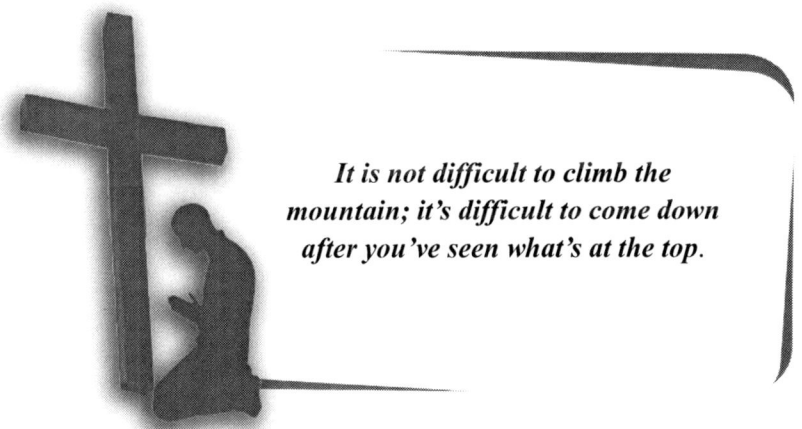

It is not difficult to climb the mountain; it's difficult to come down after you've seen what's at the top.

While driving home after "getting rid of the business," I prepared myself to break the news to my cousin. Then I got a word saying to prepare myself even more because he could not go with me to North Carolina. I beat myself up over it and even spoke with a couple people before actually breaking the news to him. God brought me back to a conversation I had with my cousin a couple months prior that I had completely forgotten about, because it was not a word for me but a word for my cousin. God put something on my mind and I simply relayed the proposition from God to him. My cousin had been battling with a couple of habits, and my message to him from God was to give up his habits for just two months and be part of a major move of God that is going to happen. You are not happy when you admit you have a problem; you are happy when you deal with the problem. Now it all made sense. My cousin, unfortunately, didn't commit to the proposition, and I realized why God told me to go on my own. He did not commit to God, and the move was starting to happen. God must be the great ruler of any wicked man, because enforcement is what controls anarchy from being affluent. Yet He does indeed pardon men who truly live beyond any form of treason or rebellion. God will pardon those who keep the Christian covenant, which is to live, obey, and believe, or perish.

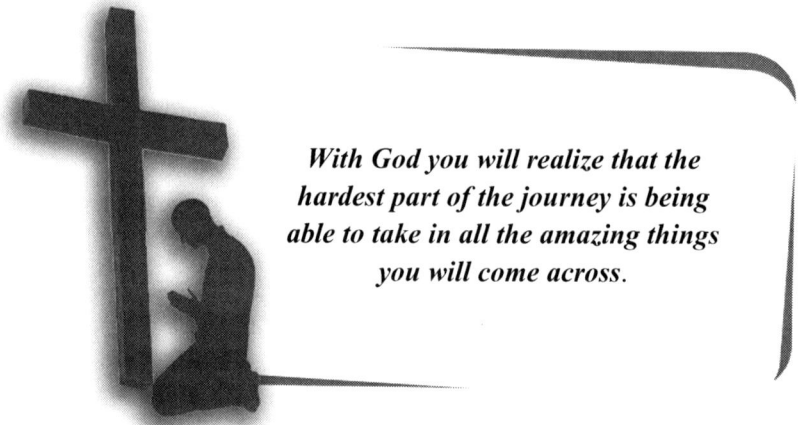

With God you will realize that the hardest part of the journey is being able to take in all the amazing things you will come across.

I am now heading to Kannapolis, North Carolina. It's amazing when God puts the perfect people in your life to arrange His purpose and intentions, how everything becomes quite clear and unbelievably acknowledged. Many friends throughout the years tend to drift apart, but this particular person I have always considered to be my best and most genuine friend. You can tell when you are close to your best friend when everyone assumes you are brothers. When people would say I would never amount to much, he would always give me a portion of his worth.

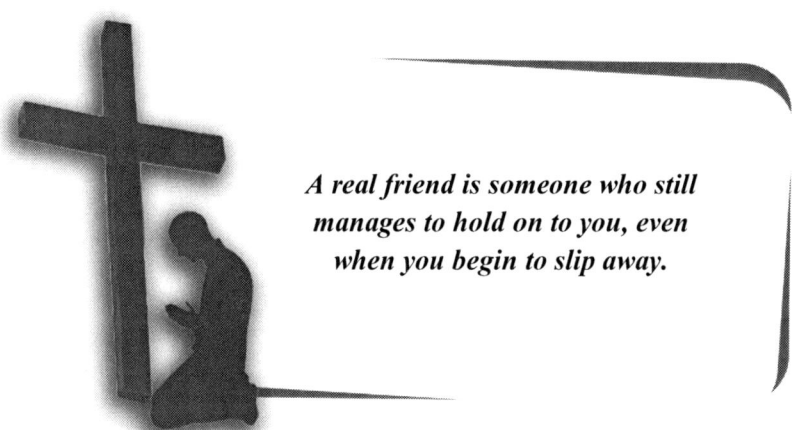

A real friend is someone who still manages to hold on to you, even when you begin to slip away.

He has always looked out for my well-being. He was probably the only person I could honestly say I would let call me "stupid," only because he knew I was different than what I made people think. He knew God, and I didn't. He knew how to be alive, and I knew how to be a dead man strutting. It is truly remarkable how reading the Word of God as a child can play a crucial role in changing your friends' lives later on down the road. He would always talk about God, and even when I ignored him, he would still tell me that he and his family would keep me in prayer. His parents standing solid on the reading of God's Word allowed him to know the source of deliverance and in return deliver the message to me. He would always tell me that God can change my world, but I never believed him. Now, he is not saying "I told you so" and laughing at me, but he's saying "thank the Lord" and smiling with me (Isa. 29:18).

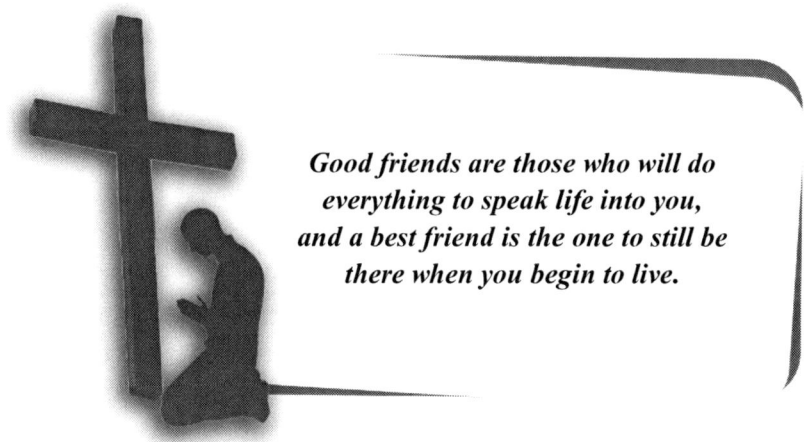

Good friends are those who will do everything to speak life into you, and a best friend is the one to still be there when you begin to live.

He moved to Chicago, but we still kept in touch. God told me that instead of keeping us simply in touch, He was going to now bring us together in North Carolina, where he now lives. I had many conversations with him about my transformation with God, and he became as excited for me as I did when I first realized God was an actual *"real"* living God. His excitement for me got me excited.

Best friends are those who see more in you than you see in yourself, who can see past the stranger you've become and love you until the right person is brought out of you.

As I was driving up to North Carolina, I made a pit stop at a friend's house. In the middle of the night I woke up with a picture of an unknown man's face on my mind (Acts 2:17). I went back to sleep and woke up that morning, again picturing the same man's face. Every dream that God has used as a message and outreach has come in a realization form, as if things in my dreams are not actually dreams, but physically occurring. This man was not doing anything but was just standing there. All day I was trying to relate his face to anything I could possibly remember. Then, I stopped everything I was doing and got in contact with my friend in North Carolina. I asked him if I had ever met his pastor before, and he said, "No. Wait, yes, he is the one who married my wife and me!" Now, this is a man who I paid no attention to at the wedding—he was there, but not really there because I didn't in reality analyze him or give attention to him. His pastor was the man I saw in my dreams!

When I arrived in North Carolina, I put aside the thought of his pastor and went back to *"purchase the lot to obtain the dream."* For two days we drove around looking for land and lots. I kept praying to God to reveal to me whatever He had intended for me out of this trip to North Carolina. For two days I was extremely confused because there were numerous lands available, but I had no direction from God. Then, on Wednesday night I got back into my blessing zone in the church atmosphere. Throughout the service I could feel the heavy presence of God and the Spirit moving in me. My body was shaking and my heart was pounding. Eventually, a complete stillness came over my body, and I felt extremely calm; then the Lord spoke to me and said, *"This is the man you need to talk to, go talk to him."* So after service, I gently walked over to him and said, *"May I have a moment with you alone? I think I am supposed to talk with you."* Benjamin May, the Pastor of Restoration Tabernacle, walked with me and his armor-bearer to his office, where we sat down and started to talk. Through most part of the meeting it was me who spoke with an open heart. When I was through, he brought up the first great patriarch in ancient Israel, Abraham.

> The *Lord* had said to Abraham, "Leave your country, your people and your father's household and go to the land I will show you. I will make you into a great nation and I will bless you; I will make your name great, and you will be a blessing. I will bless those who bless you, and whoever curses you I will curse; and all peoples on earth will be blessed through you" (Gen. 12:1-3).

Yes, Abraham was where the initial message began. Now, what was so significant about everything that had been occurring in my seven months with God was that my obedience enabled me to receive and place pieces of the puzzle together that I had been collecting throughout my journey. Remember, the first message I received was back in August, which was the letter God wrote, sealed, and gave to me personally. This letter also reflects and demonstrates many characteristics and details of Abraham.

Then I received a word of knowledge—*"Your dreams are buried in the middle of the lot, but you have to purchase the lot to obtain the dream. You must draw attention to your opportunity and God will prove the impossible!"*

My zealousness took me past the Cross, and I began to get ahead of God's development. You see, I realized when Pastor Benjamin May said "*Go to the land I will show you,*" that "purchase" simply meant *to get a hold of*, and "lot" simply meant c*hance.*

Get a hold of your chance and obtain the dream.

I have had several dreams by this point, and they all led me to one thing . . . God's purpose. I knew I had to be obedient and leave everything I had behind—my family, friends, and comfort zone, and go to North Carolina—and on the mountain of the Lord I will be provided.

North Carolina would take me into a secret seclusion far away from what I was familiar with, and into a place of complete trust in God. Envision being in a place where you don't even know where the nearest gas station is, and going from the city to the country with no friends and no family to support you. My only reliance was in Jesus Himself. I now had to trust Jesus for *everything* I did, and He had me right where He wanted me.

It's not complicated; it's mind-blowing how God's timing is always the right timing. The work project I was involved with in Florida was finished, my lease was ending the following week, and that same week my friend and his family had planed a vacation to South Florida, the same friend who God always kept around. I was leaving everything behind to go live with him and his beautiful family and wait patiently for the next move of God.

This has been my confirmation of truth and a rising power of good inheritance. Do not follow my word; "it's testimony" of the truth because of *God's Word*. His Word is the only word that is relevant. I am just speaking the evidence of God through my life. This has been my seven months with God!

My Continuing Journey

As I am continuing my journey with God, I am bringing you past the seven months for an important message. I came to North Carolina when the job world was in turmoil. My only job was to trust God to do His job. I was in North Carolina for only three days before I got work with a carpet company. At the end of the second week I was working on my own doing a punch list and carpet repairs. I was really at a loss, because a few months before leaving Florida, I had been praying to God to remove me from that same work environment, but once I was in North Carolina, He put me right back into the same environment. Pastor Benjamin May told me, *"Don't pray to God to change your environment, because maybe you're there to change the environment."*

I really wasn't talking about the people, but really the learning environment. I wanted to be around Godly people and in a Godly environment strictly to learn. But what Pastor Benjamin May said was completely accurate, because I did learn something extremely important . . . that environment is the perfect environment to learn in.

Before this point, I had so much of God's Word wrapped up in me. Staying in the garage of my friend's house, I lived in the Word of God and slept in the Word of God, pacing back and forth preaching like there were crowds of people waiting to receive this Word. I wanted desperately to *"proclaim the Gospel of God"* to everyone! (Rom. 15:16) The very next day after speaking with Pastor Benjamin May, during my lunch break at work, I got on the phone with my mother and told her that I wished I could liberate all the greatness of the Gospel that was being built within me. When our conversation was over, it was like God was saying, *"Yes, you've got it!"* After my lunch break, I went back to the second floor where we were hanging carpet base, and wouldn't you know, the first question to come out of my co-worker's mouth was, "So I hear you are a church person?" I said, "No! I'm a God person." For the next forty-five minutes I stood there and sent a message of God's Word with such depth that I believe I took notes on myself that day. The electricians even stopped what they were doing and began asking me questions, and at that moment I knew "The Gospel of Jesus" was now the only subject that was relevant to me.

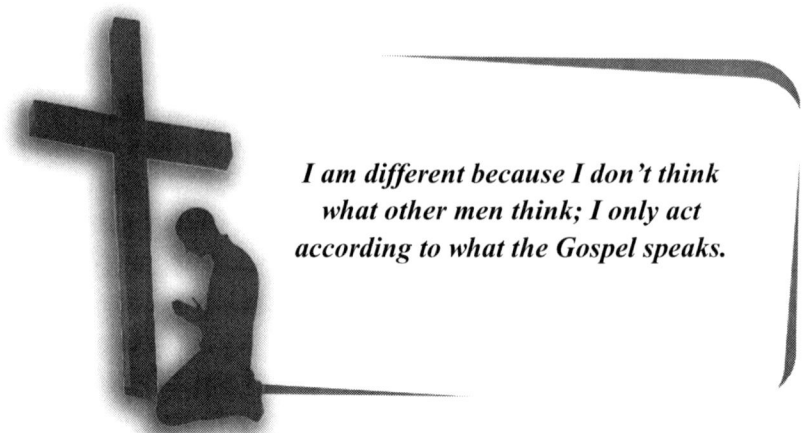

I am different because I don't think what other men think; I only act according to what the Gospel speaks.

That night God spoke and told me, *I know you want to be around people of faith to build your confidence, knowledge, and approach in the Word. Believe Me when I say that the majority of your purpose will not be around Godly people, but rather those that are lost, those who think they know Me, and those who are so close to the Cross but don't even realize it. These are the people I need you to be around. Stay in the Word and I will give you remembrance. There is something coming for you in the form of a divine outreach that you could never possibly fathom, until it has already captivated you. My time is the right time. And remember, on the mountain of the Lord you will be provided . . . but before I provide you with what I am going to provide you with, I am going to test you first* (Matt. 9:12).

As soon as the installation for the carpet company I was working with was complete, my work ended as well because the carpet company relocated to another state. Over the next several weeks, I began my search for a reasonable job, but I couldn't find one. God is inconceivable at times because He put me back into an environment I prayed to get out of, just so I would have the ability to embrace His perspective and cognitive process. He then put me in a situation where I could no longer financially support myself. My test! I knew the very first thing that needed to be done because I could hear pastor May saying in my ear, "It is a season to bring men to their knees."

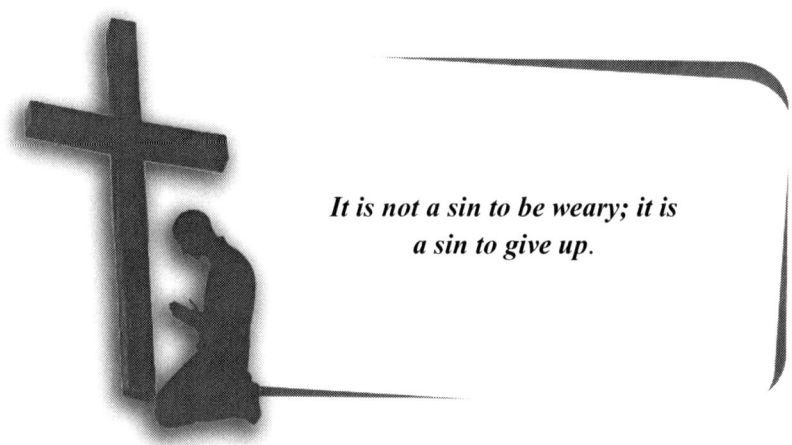

It is not a sin to be weary; it is a sin to give up.

I have to smile at the specific course God situates His people of faith on to acquire a personal willingness to stand for a broader principle. I am motivated by the truth in the Gospel, and I understand that now is my time for correcting, equipping, and revelation (2 Tim. 3:16-17). I also realize that any standardized procedure that we must endure is to test and build our faith, which gives us a measure of boldness that enables us to stand completely on the Word of God. If God says I can have it, then I refuse to leave until He has given it to me. God, prove to these people that you are on my side! I refuse to be overlooked, I refuse to be denied, and I refuse to leave God until He brings out of me what He promised was in me. God has put me in a position where I can no longer provide for myself, so literally, if God doesn't do it, then it's not going to get done. God is going to take me to nothing and make me preach my way out. God has said, *Can you still stand on the Word, even when your world has fallen . . . and if you can do it, I will put you on display.* When people ask me if I am working, most of them do not understand why I have such a huge smile on my face, because on the inside . . . I am working . . . I'm working on God and God is working on me. I am a product of God's divine favor, and He is testing me to see if in spite of not having anything to physically show for it, will I still proclaim the power of God and reveal the truth in the Gospel to this generation.

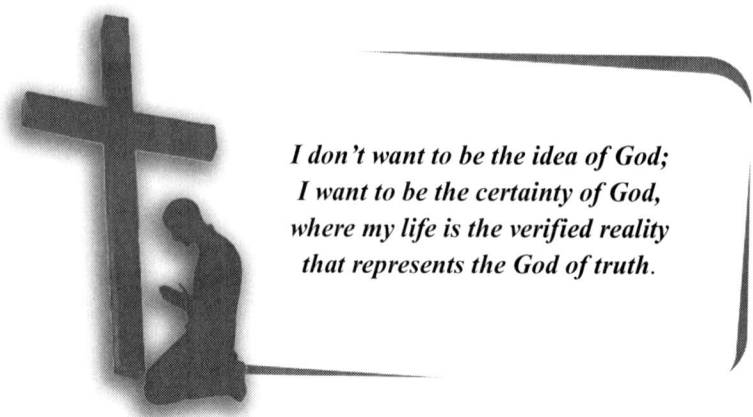

I don't want to be the idea of God; I want to be the certainty of God, where my life is the verified reality that represents the God of truth.

Plainly, our purpose as Christians is "The Great Commission" where we call people to their responsibility to do what they were called to do: live according to God's Word and come to the understanding that the Word is a direct source for hearing God Himself. We cannot be timid in speaking to those who don't want to hear the truth, because they are the individuals who need to hear the truth (Job 32:20). I am not here for man's approval; I am here for the Creator's approval. My job is not that they have a dynamic change or conversion. My job is laying out the truth of the Gospel, which leads them to a door that has been opened for them, but only they will choose whether they walk through it or not (1 Pet. 4:2).

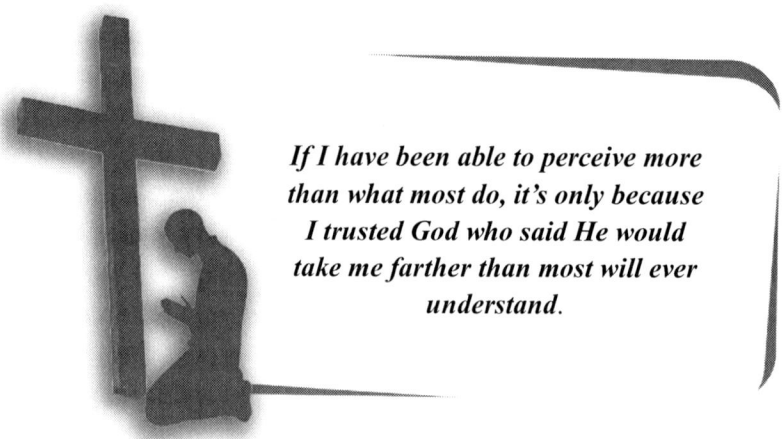

If I have been able to perceive more than what most do, it's only because I trusted God who said He would take me farther than most will ever understand.

This is the important message and the reason why I especially went beyond the seven months. I was closed off from conviction because I didn't meet the requirements of being convicted, because I didn't see it as a problem that needed to be personally dealt with. God's conviction of sin enables us to stand the test of fire and live a life free from bondage. Once we begin to bust out of our confinements, we enter into our right mind, and the devil begins to lose his. Prior to my intimacy with God, I made a vital decision to end a life by convincing my girlfriend at the time to have an abortion. It has been a while since the abortion, and I have not dealt with this restraining regret that has been piercing my sense of complete peace. I cannot say at the time I didn't want to do it, because I fought with her and despised her for no cause or reason. My only logical cause for wanting the abortion was that I didn't see us being together forever. We literally began to hate each other over "life." When it was all said and done, I felt at ease, but the moment I had God in my life is the moment I received burden. God had not allowed this load to be released from me. Every time the topic of abortion would come up I would shut myself out and I would preoccupy myself and convince myself God had forgiven me. The fact is I know God, and in my mind I tried to shut it out because I knew it was a completely wrong decision. I figured if I told myself that, I would be released from it. I guess you could say the day I took a life God had fire coming from his eyes in spite of me not having a relationship with Him. Up until coming to Kannapolis, I have cried, pleaded, and have been held accountable because of this inhumane decision. For two weeks I was killing myself on the inside over it and I began to try and occupy my mind with the reading of God's Word. Finally, at a Wednesday night service, I went up and prayed before church started, and I could feel the Spirit heavily on me—preparing me, convicting me, and opening me up. About two-thirds into the sermon, Pastor May broke into my heart with fumes of revulsion by screaming, *"Abortion is an abomination. How could you end a life? Can't you hear the baby screaming?"* His dismay went on and on and on. I literally was about three seconds from getting up and heading out the door, but God said, *This message is for you, and you're going to sit here and listen to it!* I put my head down, and God opened my ears. *It is wrong; hear the baby; it's a disgrace!* As a tear fell from my eye, it never hit the ground. I had been convincing myself it was wrong for so long, but never allowed myself to be delivered by repentance. God did not let me sit there alone;

He sat there with me crying as well. At the end of all this, God said, *It is not okay. You destroyed a purpose. You did the very thing I hate. When I cry who catches My tears? How can you ever talk about it, if you want nothing to do with it? How can it plead its case, if you won't receive its face? Now, you don't have to convince yourself it was wrong; now you know it was wrong because now you hear its pain. I have never hated you, but I have hated the decisions you have made. Now take a complete look back. I have always been with you, and I have always provided for you. Even with this burden still at large, I placed it behind you for a moment, and I cried as it lay in front of Me. Now that you know Me and have My statutes and morals, we can both cry together and then put that day, but not its important message, behind us as we continue on our journey.*

FURTHER THAN EXPECTED

Each one of us has the capability to push beyond human measure. It is not a matter of physics; it is the interaction you have with divine logic. It is the reflection of a guiding principle that involves reasoning beyond human thoughts. It is not the ability to lead and inspire; it is the importance of how we were led and inspired. An impact is only effective because of its momentum, when the momentum has enough influence to become insurmountable. We don't take risks by trying to push the limits; rather, we make continuous attempts to find the right placement on the other side of divine opportunity. We cannot submit our life by reason of opinion, because opinion is based on what others have failed to attempt.

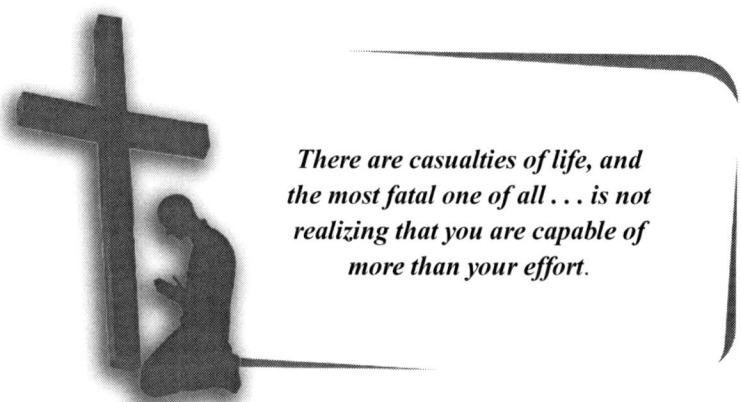

There are casualties of life, and the most fatal one of all . . . is not realizing that you are capable of more than your effort.

My conclusion with God in seven months contains an assembly of truth, where I have gathered a quantity of divine logic—not reasonable judgment, but a system of God's Word. If you still have uncertainty that God can elevate your life to a different degree in seven months, you have not thoroughly read the message intended. I have never had a resource to improve the condition of my intellectual ability, until now. My message is clearly expressed by the apostle Paul in 1 Corinthians 2:4-5: "*My message and my preaching were not with wise and persuasive words, but with a demonstration of the Spirit's power, so, that your faith might not rest on men's wisdom, but on God's power.*" Everything that has happened to me has been fully God, but it took me completely surrendering to God for Him to be fully expressed.

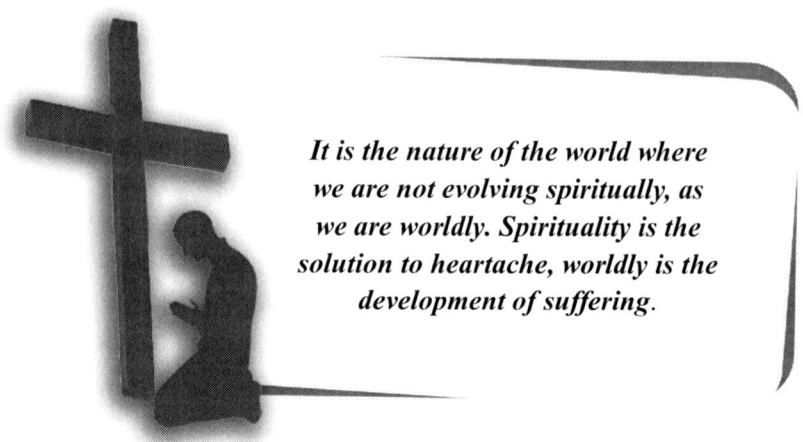

It is the nature of the world where we are not evolving spiritually, as we are worldly. Spirituality is the solution to heartache, worldly is the development of suffering.

If you were to detach yourself from the worldly impression, you would promptly realize that our personal division is God's opportunity for provision. We are suffering personally, because we are affected worldly. It's not that God isn't as powerful as He used to be; it's that we are more worldly than we have ever been. There are people in this world who are thanking God for life and committing sin all in the same breath. What is the world saved from, if we haven't yet realized that we have been saved from the world? We must reevaluate the portion of space we occupy every day, because false impression makes you think problems keep coming your way, when actually it's the same problem that just keeps getting worse—it's based on the circle you stand in. Don't allow a few bad apples to discredit the truth.

The only substance in this world that surpasses knowledge is love. Love is a profound passage that comforts the hardening of hearts. It is more valuable than words itself. It is absolutely essential that we submit to one another to obtain the necessity of one body, because we are artistically designed to be undivided. A difference of opinion between people will occur, but that is not what detaches holiness and compassion. It is allowing each other's disapproval to hinder clarity and forgiveness that begins breaking our branches of responsibility to love in spite of.

If a Christian is ever offended and holds a grudge, he has simply forgotten what he has been forgiven of. Do not categorize your opinion of a person's estrangement from God as if his bondage and your bondage are not comparative. Homosexuality, adultery, addiction, prostitution, profanity, temper, lust, pornography . . . yes, we all have issues that we are trying to work out to have a different and divine experience that's emanating from God. But do not be ignorant by rebuking someone when all he or she actually needs is to be loved. You don't love the sin in them, but you love the sin out of them, until you see the person he or she was called to be. We are divided from our sin, not from each other. What would be unity if you made someone stand alone?

The Gospel makes you "heavenly and kingdom-minded."

There is a reasonable understanding, why, when you have a misinterpretation of the Gospel, you are persecuting its reason of life. You can mean no harm, but the result of your misunderstanding will be your life not lining up with your pursuit. When your desire for the Gospel begins to signify your principal interest in a kingdom reward, and not a worldly reward, that is when your spiritual journey becomes a way of life. This course of experience, however, will only begin the instant you acknowledge that God has already sufficiently filled you, even in the midst of feeling empty. There is an incredible unveiling of glory in your life when the glory is given fully to God.

Money, prosperity, success, testimony . . . let's understand this! I am one of the wealthiest people in my county, but yet I have less in my bank account than most people in my county do. People are being blinded! God does not want you to be financially stable, healthy, prosperous, and unbeaten before you begin spreading His glory. Do not wait until you prosper to tell people that God allowed you to prosper. God wants you to tell them this: *Even though I have nothing, the God worthy of high honor and glory will bring me out! Even though I am in poor health, God will make me greater than expected and stronger than I have ever been! Even though I have not a penny to my name, God will never allow me to go without! My richness comes by conveying Christ's message, and I can do this all in the midst of having nothing!* And then, you can listen to God tell you: *Because you have stood for My name, I will not make you a lie! I will reveal your life to the world! It is not a miracle; it is the truth of the Gospel!* Now that is prosperity and success!

Where did your failures go?

You will know me as a success because I refused to let failures allow me to fail. I was not motivated by success; I was motivated by failure. My determination is what leads people to believe that the journey was easy. My hard work is overlooked because it continues when nobody is watching. I made success look easy, because prevailing made you forget my failures.

My attainment of favorability with God in seven months has been anything but easy and has not been obtained with little effort. You must realize that prior to my seven-month journey with God I spent two difficult years completely spinning myself in a circle. Meaning, I was going nowhere and still feeling unbalanced by life. It was not until the moment I entered through the gateway of clarity we call the Bible that my guiding course, identity, and purpose were communicated by God's own Words. Throughout the seven months I encountered intense opposition. But now I was fighting with a valid reason to believe that I would benefit for my services rendered because of God's guarantee. The devil never wins unless you don't fight. So my continuous fight was a full effort attempt to achieve something in spite of its disappointments. The worst perception you can ever settle conclusively on a person of relatively large feats is that the person traveled a course posing no difficulty. Success will always close the eyes to failure because it allows you to be known in a victorious manner. The only reason why people notice failures is because individuals who are seeking success decide to settle into a position where they believe they have failed. Failure is voluntary, not forced. Failure is simply a word that we use to gently describe a vain attempt at success, rather than directing the responsibility to the person himself. The more accurate assertion should be "you gave up."

Is God not revealing the church, or is the church not revealing God?

Do you know the God of the Bible or the God of Sunday? People are not in conformity with the presence of God because they are becoming preoccupied by an incorrect conception of church. As an example, let's use a pointless decision we as Christians make before we enter a church building—denomination. Well, what is denomination? Who knows? The more accurate description should be "God among the nations." What denomination really refers to is "recognizing a church's belief." This, I am yet to understand, because do we not read the same Word and believe in the same Mighty Majestic God? Church should be based on the Word of God, "Bible believing," where God Himself speaks, moves, and redeems. Why would you constrain God by placing Him in a subgroup or by categorizing Him in a particular identity? How about we just let God be God and concede the truth in the Bible where it is the only Word that is applicable and without void? People are speaking too much of their opinions, and not allowing God to exult the truth. *It is the house of God, not a place where we can experience half, some, or none of God!* When people of faith look at me, they are thinking, *"Why is he so different?"* Because, God is raising up an abnormal generation that expresses opposition in a preconditioned personal view. This simply means that I am different to you because I am not what you were expecting. *Why do I go crazy during praise and worship?* Well, God moves me, and it just feels normal to be radical for God. *Why am I so different from church people?* I believe I am the church where I can introduce continuously the Word of God to people with an intended result. *How am I experiencing in seven months what lifetime church members have never experienced? How do I do the unlikely to the highest degree?* It is quite easy for me—I don't know church, because I never knew church . . . all I know is God!

Pay close attention to the truth I am about to reveal to you, because not only will it change you, but it will change the world!

Undoubtedly, money does not specify the origin of redemption, when in the richest nation of the world over 37 million Americans live below the official poverty line. It is not a disgrace that people are suffering—it's painful—it's a disgrace that millions of Christians claim to know the extrication from bondage, yet they deprive someone's life by being silent and passive. What would happen if you were to change a person's routine to a consistency with God? It would no longer be a routine, but an exhilarated variation of life. People who are hurting don't need support; they need a cause for transformation. Imagine the possibilities if every person would wrap his mind around the idea that his life is meant to make a difference in the lives of others. Imagine the possibilities if every person had a deep concern that had nothing to do with himself. The greatest act of concern and attention is understanding the responsibility of a delegate power. It is not seeing a broken heart and giving words of comfort. It is seeing a broken heart and committing time to mend it. You would be able to pass on a controlling influence simply if you would control what you focus on . . . focusing until the point of a person's heavenly convergence. Imagine if every person's happiness wasn't based on his own story, but on the inspiration that he expressed enabling somebody else to have a happy story. Ask yourself what in your life you feel proud about right now. Naturally, we would begin with our own self-accomplishments, but according to 1 Peter 5:5, "God opposes the proud but gives grace to the humble." Excluding your own self-interest, what have you done to drastically change the condition of another person's way of living? How quick you realize that when you are kingdom-minded how much more gratifying and humbling it is to know that your position in the Body of Christ allowed someone else to find divine placement? If you were to direct your responsibility to someone other than yourself, your state of mind would then be a Gospel state of mind. As a result, if you were to get yourself into that strong state, you would never be withered away from God's sovereign power. I believe that God's intention for each individual is to improve the condition of someone else, and it is meant to show that the result is contagious.

It is imperative that God persistently pursues people in order to establish an abounding life in them through Christ. When your purpose is no longer hidden, it exposes a light that is easily released as a manifestation for others' lives. By fulfilling your purpose, you enable a multitude of other people to understand and harbor their purpose. Yes, the Gospel starts off being about you, but when you begin to understand it, it becomes about everyone else! We become a part of the Body of Christ, simply so we can touch the lost world. The fact is millions of people are living outside of their purpose every day, and even Christians are having severe impairments about their duty of being Christlike. When you do not inhabit the great importance of "preaching the Gospel to the four corners of the world," the one person that you could have touched may never know true freedom. Remember, when God affects one person, He affects a multitude! I get an uncontrolled excitement knowing that giving the shirt off my back to someone in need and then imparting the Gospel News can change multitudes! I know where I am when I stand on God's Word. Yes, changing multitudes!

You can affect a multitude of lives by affecting one person, but these people who don't know the Gospel of Christ are waiting on you to begin living within God's purpose so they can begin theirs! So they can have hope! So they can have peace! So parents can be changed! So children can be changed! So decisions can be changed! So hunger can be quenched! So you can change a person on the verge of irreversible ruins! The only way to change something is through understanding, and then becoming responsive to that change. Yes, you can be experiencing your own level of dilemmas at the present time, but here is the understanding—your own life doesn't need to be organized to impact others. The majority of our diminutive predicaments have a way of disappearing once you interact with people who face conditions of death every day. These people are waiting for you! You are counted on by God! You are counted on by mankind! *When are you going to understand that you were counted on yesterday . . . so . . .* where were you when over eight hundred thousand people were killed within hundred days in Rwanda? Where were you when sixteen thousand children died last year from hunger-related causes—one child every five seconds? There are over 2 billion children in the world and almost half of them will face poverty, and thirty thousand of those two billion children will begin dying every day due to malnutrition. Every three seconds a child in Africa will die! In Africa, more than 800 million people go to bed hungry every day, 300 million of which are children. On average, twenty-six thousand children under the age of five die around the world, mostly from preventable causes. *These are the faces of hunger*! Over 1 billion people worldwide don't even have access to safe water! Where were you when almost 100 million children were forced to live in the streets? Where were you when over 100 million children worldwide didn't get to attend school or have a chance at an education? Where were you when an estimated 1.2 million children were trafficked last year for prostitution? Where were you when 684,000 children died because of a measly lack of vitamins!

Where were you when thousands of people became mentally disoriented and almost eight hundred thousand children were reported missing last year? Where were you last year when adults and children started losing hope and eighty-six suicides occurred per day?—That's one suicide every seventeen minutes! Where were you when there were 248,300 forcible rapes taking place last year? Where were you when parents didn't have it all together and over 4 million cases of child abuse and neglect were reported—children being internally crushed having to walk around and pick up pieces of themselves? *Mommy, I know I have a hard time listening, but who punishes you for a lack of patience? Daddy, I know you don't like it when I cry, but you are yet to teach me how to smile. I've become so bad, because you made me think everything about me was no good.*

***The problem is I can see myself in their eyes*!**

Where were you last year when almost four hundred and fifty thousand people died in the United States from smoking tobacco? Where were you when every day last year more than seven hundred thousand Americans were treated for alcoholism? Where were you when almost seventeen thousand people died last year because of alcohol-related accidents . . . it may seem small, but alcohol-related accidents accounted for 40 percent of all traffic deaths! Oh, and over five hundred thousand people will be injured because of a drunk driver every year!

Where were you? This is the reality of lost souls!

How would you feel if you were the one staring out of the window waiting for hope to show up? They wait in vain . . . you cannot deny it. Now that you've heard it . . . you can't erase it!

Part Three

MY FIRST WRITINGS IN PRAYER WITH GOD—THE PRINCIPLES

I almost did not put these principles in, but it would have been an injustice to abandon and completely desert the uniqueness of God's approach in my life. The principles, which are based on the Word of God, brought my renewed mind into careful thought and evaluation of false teachings; more importantly, they brought me into truth. Truth cannot and will not take the backseat to religion or cultural church messages. I sat there in my room with one question on my mind: *Who is this Man that in only three years of ministry has made millions of people follow Him?* What I thought I knew about God, I didn't. Because I thought I knew God, I assumed I didn't need the Bible. How wrong I was. There are no new truths, only a misconception of text used falsely, and unveiled as truth. Without knowing the Word of God, Christians are living their lives as if Jesus is not the Son of God, but Joseph's son.

These principles were the first in my writings with God, and they were His distinct structured transformation for my life. My devotional time with God is what has changed my entire perspective, which in turn gave me these precise principles. I used what God gave me, and I embedded this declaration as the course for my life, which may help you. Here it is. *If your time is spent more in front of the television than with the Bible—that is idolatry. If your time is spent more in entertainment than in church—that is idolatry. But wait! God doesn't want your time; He wants your life. So with that said, if your life is not spent with God—that is idolatry.* The unfolding of change throughout the entire extent of living my life based on these principles, which were developed from the assurance of God's Word, is what deposited motivation for me to continue to write and express my strong desire to grow in God. These principles have given me a continual need for a revival and an awaking of God's touch. Everything started with the principles, and many of our blessings are predicated upon the principles of God.

These principles are what gave me hope, and whenever I was in a situation or going through a time of confusion, I would devote myself to reading everything I wrote from God. These writings are what brought me through and encouraged me to prevail when I didn't know I had any more fight left in me. I would constantly tell myself that I have to get out of *my* own way. Until you get yourself out of the way, you'll never know what you can be outside of *you*. I learned to fight with my face toward the Cross and my knees toward the ground. I am confident in knowing that in my times of affliction and persecution I am no longer forgotten. If you look beyond all my scars, you would notice one thing—that I made it here literally untouched.

I cannot rob the Gospel from its intention, which is to live my life based on truth. I tell people all the time that it is impossible to see the unveiling of your purpose without the infilling of God's Word. Then their next reply is always this: *Why do you believe in the Bible?* I believe in the Bible because it is a dependable collection of divine writings and historical recordings, documented with an ancient historian truth. It was written with prologue material clarifying a Redeemer to come, a Redeemer in whom undeniably walked among you and I—the only Savior given to this world Who even exemplifies Himself as the self-revelation of God; with an identity complex that no other human being on the face of this earth has ever seen; accomplishing a divine destiny with a fulfillment of over forty prophesies, the only One to ever match and carry out such impractical prefigures, which was evidenced by over five hundred eyewitnesses, and with a written documentation in the lifetime of other eyewitnesses, which signifies a Spirit led inscription for the exactness of the Messiah's life. Which means this: *The moment I touched the Bible I felt something different, the moment I opened the Bible I could see something different, and the moment I started reading the Bible I became something different.*

The principles you are about to read will exemplify God's enduring love. It was the principles that got me started, but what kept me focused was God's love for me. As you begin to read, this was the beginning of my changing choice and growth with God from the bottom up, and my levels of intellect advancing—or should I say, my understanding of truth and intelligence finally being exposed within myself? What you read is based on God's development and process of change for me.

These principles have been my inspiration, but most often, inspiration is not orchestrated in the middle of victory, but generally enriched when a person considers himself irrelevant in life, and then prevails. This simply means that your moments of feeling insignificant are well intended for others to obtain a lifelong conversion based on the evidence of God's hands at work in your life. Your greatest joy will become visible when you verify the insignificance in your life to be . . . *relevantly significant.* There is a reason why there is the word "test" in testimony, because the example of your life declares the glory of God to others. Being of small worth and little importance to people is powerful. God loves you and wants you to excel, so it's powerful because God makes it intimate and personal for Him to prove otherwise. Jesus took twelve uncommon men and led them to do extraordinary things. It is important to know that the disciples changed not only the condition of their own history, but history as we know it. That power also gives you the power to go beyond yourself.

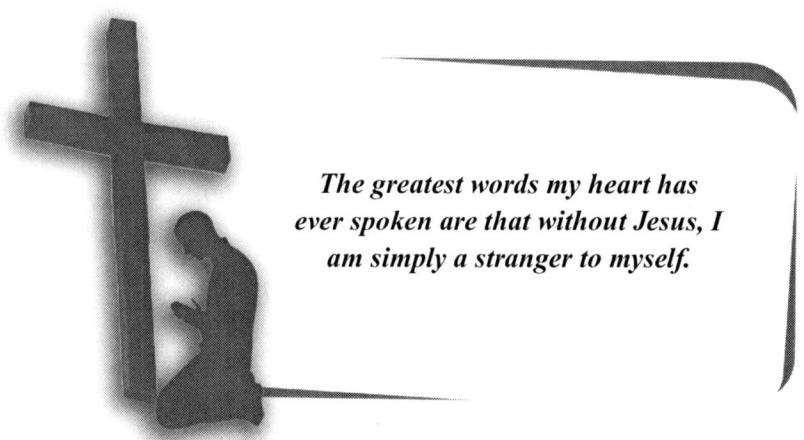

The greatest words my heart has ever spoken are that without Jesus, I am simply a stranger to myself.

I took an undesired trip through the devil's front gate and became accustomed to being alone. I was lost, broken, and mentally perplexed. My sanity became worlds apart and soaked in regions of despair. I had a lot to say to God, but my words constantly became an unspoken scream. In my way of living, I literally let "Life" pass me by. I was building up an aversion for myself. I hated the night, yet when I fell asleep I wished *my* sun didn't rise. I was depleted of strength, working my whole life on my hard appearance, and for all my effort, in the end it just made me extremely fragile. I was alone, learning to survive on instinct . . . and yes, being alone allowed my heart to have no supervision.

God would wrap His arms around me, but I was too afraid to hug Him back. I was standing on the highest point of nowhere with only one way out, and that way out was jumping off the top and going down. *"Lord if I am part of You, and You have wings, then please let me fly."* I just needed to know that there was someone who could not only feel my pain, but take it away. God looked into my heart and knew I needed something different, something more than just a chance, something more like freedom. I was a tragedy in the making until I realized that my life had already been made—in the hands of God! I remember lying in my bed one night, my head wedged between two pillows, feeling as if everyone I spoke to about Jesus Christ blatantly laughed at me. Because I stood alone among men, I felt as low as men. Lying in my bed, tears running profusely down my cheeks, I reached one hand up and gently said, *"Jesus I love You, and because You love me I will continue to show how much I love You."* I broke out of hell just so I could have the chance to walk in the fire of God, and to be able to preach the Gospel in the most desolate places. God in my life has been a match that has been struck that no wind has ever blown out.

This is my seven months of inscription for a direction in change. People have asked me, *"Can you actually hear God?"* Well, I definitely wasn't talking to myself, because if it were up to me, I would have just been convincing myself how much life hated me, and instead God *literally* spoke life into me!

I can remember driving in my car, hearing what I thought to be a commercial on the radio—but my radio was never on. Out of natural instinct, I guess, I tried to turn the radio down. The sound was like a short, loud whisper with an echo. The more I found myself in prayer "conversation" with God, the more that voice began to draw me in. In the beginning it was hard to decipher because I thought I was going crazy—it sounded like a bunch of clattering and voices overlapping each other. As I stayed in constant prayer, I began to make sense of the clattering and overlapping voices, which eventually slowed down until I could positively hear a dominative sweet whisper—God's voice—and believe me, prayer is what ushers you into conversation with God.

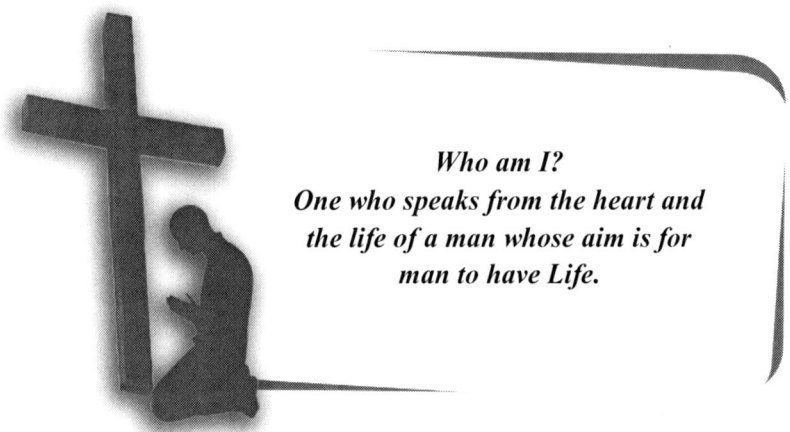

Who am I?
One who speaks from the heart and the life of a man whose aim is for man to have Life.

What I am about to say is by no means meant to discourage you, but to encourage you with a challenge of truth. If you never know where God stands, you'll never know where to kneel. I never asked God to give me what He has given me. I've actually, more times than I can explain, asked Him to take it away. This precise understanding was given to me, and it has absolutely changed my life, and now you can experience this perspective through the eyes of my journey. A pastor once asked me if I believed in *once saved always saved*. I said, "You know as well as I do that in all of the Bible's honesty you're *not* actually saved until your footprints are embedded in heaven." He asked, "So you don't believe that you are saved?" I quickly replied, "I believe that I have had a dynamic conversion in which God has saved me from my old lifestyle. My understanding of being saved is that I have been set free. However, that old lifestyle is still at large, so it is an every-second fight to stay safe, until I am truly saved." The majority of evangelists, pastors, and preachers are trying to cure an awful and horrifying disease called *lost souls* by prescribing the wrong prescription. I challenge you to take this survey of truth. Ask every pastor or minister you know if they believe that they are "saved" and why. They will respond with yes—and then here comes the truth—because of *my* striving to be pure and blameless—the process of sanctification. Now, ask the most defiled people you know, who "believe in God," if they believe that they are saved and why. They will respond with yes—and then here comes the truth—because I welcomed Jesus into my heart. Great! *How?* One Sunday I went up the altar and said the sinner's prayer. Always remember that *justification means nothing without transformation.* It is brokenness that causes God's mending process to begin. It is a cry of heart that allows prayers to be heard. I told the pastor that the motive behind the prayer that the churches are praying is not wrong; it is the misconception held by those who are doing the praying that is wrong. What are you actually saved from when you continue to do the things you've always done? That prayer does not change you, nor does it lead the Spirit to fall upon you. Conviction and faith establishes that. He was silent for about fifteen seconds, and then said, "Twenty-three years ago I sat in a pew broken in anguish. I walked up to the altar and prayed that prayer and believed that it changed my life. Twenty-three seconds ago I just realized that I was broken before I even got to the altar."

People continue to ask me what happened to me in less than a year. People have told me that my passion for Christ and the message I deliver may cause me to lose it all. My only reply to them is then I lose it all. I don't want to lose friends! I don't want to be without fellowship! I don't want to be unaccompanied . . . but I will tell you this—*I will not deny Jesus.* I will fall flat on my face and worship, just to see God raise up a generation that understands His pain! I am going to walk into a war zone, and even if my life is on the line . . . *I will not deny Jesus.* False Christianity is no new invention. It has been passed on by a culture of followers and counterfeit messages. *I love God, but I party on the weekends! I love God, but I still like to drink! I love God, but He is not evident in my life!* Yes, you may love God with the best of false Christianity, but it is not so much loving God these days that puts you in a right standing with Him. Rather, it is hating everything that He hates which puts you in right standing before Him. The question is, *do you tend to love what God hates?* How much do you really love God if you say you love Him, yet live a life full of what He hates?

Pardon me for stepping on your toes, but I'm aiming for your heart.

I remember a woman telling me that she has been trying to convince people of truth and Jesus for years. You don't convince people of God; you lead them into a conviction, which in turn will then establish their own convincing. My heart would've failed if I had never understood that the soreness of conviction has enabled it to beat. It brought me to the front door of repentance, and repentance is simply giving up. I have nothing to bring to you Father God, except me. I have prayed to God for so long to take my pain away . . . and now at last that I understand Him, I pray that He places me in the deepest and darkest parts of the battle . . . and if only one person witnesses the light where truth is exposed, it will be worth the sacrifice. I will chase the beauty of Jesus until the Holy Spirit imparts the nature of God, and His power has been thrown before my very eyes. I am not going to pray a prayer and believe that I am going to heaven. I'm going to cry out to God day after day and ask that He sanctify me by the truth to be certain that I am going to heaven. There is only one thing that I will lose sleep over. It is not worrying about whether my bills are paid. It is not worrying about whether my retirement is secure. It's not even worrying about whether I am in good health. Again, there is only one thing that I will lose sleep over . . . and that is whether I am doing the will of God, by finding myself on that narrow road that leads to life that only a few people will find. People have asked me what I am so moved and encouraged by—*He saved me*—and just because of that He doesn't owe me anything, but I owe Him my life!

The world is yet to conceive the idea that the importance of making the Godhead a priority will inevitably change the face of the world.

THE CHOICE OF CHANGE

The reason why we yearn for change is because we are in an uncharacteristic condition of "not being who you were meant to be."

Jesus said to me, *The power I give man is in choice, the love that I show is my influence in choice. I am consistently revealing Myself, but I'm routinely seen when secluded without hope and at a dead end with no turning point.*

Due to God's influence in choice, namely, love, we all have this drawn image of God, but the majority of us see this image of God without seeing or understanding the heart that makes this image come alive—namely, love. I quickly learned that aspiring bliss is the counter motivation in situations of uneasiness. Meaning our greatest accomplishments can soon come after our most trialing and most perplexing afflictions. In these same moments of uncertainty, sadly enough, *the opportunity to discover our last resort presents itself—the exact resort that should have been our first priority.* It is in that instance of turmoil when we have no place to go that we resort to exploring the curiosity of Jesus, and inevitably we find ourselves with "choice." The choice confronts the option to either continue to be overpowered by the devil's animosity or to find a cornerstone in the presence of the Lord. I told a friend that I felt as if my life was standing at the edge of the highest mountain. She told me to change my perspective, and that you don't ask God why and tempt Him by jumping, but enjoy the view and thank Him for taking you so high.

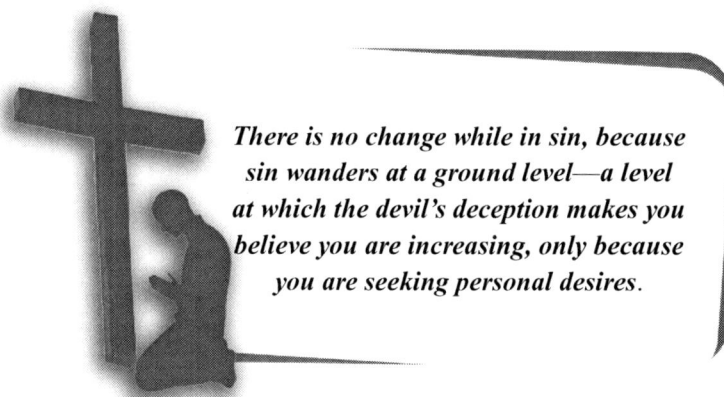

There is no change while in sin, because sin wanders at a ground level—a level at which the devil's deception makes you believe you are increasing, only because you are seeking personal desires.

Change with God appears to be unbalanced because God is rearranging your life's priorities, dropping your personal desires and filling it with His intentions, and making you decrease so God can increase, but, ultimately, bringing you to a level you could never possibly reach without God putting Himself above everything in your life.

You can work your entire life to change your own personal welfare, yet it will be meaningless. You can devote yourself entirely to a road that appears to possess the possibility of future success, yet it will be meaningless. Consider that your role in life is meant to be in the hands of God and is made up of an outstanding importance that when revealed will acknowledge that you were predestined for greatness. The problem occurs when we draw attention to everything our own hands have accomplished; only nothing really has been accomplished because God has been sitting with His hands folded the entire time.

Yes, we may all have God, but the majority of us "have" Him not working.

It is a choice that comes with responsibility. Some roads we take and choices we make in life may seem enjoyable and beneficial at some point, but many of us never realize that our decision resulted in a momentary pleasure, not an abiding benefit. Here is an encouraging word for those who are giving up on God's road: God's road is the hardest one you will ever take because it makes you break routine and eliminate bad habits. What you were once accustomed to needs to become a major separation from your habits, leading you into a place of unfamiliarity. The most difficult part of going from an old job to a new job is learning a new sequence of steps, but continual performance makes it a habitual act.

I have always said, *"Just point me to the Cross and I can find my way Home."* The Cross shows how unworthy I am to be worthy of God. It shows the immeasurable love given under desperate measures. The Cross shows me in my weakest hour pleading for help out of the belly of hell. To bear this precious Cross simply means that in the midst of my weakness and tears it has given me the understanding to move into *Gospel-spreading* action.

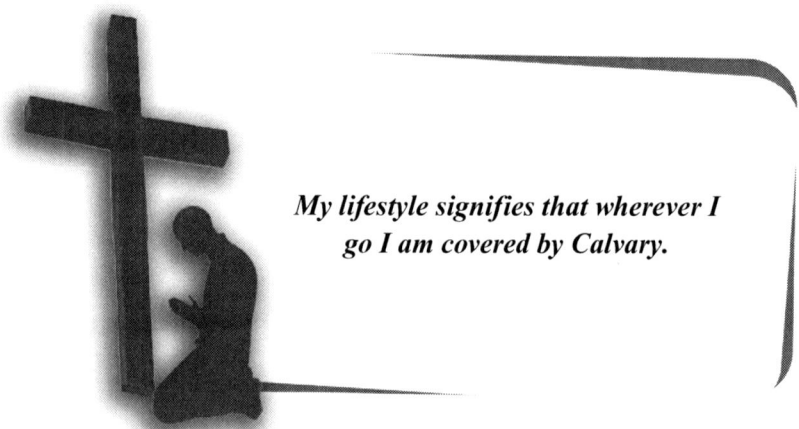

My lifestyle signifies that wherever I go I am covered by Calvary.

We must understand that Jesus put Himself in an uncompromising position so that you could not be categorical with your life. Jesus became a man not so we could give Him portions or certain aspects of our lives, but our entire life. His uncompromising position calls for an uncompromising ultimatum—all or nothing, not a call for lukewarmness.

I've given Him my all, and "*I don't see change!*" Again, do not base your approval of God on wealth, a new relationship, a perfect job . . . because this is all based on being "selfish." Change happens when God makes you "selfless." The Holy Spirit doesn't necessarily want the heart and the mind, but first the man who covers the heart and the mind from being changed. People have the tendency to say, "I feel like I am worse off than before." Yes, I believe that, because your perspective was reversed. What was bad seemed good, and what is good now seems bad. Relax, because this will be the easiest transformation you ever will make on your road with God, because you don't even need to change location to witness something different, you just need a different perspective to understand everything is different.

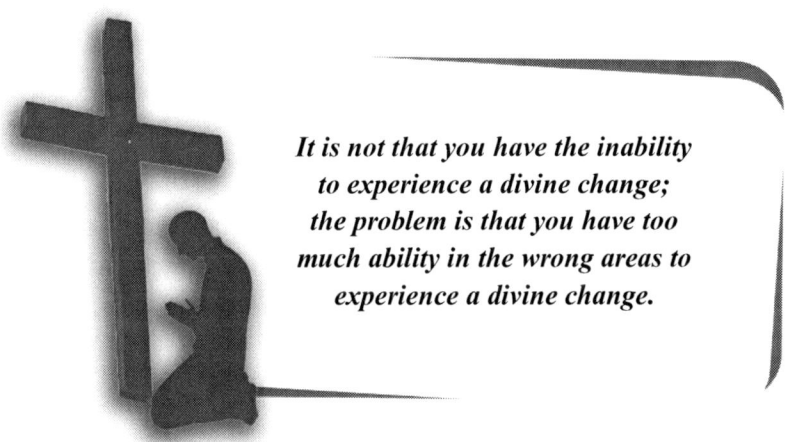

It is not that you have the inability to experience a divine change; the problem is that you have too much ability in the wrong areas to experience a divine change.

In this generation we are hearing so much of "*it is hard to believe*," not understanding that believing is more than just a consideration—it is an unassailable attachment to faith. What is faith? Faith is God's duty to reveal Himself to you. Believing is established by a series of events: Will you still believe even when your bills have not been paid? Will you still believe even after getting laid off? Is it possible to still believe even in the midst of a severe downturn? You do not establish the validity of faith when everything goes according to your perception of freedom. Keep in mind that before believing must come our growth in faith. If you don't have faith, then what exactly are you believing in? Faith gives your eyes understanding to believe in everything you hope for. Faith is not established when everything is peachy keen; it is established during disorder and chaos. It is created this way to test your trust and faithfulness in God, because doubt must not, and cannot, be entangled with faith. *If you have faith, then you will have no doubt in believing God will see you through your troubles.* It is not hard to believe; it is just unusual for people to actually experience change. Change has its uncomfortable stages, but it's not the uncomfortable moments that obliterate us, but it's the decisions in those moments that obliterate us—*when we give up or throw in the towel.* The biggest blessing you will ever receive is probably the most disregarded and least acknowledged—the removal of your sinful nature. Blessings aren't always something God deposits in your life, but above all, blessings come from what He withdraws from your life.

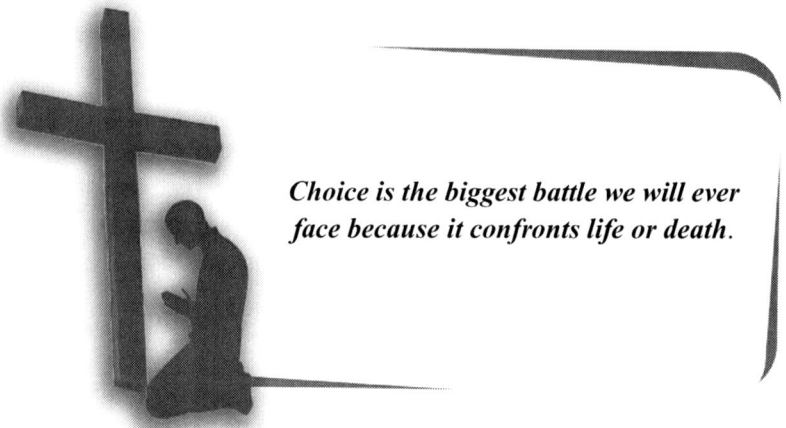

Choice is the biggest battle we will ever face because it confronts life or death.

Change enables a view of life from a different perspective. If you can change your mind-set, you will certainly shut the front door to the devil's entrance in persuasion. Change enables God to break grounds to establish new grounds. Change enables God's voice to push through the barrier of rejection. Often, we as people get tired of struggling, but always remember this: *fatigue is the Lord's opportunity for an awakening.*

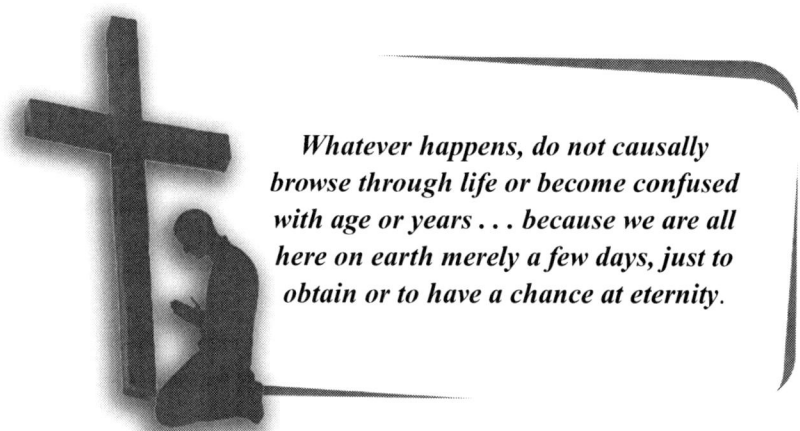

Whatever happens, do not causally browse through life or become confused with age or years ... because we are all here on earth merely a few days, just to obtain or to have a chance at eternity.

Change may not happen in a day, but the mind-set of change can happen in an instant. Prepare your mind because the devil is easily annoyed by our eviction notice, and the second we modify our choice in change, the devil will take forceful action and tempt us. Even though the devil knows your weakness, he is very impatient and will not slumber there long. Just remember that change will always have a shadow of temptation. Temptation is simply desirable conveniences. It only becomes inconvenient when we see it as a barrier to God's promises. We destroy our sinful nature by rejecting the desire of flesh, which is God's forbidden fruit. It is extremely important to understand this in context. *We are all sinners,* which means we go to God as sinners, and God begins His work where sin begins—it does not mean that you continue to sin.

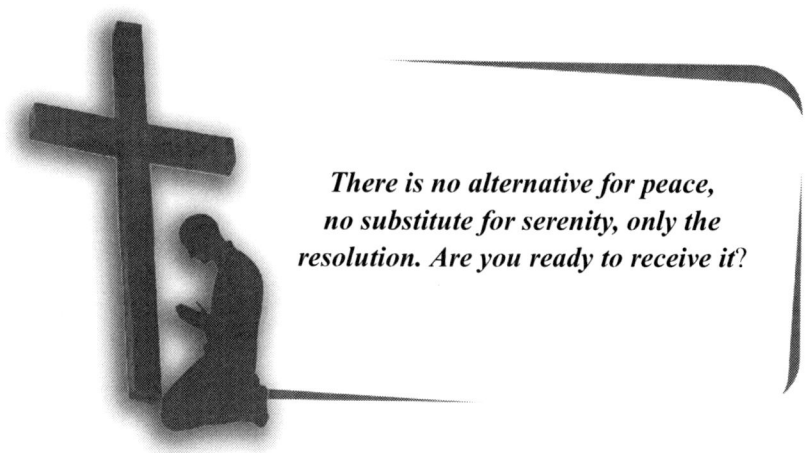

There is no alternative for peace, no substitute for serenity, only the resolution. Are you ready to receive it?

The main objective for God to change your life is for you to not only experience divine difference, but to become an attraction for others to experience it as well.

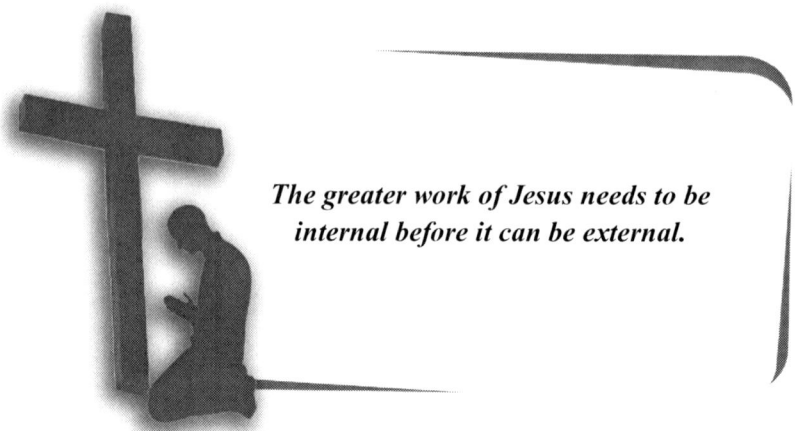

The greater work of Jesus needs to be internal before it can be external.

I had been worrying about my family, but Jesus allowed me to realize that my worries for my family will disrupt my transformation with Him. Jesus said, "I will make you a magnet for blissful change. But in order for this to happen . . . I must have you first! *Do not worry about your family anymore, but first change yourself and then use Me as a way to change them. If you surrender and seclude yourself with Me, then the love that your family has for you will ultimately make them go in search of you, which will bring them to My front door of change.*"

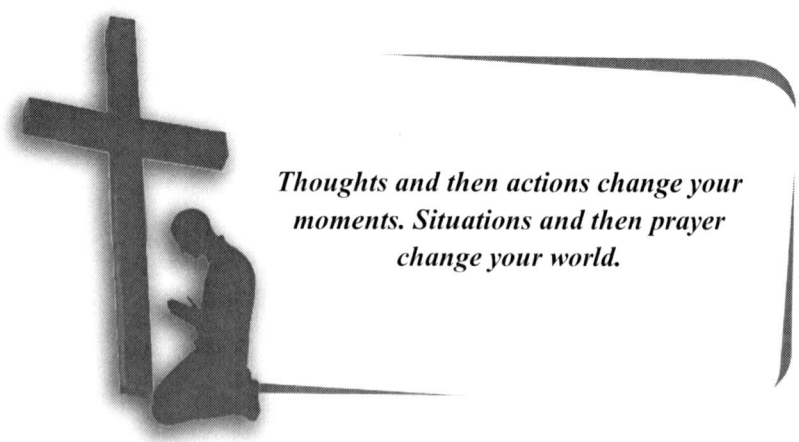

Thoughts and then actions change your moments. Situations and then prayer change your world.

Many people raise the following questions: *Why can I not find happiness? Why does God not save us? Why must I struggle?* In any condition the only method to obtain strength is by not faltering in the midst of trouble, but believing that the Lord is greater than any of our problems. *We could never* possibly know how mighty God is if He never reveals His might to us. The Lord walks with those who believe He exists, and the choice of fulfillment is yours.

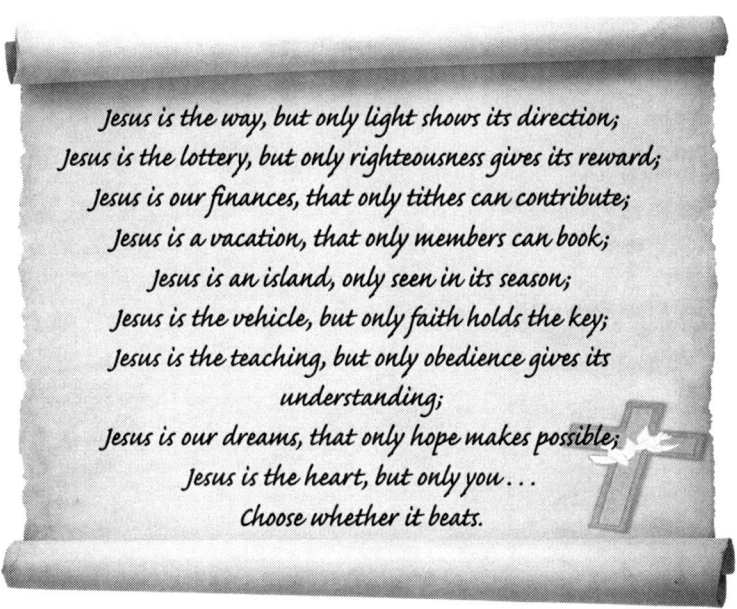

Jesus is the way, but only light shows its direction;
Jesus is the lottery, but only righteousness gives its reward;
Jesus is our finances, that only tithes can contribute;
Jesus is a vacation, that only members can book;
Jesus is an island, only seen in its season;
Jesus is the vehicle, but only faith holds the key;
Jesus is the teaching, but only obedience gives its understanding;
Jesus is our dreams, that only hope makes possible;
Jesus is the heart, but only you . . .
Choose whether it beats.

So why is it not until the moment of difficulty when clarity calls? At what rate do we find happiness? Often we confuse the pursuit of happiness with a predetermined location, not realizing that in reality we may search an entire lifetime for something that has no contentment. Happiness is within peace derived from the journey of life, a life that only God has the map for. Change somehow has the ability to give you a surveillance of awareness, to notice the small things God has a major impact on.

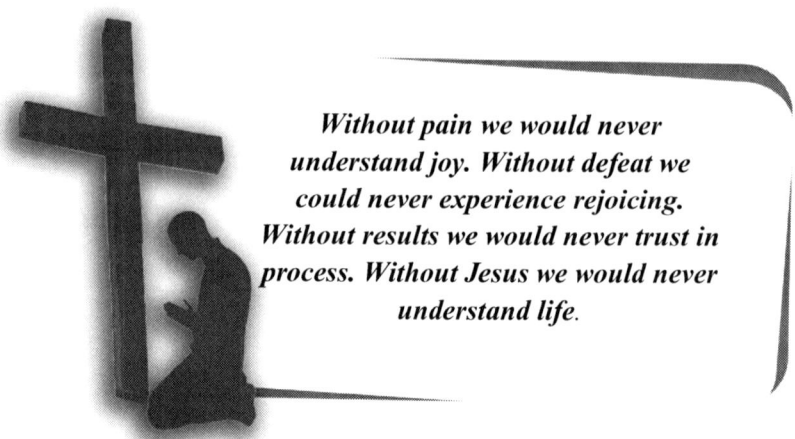

Without pain we would never understand joy. Without defeat we could never experience rejoicing. Without results we would never trust in process. Without Jesus we would never understand life.

The logic of God is based on the principle that Life has a purpose, for your purpose in life. It is not philosophy or therapy that reveals a better you. It is impossible for you to know your purpose without seeking the Lord first. Man's philosophy has no geographical meaning, which means it does nothing to change my current condition or location. The Lord will not only impart divine life, but open up a door to receive what comes with change, a change where you are made in His likeness—I not only *do* what I believe, but I *become* what I believe.

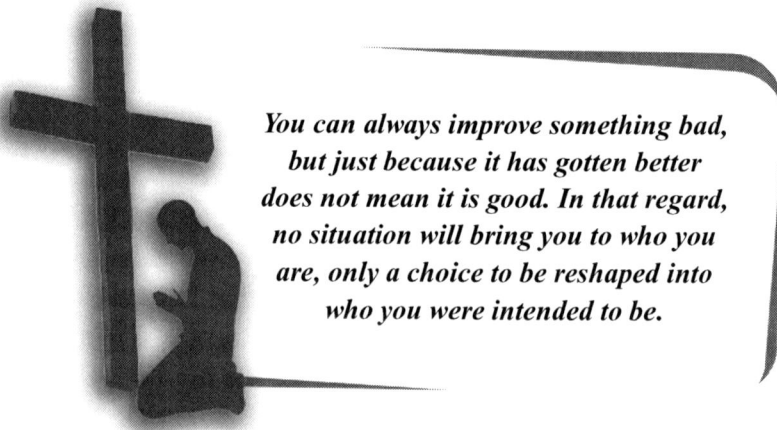

You can always improve something bad, but just because it has gotten better does not mean it is good. In that regard, no situation will bring you to who you are, only a choice to be reshaped into who you were intended to be.

The choice of change provides human beings possession of a special "quality of life," allowing an awaking of humanity, which is recognized as the beginning of an amazing journey.

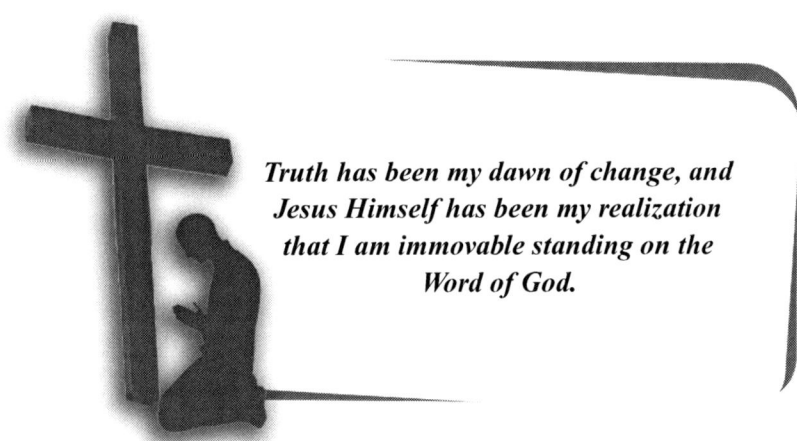

Truth has been my dawn of change, and Jesus Himself has been my realization that I am immovable standing on the Word of God.

Contrary to how numerous people find God as their last resort, now is the time you formulate it into your most crucial priority, beginning your life-saving devotion immediately. Take a grip on the journey because where you will find fulfillment is in understanding that our God is truthful, and change is something you can guarantee. I asked God what His reason was for not changing me instantly. His reply was, *Because you still had doubt, and doubt will always fail to notice the purpose. I didn't give you change, but the promise of change. It was your first possibility and your attachment to faith. If I were to instantly change you, you would assume that it was a natural change, not a God-given change, so instead I gave you the possibility of change to build your faith.*

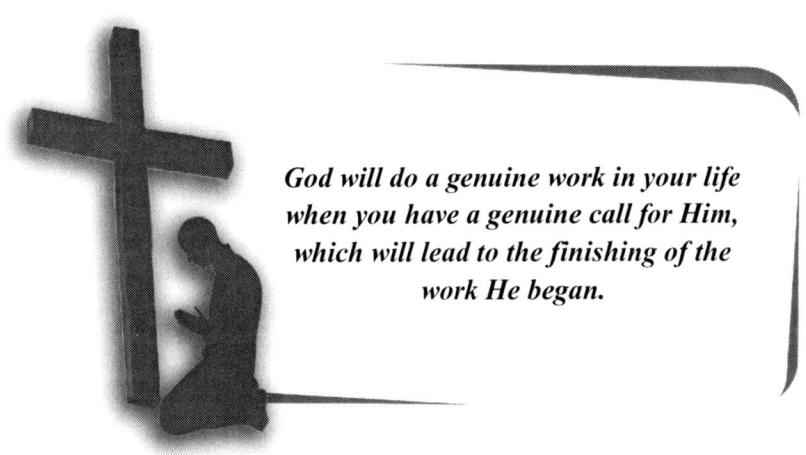

God will do a genuine work in your life when you have a genuine call for Him, which will lead to the finishing of the work He began.

The most vital principle in God's approach to change us will be when antagonizing us with our own sin, which is done strictly to lead us to conviction. Conviction will cut deep in the heart, and as your heart utters its brokenness, it is conviction that reconnects what has been unhinged. Conviction is what led me to a personal knowledge of my existence. Conviction will allow you to see and feel everything that you are doing that is detestable to God. We stop conviction and move toward God with a genuine repentance. True repentance will show in your lifestyle, when turning away from everything you were accustomed to, *never to go back to it again*. Then it is allowing what is pure and the things that God loves to manifest in your life. Keep in mind that God didn't say that as a Christian you would never sin again; He just reminds us to work out our salvation with fear and trembling. Meaning if you fall off the narrow road, you better believe there will be some consequences and a reprimand that will petrify you and force you back into the position of His sovereign will.

By prioritizing scripture it simply means that you are neglecting the Gospel.

I did not come across change by glimpsing through the layers of the Bible, but I grabbed a hold of change by digging into the depth of God's truth. There is a specific place for every person in the Body of Christ, and it all begins with a welcoming into His arms. There were so many times I just did not understand; there were so many times when I just wanted to give up. However, the best decision I have ever made was a choice to get through the pain. Now, I no longer have to ask why, because as heartwrenching as it was, I can see my strength because of it. As heartwrenching as it was, I can now see daylight because of it. As heartwrenching as it was, for the first time in my life . . . I am not alone. If I could characterize my understanding and put into perspective what my heart now feels, it would be this . . . God loves me. The fact is I do not deserve what God has given me, but because I made a choice to put all that I have into His Word, He has shown me mercy. All that I have received and all that I will receive is a truth in God's Word, that as long as I follow Christ, I will always receive because of it. You will come to a point when all you will want is for God to *use you*. It is God's love that puts you in a mind-set that I am a mortal man fighting for eternal rights. I *will fight!* I will step outside of the pillars and away from the city of refuge, walking beyond the four walls and striving toward mountains. Lord, send me into darkness and grant me the power that rose with You from the grave. Let me stand in the haze after sundown and let me dive out of the ark and into the hasty waters. Use this sheep to shut the lion's mouth, and I will take hold of the milestones that come with living for Christ. I am to bear Your suffering . . . and Lord I am ready to fight!

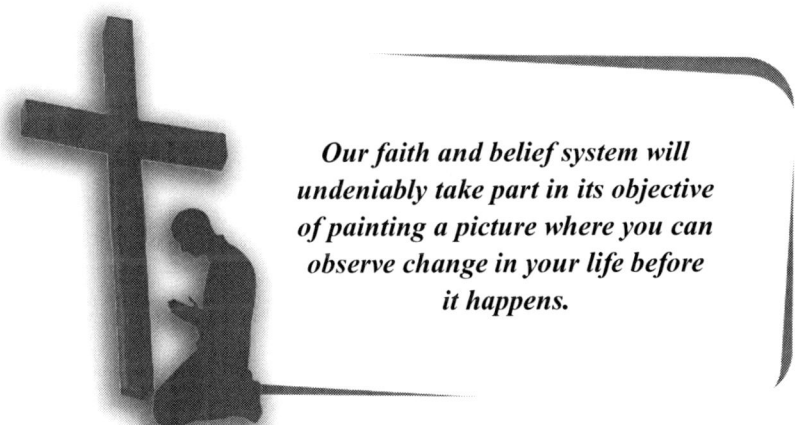

Our faith and belief system will undeniably take part in its objective of painting a picture where you can observe change in your life before it happens.

How do we get to where God wants us? By positioning your life to where it evolves into your devotional life and not your church life. It is when you find it worthwhile to retain the knowledge of God based on your self studies that God will begin to stand for you because you are in right standing with Him. Your church life is meant to lead you into a devotional life, because it is in your devotional time when you learn that the only thing that is applicable is God's Word—sound doctrine. The Word of God is inseparable from freedom. This also means you must not separate your belief system from the faith you put into where you are going, because both are ordained to work simultaneously. It is a divine arrangement where the Word of God will set you free into a belief system that will allow your faith to take you to a place you could never dream of. Now the process becomes quite unique because your devotional life will lead you back to church for the rest of your life. *How is this so?* Because, now, you are the church!

The Choice of Fulfillment is yours!
My story of understanding...

I strolled into work expecting a raise
Only to have spoken to my boss and I was reduced in days;

I am behind on rent, hopefully my landlord will help me through
Only to receive a message and find out my grace period is a week overdue;

I have descended unwell, but it's nothing a doctor can't solve
Only to be told "there is nothing we can do and the time isn't long;"

I went to a counselor to find some type of peace
Only to get explained they were booked for the week;

What can I do, God?
Maybe I would pray, but I suppose I would be denied

Then the Lord replies:

I know all of your problems and everything you need
You could have had all this and more than you can see.

If simply...

You would have asked Me.

1 Peter 3:11: "Let him turn away from evil and do good; let him seek peace and pursue it."

Peter an apostle of Jesus Christ is speaking to God's elect who have been chosen according to the foreknowledge of God. (*Refer 1 Pet. 3:11-14.*) Because of your suffering for doing good you were called so that you may inherit a blessing. Who is going to harm you if you are eager to do good? (14) But even if you should suffer for what is right, you are blessed.

Deuteronomy 30:19*: "This day I call heaven and earth as witnesses against you that I have set before you life and death, blessings and curses. Now choose life, so that you and your children may live."*

The fifth book of Moses. These are the words Moses spoke to all of Israel in the wilderness east of the Jordan River. (*Refer Deut. 30:11-19.*) This was the Lord's offering for choosing life or choosing death. (11) Now what I am commanding you today is not too difficult or beyond your reach. It is not in heaven that you have to ask. It is not beyond the sea that you have to cross to get it. (14) No, the word "a choice" is very near you; it is in your mouth and in your heart so you may obey it. (15) See I set before you today life and prosperity, death and destruction. If you love the Lord and keep His commands, keep His decrees, and walk in His ways the Lord your God will bless you and give you the land "purpose" you are entering. But if your heart turns away and you are not obedient, you will certainly be destroyed. Now choose life, for the Lord is your *life*.

Isaiah 40:29*: "He gives strength to the weary and increases the power of the weak. Even youths grow tired and weary, and young men stumble and fall; but those who hope in the Lord will renew their strength. They will soar on wings like eagles; they will run and not grow weary, they will walk and not be faint."*

The vision concerning Judah and Jerusalem that Isaiah saw during the reign of Hezekiah. Hezekiah was the king of Judah, and he began to lose his best cities because of war. Hezekiah not only started paying tribute to Assyria, but entered into an alliance with Egypt against God's will (Isa. 31). If you want help, then you must seek the Lord your God. How wise for Hezekiah to turn to the Lord for help by going to the temple and sending for Isaiah the prophet. Hezekiah began praising God for who He is. Even after this call of praise and prayer, Hezekiah still faced tribulation by falling ill to the point of death. Hezekiah turned to the wall and cried out to God, and then God said, "Not only are you healed and will live for another fifteen years but I will deliver you from the king of Assyria and I will defend this city." However, Hezekiah didn't comprehend that he shouldn't depend on anyone but the Lord. The crucial mistake Hezekiah made after his illness was showing the Babylonians his entire treasure in his palace. Isaiah then prophesied and said, "You would lose it all and your descendants will be taken away." However, in Isaiah, chapter 40, God comforts all His people by saying, "I am sending good tidings to Zion who comes with power, so prepare a way for the Lord (Jesus). Through Him with obedience to the Word of God you will be strengthened; you will not fall, and if you live for Him, you will be saved! Trust in the Lord above all!

2 Peter 3:9: "*The Lord is not slow in keeping his promise, as some understand slowness; He is patient with you, not wanting anyone to perish, but everyone to come to repentance.*"

The Second Epistle of Peter, a servant and apostle of Jesus Christ, who through the righteousness of God and the Savior of Jesus Christ has received faith. (*Refer 2 Pet. 3:1-18.*) Peter writes concerning everyone that they should turn to repentance before the time is too late. As it was written by the holy prophets and the commands given by our Lord, everything will go on as it has since the beginning of creation. Earth was formed out of water and by water, and then by these same waters the earth was destroyed. Heaven and earth are reserved for fire, being kept for the Day of Judgment and destruction for ungodly men. Meaning the Day of Judgment is near, but the Lord is patient in hopes that every man should repent and turn to Him. With the Lord a day is like a thousand years, and a thousand years is like a day. This simply means not to hold off your repentance and pleading for God, because this Day of Judgment will come like a thief. (10) The heavens will disappear with a roar; the elements will be destroyed by fire, and the earth and everything in it will be laid bare. (11) Since everything will be destroyed in this way, what kind of people ought you be? You ought to live holy and godly lives (12) as you look forward to the day of God and speed its coming. Find yourself spotless and blameless; the Lord's patience means salvation—entering into the Home of righteousness!

Romans 10:17: "Consequently, faith comes by hearing the message, and the message is heard through the Word of Christ."

Paul, a servant of Jesus Christ, called to be an apostle and set apart for the Gospel of God speaking concerning the Spirit of holiness, who declared Jesus with power to be the Son of God to all of Rome. (*Refer Rom. 10:1-21.*) My heart's desire and prayer to God is that you *may* be saved. You do not know righteousness because you have yet to submit to God's righteousness. Righteousness is in Christ for everyone who believes, a righteousness that is by faith (Rom. 1:17). The word is near you; it is in your mouth and near your heart (Prov. 3:3). Everyone who calls on the name of the Lord will be saved, but you must have faith, because without faith it is not only impossible to please God, but it is impossible to believe. (14) How, then, can they call on the One they have not believed in? How can you believe in the One you have not heard? How can they hear without someone preaching to them? Faith first comes in the Word of God and believing in the message that you hear. The Word of God has been proclaimed to the ends of the world. The Word of God is all around you, but it is literally impossible for anyone to advance in faith and toward the will of God without an open Bible before them. The Bible has been positioned in front of you by the hands of God for the advancement of your life by faith. (21) All day long I have held out my hands to a disobedient and obstinate people.

Regardless of where you think your position is in life, there is always somebody replicating your way of living. If you can change your influence, you can certainly change what others are influenced by.

CHOICE OF INFLUENCE

An individual who has pledged to do evil disregards his own integrity and turns his back toward morality. The individual will fall and keep falling into a pit that denies the certainty of sincerity.

Jesus said to me, *The influence you keep influences your intentions . . . you want change . . . remember that your influence influences Me.*

A behavioral pattern that is dominated by altercation is created by habit, which gives the illusion of pain, causing us to think illogically—*the world is out to get me, so I am going to fight the world before it has a chance.*

This activates the imagination and causes you to feel threatened. These feelings arise merely from false belief and are not based on anything that is presently happening. Meaning if we entertain ourselves with the obscurity of life for a prolonged period of time, we will build it into our daily lifestyle, reacting to situations with sensitivity and becoming melodramatic regarding circumstances that need no action. Routine anger is not formed by personal objectives, but is entrenched in the company you surround yourself with.

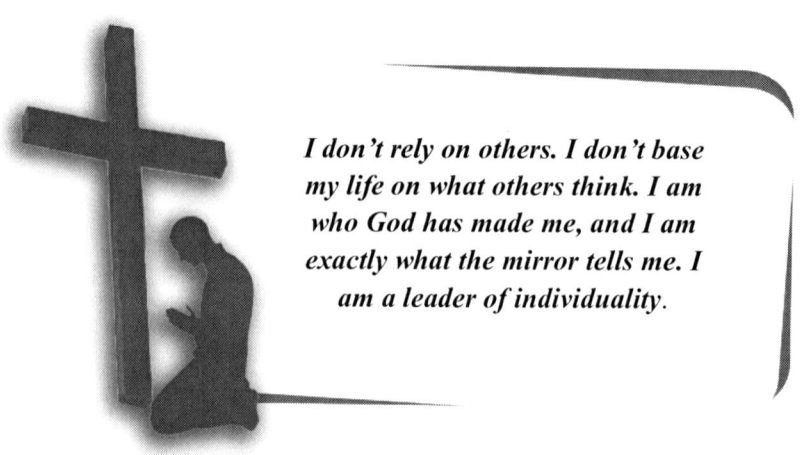

I don't rely on others. I don't base my life on what others think. I am who God has made me, and I am exactly what the mirror tells me. I am a leader of individuality.

Respect isn't developed from lack of fear, but rather you fear that you won't have respect. So it's not actually respect; it's better defined as peer pressure. Respect, admiration, choices, and fitting in are all influenced by fear. Influences are fear-driven.

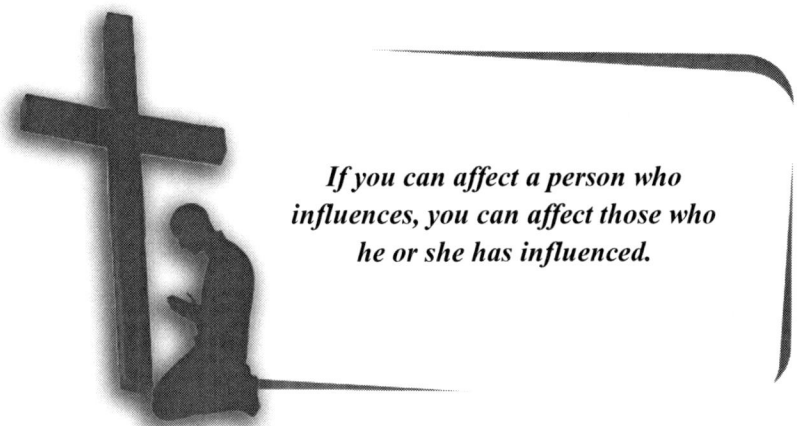

If you can affect a person who influences, you can affect those who he or she has influenced.

People become inclined out of fear to do what they normally wouldn't do "*alone or on their own*"—a fear that is strictly based on "*what other people would think*." Do not choose the wrong path in life based on a circle of misdirection, because that circle will mold you into thinking "*you can never fit a square inside a circle*." Well, what are squares? Squares are defined by categorizing above-normal people, intellectual human beings, and smart decision-makers into a box we place aside from a circle. A circle is defined by illustrating a dominate zone of *followers* who lead based on a single person's motive. Have you ever heard the phrase, "*You are who you hang out with*"? Well, it is perfectly phrased because it is exactly right. If you hang out with immoral people long enough, you will become accustomed to their standard of living, which goes against the unique course of individuality God has for your life.

When you as a child say, *You don't even know my friends! They are not want you think! I don't do what they do!*—Yes, of course you do! The reason why we have friends is not always because we have the same "likes" in common, but more importantly because they already had a distinctiveness that intrigued you and made you want to be like them or become a part of what they were doing.

The main hindrance that keeps us from going to God and exploring our true intention for our lives is influence. The wrong influence will always keep you away from the proper choice, and, yes, the most crucial one at that—the influence of God.

I used to say, *I am a leader; I am not a follower. My friends don't influence me.* Jesus, again, made me realize something. If your parents were to take your best friend to church every Sunday, I guarantee you would eventually start going too. Why? Because you do what your friends do; their influence influences you.

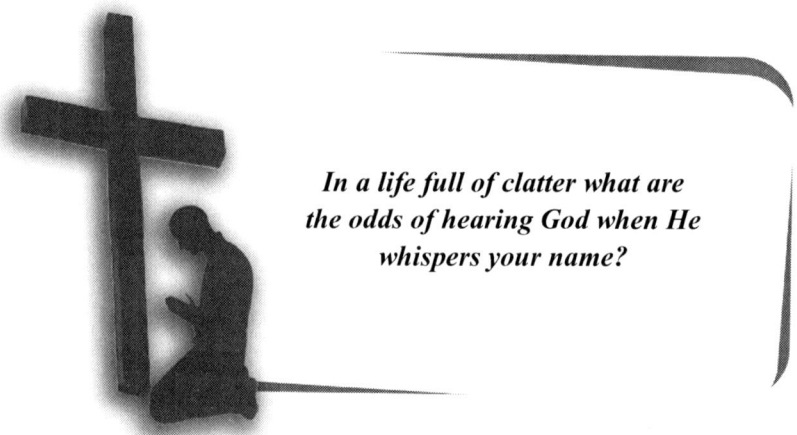

In a life full of clatter what are the odds of hearing God when He whispers your name?

You must know that every individual on the face of this earth has been called to do something according to God's plan. God has ordained and sanctified each person before he or she was born. The problem is until you decide to pick up the phone . . . you are simply being called. The moment you answer the calling is the moment you become a called believer. This irrevocably means that unless the Gospel is errant, you as a called believer are to be part of greatness. You will know when you have received the greatest gift when you cannot stop addressing it. Here is the secret to how God's power and strength is revealed in your life. Ready? Here it is—ask for it!

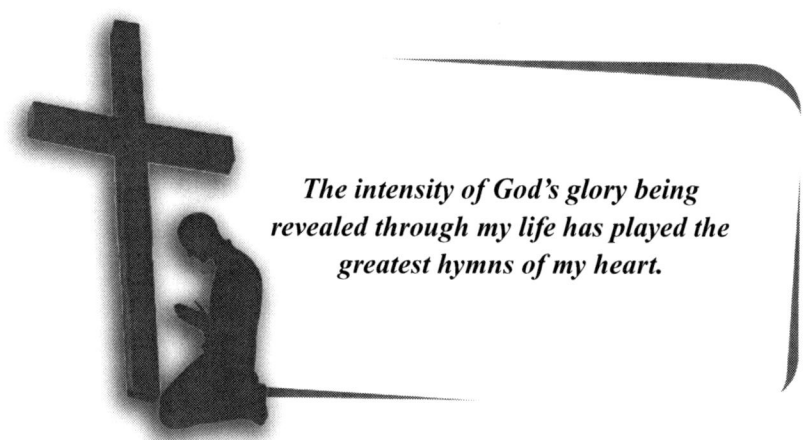

The intensity of God's glory being revealed through my life has played the greatest hymns of my heart.

Bad company will create a state of mind of "settling and adapting," which will delude your mind into thinking that the cards life has dealt you are the only allusion to what you are or what you will become. You can always view the road as rugged, but if you never walk out in faith, you will never know what comes after the ruggedness. In no way has God created a misconception of right and wrong, because God has created the image of Him in you. You were born into the image of perfection regardless of whom your family is or where you live. The layout of where you are from should never identify who you become. Never allow influence to dictate your capabilities.

Well, let me ask my friends for their opinion. If God has called you to do something, why would you ask for an opinion before doing it? It does not mean you are not hearing God; it means that you are not trusting in the God that you hear. Why would you ask your friends for support while walking into God's unique course *for you*? It does not mean that you don't believe that God is all you need; it means that you've chosen to take support until God meets your need. The wrong opinions or wrong influence will control your mind and overrule your heart into believing it's not meant to be, you are inferior, or "one of them."

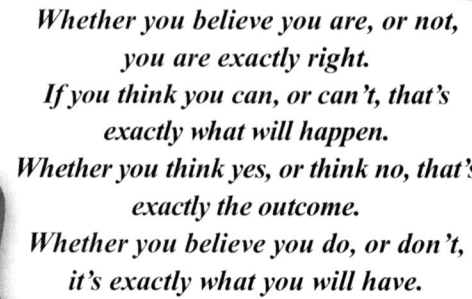

*Whether you believe you are, or not,
you are exactly right.
If you think you can, or can't, that's
exactly what will happen.
Whether you think yes, or think no, that's
exactly the outcome.
Whether you believe you do, or don't,
it's exactly what you will have.*

*I have prayed, I have cried, I have sought God, and
He still has not saved me.* **Yes, I experienced the same
circumstance; the only difference is I did it until He did
save me**.

I am hurting because people I love are saying "*I am having a hard time believing*!" Then I ask, "How can you believe in a god that you have no faith in? How can you trust in God's road when you have blind people leading you to a place that they have never seen? How can you say you are yet to feel God at church, when you are yet to understand that just because a group of people come together once a week, *does not make it church*? If there isn't faith, if there isn't trust, if there isn't belief where the Spirit of God can fall . . . then God is not there! *I read God's Word but nothing happens; surely it can't mean what it says*. The fact is we are waiting for what comes with the Word, instead of walking in faith and believing to receive because of the Word. It is not that God didn't open the door to you; the fact is you are yet to walk through it! It isn't that God didn't allow you to receive what you believed; the fact is you didn't believe enough that you would receive. It isn't that faith made you doubt; the fact is you doubted before you could have faith!

I could never turn away from a Man who has saved my life.

The wrong choice of friends will make you think you are bigger than what you are until your time is cut short by *prison or death*. Go to prison and you'll know who your friends are. Experience death, and then search your friends' hearts to see if you linger in their pain. The choice of our friends will determine what highway we choose to take in life. Be careful of the highway that intersects with prison and death—it's called highway robbery.

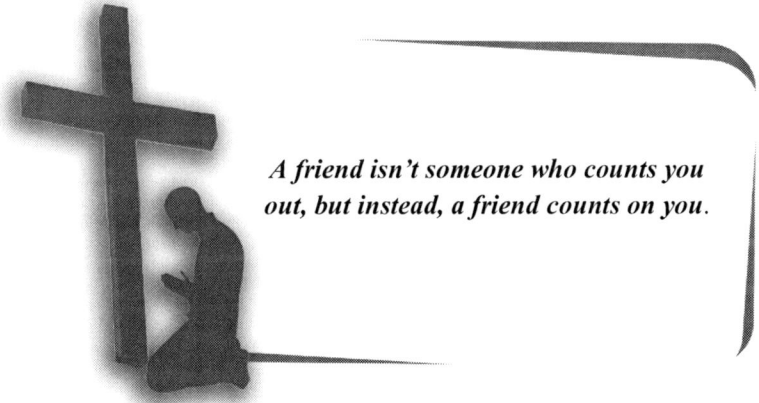

A friend isn't someone who counts you out, but instead, a friend counts on you.

How do you get respect when you sit alone? How do you have choice, when you are left with no options? I get respect with my friends, and my friends will never turn their back on me! *What kind of respect does a man have if no one wants to be around him?*

An angry man stated he would die for his respect, yet nobody knows he exists;

*An angry man said people love me because I get respect, yet
nobody takes pleasure in his company;
An angry crowd mocked people want to be like us, yet no
one wears their costume;
"What kind of respect does a man have, if no one respects
him at all?"*

Do not find yourself swimming in the devil's water. There is a sort of water that presents a mirage of counterfeit bliss, and many of us jump into the water not realizing what's in force below. Just below the surface of these "persuading" waters lurk betrayal, deceitfulness, unfaithfulness, misinformed respect, criminal mischief, drugs, anger, and a list of unlawful conduct. The devil will persuade a single person into believing that this water is agreeable, just so that one person can mislead others into the water as well. Once the water is filled with the influence of lost souls, all the devil has to do is drown one person to destroy the rest.

Imagine a person who is drowning in the middle of a lake surrounded by five individuals. When that person begins to struggle to stay afloat, their deceptive "survival" instincts take over, and they will do whatever possible to stay above water—even if it means using someone else as a buoy—the outcome is a domino affect.

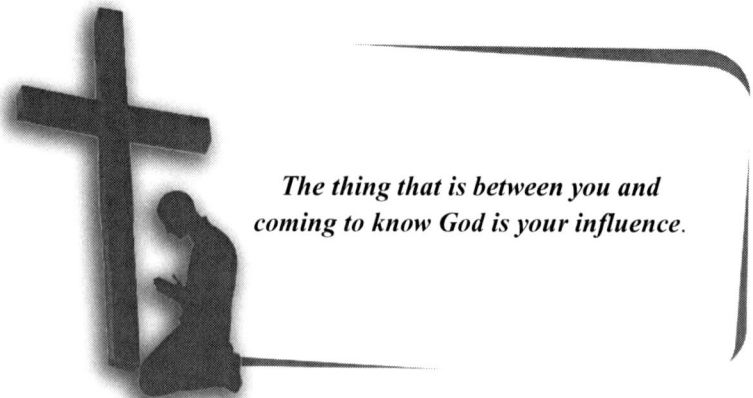

The thing that is between you and coming to know God is your influence.

You must avert your attention from your misleading crowd and the problems that can and will occur while occupying their customs. Simply being in the presence of God will keep you from the presence of evil.

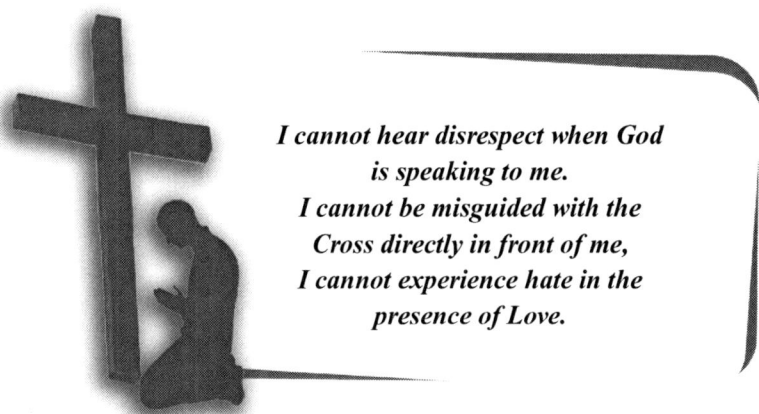

*I cannot hear disrespect when God is speaking to me.
I cannot be misguided with the Cross directly in front of me,
I cannot experience hate in the presence of Love.*

You must realize that men who are consumed with immoral habits and pessimistic exploits have constructed a root of bitterness. Nourishing this root with unconstructiveness will only permit the root to grow and cause trouble to many. We are obligated to reevaluate what we accept into our garden—one bad root can spoil the entire harvest. You cannot change the fruit without changing the root.

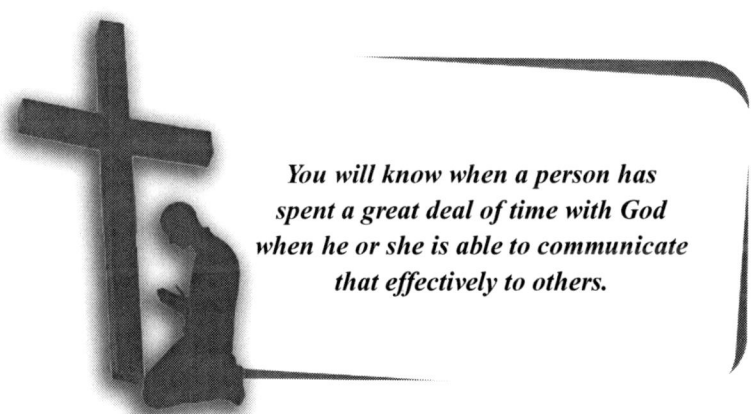

You will know when a person has spent a great deal of time with God when he or she is able to communicate that effectively to others.

I cry and cry and cry because I have begun to understand the Gospel. When you begin to understand Christ, you will begin to know more about other people's lives than they do. Without a doubt, Jesus is dispassionate about your conforming influence because it causes you to be spiritually inactive, but we must realize that by allowing God to influence us it will not be impossible for Him to bear life out of stones. It is a shame when your friends have more influence over you than God does. The majority of our friends work from the wrong side of our lives. It is not pain that hurts the most; it's usually always the source of pain that hurts the most. A work of pain that is established on what we call our blind side. Parents hold the arrow that points the way for the proper arrangement of change in their children's lives. If you stop positioning God in your children's lives, who will ever be the one to lead them to the accurate path? If you stop praying, who will ever intercede for them? For anyone who says to his or her parents: *Stop pressuring me to go to church*! *Stop talking about God! Stop trying to make me something I'm not! Stop judging all my friends!*—Parents, **don't stop doing it**.

Jesus said to me, *If your mother would have ever stopped being "a mother," you would have never known how much she loved and cared for you. When your family was behind you pushing you in the right direction, I stood in front of you trying to drag you into your purpose as well. The reason why you hate your family's concern is because you're yet to appreciate their love.*

THE INFLUENCE OF CHRISTIANS

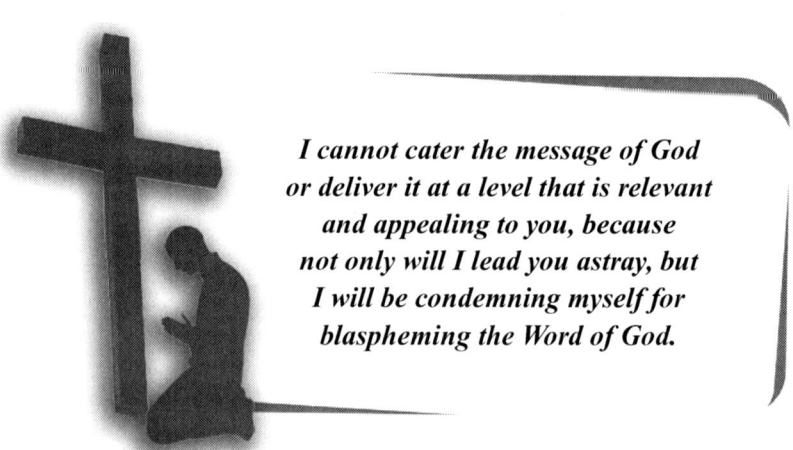

I cannot cater the message of God or deliver it at a level that is relevant and appealing to you, because not only will I lead you astray, but I will be condemning myself for blaspheming the Word of God.

Christians—you describe the love of God, you describe the success of God, you describe the money because of God, you describe the promotions due to God—but you are yet to describe the reality in *battleground of the true*

Gospel! I am not talking about a church or people of faith with liberal and conservative doctrine. I am talking about people with biblical backing and who implement Christ with "authority" and who are directors of genuine repentance. You describe the love of God, but you forget to explain that His love is meant to break you first, to make possible for His Spirit to fall upon you. Are the eyes of your faith big enough to not merely see the suffering, but the Savior of the suffering? You describe the success of God, but you never mention that it has nothing to do with money, but most importantly our reward in the kingdom of heaven. When you delude the Word or the power of God, it takes away the effect. *Fight*! God's Word is at the top, and He will never go below His own Word to appeal to man or culture. *Fight*! You tell people to seek the face of the Lord, but you never mention that the tears that trickle down His face are meant to show His pain, and illustrate what He has endured over the years because *He loves you*! If Christ can be loved under unbearable conditions by martyrs who risk their lives every day, then there must be a personal evidence to what most see as invisible. There is a short slogan to the early Christian world that navigated its way to becoming a nationalistic movement—I Am. We must ask ourselves what we want and need out of this life. The response of Jesus will always be, *I Am*, because it is a prophetic picture that reaches no maximum bounds. Its only incarceration is the heart that disbelieves or the individual who is kept from truth. It is important for Christians to know that the battle is not being blind and coming to the light; it comes when you become the light trying to lead the blind. The only way blind people end up leading blind people is when they speak about the greatness of God and don't involve in the great battle we will face to overcome our sin to experience all of God. Without honesty, you will keep the experience of God's love too far away for any affection. People should be able to see the face of God through your eyes. It is not hard to fight; it's hard getting people to comprehend that *there will be a fight*! It is not a terrible process; it is an incredible process! God will do all of this for you, just to put your life in position to do only what God can do!

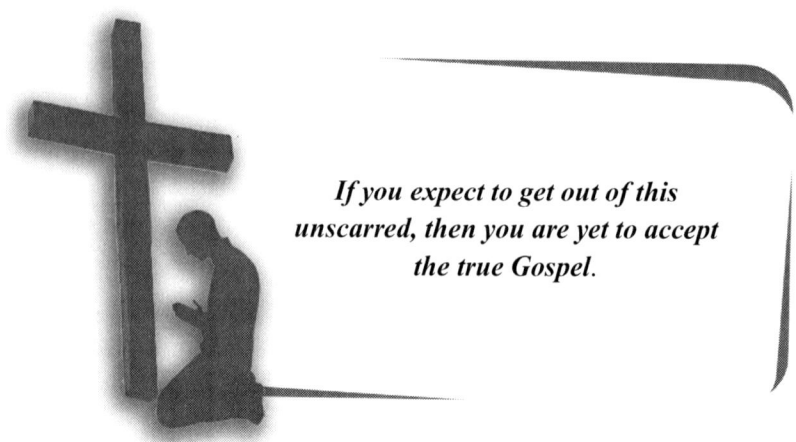

If you expect to get out of this unscarred, then you are yet to accept the true Gospel.

What are true Christians? A Christian is one who establishes the visions of faith to be reality. Christians are not the people who you follow because of the big picture that they are pointing at, but instead you go to the picture Christians are starring at, wondering what they are so intrigued by—a vision of certainty we call faith.

Try to understand this illustration on how important your faith is to those who do not believe in your faith, a faith that you don't necessarily need to talk about, but a faith that is demonstrated because you are not afraid to show it. If you walk by someone standing motionless in the middle of the parking lot looking up toward the sky, you too would look up and ask what is going on, not because the person told you to look up and there is actually something to look at, but because what the person is doing is distinctly unusual. The Christian life is meant to be exemplified as distinctly different, because you are looking at a picture that no one else sees—looking, starring, and believing that it is there. You must have a faith that is so astounding that you are willing to be rejected by thousands, so you can be accepted by One. The problem that I am having with people of faith is that you can't even walk into a crowded mall and know who a Christian is by their appearance and actions.

I will stare at the sky and tell the world about the beautiful picture I see even when nothing is there, even when thousands of people will walk by and believe that I am insane. I will stand there until God begins to paint! Then, not only will those thousands be proven wrong, but my faith will become the reality of millions!

Proverbs 23:9: "Do not speak to a fool, for he will scorn the wisdom of your words."

The Proverbs of Solomon, the son of David, king of Israel—to receive the instruction of wisdom, justice, judgment, and equity. The fear of the Lord is the beginning of knowledge, but fools despise wisdom and knowledge. (*Refer Prov. 23.*) Apply your heart to instruction and your ears to the words of knowledge. Your heart will be glad when it speaks what is right. By fear of the Lord there is surely a future hope for you, and your hope will not be cut off. Listen, be wise, and keep your heart on the right path.

Genesis 1:27: "So God created man in his own image, in the image of God he created him; male and female he created them."

The first book of Moses, the beginning of creation. God gives dominion to man over everything that moves on earth and leaves him with three requests: be fruitful and multiply, replenish the earth, and subdue it (control it). We are in the image of God, a molding in the potter's hands, but because of the fall of man "Adam" (Gen. 3), we must now have God's life-giving wind or breath of life to reshape us. It is an outpouring of God's Spirit not to reshape our physical form, but to reshape our moral and intellectual qualities. It is reconciliation through His Son Jesus Christ by whom we are set free from the law of sin and death (Rom. 8:1). Through Jesus Christ we are now a crowning masterpiece where we are taken back to the beginning of God's creation when "it was good."

Romans 12:21: "Do not be overcome by evil, but overcome evil with good."

Paul, a servant of Jesus Christ, called to be an apostle and set apart for the Gospel of God speaking concerning the Spirit of holiness, who declared Jesus with power to be the Son of God to all of Rome. (*Refer Rom. 12:9-21.*) (9) Love must be sincere. Hate what is evil; cling to what is good. (10) Be devoted to one another in brotherly love. Honor one another above yourselves. (17) Do not repay anyone evil for evil. Be careful to do what is right in the eyes of everybody. (19) Do not take revenge, my friends, but leave room for God's wrath, for it is written: "It is mine to avenge; I will repay," says the Lord.

2 Timothy 2:3: "Endure Hardship with us like a good solider of Jesus Christ."

The Second Epistle of Paul, the apostle, to Timothy. Paul, an apostle of Jesus Christ by the will of God, according to the promise of life, which is in Christ Jesus. (*Refer 2 Tim. 2:3-13.*) (3) Endure hardship with us like a good solider of Jesus Christ. We must endure hardship because we don't set out to please others, but we must do this to please God. Paul said, "I am suffering even to the point of being chained like a criminal. But God's word is not chained! (10) Therefore I endure everything for the sake of the elect that they too may obtain the salvation that is in Christ Jesus, with eternal glory. (11) Here is a trustworthy saying: If we died with him, we will also live with him; (12) if we endure, we will also reign with him; if we disown him, he will disown us; (13) if we are faithless, he will remain faithful, for he cannot disown himself. Yes, if we suffer, we shall also reign with Him!

1 Corinthians 15:33: *"Do not be misled: Bad company corrupts good character."*

The First Epistle of Paul, the apostle, to the Corinthians. Paul called to be an apostle of Jesus Christ through the will of God. May every place call upon the name of Jesus Christ our Lord to the church at Corinth. (*Refer 1 Cor. 15:22-58.*) (22) For as in Adam all die, so in Christ all will be made alive. Jesus must reign until all His enemies are put under His feet. The last enemy to be destroyed is death. Christians will suffer every day just so the dead can rise—those who walk around in sin. Our lives can enable the dead to rise. (29) . . . If the dead are not raised at all, why are people baptized for them? And for us, why do we endanger ourselves every hour? Paul said, (31) "I die every day"! Paul then says, "Come back to your sense as you ought, and stop sinning; for there are some who are ignorant of God—I say this to your shame." Be careful of your company.

Anger is the root of bitterness that develops a vein of instability and forms branches of opposition.

INFLUENCE OF ANGER

Love has a face, but anger demands its disguise. You can never appreciate people without the expression of appreciation.

Jesus said to me, *We get rid of anger simply by putting it in the shadows behind love. When love isn't primary, anger has a way of being exposed.*

Following the Word of God is the confinement of the possible cruelty and evil that can come out of a man. Anger doesn't necessarily keep your mind closed off; it just keeps it filled with *a possession that's unnecessary*. Either way it sends a signal of rejection or gives an occupied notice to love. When anger isn't taken out of the routine of your life, it plays an essential role in eliminating a sound mind. Your character is built in moments of disagreement, and in those moments the importance of your life is uncovered, because it is in those moments where your heart begins to prove that anger was never meant to be part of your nature. Because I have moral tendencies, I am obligated and actually obliged to take my spiritual medicine by ingesting a daily overdose in the Word of God.

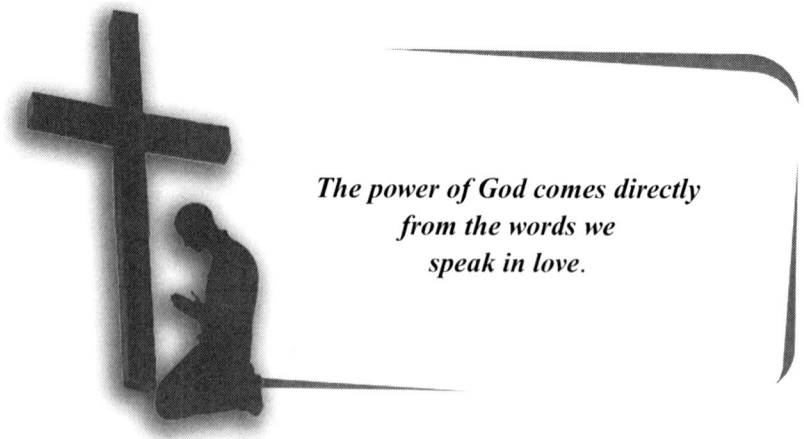

The power of God comes directly from the words we speak in love.

Anger disconnects you from the power of God, drawing you into a vulnerability, leaving you with no power of protection. Be sure you are rightly connected. You cannot expect to have power if you take the plug out of the outlet. If you feel you are losing strength or the power to control yourself, plug yourself into Jesus.

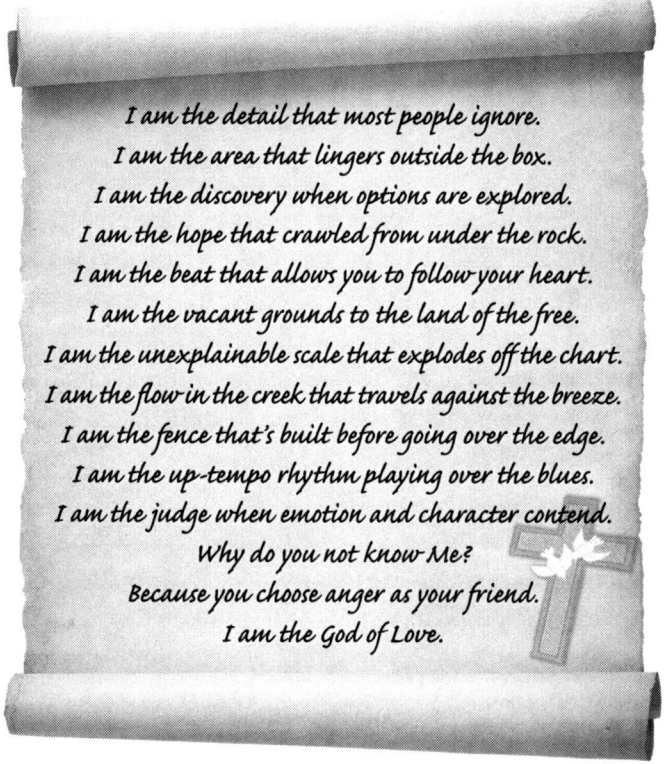

I am the detail that most people ignore.
I am the area that lingers outside the box.
I am the discovery when options are explored.
I am the hope that crawled from under the rock.
I am the beat that allows you to follow your heart.
I am the vacant grounds to the land of the free.
I am the unexplainable scale that explodes off the chart.
I am the flow in the creek that travels against the breeze.
I am the fence that's built before going over the edge.
I am the up-tempo rhythm playing over the blues.
I am the judge when emotion and character contend.
Why do you not know Me?
Because you choose anger as your friend.
I am the God of Love.

Resentment in your life alerts an empty place in your heart for the need of restoration. Ironically, a place of restoration isn't built by tools; it's built by love.

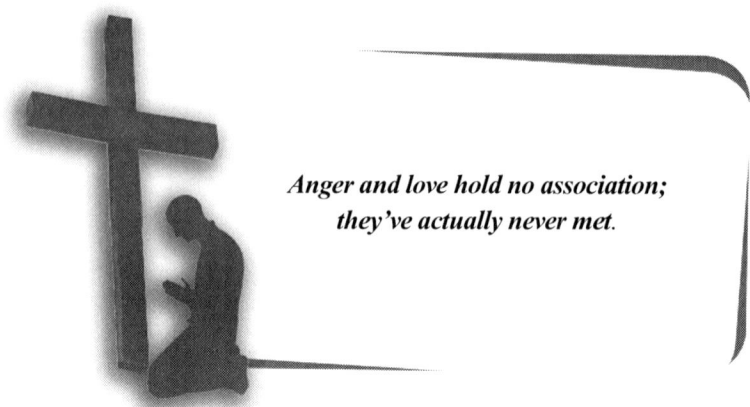

Anger and love hold no association; they've actually never met.

When you allow anger or hate to overrule your ethics, you lose the constancy on the calling on your life. When you possess anger, you actually are giving access to the devil to converse through you. Anger has a way of segregating people from general conversation with you, because general conversation about you tells them to segregate themselves from you. Have you ever wondered what kind of man Jesus was? When He was made in our likeness—flesh—the Bible says that He made Himself nothing. So the question is, what kind of people are we that God would detach His Son from the throne to wither in a low place and eventually be crowned with thorns? A man who was overwhelmed with human feelings and trials. A man who could have put every man on their face, but instead chose to embrace their hearts. Amazing! He has done all this so that we may live a life experiencing Emmanuel—God with us.

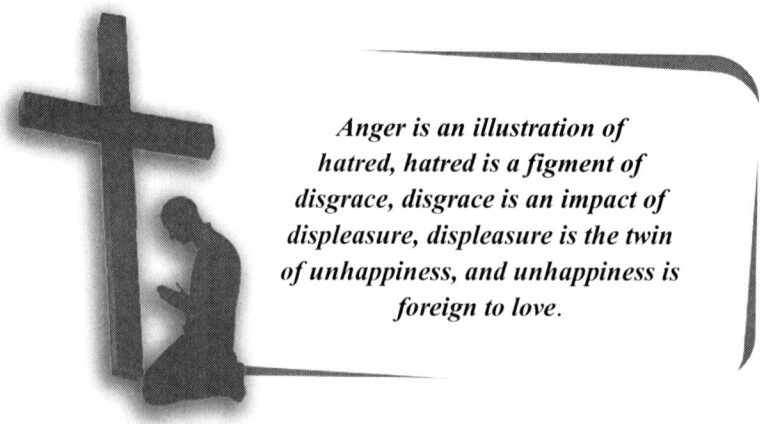

Anger is an illustration of hatred, hatred is a figment of disgrace, disgrace is an impact of displeasure, displeasure is the twin of unhappiness, and unhappiness is foreign to love.

Always remember that you have to desire more in order to receive more. Smiling keeps you content; laughter keeps you happy. If you are waiting for God in order to change, then there is a problem . . . because He is waiting for you! Anger will always keep your faith unresponsive, but one of the major ways to activate your faith is with love. If you can place anger behind love and set your mind strictly on the Gospel's belief, it will penetrate the heart for faith to gain access, which will prove to the eye that faith is a living substance—reality. Until our faith is awakened we will live in the darkest reality of our time.

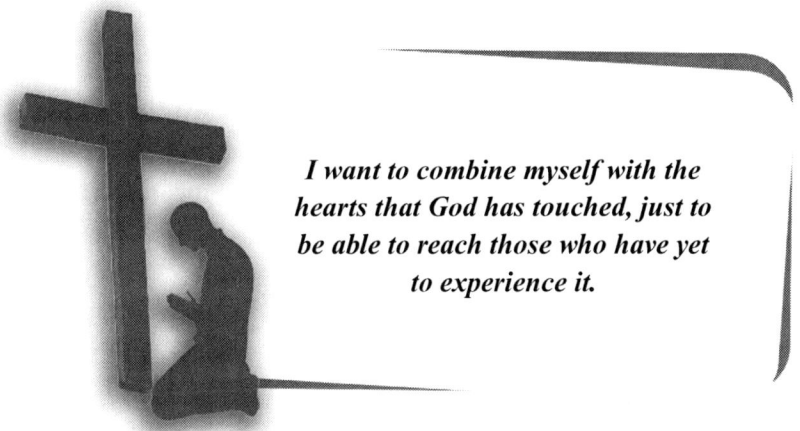

I want to combine myself with the hearts that God has touched, just to be able to reach those who have yet to experience it.

THE INFLUENCE OF MY LOVE, NOT ANGER, BUT PASSION

Who is this man that I cry for? Who is this man that I yearn for? Who is this man that I am willing to die for? I am deeply passionate for the passion of Christ. You have asked who, and now I will explain it with why. Why can I live? . . . *He died*! Why can I breathe? . . . *He died*! I want the chambers of my heart to shake not because I can live, but because the light of the world has died and now through me He can live!

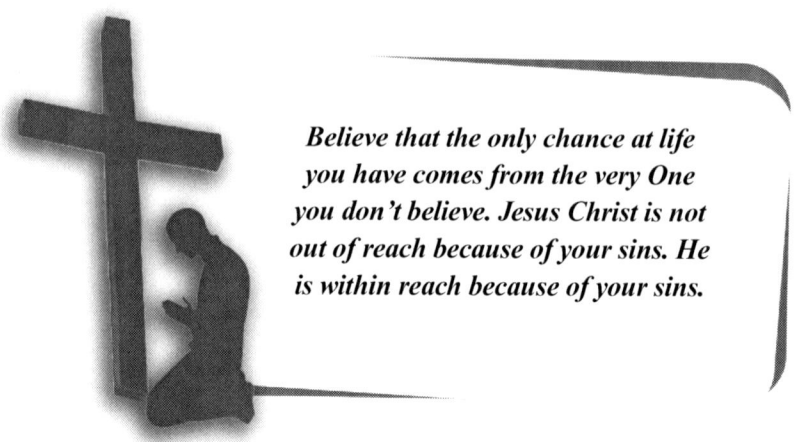

Believe that the only chance at life you have comes from the very One you don't believe. Jesus Christ is not out of reach because of your sins. He is within reach because of your sins.

The Gospel is the news of Jesus Christ, who died for our sins to be embraced in the grace of God, that whoever believes in the sovereign name of Jesus would not receive condemnation but joy in eternal life. We are strengthened by God through the Gospel, the effect of which is not just a preaching to others, but an everyday preaching to ourselves. The Gospel is what has brought about faith because we now can acquire the mercy of God through His Son Jesus. We, immediately, through Jesus, can expect a regeneration of living and an understanding of life. Through the Gospel we can be in right standing with God.

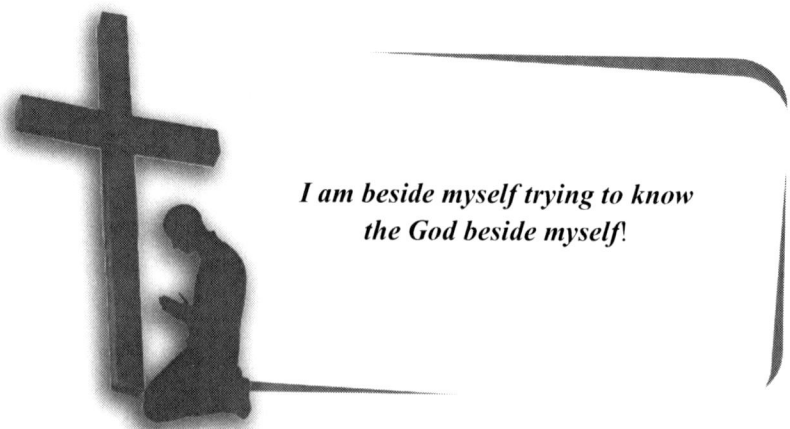

I am beside myself trying to know the God beside myself!

You wonder why God is not supplying for your every need, because the very things that mean so much to you in this world mean so less to God. Are you as excited about the love of God as you are about the promotion at your job? Let me ask you . . . have you denied the name of Jesus? *We speak verification that the Son of God is Lord of our life. We would never say that God doesn't exist! We would never say there is no Higher Power!* Yes, but here it is; we speak verification, not with our mouth . . . *but with our life*! Now, again I ask you, have you denied the name of Jesus?

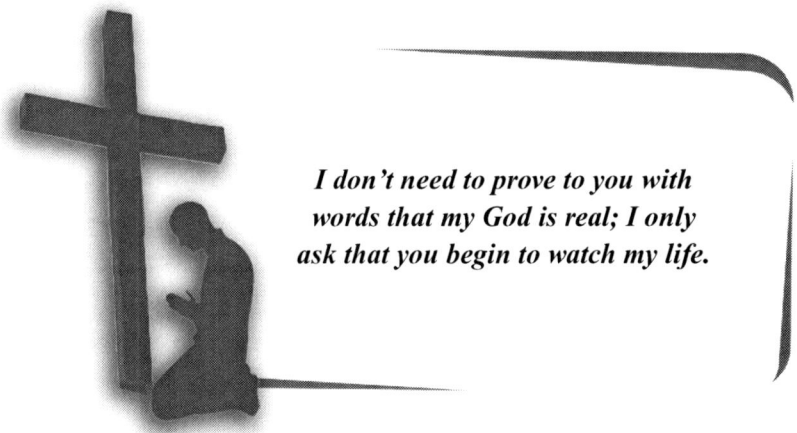

I don't need to prove to you with words that my God is real; I only ask that you begin to watch my life.

You can hover over doubt and wait on God's sympathy, but while you have mountains burying you, I am burying mountains and turning them into valleys! While you have waters drowning you, I am engulfed in living water, turning it into a desert preparing a way for the Lord! Jesus does not have to apologize for you falling outside of His mercy, because His grace was like an extended hand throughout your life that was meant to pull you into His mercy. Jesus doesn't have to show compassion for your unrighteous living, because just by you living demonstrates Jesus's compassion in spite of your unrighteous living.

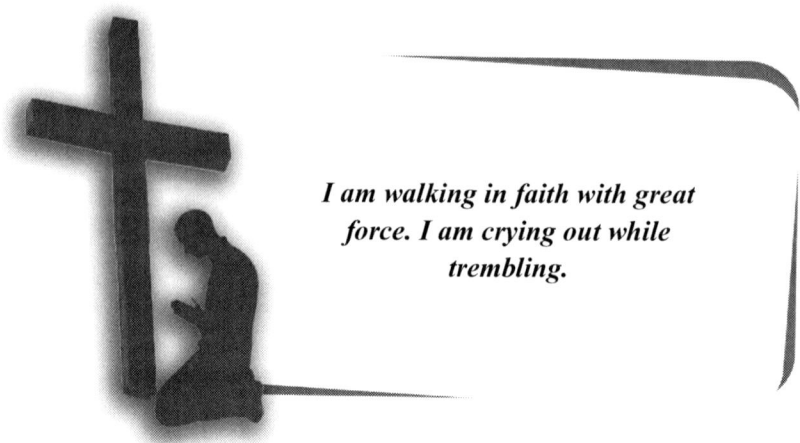

I am walking in faith with great force. I am crying out while trembling.

I am the one who should be angry . . . because God has taken everything from me . . . but now amazed, knowing it was only meant to help me understand Him and His love. God has put me in isolation where I see nothing—nothing on the walls and nothing all around me. God has done this and left me with nothing but the Bible. If I have nothing, then I cannot have opinions and I cannot be preoccupied by anything. If all I have is the Bible, then when God opens the door, all I will have to talk about is Him!

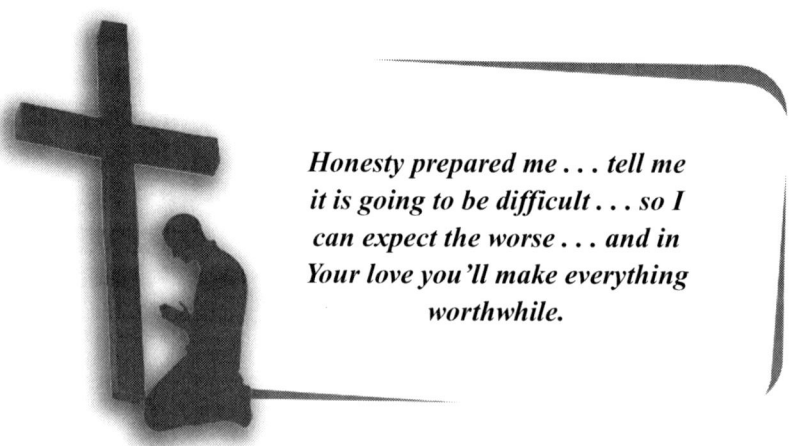

Honesty prepared me . . . tell me it is going to be difficult . . . so I can expect the worse . . . and in Your love you'll make everything worthwhile.

Why am I so passionate? As I smile while saying this . . . I have no substitution of truth. I am the ear that heard God before tradition. I am the voice that spoke before religion. I am not an accommodator of practical thinking. I am a radical for dangerous missions. I have never gotten enough of God's love because I learned through the Gospel about the fight it will take until you breathe your last breath . . . because of tough love.

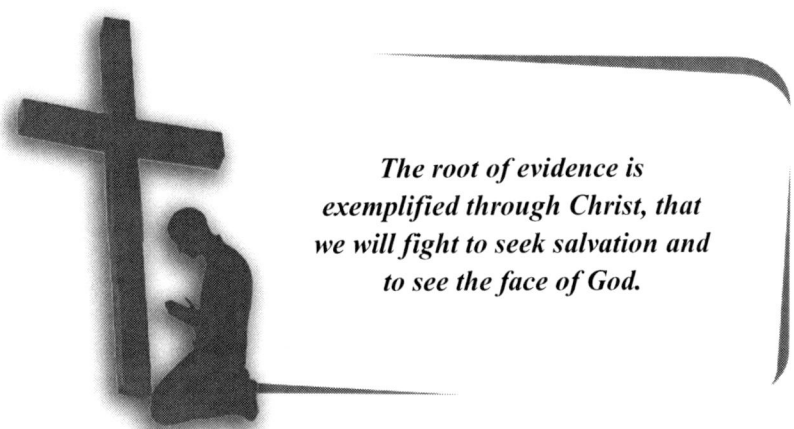

The root of evidence is exemplified through Christ, that we will fight to seek salvation and to see the face of God.

Here is where I stand—beside God's anger with love. There are billions of people who have never been touched by the name of Jesus and who have never been reached by the Gospel. What does this mean? It means half the world is yet to hear! As it begins to soak in, let your heart begin to pierce as you realize . . . that it means *you* are yet to open your mouth! Mission is not a travel, it is a mission to deliver!

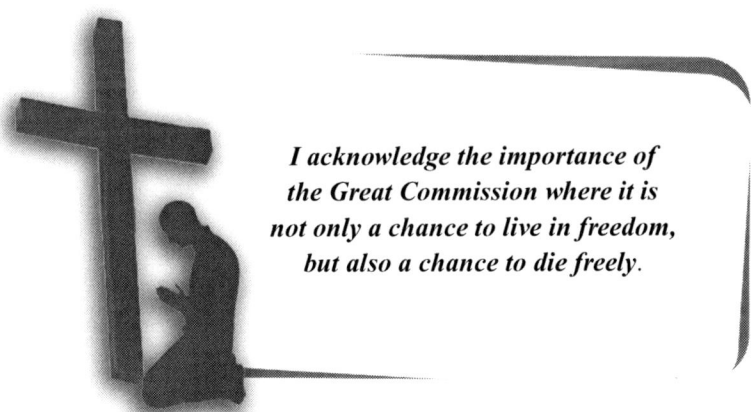

I acknowledge the importance of the Great Commission where it is not only a chance to live in freedom, but also a chance to die freely.

2 Thessalonians 3:16: "Now may the Lord of peace himself give you peace at all times in every way. The Lord be with you all."

Paul, Silas, and Timothy to the church of the Thessalonians. (Refer 2 Thess. 3:1-6.) The apostles said, "Pray for us that the Gospel will be spread by delivering us from wicked and evil men, for not everyone has faith, but the Lord is faithful, and He will strengthen and protect you from the evil one." (6) Keep away from every brother who is idle and does not live according to the teaching you received from "The Word."

Philippians 4:7: "And the peace of God, which surpasses all understanding, will guard your hearts and your minds in Christ Jesus."

Paul and Timothy, servants of Christ, to all the saints, deacons, and overseers at Philippi—(1) Paul said, "You are my joy and my crown, stand firm in the Lord." (3) Women you have contended at my side for the cause in the gospel and fellow workers whose names are in the book of life. (4) Rejoice in the Lord always. (5) Let your gentleness be evident to all. *The Lord is near.* (6) Do not be anxious about anything but in everything by prayer and petition present your requests to God. *And God's peace will be with you.* (8) Whatever is true, whatever is noble, whatever is right, whatever is pure, whatever is lovely, whatever is admirable—if anything is excellent or praiseworthy—think about such things. (9) Whatever you have learned or received or heard or seen from "The word" put into practice. *And the God of peace will be with you.*

Proverbs 10:12: "Hatred stirs up dissension, but love covers all of wrongs."

The Proverbs of Solomon, son of David, king of Israel: For acquiring a disciplined and prudent life. Let the wise listen and add to their learning, and let the discerning get guidance. (*Refer Prov. 10:2-12.*) As we build up anger, we must know that ill-gotten treasures are of no value, but righteousness delivers from death. Do not curse a man whom God has not cursed (Num. 23:8) because blessings will crown the head of the righteous. (7) The memory of the righteous will be a blessing, but the name of the wicked will rot. (10) He who winks maliciously causes grief, and a chattering fool comes to ruin. (11) The mouth of the righteous is a fountain of life, but violence overwhelms the mouth of the wicked.

Hebrews 9:15: *"For this reason Christ is the mediator of a new covenant, that those who are called may receive the promised eternal inheritance—now that he has died as a ransom to them free from the sins committed under the first covenant."*

The Epistle to the Hebrews. (*Refer Heb. 9:11-17.*) Calling people not only to who they were called to be, but more importantly who we are called through—Jesus. Jesus came to us through a channel that is not of man-made creation. He did not enter by means of the blood of goats and calves, but He entered through His own blood—The Most Holy Place of all. The blood of goats sprinkled over those who are unclean will only make a person appear to be outwardly clean. The blood of Jesus is the only new covenant of blood that can offer a full redemption. (16) In the case of a will, it is necessary to prove the death of the one who made it, (17) because a will is in force only when someone has died; it never takes effect while the one who has made it is living—meaning Jesus had to *die for you* so you can *live* and be pure and blameless before the throne of God!

1 Peter 4:12-13: *"Dear friends, do not be surprised at the painful trail you are suffering, as though something strange were happening to you. (13) But rejoice that you participate in the sufferings of Christ, so that you may be overjoyed when His glory is revealed."*

The First Epistle of Peter, an apostle, of Jesus Christ, to the elect according to the foreknowledge of God the Father, through sanctification of the Spirit, and unto obedience and the blood of Jesus Christ. (*Refer 1 Pet. 4:12-19.*) (14) If you are insulted because of the name of Christ, you are blessed, for the Spirit of glory and of God rests on you. (16) . . . If you suffer as a Christian, do not be ashamed, but praise God that you bear that name. (17) For it is time for judgment to begin with the family of God; and if it begins with us, what will the outcome be for those who do not obey the gospel of God? (18) And, "if it is *hard* for the righteous *to be saved*, what will become of the ungodly and the sinner?" Commit yourselves and continue to do good.

> *If you become too concerned with what mess you will step into, you'll never enjoy what you just stepped out of.*

INFLUENCE OF WORRIES

> *Worries are a disruption to progress—a major setback from increase.*

Jesus said to me, *Worrying has everything to do with a lack of trust in Me. Worrying is a fear of the future, not the present. Why would you worry about something that hasn't happened yet if I am in control?*

What are worries? Worries are like change building in your pocket; the more you have, the more it weighs you down. You see, worrying will always occupy your mind and keep your heart from where it is you want to be. Whatever we give attention to gives attention back. Did you know the greater part of divine chance or opportunity becomes a success in our lives, not as a result of dealing with our worries or fears, but actually because we were smart enough not to give attention to them?

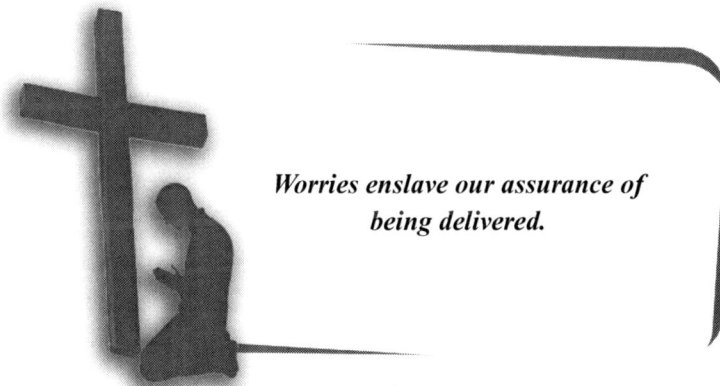

Worries enslave our assurance of being delivered.

Now, what is the main purpose for why we worry? Nothing. Worry only results in agitation and abnormal reactions. What is the devil's main purpose for worry? It is a direct and indirect source from which we can literally worry ourselves to death. Worries are life's main cause for interruptions and delays that pull us off our destined course. What makes the Lord's presence so dynamic is that His chosen moments for serenity can be found in those interruptions.

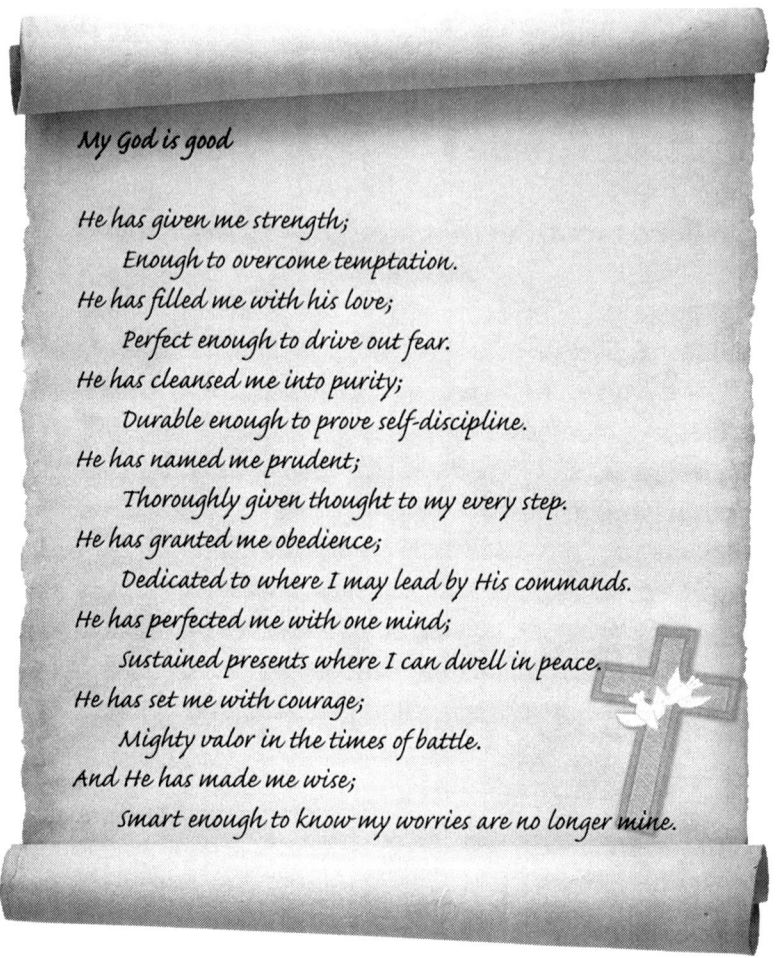

My God is good

He has given me strength;
  Enough to overcome temptation.
He has filled me with his love;
  Perfect enough to drive out fear.
He has cleansed me into purity;
  Durable enough to prove self-discipline.
He has named me prudent;
  Thoroughly given thought to my every step.
He has granted me obedience;
  Dedicated to where I may lead by His commands.
He has perfected me with one mind;
  Sustained presents where I can dwell in peace.
He has set me with courage;
  Mighty valor in the times of battle.
And He has made me wise;
  Smart enough to know my worries are no longer mine.

> **You cannot fix a worry because "you cannot fix something that isn't broke." Worrying is an emotional paranoia for something that has not happened yet, and may never happen.**

I used to worry about what to say to people who needed some life spoken into them. I used to think to myself that I was not a talker, saying over and over in my head that being a conversationalist is not for me. What changed? I handed over my worries, and I began to speak and preach about conditions that I literally had no answer to, until I began to open my mouth. Whenever you approach a wall of concern in your life, just remember that God is in control, which means worries are never what they appear to be because they were never meant to be there. The problems we face and the worries resting on us are not prearranged punishment; they are *resulting punishment* that we have placed on ourselves. Our concerns were never part of the arrangement or process that allows us to grow in the purposeful life of God. It is crucial that you understand that worries are the devil's way of distracting you from what God is trying to tell you. The devil cannot physically destroy our progress to prosper; he can merely avert our mind to ravage our own hopes and beliefs. Hope will never allow you to fall upon troubled thoughts. Therefore, if we occupy our mind with worries, it distracts us from anything we may gain in our steps or leaps of faith. The only way to plan ways out of worry is by planning today for the days to come that your worries are out of your control, because faith gives away our worries to God. Give yourself a fresh start by being worry-free. *Place your dirty clothes in the washer.* Don't allow your dirty clothes to pile up, because it takes up unwanted space and leaves behind a situation . . . that just stinks! Worries, fears, troubles, dilemmas, failures, and obstacles—the Lord will not give you back anything in its original condition—it always comes back better. *"It will all come out in the wash."*

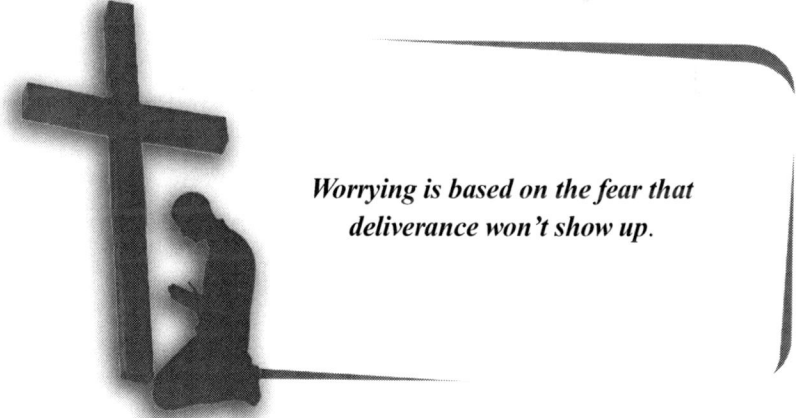

Worrying is based on the fear that deliverance won't show up.

Before the reward comes the fight. This particular fight is not fought in the physical realm, but in the spiritual realm. We do not have to face something to fight it; the fight is done and won by overcoming the situation whether it be facing it or ignoring it. Everything we overcome has a reward standing right behind it.

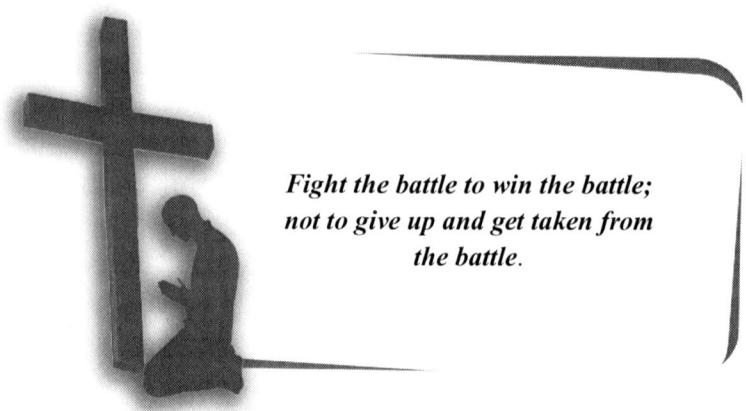

Fight the battle to win the battle; not to give up and get taken from the battle.

I am in no way saying that you will not worry, because even Jesus showed a state of being worried in His prayer at Gethsemane. What I am saying is always remember that God will never give you more than you can handle. If we never pushed ourselves, all we would know are limitations. If you are in a current battle, do not pray for God to relieve you from the battle, but pray for renewed strength and assistance to get through the battle. Worries are a major battle that comes with great reward.

I can remember so clearly walking down a strip mall with one of my friends, and an ignorant man said to me, "*What's more important, the Cross around your neck or the tattoos on your arm that contradict it?*" I smiled and responded, "May the eyes of your heart understand, God bless." My friend was shocked and told me to say something to him. I told him there was no need. With his arms up and eyes wide he expressed that I would never achieve anything if I didn't find myself in the battle. I smiled and replied, "My friend, I've just won that battle" (2 Tim. 2:22-26).

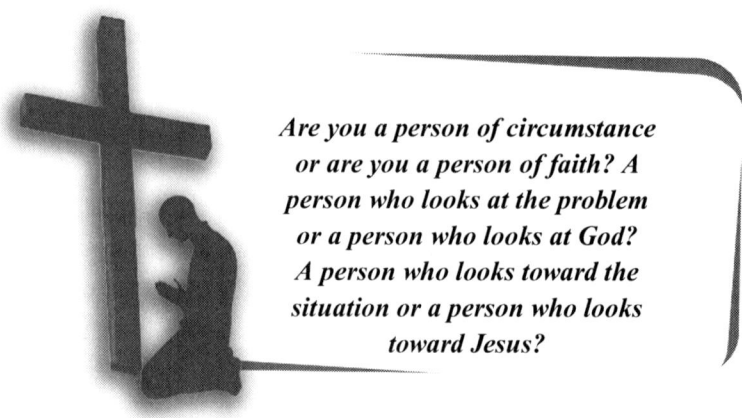

Are you a person of circumstance or are you a person of faith? A person who looks at the problem or a person who looks at God? A person who looks toward the situation or a person who looks toward Jesus?

I Am Not Worried; I Am Troubled

What I am most troubled about is how we are going about expanding the kingdom in the Body of Christ. The worst thing you can do is live in half of the truth, believing that your belief is justifiable before the throne of God. There is no ordinary with Jesus, only the extraordinary. We lack the understanding of God, because we work through tradition and religion. It is not that you have betrayed your faith, but rather your faith has been entangled and trapped in a bed of tradition and custom. Truth screams, arise and shine, awaken to the power! It is the commonplace of Christianity where we are believing that our belief is permissible, and subsequently moving our lives in the direction of sin. You will never be able to see God if it is based on human reasoning because the Spirit of God has no interaction with the flesh. You must come to a point of conviction where you can take on the Holy Spirit's heart. The believing in your heart must be immersed by the Spirit of God, as a filler and leader in your life, because when it is not, the heart is still considered to be most deceitfully wicked.

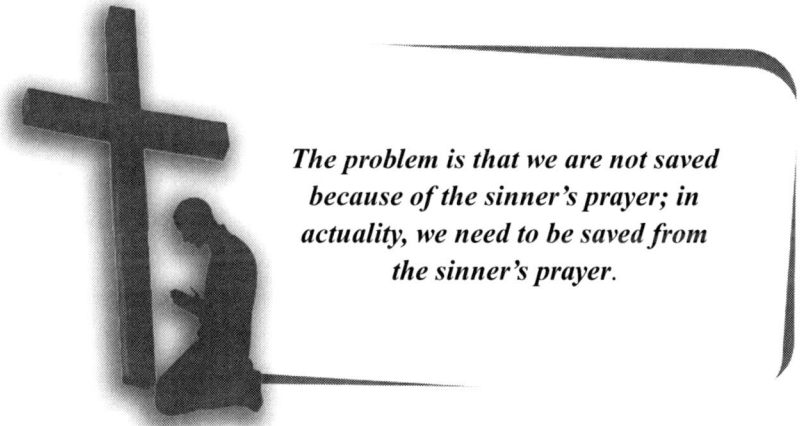

The problem is that we are not saved because of the sinner's prayer; in actuality, we need to be saved from the sinner's prayer.

I will not be the person that pats you on the back and tells you that it's going to be okay and Jesus loves you. I will plead for the Spirit of God to fall, which will bring you to a point of conviction, so that *you can feel* the love of Jesus! I will not say things to you that are acceptable. I am going to penetrate your mind-set and inject some truth. I am not trying to call you out . . . I am trying to bring you to who you were called to be. This should be the mind-set of Christianity! Truth is not hidden from us; it only appears this way because misunderstanding has become too common. Jesus carries the great truth. This is why we follow Him to be led to a place where misunderstanding is corrected.

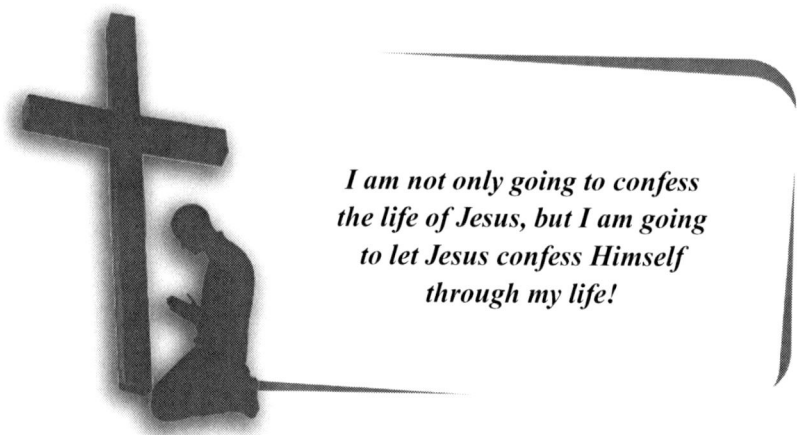

I am not only going to confess the life of Jesus, but I am going to let Jesus confess Himself through my life!

I am most troubled by Christians saying, "I have professed His name, I have called unto Him, and I have done the works of the Lord"! Remember that you are not fooling anyone, because God knows the heart and the intent of men. Not everyone who preaches "the understanding" of the Gospel is a steward of the mysteries of God. This means that not everyone is a servant of Christ. Not everyone who says Lord, Lord will enter into the kingdom of heaven (Matt. 7:21). This means that not everyone who says Lord, Lord is really a Christian! He says that he understands the pain of God but has never shed a tear! He says he preaches the Gospel, but it's to the same people in the same place, year after year! He says that he prays, but only declares His name and never communes with Him! He says that he is saved, but after the "simple prayer" he prayed, he never endured the difficult struggle! He says that he is filled with the Holy Spirit, but has no remembrance of the truth! He says that he is radical for God, but the only reason why we know is because his T-shirt told us! He says that he has found God, but yet he has lost souls all around him!

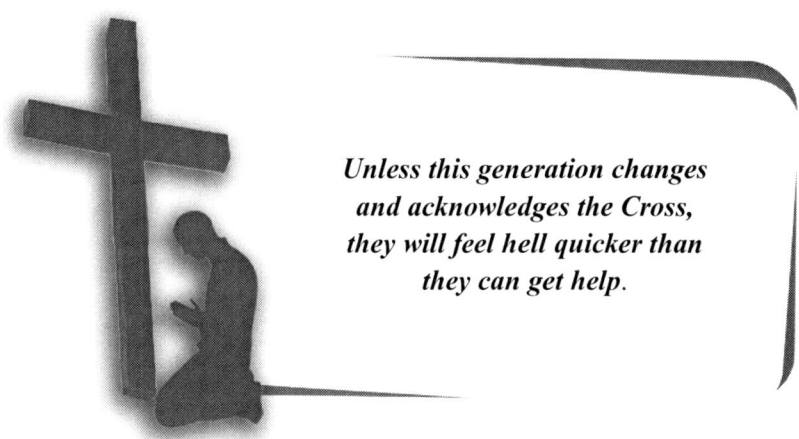

Unless this generation changes and acknowledges the Cross, they will feel hell quicker than they can get help.

I am not satisfied with people knowing there is a God or even believing there is a God, because much of today's believing and knowing is wrapped up in the midst of condemnation. The intent of my heart is that men would assemble their understanding of Christ through His pain at Gethsemane, and have a constant commemoration of His love while placing their lives on the Cross at Calvary, as my knees fall and my hands extend high, longing for God to be exhaustively honored among you and me.

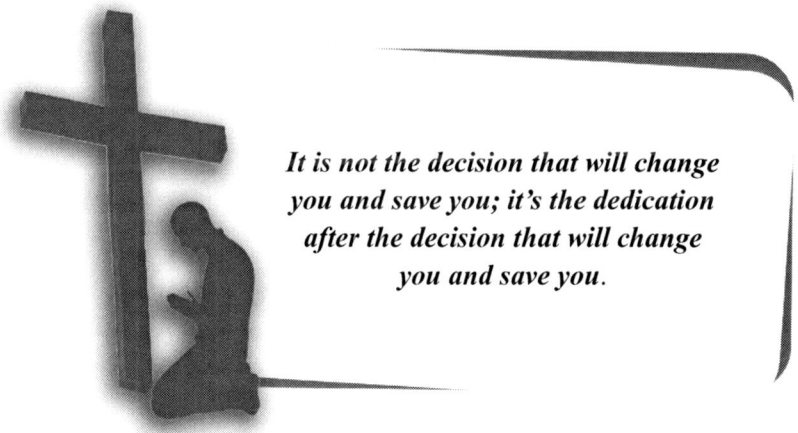

It is not the decision that will change you and save you; it's the dedication after the decision that will change you and save you.

It is not after we go to God when we become most powerful; it is when we are most delicate and weak when we become most powerful. It is not when we are standing on the peak of the mountain that we will find our strength; it is just before we hit the bottom of the pit and God tosses us a rope and says "climb your way out"—that is when we will find our strength! It is not when you are swarmed by a crowd of people screaming that you will find your greatest desire; it is when you are embraced by a solitary person who is weeping in conviction that you will find your greatest desire!

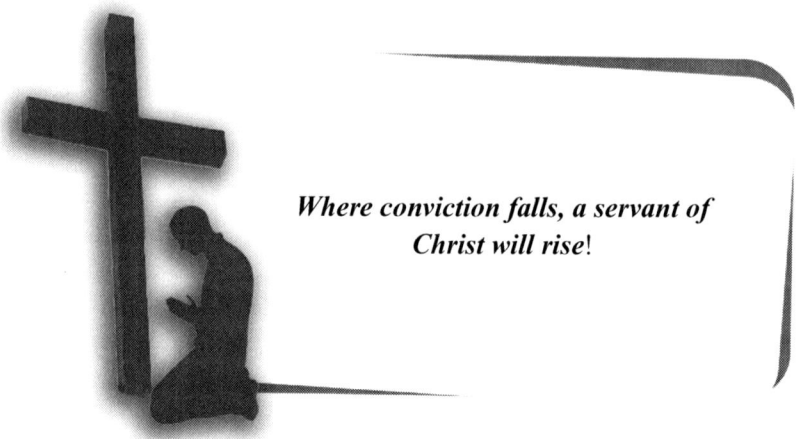

Where conviction falls, a servant of Christ will rise!

One of the most absurd questions that I am constantly hearing is, *when did you make Jesus Lord of your life*? Personally, I will not ask anyone to make Jesus Lord of their life, because whether you believe or not . . . Jesus *is* . . . Lord of your life! How can I make Him Lord, when God has already made Him Lord? What enables His grace and mercy to pour out over our lives is when we *acknowledge* that He has already had that position.

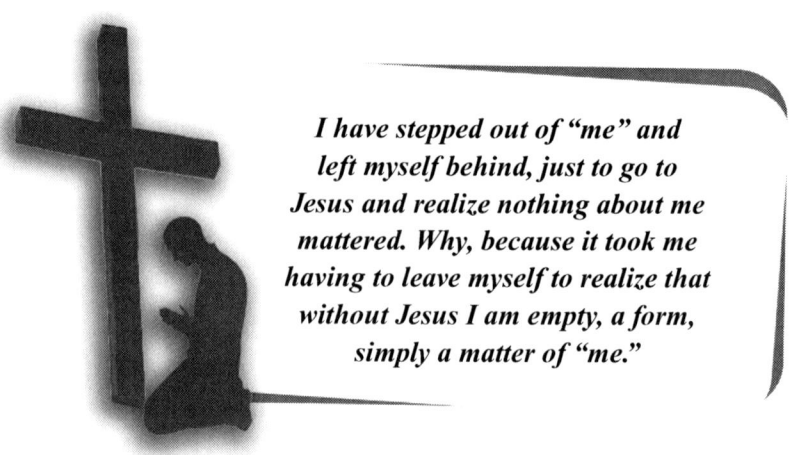

I have stepped out of "me" and left myself behind, just to go to Jesus and realize nothing about me mattered. Why, because it took me having to leave myself to realize that without Jesus I am empty, a form, simply a matter of "me."

We have all been born radically depraved as sinners, so the only way to experience change and to be saved from our sinful nature is this: We must *repent* and turn to God! *Repent, repent, repent* and believe! Peter, an apostle and a servant of Christ, *did not* console wicked men by saying Jesus loves you, but he *warned* and *pleaded* for wicked men to repent, and then understand the love of Jesus. Peter said, "Repent in the name of Jesus Christ *for the* forgiveness of sins!" *Save yourself* from this corrupt generation! People were *devoting* themselves to prayer and thanksgiving, coming together with sincere hearts and praising God . . . and these were among those being saved! It is not a prayer we pray that saves us . . . it is the repentance of our ways and a dire devotion to crying out and giving thanks for mercy, grace, and compassion (Acts 2). It is not a prayer that makes you a Christian! You become a Christian when you begin to suffer on behalf of God's pain, exclaiming the need to be used like a sheep among wolves, and for God to toss you into a world of hate to be used as a lure of love! Until you are Christlike, you are not a Christian; you are someone seeking to be a Christian! *Seek the face of the Lord*, and until you see the tears running down His face . . . you will never know what you are crying out for!

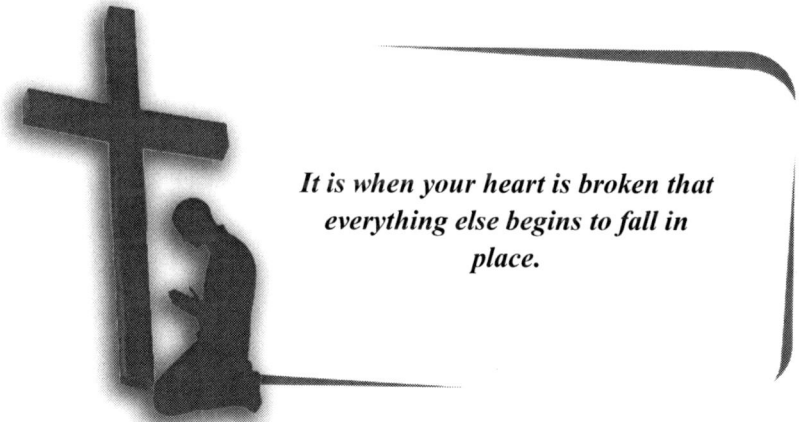

It is when your heart is broken that everything else begins to fall in place.

A friend told me that all he had to do is say the sinner's prayer on his deathbed and he would go to heaven. Religion! Accommodation! Tradition! Blasphemy! This has brought so much *condemnation* to the lives of millions! A misconception of this prayer has led millions in the wrong direction. I am not trying to tell you how you may or may not be saved . . . I am here weeping for you to understand the way in which you will be saved. Pleading for repentance of your sins and crying out for mercy lead to devotion and a life of being Christlike. You called on Jesus to begin a work in your life. The evidence of deliverance and being one who is guarded by heaven is when the work Jesus starts He is able to finish unto completion. You will find yourself in the worst battle of your life, yet living the best part of your life.

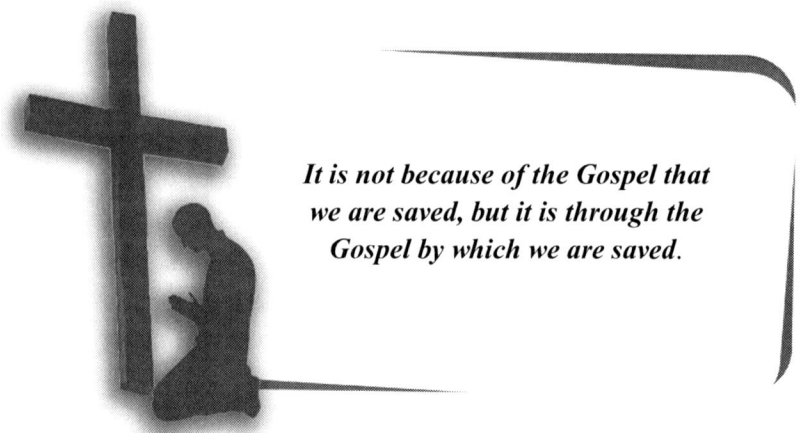

It is not because of the Gospel that we are saved, but it is through the Gospel by which we are saved.

Have you heard this before? *Maybe you came here tonight and you didn't know Jesus.* You think that by walking up and standing before a church altar because someone told you to go up, you will be saved . . . you will not be saved! You think that by deciding to go because a friend or family member walked up there first, you will be saved . . . you will not be saved! Even thinking that by walking up leisurely before a congregation and saying to yourself that you want to be saved . . . will not save you! Yes, and this is statistically proven. *So how then can I be saved?* You are saved when your heart has been broken, when your togetherness all of a sudden begins to lack portions, when repentance runs down your face, when your world begins to separate into pieces, when you are obsessed with a devotion to the king of glory and are falling on your face knowing you are not worthy of such a sacrifice! Believe in His name, and *you will be saved*! However, I must warn you. It is not crying out to Jesus once in your life that saves you; it is walking with Him for the rest of your life with assurance that you are saved that saves you! This is when we are secured with eternal life and lives are inherited into the kingdom of God!

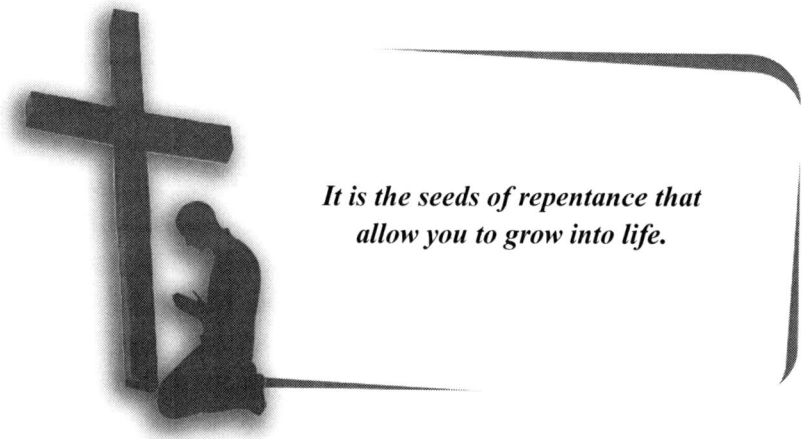

It is the seeds of repentance that allow you to grow into life.

I am not worried; I am troubled . . . without understanding the pain of God, you are not welcoming Jesus into your life; you are welcoming yourself into American Christianity!

Matthew 6:27: "Who of you by worrying can add a single hour to his life?"

> The first Gospel in the New Testament according to Matthew (tax collector), the evangelist and one of the twelve apostles. The account of life, ministry, death, and Resurrection of Jesus of Nazareth. (*Refer Matt. 6:19-34.*) (19) Do not store up for yourselves treasures where moth and rust destroy, and where thieves break in and steal. But store up for yourselves treasures in Heaven where moth and rust do not destroy. (21) For where your treasure is that is where your heart will be. Heaven is what truly matters because it is where the reward of our salvation subsists. (25) Therefore I tell you, do not worry about your life, what you will eat or drink; or about your body, what you will wear. Is not life more important than food, and the body more important than clothes? The birds are fed, and are you not much more valuable then they? O you have little faith. I *will provide*!

(34) Therefore do not worry about tomorrow, for tomorrow will worry about itself. Each day has enough trouble of its own.

Jeremiah 17:8: "He will be like a tree planted by the water that sends out its roots by the stream. It does not fear when heat comes; its leaves are always green. It has no worries in a year of drought and never fails to bear fruit."

The words of Jeremiah, the Jewish prophet who lived at the time of the destruction of Solomon's Temple in Jerusalem during the fall of the kingdom of Judah at the hands of Babylonia, predicting the reign and judgment of God. (*Refer Jer. 17.*) Jeremiah the prophet has felt more affliction than having favor of being blessed by God, struggling to walk in the will of God, believing that he was too young for the calling of being a prophet. Jeremiah began to believe that God was merely using him as an example of pity. Later we learn through Jeremiah that God calls us by blessing for blessing. We also learn very quickly that no matter what storm is pushed against us, as long as we stand on the Word of God, we cannot be withered! (7) . . . blessed is the man who trust in the Lord, whose confidence is in him. (10) I the Lord search the heart and examine the mind, to reward a man according to his conduct, and according to what he deserves.

Deuteronomy 1:32-33: "In spite of this, you did not trust in the Lord your God, who went ahead of you on your journey, in fire by night and in a cloud by day, to search out places for you to camp and to show you the way you should go."

The fifth book of Moses—these are the words Moses spoke to all Israel in the wilderness east of Jordan. (*Refer Deut. 1:6-40.*) Moses began to expand the law and said to all of Israel at Horeb that they would take possession of the land that the Lord had promised—not to be afraid, just go get it. After Moses appoints twelve leaders, one from each tribe, to help bear the burden and hear the disputes of the people, they set out for Kadesh Barnea. The Lord said, "Go take the land of the Amorites that

I swore would be given." The people went to Moses and asked to send spies to the land to bring back a report about the route they would take and the towns they would arrive at. So Moses selected another twelve to go ahead and spy out the land, and only two (Joshua and Caleb) returned with reports that the land the Lord was giving them was good. But the people were unwilling to go up and began to rebel against the Lord. The people thought the Lord brought them out of Egypt just to destroy them in the hands of the Amorites. "The people are stronger and taller than we are!" Then Moses pleads by saying, "The Lord is going before you and He will fight for you! In spite of the Lord helping you in Egypt and in the wilderness, you do not trust in Him!" Now the Lord heard what was said, and with anger claimed "Not a man of this evil generation shall see the good land I swore to give your forefathers." We learn in the opening of Deuteronomy that we must trust in God and not to worry even when the situation doesn't appear to be in our favor. *He is with you!* Always remember if God did it for you once, then He can surely do it again.

Philippians 1:6: "Be confident in this, that he who begun a good work in you will carry it on to completion until the day of Christ."

The Epistle of Paul. Paul and Timothy, servants of Christ Jesus, to all the saints, overseers, and deacons at Philippi. (*Refer Phil. 1:3-9.*) Paul wrote this Epistle while in prison, confirming and defending the Gospel. Paul prays on their behalf that their love may abound more in knowledge and depth of insight so they may know what is best and continue to do what is pure and blameless until the day of Christ. Praying that the work they called Jesus to begin in them, Jesus is able to carry on to completion until the day they meet.

Matthew 7:21: "Not everyone who says to me, 'Lord, Lord,' will enter in the Kingdom of Heaven, but only he who does the will of my father who is in Heaven."

The first Gospel in the New Testament according to Matthew (tax collector)—the evangelist and one of the twelve apostles. The account of life, ministry, death, and Resurrection of Jesus of Nazareth. (*Refer Matt. 7:15-23.*) You will recognize a Christian, preacher, person of faith, or prophet by their fruit. (15) . . . They come to you in sheep's clothing, but outwardly they are ferocious wolves. (18) A good tree cannot bear bad fruit, and a bad tree cannot bear good fruit. (19) Every tree that does not bear good fruit is cut down and thrown into the fire. (20) Thus, by their fruit you will recognize them. (22) Many will say to me on that day, Lord, Lord, did we not prophesy in your name, and in your name drive out demons and perform many miracles? (23) Then I tell them plainly, I *never knew you. Away from me, you evildoers!* (emphasis mine)

*What is the difference between patience and laziness?
Patience is always eager for something to happen, while
laziness is hoping that nothing will ever happen.*

INFLUENCE OF PATIENCE

*A restless individual will stumble upon a premature
opportunity, but a patient individual will humble himself
into a prepared opportunity.*

Jesus said to me, *Patience gives Me time to work, arrange, and develop.*

Patience is an endurance that exhibits a type of courage that a single person demonstrates in order to overcome various conditions. The level of endurance that must be sustained in order to pursue, obtain, and achieve is the most difficult part of any success in life, and it is the most crucial aspect of acquiring Godly desires. Patience gives you a portion of life that is so crucial—time. Time allows you to be collective, controlled, and unchained about the worries of being rushed. When your patience runs thin, sit it on the couch and give it some food. Every necessity we desire in our daily life should always start off with a plate of patience because the ingredients in patience calls for milk and honey—riches and glory. Having Jesus fully expressed in your life is the equivalent to receiving the greatest representation of riches and glory.

Patience will always present our milk and honey.

Let's use the sport of boxing as an example because it is understood by those who have been an underdog in a big bout. Our biggest victories in life are like a fight against an opponent that is bigger and stronger than we are. You cannot beat them by trying to overpower them or by trying to be a warrior, but rather by being patient and allowing your opponent to grow weary and weak. You have to allow them to make the crucial mistakes of being overanxious and restless. This is a fight where irritability will cause defeat and a fight that must go the distance to be won. Being patient may seem like forever in the fight of your life, but you're wearing down your opponent's opportunities while strengthening yours. You don't have to start off stronger to end up mightier. It all begins with patience.

Patience and reward are inseparable.

Patience allows every thought to be considered carefully and permits purposeful thinking, but most importantly, it gives us time to understand what Jesus is trying to arrange in our lives. *What would be the point of rushing if it never gives Jesus time to work and we leave Him behind?* God is required!

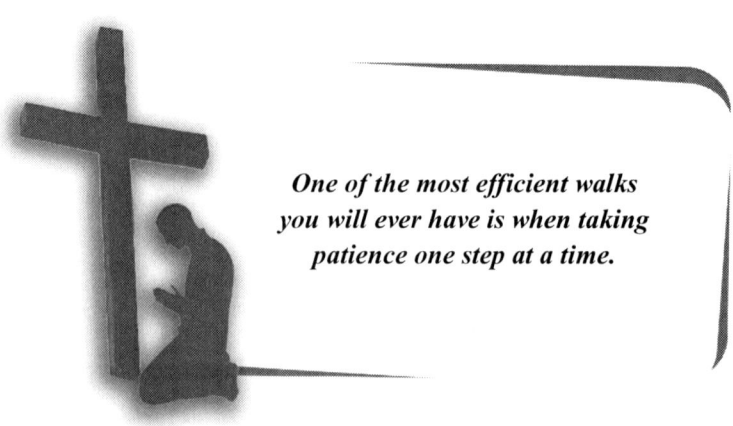

One of the most efficient walks you will ever have is when taking patience one step at a time.

Patience is closely connected to every substance that is part of God's divine purpose. It enables God to work not only in your life, but in the lives of those who are closely connected to the fulfillment of His plans. If you need finances to construct a distinct idea God has placed in you, then it is God who will work in the lives of others to provide for the idea He has prearranged.

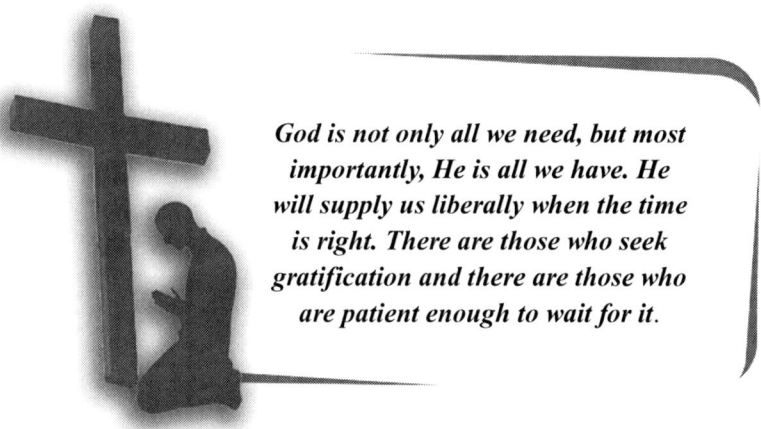

God is not only all we need, but most importantly, He is all we have. He will supply us liberally when the time is right. There are those who seek gratification and there are those who are patient enough to wait for it.

Everything God authorizes in our lives is for the purpose of a *result*. When you are patient, it is God's time to teach. He expands the mind, extends the soul, and enlarges the heart strictly for the purpose of making room for what He is going to *fill* you with. The more patient we are, the more He can teach, the more He can expand, and the more He is able to fill. How can you have the fullness of God without going through the infilling of God?

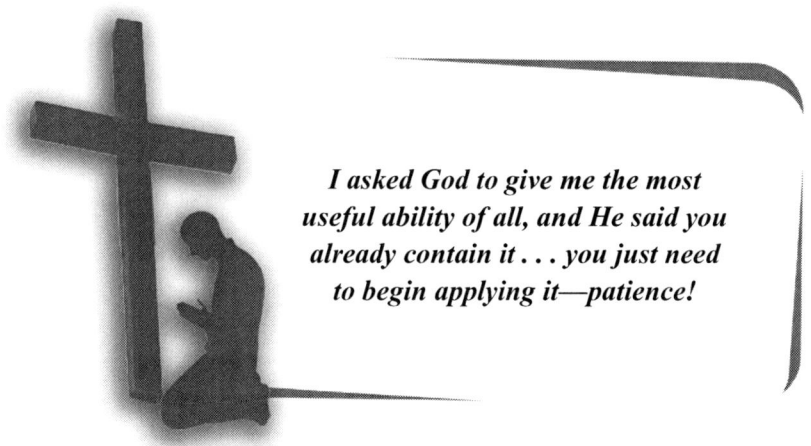

I asked God to give me the most useful ability of all, and He said you already contain it . . . you just need to begin applying it—patience!

The road to righteousness will always have pit stops of sincerity, the fueling of promise, and the destinations of rewards. Everything we receive starts with patience and ends with obedience. Remember that God's road of purpose and reward is a learning journey. You must take the time to learn what God is preparing you for, what your purpose is, and what you will do with the tools and blessings that God is constantly giving you.

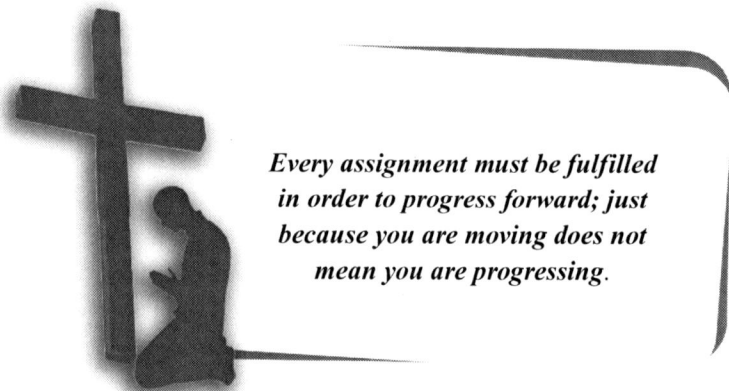

Every assignment must be fulfilled in order to progress forward; just because you are moving does not mean you are progressing.

Patiently observe, learn, and preserve the instruction and process of God. Complete the assignment! God's assignments for you now are current developments into future reasons. You must protect everything God gives because He will not give you something you have no need for.

Patience allows you to humble yourself into opportunity.

An assignment is a process in growing all by itself, but patience and obedience will determine how long you stay there. Whenever you feel moments of stillness or being secluded from the growth of God's rain, we must understand that dry time is testing time. God takes no days off, and He will not abandon you. He just steps to the side to see what you will do in moments of discomfort. The Lord's testing is out of an enduring love to show us how powerful we can be because of Him. Testing time is growing time. Whenever we are tested, we are being developed and prepared for the future. If you don't pass a test, you don't move on until you do. Study God, understand God, and when God moves, learn to move along with Him. Everything starts and ends in some form of patience.

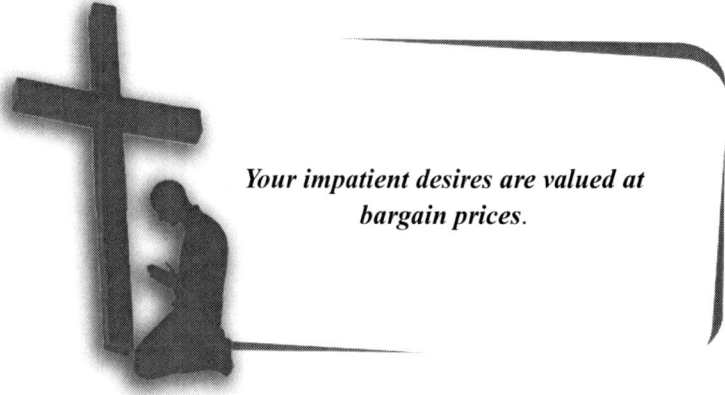

Your impatient desires are valued at bargain prices.

Being steadfast and patient will broaden the visions you have to begin noticing the small dealings in your life that are usually overlooked. Look to the small things, hope for a powerful move of God, but understand that even a nudge from God can leave a powerful impact.

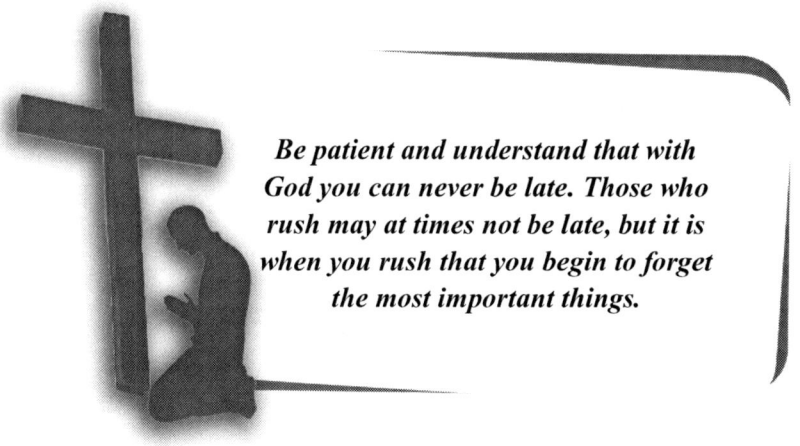

Be patient and understand that with God you can never be late. Those who rush may at times not be late, but it is when you rush that you begin to forget the most important things.

God manages the clock. God's timing is the right timing—He is never late. His time involves patience, and patience gives you experience, so when the time is right, you are able to deliver perfection. If you slow down enough to listen and see where Jesus is taking you, you might be surprised at what He is working out in your life. Don't miss that key turning point!

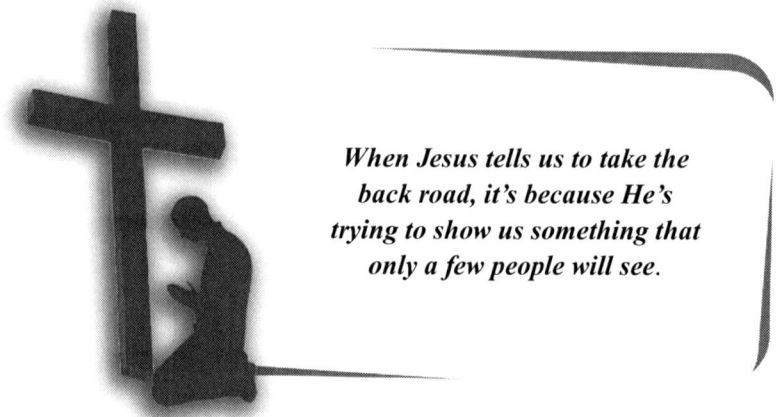

When Jesus tells us to take the back road, it's because He's trying to show us something that only a few people will see.

I Am Not Impatient; I Am Eager for People to Understand

You are not saved because Jesus hung on the Cross at Calvary. You are not saved because Jesus endured great agony. You are not saved because His blood puddle around the trunk of a rugged tree. You are saved when you lay your heart beside the Cross and your heart becomes the channel for His blood to live through you.

But I have tried it before; I gave Jesus time. **He doesn't need your time. He needs your life!**

I was told in 1997 that all I had to do was say His name and welcome Jesus into my heart and I will be saved. No, I cannot identify with that! What changed my life was almost ten years later when I hit the floor in my grandparents' bathroom screaming for His presence. Still for two years, I wanted a move of God, I wanted to feel God, and I wanted more than anything to know God! Then God did the best thing He has ever done for me when He laid conviction over me, and I absolutely fell apart witnessing my life as a manifestation of sin. I deserve His anger! I deserve condemnation! I deserve His wrath! You must know . . . it was my tears joining Jesus's blood that saved and changed my life!

This world is yet to comprehend what patience really is; it is God withholding His wrath and not spewing you out of His mouth, because of your lack of knowledge and disloyalty to the face of His Son.

I have lost many opportunities in this world, just to have one chance to find favor in God's eyes. I'll have you know that eternal life means more to me than anything this world will deceive me with. When you give everything up, it's in hope that something better will come along. When I give everything up, it goes up . . . where I am storing up treasures in heaven. Search your heart diligently, and whatsoever you desire, ask yourself if it is for God's gain or your personal gain. Is it a "*I will make it benefit God,*" or rather "*Lord give me only whatsoever is for your benefit*"? Search your heart diligently and again ask yourself, do you spend your time with God asking and then searching, or do you spend it praying and then serving?

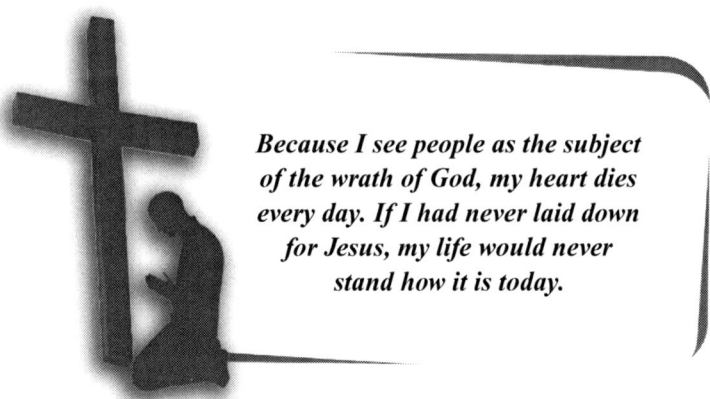

Because I see people as the subject of the wrath of God, my heart dies every day. If I had never laid down for Jesus, my life would never stand how it is today.

How did I get to this point? God took me to an unreached place to suffer in the dark, not because of the dark itself, but because of the people I see living their lives who don't realize that they are the faces of death. You will come to know who is a servant of Christ when that person's mission is to stay behind in the dark, just so he can push other people into the light.

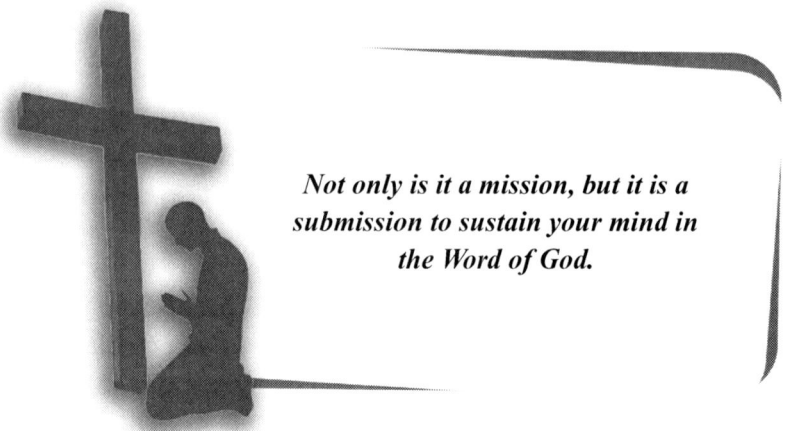

Not only is it a mission, but it is a submission to sustain your mind in the Word of God.

I am captivated by the Word of God, because the core of the Gospel is the fullness of Christ. It is the doctrine of principality and power. How do I know that Christians are not reading the Word of God like they should? Because when you ask Christians if they could ask God one question, why is it that they always ask a question the Bible has already given the answer to? Nothing is complete unless it goes through the Word of God to understand how we can live within Him. Calling on Jesus is not equal to Jesus standing with you. Professing that I am a Christian holds no validity if I have to tell someone I am a Christian. If a person can walk with God and soon turn away from Him, it is evidence that he did not have God. If a person can feel a move of God and soon turn away because he is lonely, it is evidence that he never had a touch of God. There is one thing that you can be certain of . . . if God has saved any person, then that person has been changed. It is a shame when someone tells me that I am different, because I should remind them of someone they know . . . Christ—didn't you say you had a relationship with Him?

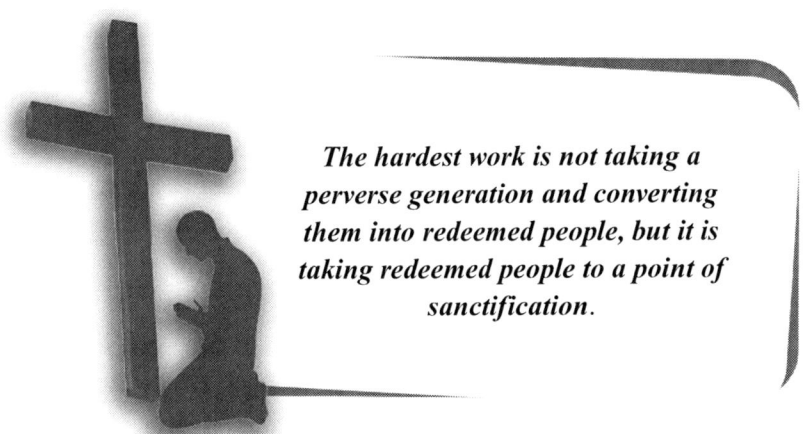

The hardest work is not taking a perverse generation and converting them into redeemed people, but it is taking redeemed people to a point of sanctification.

Proverbs 19:11: *"A man's wisdom gives him patience; it is to his glory to overlook an offense."*

> The purpose of the Proverbs of Solomon, the son of David, king of Israel, is to know wisdom and instruction, knowledge and discretion. (*Refer Prov. 19:8-23.*) (8) He who gets wisdom loves his own soul; he who cherishes understanding prospers. (15) Laziness brings on deep sleep, and the shiftless man goes hungry. Patience! Many are the plans in a man's heart, but it is the Lord's purpose that prevails. The fear of the Lord leads to life: one rests, untouched by trouble.

2 Corinthians 1:6: *"If we are distressed, it is for your comfort and salvation; if we are comforted, it is for your comfort, which produces in you patient endurance of the same suffering we suffer."*

> The Second Epistle of Paul, an apostle of Christ Jesus by the will of God, to the church in Corinth. (*Refer 2 Cor. 1:3-10.*) We serve a God of all comfort, who will comfort us in our times of trouble, so we can comfort those in trouble with the comfort we ourselves have received from God. *Very important!* (5) For just as the sufferings of Christ *flow over* into our lives, so also through Christ our comfort overflows. Just as we share in sufferings, we also share in comfort. We are under great

pressure, far beyond our ability to endure. In our hearts we felt the sentence of death. But this happened that we might not rely on ourselves but on God.

James 5:7: "Be patient, then, brothers, until the Lord's coming. See how the farmer waits for the land to yield its valuable crop and how patient he is for the autumn and spring rains."

The Epistle of James, a servant of God and the Lord Jesus Christ, to the twelve tribes scattered abroad. (*Refer James 1:7-12.*) Stand firm because the Lord is coming near. Do not place your misery on objects that corrode like silver and gold. Do not grumble against each other or you will be judged. The judge is standing at the door! There is favor and blessings that come with patience. (11) As you know, we consider blessed those who have persevered.

Proverbs 16:32: "Better a patient man than a warrior, a man who controls his temper than one who takes on a city."

The purpose of the Proverbs of Solomon, the son of David, king of Israel; is to know wisdom and instruction, knowledge and discretion. (Refer Prov. 16:17.) (17) The highway of the upright avoids evil; he who guards his way guards his life. (18) Pride goes before destruction and haughtiness before a fall. Be patient! (25) There is a way that seems right to a man, but in the end it leads to death.

2 Corinthians 4:10: "We always carry around in our body the death of Christ, so that the life of Jesus may also be revealed in our body."

The Second Epistle of Paul, an apostle of Christ Jesus by the will of God, to the church in Corinth. (*Refer 2 Cor. 4:1-18.*) Do not lose heart. Do not distort the Word of God. Setting forth plainly that we are commending ourselves to every man's conscience in the sight of God. For we do not preach ourselves, but Jesus Christ as Lord, and ourselves as your servants for Jesus' sake. Let light shine out of darkness. (8) We are hard pressed on every side, but not crushed; perplexed, but not in despair; persecuted, but not abandoned; struck down, but not destroyed. With Christ in us, glory is revealed. Inwardly, we are being renewed day by day.

Success is not always doing everything you can, but rather it's "doing" . . . what you can't.

INFLUENCE OF SUCCESS

Success is not established by following footprints; it's established by leaving imprints.

Jesus said to me, *Do not become occupied by the remaining distance to success because it is a wavering figure. Realizing how far you've come is an entrenched feat.*

In life there are so many options that affect the way the future plays out. Every person has a dream, idea, or image of what could be, what he hopes for, or envisions what would have happened if . . . I would have taken a chance.

The hardest part of a dream is knowing why it was given, the most challenging part of an idea is wondering if it would work, the most difficult part of an image is figuring out how to construct it, and the most defying part of taking a chance . . . is not taking one.

The best part about having a dream is that it doesn't come with a blueprint. A dream doesn't need to know how to work; it just needs to be started. The most powerful aspect about the dreams the Lord gives us is that the plans He has for our lives will never go unattended. Answer the phone when God calls because one word from God can change your life, and believe it or not, our biggest hang-ups are on ourselves. Don't give in—give out and fight for success, because the visions we hope for are never what we imagine—they are always more.

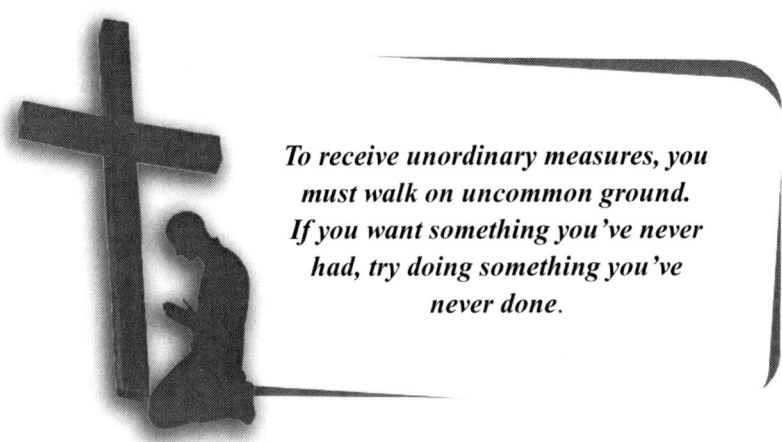

To receive unordinary measures, you must walk on uncommon ground. If you want something you've never had, try doing something you've never done.

Jesus has everything you need and is preparing a way of life for you without you even knowing it. Jesus requires attention and so does ambition—you have to desire more in order to receive more. If you falter and give up or become satisfied with where you are, that is where you will stay.

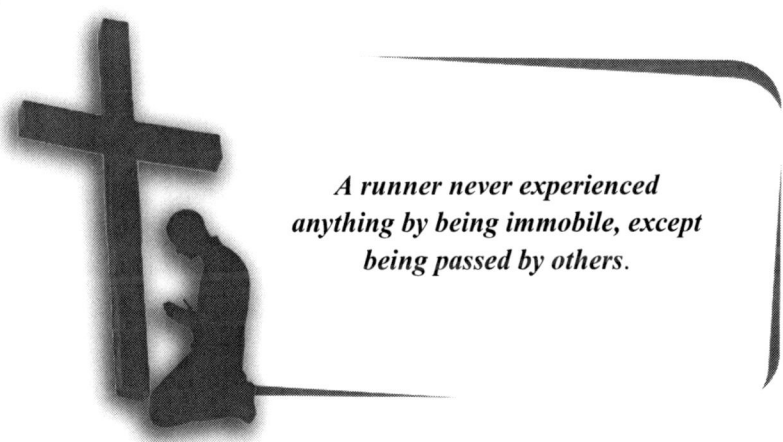

A runner never experienced anything by being immobile, except being passed by others.

Do not be discouraged by failure. Setbacks are actually a boost that brings you closer to your goals. If we never had problems, we would never know the power that gets us through them. You cannot expect to take delivery of success without expecting to take rejection en route.

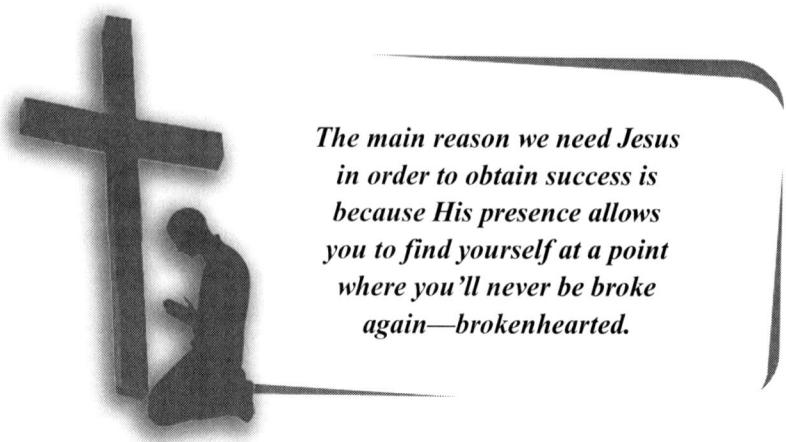

The main reason we need Jesus in order to obtain success is because His presence allows you to find yourself at a point where you'll never be broke again—brokenhearted.

It is at key points in your accomplishments when the devil stirs up mixed emotions and doubts and triggers crucial letdowns for individuals to lose hope. This is called the breakdown stage where the devil smothers you with roadblocks and wrong turns. Understand that hope is never lost, only at times, temporarily misplaced. The road promised by God is not an easy one. God allows difficulty in our lives to show us that simplicity lies within Him.

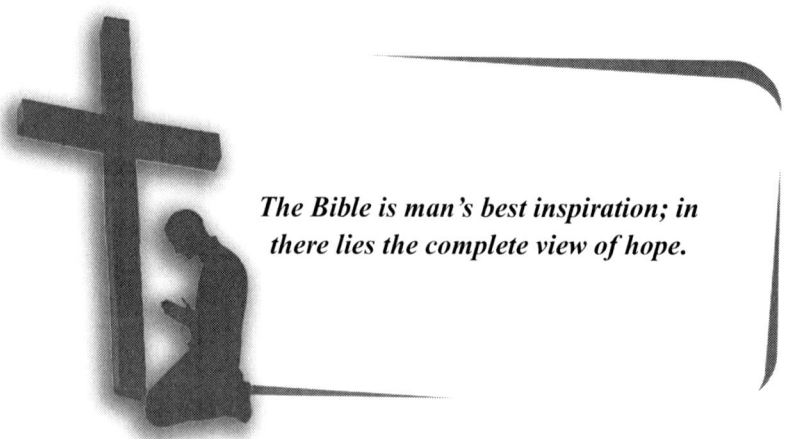

The Bible is man's best inspiration; in there lies the complete view of hope.

Allow Jesus to be a river in your life, because this means you're giving your consent for Him to have *His way* with you. Jesus will pour Himself upon you like a river, because a river does what it wants to do and goes where it wants to go. It is essential you know that by allowing Jesus to be the river in your life, it will always create a continual flow. Jesus says in John 7:37-38, "*If anyone is thirsty, let him come to me and drink. Whoever believes in me, as the Scripture says, streams of living water will flow from within him.*" We have to trust in the visions we have of where success lies, and earnestly follow Jesus, because nothing significant happens without releasing your faith. The size of the river is determined by the size of the faith in the believer. We must learn to walk in faith!

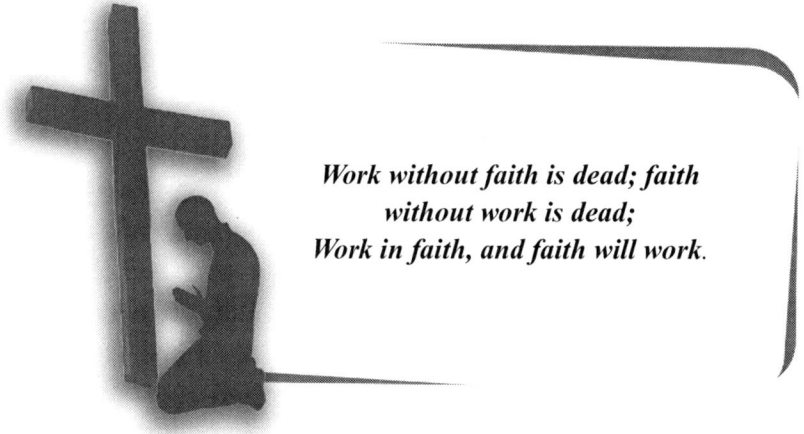

Work without faith is dead; faith without work is dead;
Work in faith, and faith will work.

If you're scared to get your feet dirty, put on your work boots.

There are two kinds of shoes that people use on their road to success—formal shoes and work shoes. Your formal shoes are the apprehensive pair that gives concern to what type of ground they walk on—they walk nervously and are conscious of each step, and they cannot be worn in bad weather or they will be thrown out or thrown to the side.

Your work shoes are your gritty, worriless, tough terrain pair that give no attention to the discomfort of the rugged road they walk on. No matter the weather, these shoes continue to serve their purpose—to work. If you're concerned about the path that lies ahead, then *you will do more worrying than actual walking*. Give Jesus the worries and put on your work shoes because "*whether you turn to the right or to the left, your ears will hear a voice behind you, saying, 'This is the way; walk in it'*" (Isa. 30:21).

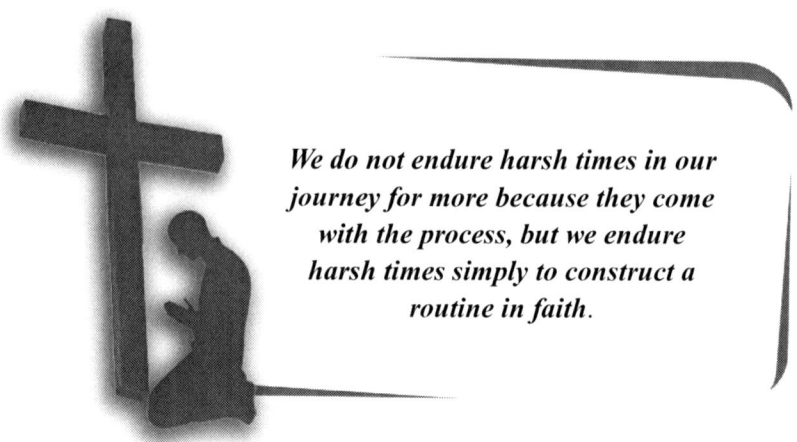

We do not endure harsh times in our journey for more because they come with the process, but we endure harsh times simply to construct a routine in faith.

Where success is found, glory is suddenly awakened. Glory is far more profound, because glory is not success; it's the beginning of God's excess of blessings. *"To whom much is given, from him much will be required"* (Luke 12:48). Glory is reaping the harvest in full, the abundance, the treasure, and the beginning of something constant that only you can choose to end. God declared that He will bless specific people according to their faith, according to the fulfillment of their assignments, and He will bless them so that through them He can bless others.

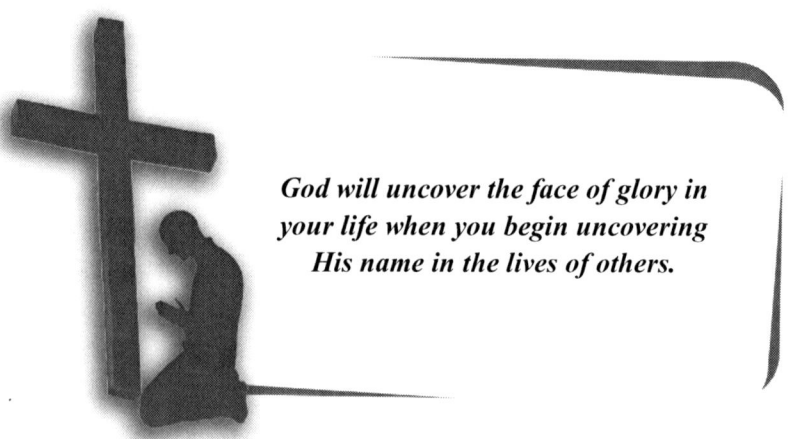

God will uncover the face of glory in your life when you begin uncovering His name in the lives of others.

This means that it's vitally important that you yearn to be a piece of good fortune for others and make yourself known to be a vessel and a blessing from God's hands, because men do foolish things when they crave wealth for their own power. Blessings can cause an extraordinary turn around in a single person's life and can give indescribable expectations for the direction of Jesus. God supplies His love of blessings upon your life for you to willingly plant seeds in other people's lives. Jesus gives glory in order to be glorified, and what He puts in you, He expects to be put out. Never lose sight of where success came from, and never curse yourself because of the blessing.

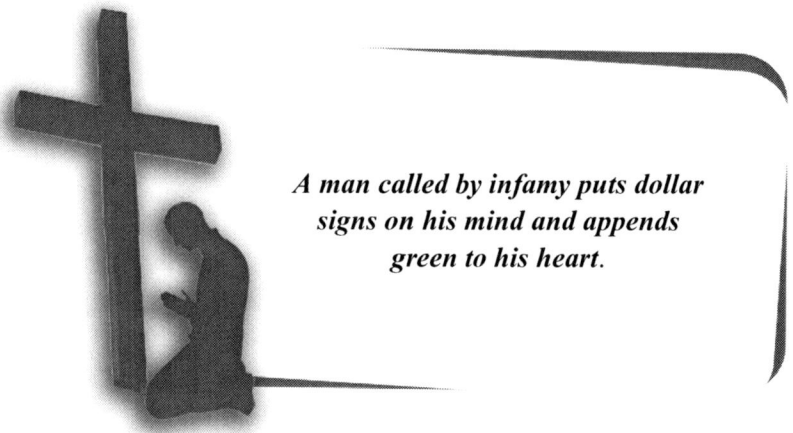

A man called by infamy puts dollar signs on his mind and appends green to his heart.

The kingdom is full of gold and riches. Money is like water to God. Don't you think that if it was the only thing He wanted you to have, then you would already have it? Instead, He knows it's what you want, and money doesn't build the heart, so before you get it, it'll be something the heart generously grows into.

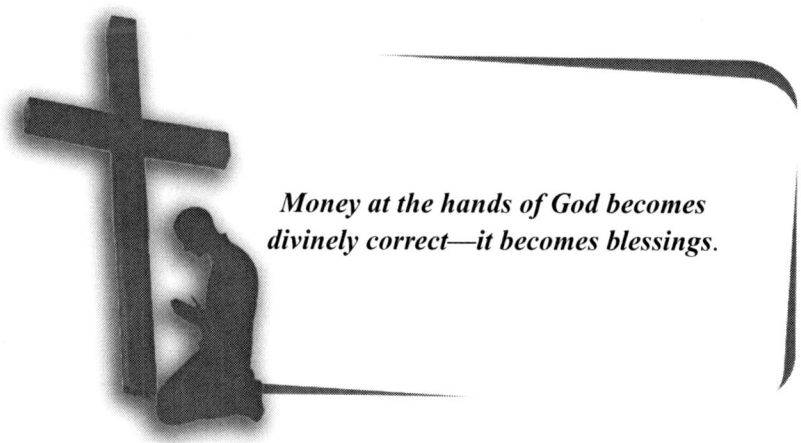

Money at the hands of God becomes divinely correct—it becomes blessings.

God uses money as a way to reveal the truth of your heart to Him, because people tend to put money before God. God gives money and success according to what your heart tells Him. God uses what most everyone desires as a way to determine blessings and establish Himself in it. God says, *What's more important, money or Me? You're pleading for money because all you have is two dollars in your pocket . . . but you have to give what you've got, in order to receive more than you've ever had. Do you trust Me enough to put Me before your money?* Your problems are not from a lack of finances; your problems are from a lack of God!

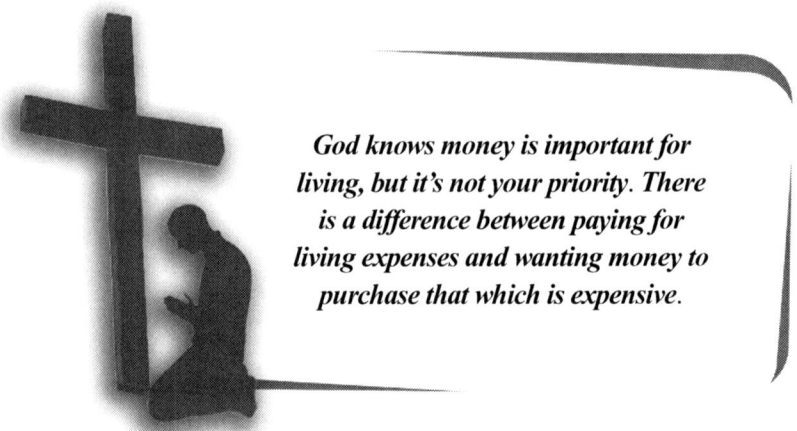

God knows money is important for living, but it's not your priority. There is a difference between paying for living expenses and wanting money to purchase that which is expensive.

So how do you receive money and how do you receive success? By not only putting God before it, but by also putting God in it. If God is not in your money, it has no value. God must have His Hands in everything. God is the accountant who dictates what comes in and out of your life account, which simply tells you that you are not in control of your money or your success. In order to receive any desire of your heart, you must go through God to get it. Do not base your income on the outcome of God, because money doesn't determine God—God determines the money.

Money is a natural disaster to the character of God, but having the character of God makes what's natural, super. Replace Me with money and this is what you will get:

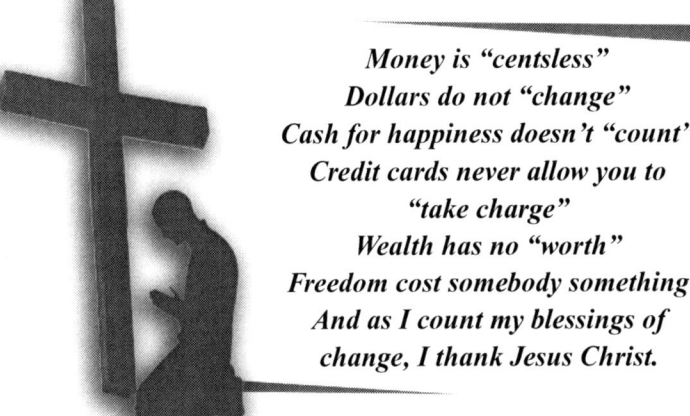

Money is "centsless"
Dollars do not "change"
Cash for happiness doesn't "count"
Credit cards never allow you to "take charge"
Wealth has no "worth"
Freedom cost somebody something
And as I count my blessings of change, I thank Jesus Christ.

In order for you to stand out . . . you must let God stand in.
If you're well-off without God,
You need to find yourself well-in His presence,
Because money will not save your well-being.

I AM INFLUENCED BY SUCCESS, YET IT HAS NOTHING TO DO WITH MONEY

Money, just like our modern-day practice of religion, wears the uniform of a prisoner. Unfortunately, in today's society money has become the central thought of Christianity. A pastor effectively told me the reason the majority of small churches cannot excel into a breakthrough is because they choose to focus on the "nice" things instead of the right things. He explained that Jesus never wanted the best transportation in His lengthy traveling, even though He could have commanded it to be done. Jesus never wanted the richness and splendor of the land, even though He could have prayed it into being. Jesus could have established empires, but instead, He focused on the right thing—touching and teaching twelve uncommon men. Churches will always establish the mind-set of men. If money is what you want, it will be greed that will always keep you *in need*.

    I fear that the world will determine the love of God on how they are redeemed in terms of money. People believe that life is established with money, when in fact Jesus tells you that money will ultimately kill people. Your greatest fear shouldn't be whether or not you will be able to pay for your bills due next week. Your greatest fear should be, *"Why am I so worried about whether or not my bills will be paid?"* Jesus will bless you with money when you realize that money is not available to you, but through you it's available for God. What kind of worth does your life have when you spend your life seeking money? Money has an enslaving effect. You see, I don't need money, because I know the value of living. My value of living is not based on the items I've acquired over the years that I will remain paying for—unnecessary bills. My value of living is not developing a financial plan to be able to acquire a future luxurious way of living. My value of living is understood and appreciated by the price that was actually paid for me. My life has been blood bought. It seems as if everywhere I go people are constantly telling me that I need money, mainly people of faith. Yes, we need money, but I don't need anywhere near what your terms of living costs! I am not focused on money, but am focused on first seeking the kingdom of God. Being as graceful as Jesus is and knowing all of our needs, that we might have life and have it more abundantly as we seek the kingdom of our sovereign Lord, everything else will be given to us. (Matt. 6:33 and John 10:10.) No, I will not be a poor man because I choose a suffering that is much greater . . . laying my life down for the Word of God, so that through my life the Word of God can be spread to the 2 billion people in the world who don't even know His name. What that simply means is you should reevaluate where your money is going and how your time is spent? What an easy solution, given that we live in a country that revolves around "entertainment," and we know exactly where our money goes. I see everything from God's perspective. I see a lost world that can be easily found. Do you seek God as much as you seek money and sources of entertainment? Where is your devotion to the Son of God? If you do seek God above everything, then this will probably bother you as well: Why is it that almost 90 percent of the Bibles in this world are printed in English, when only 9 percent of the world actually reads English? So where is your money going and how is your time spent? Why is it that over 2 billion people must go days and even weeks without eating, and you can say to yourself, "There is nothing to eat in this house," after pushing aside boxes and canned items throughout your food pantry?

So where is your money going and how is your time spent? Why is it that millions of people in the Two-Thirds World are walking around on blistering hot pathways with no shoes and wearing clothes they have been wearing for months, and you can leisurely browse through your dresser drawers and your walk-in closet and say, "I have nothing to wear?" So where is your money going and how is your time spent?

We study the Word for reformation of the Gospel, to clean up what we have misunderstood, not only for revelation, but most importantly, to know the true doctrine of Christ. I am the tallest man before men, because I live my life on my knees before the Word of God.

It is mortifying when people believe that the hardest part of the battle is waiting on bills to be paid, job promotions, business success, personal ventures, and relationships. What about your life being compressed by pain and suffering because there are un-reached people in the world, religious strife, babies dying, and you being pressed by demonic opposition every day? We should live each day as if we are on a mission—making our neighborhood, our county, our state, our country, and the world, a mission field. It is an indignity to the Christian name when people all over the world are suffering and all we talk about is prosperity! The essential shape of Christ's love for you is found in the suffering and pain you feel for others.

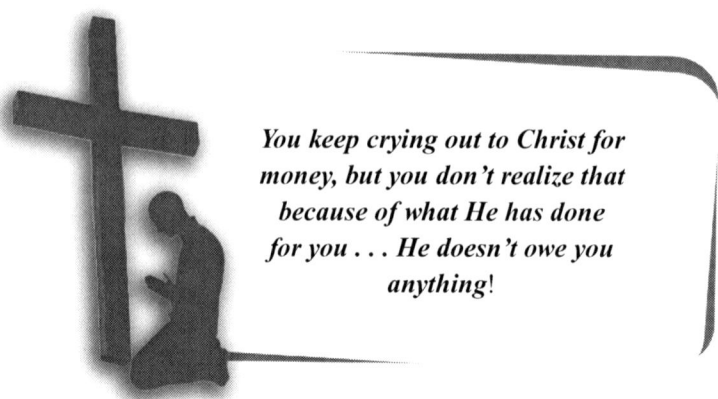

You keep crying out to Christ for money, but you don't realize that because of what He has done for you . . . He doesn't owe you anything!

If you cannot praise and drop to the ground for the sake of salvation . . . then there is a problem. The problem is not that God hasn't yet started working in your life; the problem is that you have not yet worked God in your life. The instant you feel God, you will be instantly reprimanded by guilt all in the same cry. At that point, your only sense of ease will be joining Jesus in His suffering. You will have a heavy, almost unbearable burden come and lay over your heart knowing that all around the world the Gospel has been incarcerated without visitation. There is a job that must be done without an expectation of pay, and a heaven that will open up and spit out a greater worth than gold. I live by this . . . not to compare myself to life, but to compare my life to His death. *Are you a man of God?* It isn't a fire that creates men of God; it is when the fire begins to burn in you for God to be among men. I am infatuated with Christ, and the Spirit of God is bearing witness over my life!

Somehow Christians have gotten the impression that prosperity brings happiness . . . buy into that and you are merely investing yourself into the business of religion. Have you ever seen a dying baby live? Have you ever seen a starving mouth get fed? Have you ever seen the face of suicide find hope?

Proverbs 8:10: *"Choose my instruction instead of silver, knowledge rather than choice gold."*

The purpose of the Proverbs of Solomon, the son of David, king of Israel, is to know wisdom and instruction, knowledge and discretion. (*Refer Prov. 8:10-23.*) (11) Wisdom is more precious than rubies, and nothing you desire can compare with her. (18) *With me* are riches and honor, enduring wealth and prosperity. (19) My fruit is better than fine gold; what I yield surpasses choice silver. I walk in the way of the righteous, along the paths of justice, bestowing wealth on those who love me and making their treasuries full. Now then, listen to me; blessed are those who keep my ways. Blessed is the man who listens to me, watching *daily* at my doors, waiting at my doorway.

Isaiah 52:3: *"For this is what the Lord says: 'You were sold for nothing, and without money you will be redeemed."*

The vision Isaiah saw concerning Judah and Jerusalem in the days of the kings of Judah. (*Refer Isa. 51 and 52.*) Going back to Isaiah, chapter 51, the Lord is called to an awakening and a plea for help. Then Jerusalem is called to awake from the cup of wrath in the Lord's hand. (52) Finally, Zion is called to awake and be clothed with strength. Jerusalem had turned away from the Lord our God and began to follow false gods. You have sold yourselves for nothing! Yet, because of the mercy of God, He said that they would have a chance to be redeemed without money. Because now money is worthless, it cannot bring happiness, and most importantly cannot bring salvation. The redemption God is speaking about is the price Jesus will soon pay for the deliverance and salvation of man.

Acts 8:20: *"... May your money perish with you, because you thought you could buy the gift of God with money."*

The Acts of the Apostles. Luke, the medical doctor who was converted to Christianity by the apostle Paul, began to write the accounts of the first Acts of the Apostles as Theophilus the businessman encouraged him, knowing that the inspired outcome of the Gospels would be by the Holy Spirit. (*Refer Acts 8:9-23.*) Simon, a sorcerer, had traveled around Samaria a long time astounding people with his magic. He eventually was converted into the name Jesus Christ with many others by the apostle Philip. When Peter and John heard that Samaria accepted the Word of God, they came from Jerusalem to pray that these people would now receive the Holy Spirit since none had received it yet. After Peter and John laid their hands on them and received the Holy Spirit, Simon, the once sorcerer, offered Peter and John money and said, (19) Give me also this ability so that everyone on whom I lay my hands may receive the Holy Spirit. Peter then tells Simon, (21) you have no part or share in this ministry, because your heart is not right before God. (22) *Repent* of this wickedness and pray to the Lord, perhaps He will forgive you for having such a thought in your heart. For I see that you are full of bitterness and captive to sin.

Matthew 6:24: "No one can serve two masters. Either he will hate the one and love the other, or he will be devoted to one and despise the other. You cannot serve both God and Money."

The first Gospel in the New Testament according to Matthew (tax collector)—the evangelist and one of the twelve apostles. The account of life, ministry, death, and Resurrection of Jesus of Nazareth. (*Refer Matt. 6:19-24.*) Do not store up treasures on earth, but store up treasures in heaven. Wherever your treasure is, that is where your heart will be. The eye is the lamp of the body. If your eyes are good, your whole body will be full of light. But if your eyes are bad, your whole body will be full of darkness. Now then, no one can serve both God and money!

Luke 9:3: "He told them: Take nothing for the journey—no staff, no bag, no bread, no money, no tunic."

The Gospel according to Luke, the medical doctor converted by the apostle Paul into Christianity and traveled with him in this ministry. (*Refer Luke 9:1-9.*) The twelve disciples have been traveling with Jesus, watching Him perform many miracles and healings, and drive out demons. After Jesus instructed the disciples on the Word from the kingdom of God and the faith they must have, he sent them out with *nothing*! The disciples' mission was quite easy considering the miracles that they have seen firsthand by Jesus up until this point. It was to preach about the kingdom of God, to drive out demons, and to heal people everywhere. It is important we know that this account of Jesus preparing the disciples for spreading the Good News "The Gospel" that they needed nothing but the power and authority He gave them to do it. This simply tells us that as people of faith all we need is his divine empowerment and Spirit, and it is impossible for us to lack or to be without.

I have heard so often that you don't know what you have until you've lost it, but for me I didn't know what I was missing until I found it—the God of love.

INFLUENCE OF LOVE

Sometimes it takes becoming acquainted with perfect love before all we know is how to give it in return.

Jesus said, *Love is essential to your following the will of God. It keeps hope certain, because if you look love in the eyes you will realize that love has a face of faith.*

The senses of the body have a variety of different meanings and intense emotional desires. This diversity of feelings is combined with a certain complexity that forms acts and themes into a person's heart, giving off a passionate desire that encompasses a particular wealth—and that range represents love.

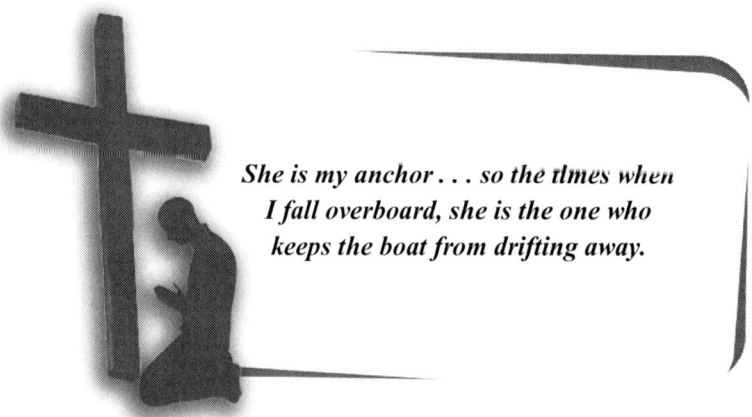

She is my anchor... so the times when I fall overboard, she is the one who keeps the boat from drifting away.

The possibilities of where love can take people are remarkable, and where many people hesitate with love is leaning on their own judgment and lack of understanding. There is a bond of love that replaces confusion with solution. There is no confusion with love as long as the foundation of the relationship is built with God. Love needs attention and a particular closeness that wraps two sternly in a womb. This bond or closeness that I am speaking of is a form of strand that when tied together with other strands cannot be easily broken. However, if a single strand would break, that strand would not stay broken and left for dead, but re-established as a stronghold, forming a weakness into strength. It is important that you know that these exclusive strands are only knitted in the hands of God.

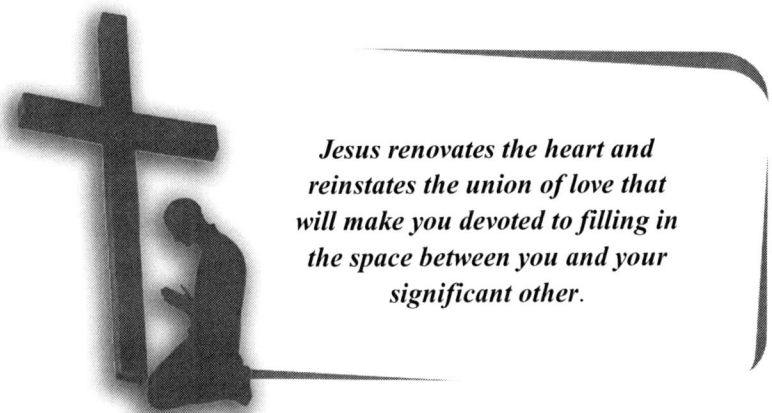

Jesus renovates the heart and reinstates the union of love that will make you devoted to filling in the space between you and your significant other.

The gift of love between two people can never be defined or be compared to anything worthy of a category. It would be a misdeed to place a limitation on something that has no limits. There is deep hole that lingers like a shadow where love is established, a hole that has no base. This hole was specifically positioned as love's shadow, so when two people fall in love, their love will never reach a base and they can always keep falling—*"falling in love."* Communication is the primary source in understanding where love can be honored and the way you keep falling in love, even after years of being together. A separation between communication and honesty is when love becomes worlds apart.

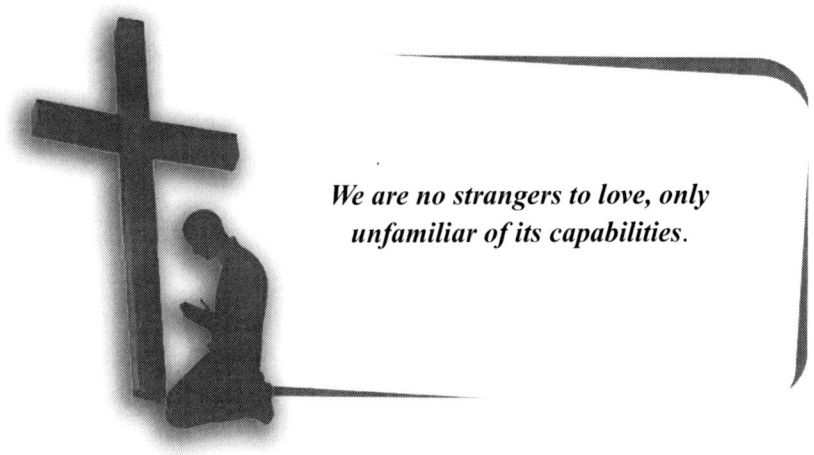

We are no strangers to love, only unfamiliar of its capabilities.

The Lord uses relationships to His advantage, placing love, faithfulness, trust, communication, and His presence within you. The Lord will deposit light upon your love to allow it to be understood. Why, because it's easy to breathe when you spread love in the air.

Perfect Love

Alone with God we can speak in neighborhoods, creating a block party of rejoicing; together with God we can speak to the city, creating a county revival; but as one with God we can reach the state, creating a world revolution.

Relationships must be consumed with mutuality. There will be plenty of occurrences when you may not accept one another's behavior, but you must keep your love constant. *I can survive without you . . . I just can't "live" without you.* Allow yourself to be patient with your significant other and yourself. Many arguments and wavering marriages are moment-driven, and often we speak out of irritation and not actuality. Sometimes we speak not out of disagreement with what the other person said, but in annoyance of why it was even brought up. Like my grandmother says, "We must choose our fights. Most are never worth it."

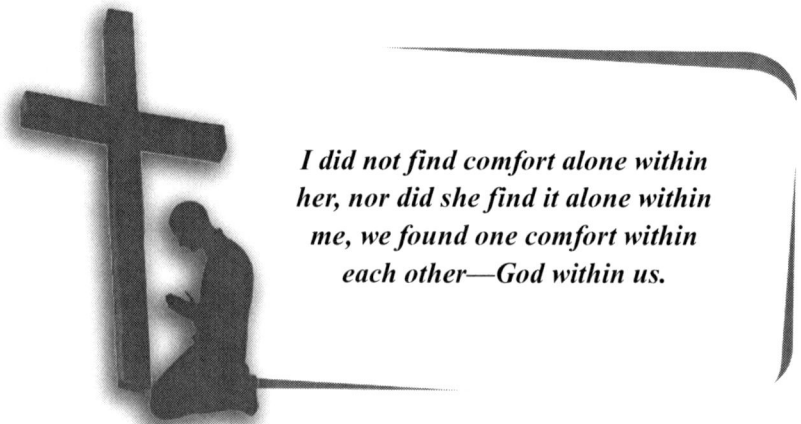

I did not find comfort alone within her, nor did she find it alone within me, we found one comfort within each other—God within us.

Love conquers even the highest aptitude of self-prosperity, and if we base our life on self-desires, such as our income, we lose the most requested yet least acknowledged achievement of fulfillment in our lives—*love*. What would be the purpose of being financially unbalanced and still lose love in the process, leaving you with less than what you started with? When all else fails . . . there is love! Place your companion above yourself and in return you will be given the same. Men, what is a married life with ignorance toward your wife? It is an overwhelming and uncomfortable picture of yourself married to *you*. No monetary value or personal desire can fill the abundance of one's heart like the love given to another person and within Christ. We must cherish the blessing of love that surrounds our life's expeditions. No matter how hellish my day has been, as long as my night ends with you, I can close my eyes and drift back into heaven.

A poor couple said, **We may not have a dollar, but with love we can still go anywhere.**

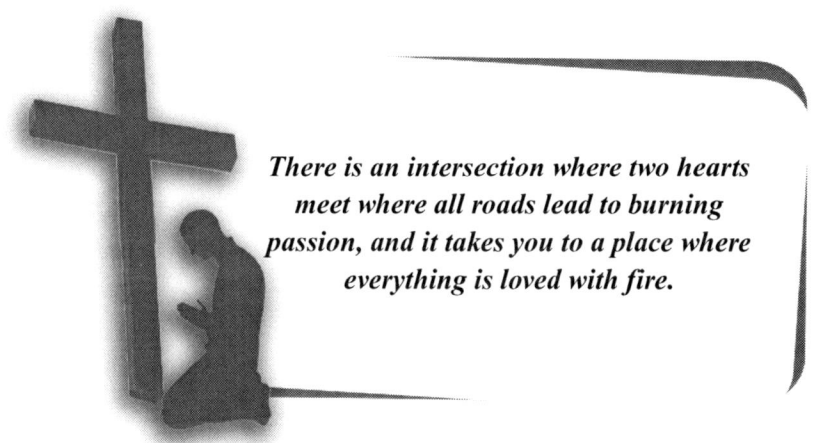

There is an intersection where two hearts meet where all roads lead to burning passion, and it takes you to a place where everything is loved with fire.

What if I am still searching for my significant other?

It is important that you establish your life on the perfect love of God, and then allow God to unite you with His perfect choice of companionship to fulfill that need for unconditional love in your life. Marriage is not only a deep desiring interest, but more important, it is a meeting of needs. Just like we have the need to know our reason for life, if we never followed God's will, then we would simply live our lives with a feeling of knowing that there had to be something better than this. It is the same with love. If you are not patient and you do not wait for God's consent to join together the perfect love for your life, you will find yourself with a feeling of knowing *that there has to be something better than this*. Love is also an original feeling that will never go away unless fulfilled.

In your beauty, my eyes have seen the sanctuary of heaven.

God will send the perfect love in your life because He is the master of love's perfection. Searching for love is the heart's dispute with the mind's urge to execute loneliness. Love is one of the few desires in life we must let find us. The more a person searches, the less particular the person becomes, consequently allowing the mind to settle *"with the next best thing."* It now becomes a great possibility that you will uncover yourself to the worst case of unrequited love, and you will find out that it's difficult to make the wrong person the right person. Ask the Lord to fill the lonely part of your heart and the need in your life for that precise indescribable love. Acknowledge that love must find you, because searching only creates a viewing from a distance and you may miss the opportunity of love within your presence. As the Lord fills this empty void, nourish it with constant love. Never let a day go by without letting somebody know they are something. Love is uncontrollable when you're with the right person; that's why we call it crazy in love.

My Story of Understanding

A woman desperately searching for the man of her dreams walked into a celebration dinner *accompanied by a prayer partner from church.*

Earlier that morning a pastor told her, "Love has found you, and it's patiently waiting for you." So the woman was enthused about the idea of the possibility of meeting her destined partner. As the end of the night drew closer, the woman still found no sign of her Prince Charming. Then, just before the end of the night, a tall man in a suede suit approached her, and they began a general conversation which led to him escorting her home. The enjoyment of her thinking that her long search for Mr. Right has finally ended came to a quick halt, only for her to find out he wasn't exactly looking for Ms. Right. The following day she told the pastor, "I didn't find love at the dinner like you thought." The pastor looked up over his glasses and said, "My dear, I said love has found you. In the disarrangement of your searching you blocked out the one person who knows you best." The woman asked, "*Who*," and the pastor responded gently, "He is probably still waiting to take you home from the dinner."

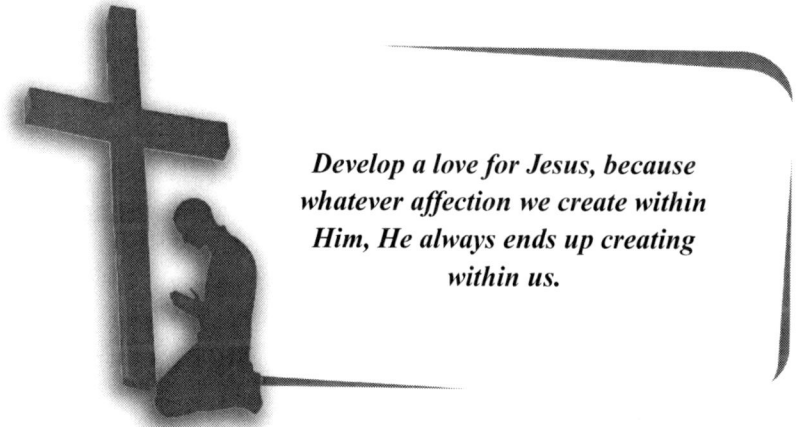

Develop a love for Jesus, because whatever affection we create within Him, He always ends up creating within us.

Love has no boundaries. Its growth depends on the providers. Be the support to each other's imperfections, and when your significant other is down, learn to bring them up or go down there with them to understand their hurting. Treat one another like a Christmas gift. Remember, when you were interested in a gift what you would do? You would go under the tree, pick up the gift, touch it, and shake it just to figure out what was in it. The best part of love is that you really never know the surprise or how special the gift inside is until it is opened.

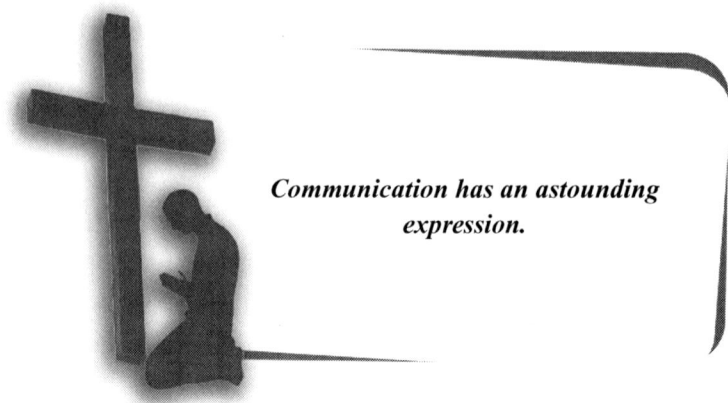

Communication has an astounding expression.

Communication is a connection with another person that permits the right of entry into understanding what's on the mind, what lies in the heart, and the direction into the furtive part of the soul. Without communication there is no sincerity, and without sincerity love diminishes. Communication is best when absent from claustrophobia, so words never stay routine or closed off, which will allow each other to open up and explore each other's ideas, thoughts, and dreams. She didn't change my life . . . she completed my life.

Communication creates a window into honesty. Honesty opens the door to trust. Trust builds a home of love. Love shelters the home from rain.

YOU ARE NOT BOUND IN SUCH CIRCUMSTANCE

Any man who is capable of hoisting his hands in anger toward his spouse formulates his own self-theories of justification or rationalization. There is no validation for peace in the midst of antagonism, nor can people be apologetic for something they are capable of repeating. Violence and abuse within a household cause the walls to plummet and brake down, leaving you with a "broken home." A man who has hostile intentions is also unreceptive to the Word of God. *"But if the unbeliever leaves, let him do so . . ."* (1 Cor. 7:15). A woman who is unsteady in mind may not logically make that vital decision to free herself from the disorder in her own home. The Lord said, "Each person should retain the place in life that I have assigned them, and to which I have called them. That is not to live in bondage! That is to live in peace, so it goes without saying, if trouble arises within those walls that take the desire of the Lord away, a believing woman is not bound to continue in such circumstances (1 Cor. 7:15).

The absolutely worse condition in a home is when children are involved in the midst of disorder. The violence alone can relentlessly impair parents' aptitude to nurture the development of their children. The love for your child is unconditional, but when abuse occurs, a mother becomes preoccupied by a feeling of hopelessness, and it results in her not being able to care for her child's basic needs. When children cannot count on their parents for practical support, it alters their development or, in severe cases, permanently distorts them. God is the shield that will protect you, to establish in you peace and comfort. He is the Father of mercy and the God of all comfort who comforts us in our time of need. Many times women convince themselves that they do not leave because of the children, but in situations of neglect the children must be disconnected from the muddled state of puzzled learning. The Lord places His children up under His wing and is the father to the fatherless. Children will be saved and will not be at fault in the midst of a crooked and perverse generation.

> *I told a woman who stated, "Mothers will never take the place of a father," that I begged to differ. I came from a physically and verbally abusive father who was content in making a product of him in me. Instead, it was my mother who taught me to be me and raised a man.*

God, Send me an Angel

The only way I can describe her love is that it's revealed as she rests her head on the chest of Jesus. Her thoughts are not of this world; they are that from above. God, send me an angel.

She sees the joy in a hurting world. She sees the possibilities in the midst of impossibilities. She sees the love in the center of hate. She sees heaven when going through hell. God, send me an angel.

She is solely given to me, yet because of the love that she has inside, I want to share her heart with the world. If ever there could be heaven in one woman. God, send me an angel.

She has Jesus in her heart. She has heaven on her mind. She has faith on her feet. She has the Word on her tongue. She has life in her hands . . . she is dressed in love. God, send me an angel.

There is a place where dreams come true, and I will take you there. There is a place where hope is alive and where visions breathe, and I will take you there. There is a place where love is the greatest of all; that's where I will build our home, and I will take you there. God, send me an angel.

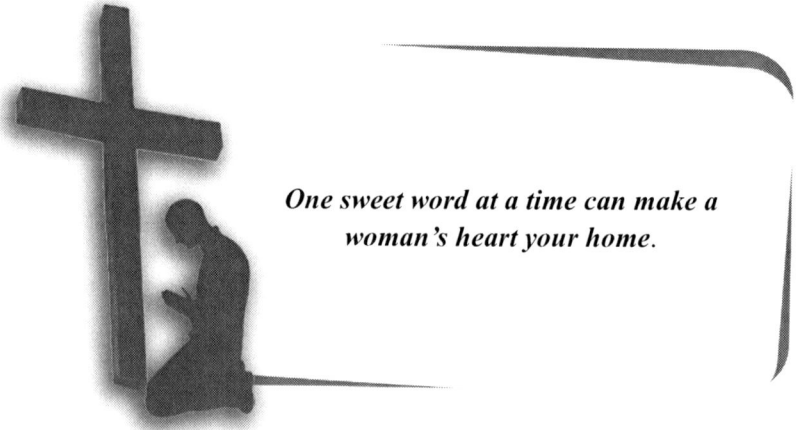

One sweet word at a time can make a woman's heart your home.

I will destroy the walls of prison that your heart has been confined to. I will place our love into the light, just so you can see behind that love is the shadow of angels. I will show you that I will never take love for granted or misuse its identity. Love is the closest understanding we will have to God on this earth, and I know that we will never get to know love by taking its name in vain. I will wrap you in my arms just to make you feel my love. I am not worried about trouble, because when you shut down and no access is possible, love will always find a way. Above all, in order for you to know the strength of my love, it is when troubles rise and hope descends that you find out what remains will be real. I will do all of this with complete liberty . . . because I want to *get* loved as well as I *give* love. God, send me an angel.

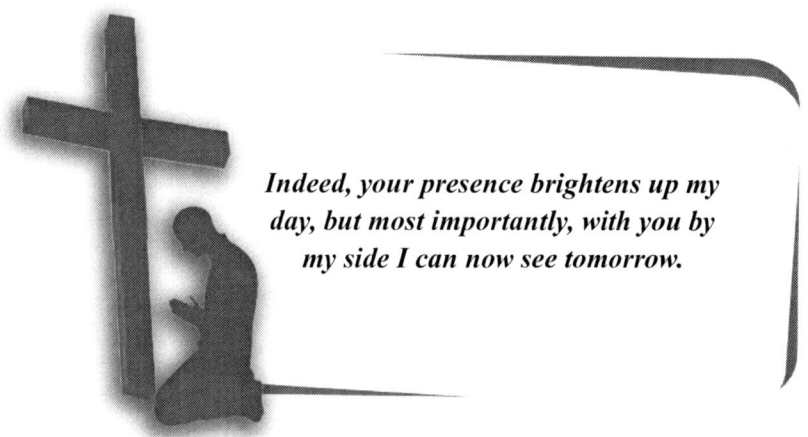

Indeed, your presence brightens up my day, but most importantly, with you by my side I can now see tomorrow.

Without saying a word, as my hands slide under your hands, I have found the greatest pleasure in your touch. I direct my thumbs under your eyes, grazing your tears just before they fall. Without breaking a beat my hands glide into gentle affection while slowly dropping down your cheeks. They are molded to love . . . these are the hands of love.

I have seen heaven in its greatest form. Laying my head on my pillow fixed on your eyes, I marvel. I have located a place of complete bliss, stopping the pursuit of happiness in your presence. I am infatuated . . . these are the eyes of love.

Without interrupting your heart that is playing my favorite beat, I draw myself closer and whisper heaven in your ear, the deserving angel that you are. What a breathtaking moment it is as I lie and listen to you breathe. This is the sound of love.

I have heard an angel speak with nothing but a smile. I will place your hands over my heart, just so you can feel it skip a beat, purely at the thought of you loving me. I have been made complete the instant that you spoke, when heaven opened up just to speak to me. This is the voice of love.

I was created by love . . . I was made to love . . . she will be loved . . . God, send me an angel.

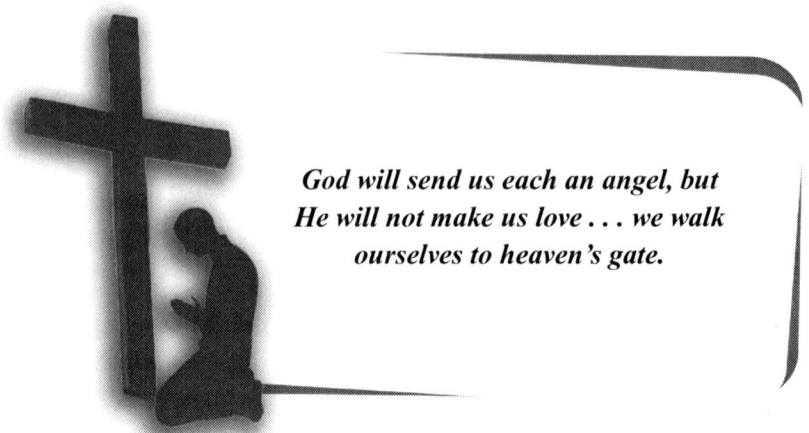

God will send us each an angel, but He will not make us love . . . we walk ourselves to heaven's gate.

Proverbs 3:3: "Let love and faithfulness never leave you; bind them around your neck, write them on the tablet of your heart."

The Proverbs of Solomon, son of David, king of Israel—for acquiring a disciplined and prudent life. (*Refer Prov. 3:3-28.*) Nothing you desire can compare with her. Long life is in her right hand; in her left hand is riches and honor. *Love.* She is a tree of life to those who embrace her; those who lay hold of her will be blessed. Wisdom in this understanding will set the heavens in place. Do not withhold good from those who deserve it, when it is in your power to act. Do not say, I will give it tomorrow, when you now have it with you.

Song of Solomon 3:5: ". . . Do not arouse or awaken love until it so desires."

The Songs of Solomon. (*Refer Song of Sol. 3:1-5.*) I look for the one that my heart loves. I will search for the one my heart loves. I will continue to look but will not find him. Let love find you!

Song of Solomon 8:6: "Place me like a seal over your heart, like a seal on your arm; for love is as strong as death . . ."

The Songs of Solomon. (*Refer Song of Sol. 8:6.*) Love burns like a blazing fire, like a mighty flame. Many waters cannot wash it away.

1 Corinthians 13:13: "And now these three remain: faith, hope, and love. But the greatest of these is love."

The First Epistle of Paul (called to be an apostle of Christ Jesus by the will of God) to the church in Corinth. (*Refer 1 Cor. 13:4-13.*) (4) Love is patient, love is kind. It does not envy, it does not boast, it is not proud. (5) It is not rude, it is not self-seeking, it is not easily angered, it keeps no record of wrongs. (6) Love does not delight in evil but rejoices with the truth. (7) It always protects, always trusts, always hopes, always perseveres. (8) Love never fails. When perfection comes, the imperfect disappears.

*Children are meant to dream freely. It is the parents' duty
to guide and protect those dreams.*

INFLUENCE OF CHILDREN

*Love for your children is one thing you can constantly
admire, because it will never be worn away with time and use.*

Jesus said, *Children are a source of pleasure from God because they are meant to make the displeasing things in life seem so unimportant. I will not only work in you, but the work that I've done in you, will also be for your children's advantage.*

The most effective results that parents will have toward their children are when disciplining *themselves* for a poor example of living. Do not teach your children not to become like you! Instead, change yourself and set high standards of character within yourself so you wouldn't mind if your children began mimicking your quality of life. If you always hide your faults, children can never learn from your mistakes, and neither will you. A child can enlighten the way for many others to grow, but parents must first be enlightened themselves before trying to impart quality principles for a child's growth.

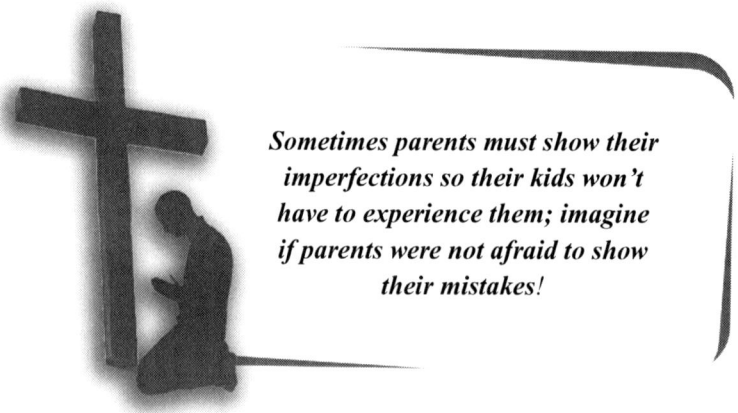

Sometimes parents must show their imperfections so their kids won't have to experience them; imagine if parents were not afraid to show their mistakes!

Children are a shadow of your every move—what you do, they will do; how you act, they will act; what you say, they will say; what you are, they will have the tendency to become. God gives children wings to fly, and their parents can show them how they actually work. Not only do your kids need your helping hand, but most importantly, they need the hand of God lying over their lives. Point your children to the Cross and allow them to understand that Jesus is the way. Imagine all the mistakes you've ever made; now imagine raising your kids around those mistakes without God. Even though you're not bringing them up in those mistakes . . . those mistakes are still there. So when you send them off on their own, it is highly possible that without your kids knowing "The Way," they may wander into the same mistakes you have built them around. If parents took the time to simply direct their children toward the Cross, it would instill in them a moral obligation to continue to follow the Cross.

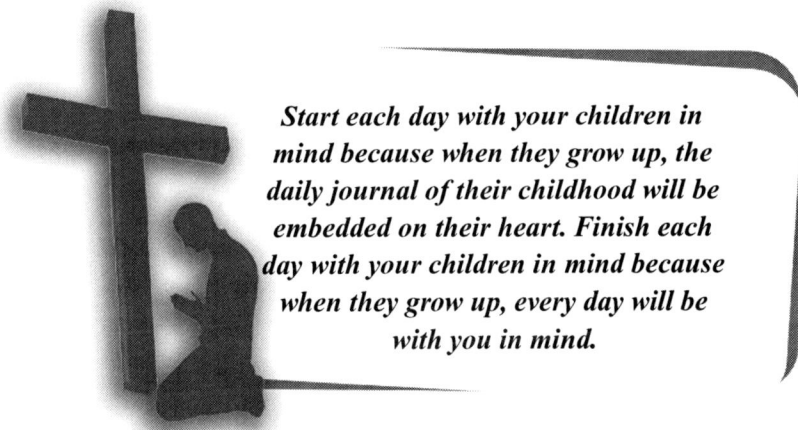

Start each day with your children in mind because when they grow up, the daily journal of their childhood will be embedded on their heart. Finish each day with your children in mind because when they grow up, every day will be with you in mind.

"I want what's best for my children." If you truly want **the best** for your children, show them who, what, and where the best is. When your children are not within your presence, their motives will be based on *who* they know, their character will be based on *what* they know, and their direction will be based on *where* they know to go. God is the best. He knows what the best is, and He knows where the best is for you. God's motive is always Himself! We are the center of His world. God is the best, and if He gives us any less, then He's not giving us the best. So where do you send your kids to receive the best life can give them? Yup, you got it! Jesus has prepared a meal that must be served regardless of whether your kids don't want to attend church, read the Bible, or listen to who He is. Your children have more of a hunger for God than you realize, but because of the table you sit at and the plate

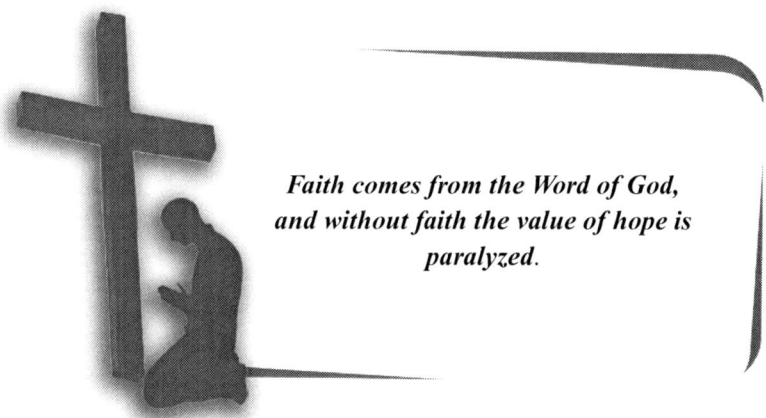

Faith comes from the Word of God, and without faith the value of hope is paralyzed.

Whatever you do, do not give your children a time frame for maturity; allow them to freely develop into what God has brought them here for. Parents, take the time yourselves to watch your children grow and see the unfolding of the Word right before your eyes. Teach your kids to understand that excellence makes people nervous. They are uniquely created by God for a unique purpose. This will allow them *not* to let people's opinions alter who they are or change their personality, because it may not mean much to that person, but it can mean the world to somebody else. Don't let "*A*" word affect you, let "*The*" Word affect you. Inform your kids about social pressure and don't let them settle for anything less than scripture. If your child asks, *What if my friends don't believe in God?* Then you tell them that sometimes the only way people will come to know God is through the God they see in you.

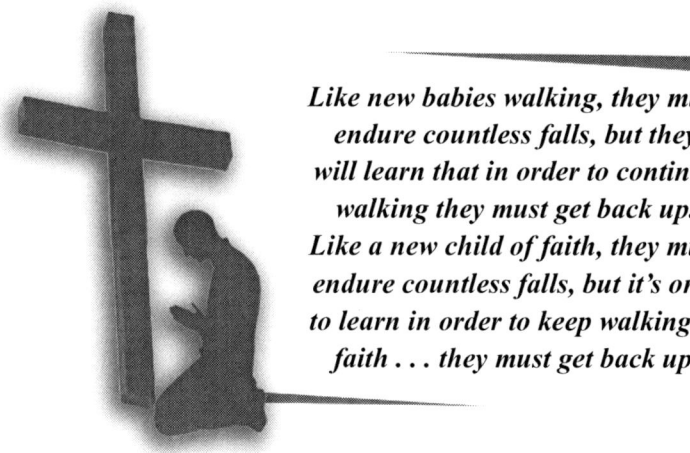

Like new babies walking, they must endure countless falls, but they will learn that in order to continue walking they must get back up. Like a new child of faith, they must endure countless falls, but it's only to learn in order to keep walking in faith . . . they must get back up.

Children need attention so they never wander into the wrong attention. Parents must stand behind the promises they present to their kids. They are no longer promises; they are obligations. Parents, be careful where you step, because you may be crushing your children's dreams without even realizing it. Most often, the most insignificant things to us that we overlook are probably the most highly regarded by our children. The absolutely worst thing you can say to a child is *"Not now," "I'm Busy,"* or *"Don't you see I'm doing something,"* because what you are actually saying is *"I don't have time for you."* Children may not know the concept of money or work priorities, but they do feel the concept of being *shut out, shut down, or denied.* When parents do this, they alert their child's subconscious to recognize when to avoid their parents *when they are busy.* Nine times out of ten it may not have been important, but it's that one time that could change and preserve your child's life; instead, they tried to avoid bothering you . . . w*hen you were busy.* As a parent, be sure to leave your children's dreams more alive than how your children described them to you. So one day you can say to yourself that my little man has found his buried treasure, and my little princess has found her castle. Then, you will be able to see your own dreams established when you have raised a tender warrior and a sovereign princess. Following your children's dreams is what makes parents heroes in their kids' eyes. As a father, you will enjoy overhearing conversations between your son and his friends, just for that moment of hearing his sentimental response: my dad can beat up your dad!

Always make sure your children know they can speak to you about anything. There are going to be conversations, questions, and problems that are going to disappoint and frustrate you, but if your children know they can speak to you about anything without worrying, those conversations will present solutions and stepping stones for learning, not destruction and life-altering consequences.

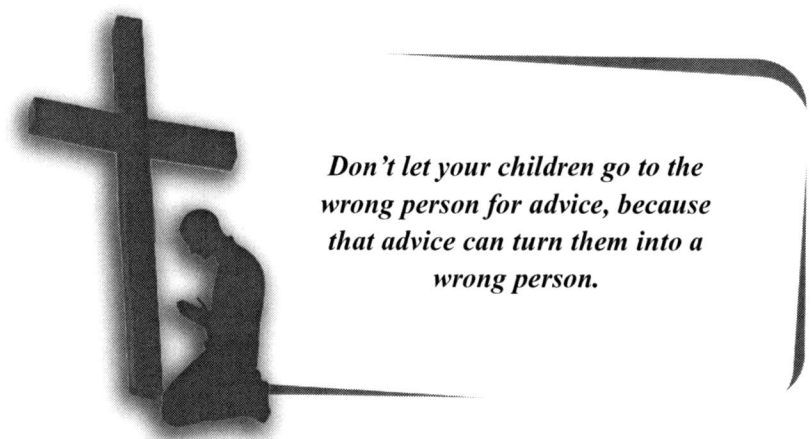

Don't let your children go to the wrong person for advice, because that advice can turn them into a wrong person.

Believe it to be true, when children feel they can talk and open up to their parents, their relationship extends farther than just being parents, but friends.

You may think your children are not listening, but they are listening.

Children have influential minds, which means they can be easily influenced into something they were never brought up to be. So, parents, go easy on yourself because sometimes children fall off course even with the proper upbringing. Just be sure to keep a close eye on the company they keep.

When you feel you have nothing inside, do you know what's important? This is why Jesus is so vital; because if you teach your children deliverance, they will know where they can go when they are lost, or when they feel they have nothing left to give, they will turn back to the only name that saves—the same name that you consistently praised. Even a nurtured bird must learn to fly on its own, but if that bird decides to fly amongst vultures and consume out of graveyards, the worst possible thing you can do is go fly with them. You must pray for salvation on behalf of your children, and it is God who hears, receives, and delivers our requests. It is the Lord who declares nothing is too big or too far-fetched for Him to handle or bring back to life. Use the power of prayer and the capabilities you have through intercession to restore lost lives. Do not go fly with them or give up on God because of the path your children stumbled onto. The restoring of their lives depends on your trust in God.

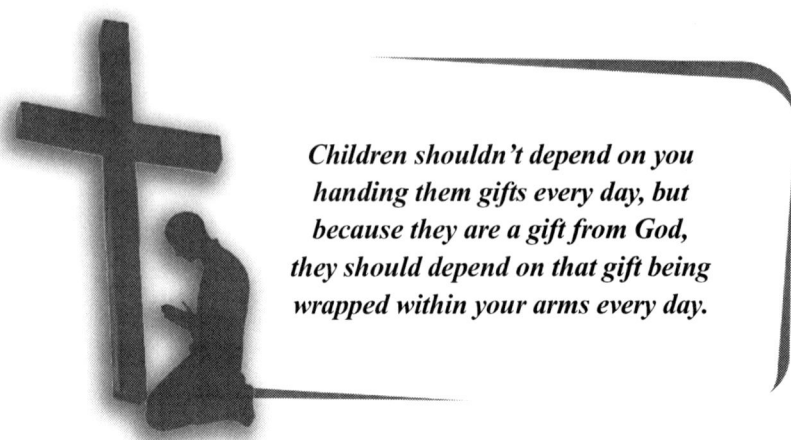

Children shouldn't depend on you handing them gifts every day, but because they are a gift from God, they should depend on that gift being wrapped within your arms every day.

Parents, live out your own instruction and pay attention to what you say and how you act, because you might be disciplining your child for simply being you.

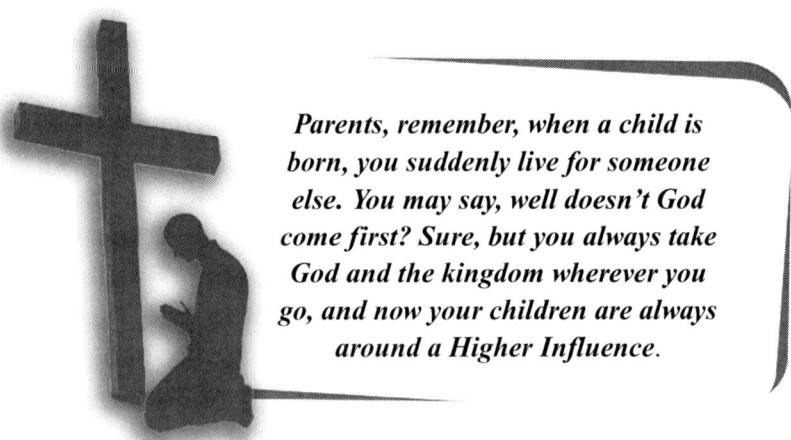

Parents, remember, when a child is born, you suddenly live for someone else. You may say, well doesn't God come first? Sure, but you always take God and the kingdom wherever you go, and now your children are always around a Higher Influence.

***Deuteronomy 4:9:** "Only be careful, and watch yourselves closely so that you do not forget the things you have seen or let them slip from your heart as long as you live. Teach them to your children and their children after them."*

The fifth book of Moses. These are the words Moses spoke to all Israel in the wilderness just east of Jordan. (*Refer Deut. 4:1-19.*) Instruct yourselves and your children with obedience. The Word of God will show your wisdom and understand to all. Listen to my Words so that you may teach them to your children. (Deut. 6:6-7.) These commandments that I give you today are to be upon your hearts. Impress them on your children. (7) Talk about them when you sit at home, and when you walk along the road, when you lie down and when you get up.

Deuteronomy 11:18-19: "Fix these words of mine in your hearts and minds; tie them as symbols on your hands and bind them on your foreheads. (19) Teach them to your children, talking about them when you sit at home and when you walk along the road, when you lie down and when you get up."

The fifth book of Moses. These are the words Moses spoke to all Israel in the wilderness just east of Jordan. (*Refer Deut. 11:2-22.*) Instruct your children to be obedient to the Lord. (2) Remember today that your children were not the ones who saw and experienced the discipline of the Lord your God: His majesty, His mighty hand, His outreached arm; the signs He performed and the things He did. You must do this so that your days and the days of your children may be many. Carefully observe the commands.

Psalms 37:25: "I was young and now I am old, yet I have never seen the righteous forsaken, or their children begging bread."

A composition of 150 different individual Psalms. It proclaims the work of God's hands, being the longest book in the Bible. (*Refer Ps. 37:3-28.*) (3) Trust in the Lord and do good; dwell in the land and enjoy safe pasture. Delight yourself in the Lord and he will give you the desires of your heart. For the sake of your children trust in the Lord, so in times of disaster they will not wither, in the days of famine they will enjoy plenty. Your children will be blessed. Turn from evil and do good; For the Lord loves the just and will not forsake His faithful ones. They will be protected forever, but the offspring of the wicked will be cut off.

Proverbs 22:6: "Train a child in the way he should go, and when he is old he will not turn from it."

The Proverbs of Solomon, son of David, king of Israel: for acquiring a disciplined and prudent life. (*Refer Prov. 22:1-15.*) A good name is more desirable than great riches, and what better name to implant in your children's lives than the name of Jesus. He who loves a pure heart and whose speech is gracious will have the king for his friend. Brighten your children's lives with the wisdom of God. The eyes of the Lord keep watch over knowledge, but he frustrates the words of the unfaithful. Discipline your children in the ways of the Lord. Folly is bound up in the heart of a child, but the rod of discipline will drive it far from him. (Mark 13:12) Children will rebel against their parents, but teach them the way that leads to life and when they fall off course they will remember their way.

you eat from, they are compelled to sit and eat as well. The greatest act of love that you can do for your children is placing them back into the loving hands of God. Save your children! Don't allow them to fall amongst the idols of the world where they will live their lives broken trying to please a mirror. Lay your children's lives before the altar before the world has a chance to alter their lives. Show your children that beauty is deeper than worldly standards and that strength can be found in the center of weakness. Push your children past barriers so they can feel what it's like to break down walls of rejection. Point out all the limits of this world, then take the time to walk your children past each limit, just to show them *there are no limits!* Allow your children to realize that trying to blend in with people will simply make them invisible to the world, but if they want to stand out, tell them to place the Word of God under their feet and stand up!

There is no greater joy than watching your children take their first step, and no joy greater than watching them take their first steps in faith.

The teaching of values is inexpensive; choose to take pride in your prize possession and don't put your kid's spiritual growth on layaway. Set an example for your kids. Don't just tell your children God is good; show them why God is good. Guide them into the right decisions, but allow them to make their own decisions . . . create independence. Independence will allow children to realize on their own that they have a purpose and an awaited promise for their lives. But instruct them not to look at the promise but the opportunities that allow them to get to the promise. Jesus has everything you hope for in your child's life. You cannot see what their future is; that's why you must have faith for everything that you hope for in their lives.

You will know if someone is reading God's Word, because he will be someone that God is working in. His appearance will start to transform. His vocabulary will begin to transcend. When God begins to work . . . the evidence will be there!

INFLUENCE OF THE WORD

We must first learn to listen to the intelligence of instruction to us, before we unintelligently speak words that lack instruction to others.

Jesus said to me, *In order to have relations with Me, you must have relations with My Word.*

I want to know the will that God has for my life! If God is going to call you to do something, it is without a doubt He is going to call you through His Word. The will of God is more sincere than we are aware of. The will of God is a distinct separation for your life to reach an elevated peak where you are not only seen, but heard for the glory of His name. The will of God is God standing in front of you dwelling in sorrow asking you a simple question—will you? Will you stand for my name even when the enemy has drawn you back? Will you still call out my name even after you sit feeling abandoned with no response? Will you behold my pain and consider nothing but scripture? Will you plead among the nation even when the gateways to heaven are desolate? Will you pour your heart out trying to save your brethren? Will you do this for God?

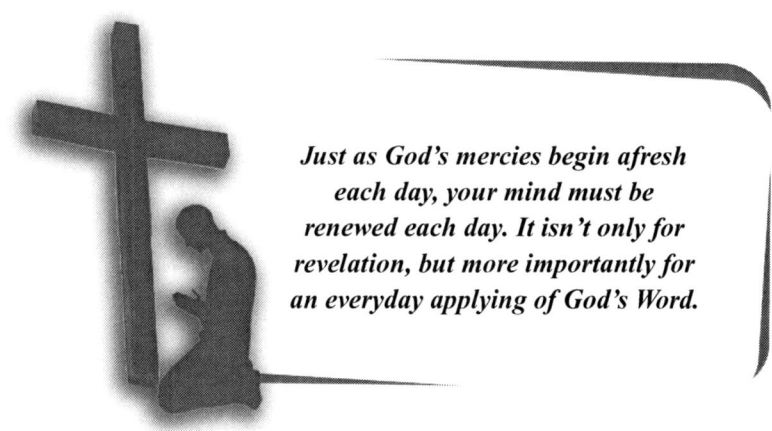

Just as God's mercies begin afresh each day, your mind must be renewed each day. It isn't only for revelation, but more importantly for an everyday applying of God's Word.

The Word of God is why we are faithful . . . simply to see if the Word of God *is* faithful. Going to God does not put you on His road; it is understanding God that puts you on His road, and it is continuing to understand Him by the reading of His Word that *keeps* you on His road. If His Word says you can have it, ask for it, and don't walk away until you've obtained it. There is a difference between ignorance and hunger for His dependable Word. My hunger motivates God to breathe over my life. Lord, you have told me that I can have all of this according to your Word. I refuse to leave Your presence until You bless me. I refuse to be denied until You lead me to the Cross and begin opening up my mind and giving me revelation without limits. I will fall before Your feet until you enlarge my appetite and allow me to drink from the cup in Your hand. Lord, if I am silenced before You, as my hands rise, fill them with a power that has been hidden since the beginning of creation. Sovereign Lord, through Your name the devil has no authority over me. I tremble before Your feet, but am filled with joy at Your presence. Deliver me according to Your Word, and as I wander amongst lions as a lonely sheep in a pasture, I will prevail against this world. Bless me O Lord! What is worldly wisdom when its wisdom is based on *a great effort of personal theory?* Filling the temple of God—yourself—with the secret wisdom of His Word creates in you an intellectual powerhouse, especially when the moment you open your mouth you can turn all worldly wisdom that opposes God on its face!

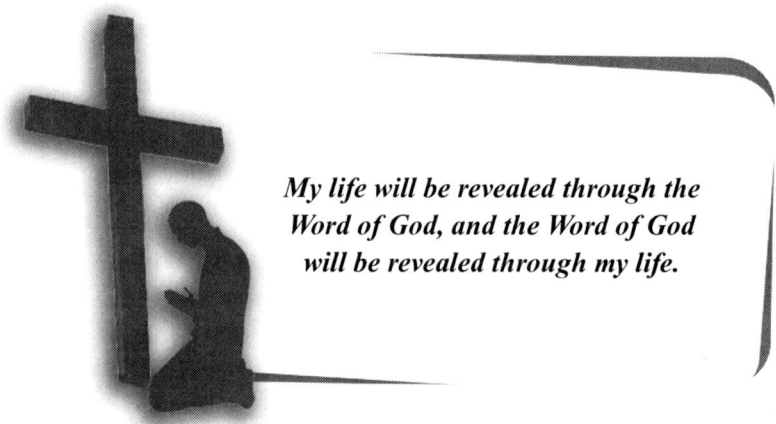

My life will be revealed through the Word of God, and the Word of God will be revealed through my life.

There is an instructive experience that the Lord gives according to the Bible. We must listen to the Word of the God, because in these Words the message of your assignments is revealed. We read the Bible because it has the confirmation of God's truth. This is significant because it allows mankind to be acquainted with the words God Himself spoke. The Word is also the passage that directs us into righteousness. The foundation of living or life is established based on the Word of God. The Bible shows God is God, the Bible demonstrates the incredible, and the Bible establishes the impossible. Scripture is not difficult; it is just undeniably different than what you are accustomed to. Scripture is a supply of sheltering bliss. *Why do we choose to take an axe and chop down scripture when we don't understand what it means right away?* When doing this it does not provide room for opportunity, but rather widens the area for unwanted development from the devil's senseless diversions. Whenever you assume situations in life are difficult, you are blatantly confining God that has no limits with a boundary line. If something appears to be hard or difficult to do or comprehend, look beyond the adjacent "impossible" sign and realize it's God waving you through. The purpose of reading the Word is to gain knowledge and instruction for our righteous way of living. Jesus taught His disciples that the power behind miracles is the belief you put in front of it. The Word is as important as your prayer, because the Word is what allows God to be heard . . . and prayer is what allows you to be heard. This question, not too long ago, was brought to my attention. Sin is simply anything that separates you from God. So would *your* choice of not reading the Bible consist of separation? Considering God will only call you through His Word, the answer is quite evident, but you decide! The Word of God must be grounded and rooted in the heart for an effectual working of divine power. In all honesty, I just want people as well as myself to have a foundation of biblical truth.

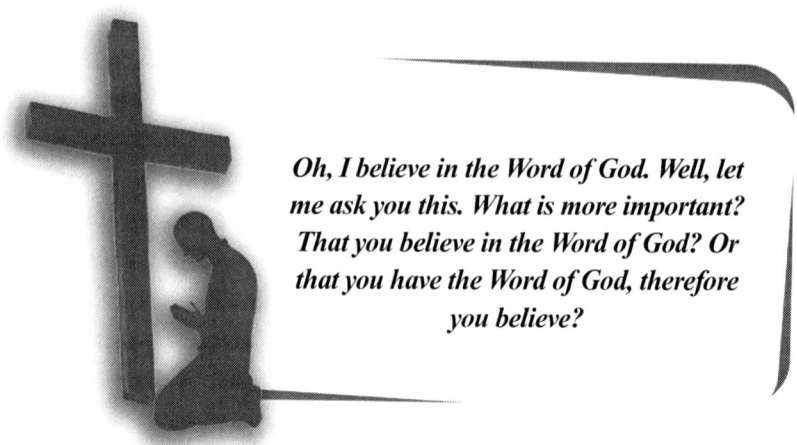

Oh, I believe in the Word of God. Well, let me ask you this. What is more important? That you believe in the Word of God? Or that you have the Word of God, therefore you believe?

You may wonder how to know if it is God who is speaking to you. Well, imagine yourself as a kid playing with a group of children who are all being watched by their parents. Why is it that when your mother calls your name you quickly look even though you are distracted by your playmates? It's because you recognize the voice that you are accustomed to and it's a voice you have spent a great deal of time hearing. The more time we spend with God, the more we fall deep in His Word and the more God will reveal. Build a relationship with God and give Him the time, which will instinctively allow you to recognize His voice. Yes . . . you will know the voice you have spent so much time with.

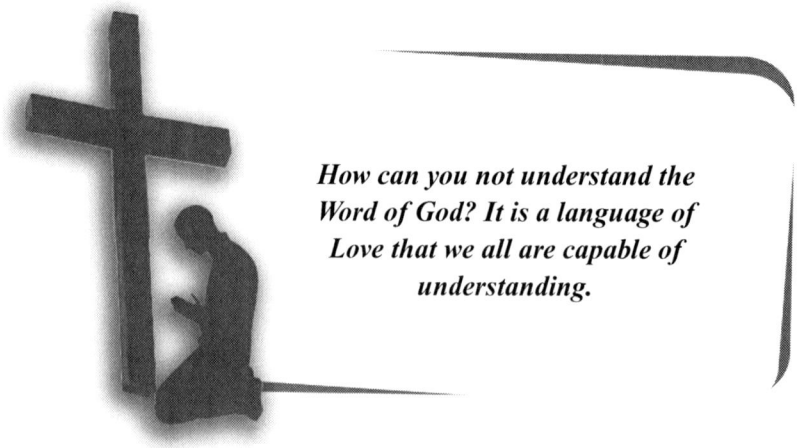

How can you not understand the Word of God? It is a language of Love that we all are capable of understanding.

God's love is demonstrated by His justification toward wicked men who have depraved their minds because of a lack of knowledge. His love gives you a channel by the name of Jesus Christ for grace to flow in your life. His love leaves you with a doctrine of righteousness through the Gospel at which you will fight to seek salvation. Tradition has made people believe that a short repetitive prayer has saved them without the need of sustaining their life in the Word of God! It is sad to say that religion and American theology will have more "Christians" standing condemned before the Son of Glory than the handful that have found favor in God's eyes. The Word of God is an operative power. The God of love is not only the doorway, but most importantly, the narrow road that enables you to reach a point of glorification. The Word of God is meant to bring fear! So you have no choice but to lay your life down to be saved. You can love God all you want, but your following God will not be noble without His Word under your feet, standing as you walk. Just because you go to church every Sunday does not mean you will be lifted up as a righteous man on the Day of Judgment. If you do not constantly nourish your mind with the Word of God, all you will know is the God you hear about one day a week. As horrible as this may sound, it is true that the majority of churches in America are teaching you about a different god than the One who reigns in the Bible, with dominion and authority over both the wicked and the righteous. Without submitting your life to the reading of God's holy scripture, you may be devoting your time to a god that the Bible declares as an *idol*! Without personally knowing and understanding His love, it is going to be a shock to most people when they face a God different from the one they have been worshiping. God is not in every church! Well, what church is God in? If you would find it worthwhile to mediate on God's Word and come to an understanding of God's truth . . . when you walk into a church you will know instantly if God moves in there because the Word that you have read will align with everything that is said! Now with the right church, Monday will be the most important day of the week, because it puts you in position for what Sunday prepared you for.

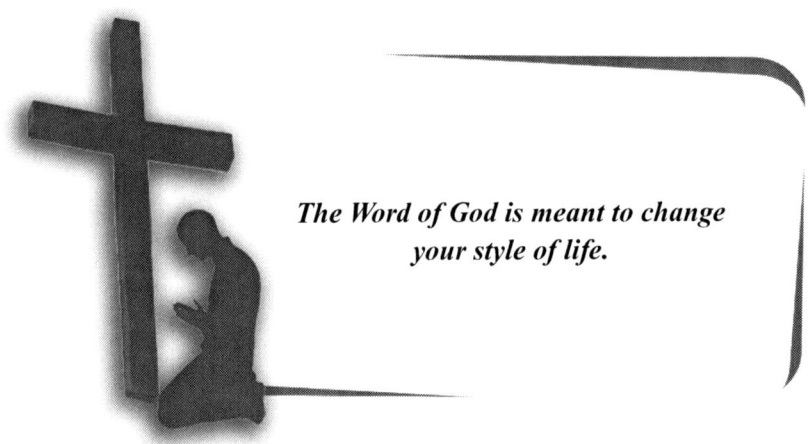

The Word of God is meant to change your style of life.

The Gospel is the response to the image of Christ, where you will fight for salvation. You will plead for mercy. You will endure pain for God's people. You will weep when understanding the true meaning of the Gospel. The Gospel is Jesus dying under the wrath of God, which alone will not save you, but now gives you the only possible way of eternal life. Prior to the Gospel of Jesus, we all stood condemned as subjects of the wrath of God because we knew nothing but lawlessness and sin. Jesus became "The Way," but for most us because of our choice of modern-day living, Jesus is just *in the way*. Understand that a prayer will not save you. Scripture will help you understand that. Going to church does not make you a Christian. Scripture will help you understand that. Telling people that they are saved does not make you God, but scripture will help you understand that. Who are you to tell anyone that they are saved? You are in no place of judgment. If you speak to a person straight off the street who has never known God and tell them after a series of questions and a simple prayer that they are saved, they will never strive to grow in holiness and godliness. People, salvation is in faith and faith in Christ alone, because we are called to repent through that faith. *How do you know you are in conversion?* Examine yourself and test yourself to see if you are in the faith, by scripture, which then leads to salvation, but know that it is only obedience, discipline, love, trust, and faith that give you the protection as God's people. This is why you must read the

Word of God because you will get the indisputable attributes of God, and not religion's version.

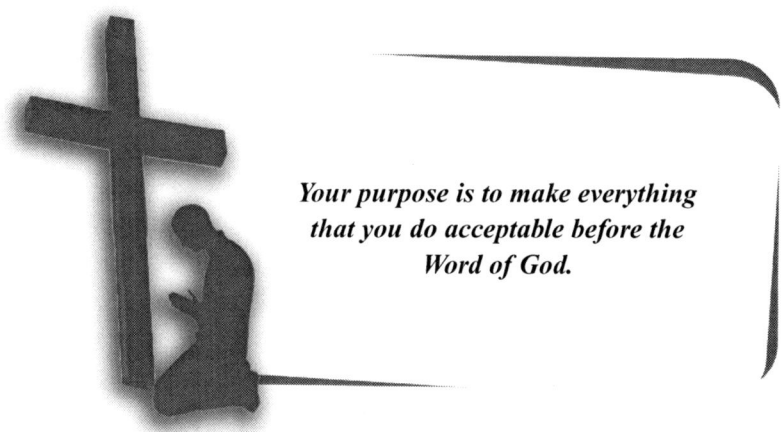

Your purpose is to make everything that you do acceptable before the Word of God.

Can you grasp the mind of Jesus where His equality toward you says, *though you are a sinner who sins without excuse, drop to your knees and plead for mercy and forgiveness. As you rise I will look you in the eyes and before every man, in spite of you being you, I will point you out and call you . . . righteous!* That is the grace of God and His infallible Word!

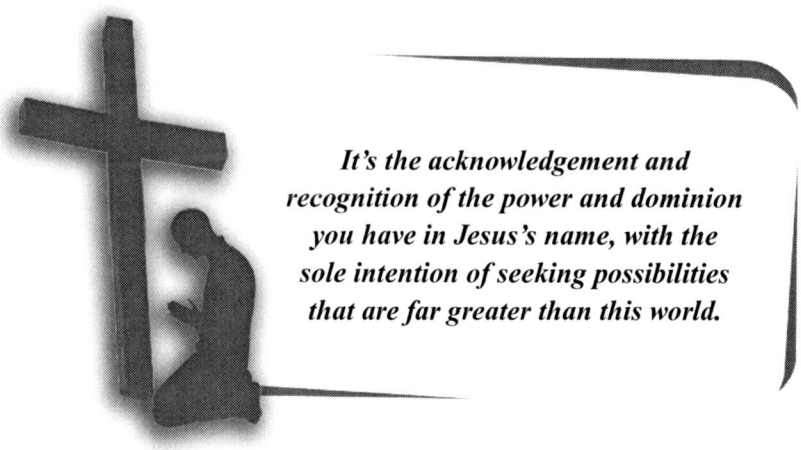

It's the acknowledgement and recognition of the power and dominion you have in Jesus's name, with the sole intention of seeking possibilities that are far greater than this world.

By becoming entangled in American Christianity, I have climbed mountains the majority of my life. Until I fell under conviction standing on God's Word, I never realized I only had to move the mountains. God wants you to stand before men, and fall before Him. The moment you fall at His holy feet you will have millions of angels in heaven standing in high regard in favor of you. The Gospel is the only way a man can manifest within Christ. We are divorcing the Word of God and finding our way into a marriage with a set of our favorite scriptures, then standing before the judgment seat of God realizing our whole life that we have been committing adultery with a false way of righteousness. The Gospel shouldn't be reduced to our favorite scriptures; it should be accelerated to a point of weeping because you see yourself standing under the Cross, crucifying a Man who knew what you needed so you could have a chance before His Father. Jesus is not a servant of men; you are a servant of Him. Jesus ended the law in terms of our new relationship with God, but He did not eliminate His standards in the law. American Christianity is what your life is apart from the law and the Gospel, where we sprinkle some scripture over our sin and begin signifying it as acceptable with baptism. I am here to open the Word of God and silence the mouth behind religion.

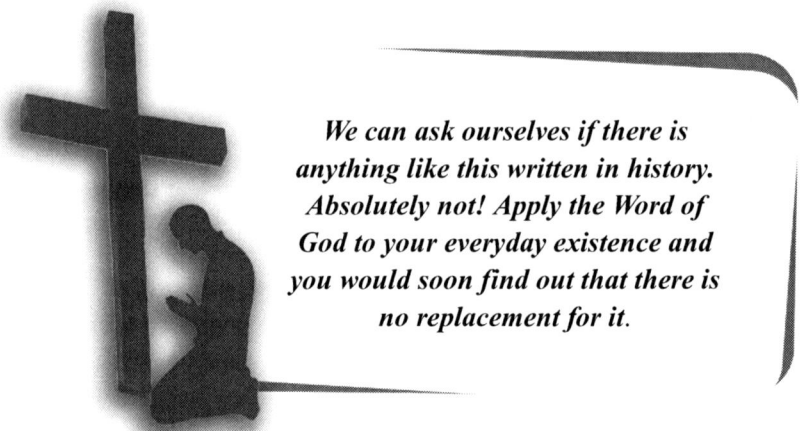

We can ask ourselves if there is anything like this written in history. Absolutely not! Apply the Word of God to your everyday existence and you would soon find out that there is no replacement for it.

Psalm 119:9: "How can a young man keep his way pure? By living according to your Word."

A composition of 150 different individual Psalms. It proclaims the work of God's hands, being the longest book in the Bible.

(*Refer to all of Psalms 119.*) (2) Blessed are they who keep *his statutes* and seek him with all their heart. (4) You have laid down *precepts* that are to be fully obeyed. (6) Then I will not be put to shame when I consider *all* your *decrees*. (10) I seek you with all my heart; do not let me stray from *your commands*. (11) I have hidden your *word* in my heart that I might not sin against you. (15) I mediate on your *precepts* and consider your ways. (25) I am laid low in the dust; preserve my life according to *Your Word*. (27) Let me understand the teaching of your precepts; then I will mediate on your wonders. (30) I have chosen the way of truth; I have set my heart on your laws.

Isaiah 40:8: "The grass withers and the flowers fall, but the word of our God stands forever."

The vision of Isaiah, the prophet, concerning Judah and Jerusalem in the days of the kings of Judah. (*Refer Isa. 40:1-8.*) It is the set of scripture to comfort all of God's people that will soon be taken over to the king of Babylon. It is God who is saying that I am going to send a man to prepare the way for the Lord (John the Baptist) and someone who is going to be the answer to your deliverance and salvation (Jesus). God speaks and says that all men are like grass and their glory is like the flowers of the field. The grass withers and the flowers fall because the breath of the Lord blows on them. So now the *only* way to stand firm and never be withered is not to trust or lean on man for comfort, but to *stand* firm on the *Word* of God, because it stands *forever*!

Romans 8:4: "In order that the righteous requirements of the law might be fully met in us, who do not live according to the sinful nature but according to the Spirit."

This is why following the requirements of God's *Word* is so vitally important in our lives. We learn in John 3:16 that Jesus became the sin offering that when we believe in His sacrifice and not only live in Him but for Him, we would not see condemnation. Prior to this everyone was a subject of God's wrath and condemnation because no one could pay for their debt, but Jesus paid it. Many people get this scripture confused and say, "*Well, all we have to do is believe and we will receive eternal life.*" Like everything else in God's Word, there is a process we must follow because there is so much more behind that belief . . . it is giving your life for Christ and letting the greater works of God be exemplified through your life (*John 3:21*). There is no glory, unless glory is revealed. It has nothing to do with you; it has everything to do with what God is going to do through your life. "*I believe! Yes, I am going to heaven.*" No! Even Jesus said (John 8:54) if I glorify myself, my glory means nothing. My father whom you claim as your God is the one who glorifies Me. It is not God's will for you to believe and go to Heaven, it is His will that you believe in His Son, follow His Word, and allow *your life* to be an example of His glory. People, transgression is living outside of God's will . . . condemnation and sin are the equivalent of death, meaning you are the subject of judgment . . . (1 John 3:4) *sinning*! Most importantly, after you put your faith and belief in Christ, there is still a requirement of God's *Word* to be met, even if you believe and have faith . . . *you must* still *meet* the requirement of why Jesus died: "for us to work and fight in Him" and follow the *Word* of God. (Rom. 8:1-4). Again, not everyone who says they believe, really believe. Not everyone who says that they are Christians are really Christians. And sadly enough, not everyone who goes to Christ *lives* for Christ.

Deuteronomy 8:3: ". . . man does not live on bread alone but on every word that comes out the mouth of the Lord."

The fifth book of Moses. These are the words Moses spoke to all Israel in the wilderness just east of Jordan. (*Refer Deut. 8:1-3.*) Be careful that you follow every command that the Lord is giving you so that you may live and increase in all of His promises. You have been through tribulation, but it was merely a test to humble you in order to know what was in your heart. The Lord humbled you, causing you to hunger and then the Lord fed you manna (a sweet-tasting food from heaven), which taught you that man can and will *only* live on every *word* that comes from the father's mouth.

The moment you have faith, there is literally no doubt that you will approach an unrealistic encounter, where supernaturally it will be a portion of miracles you could have never envisioned without having faith.

INFLUENCE OF WITNESSING

Talk to an individual who is completely committed to God, and you'll realize God is a visible thing.

Jesus said to me, *I am-self-evident*!

In order for any individual to "*relate*," he or she must accumulate "*relation*." Certainly we know the word "*life*," but do we know what it's like to "*live*?" You may say you know God, but how can you say you know of something you've never taken the time to understand? God is self-evident.

EVIDENCE FOR ATHEISTS

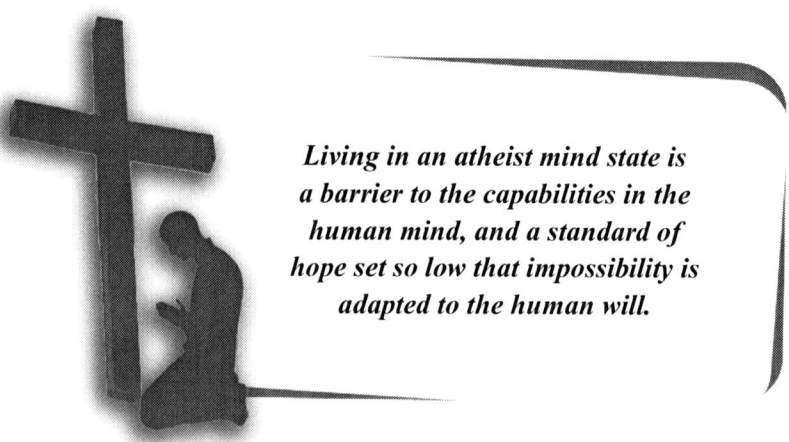

Living in an atheist mind state is a barrier to the capabilities in the human mind, and a standard of hope set so low that impossibility is adapted to the human will.

My position in the Body of Christ is not to tell atheists that they must believe in God, because even if these nonbelievers choose to continue disbelieving and decide not to walk through the door that has been opened for them, their choice does not and will not threaten the throne of God. For any atheist to say to me *"prove God's existence,"* they are blind to the person they see before them. My evidence for you is me. Again, whether you believe or not is not my worry. I cannot elaborate on historical facts, the witnessing of God's holy power, and the truth that the Gospel is infallible. I cannot explain this to you because it would be a waste of time to paint a picture to a blind person who is deaf by choice. The only thing that I can tell you is based on a "choice"—you must make God self-evident. It really confounds me when atheists say, *Belief should only be founded on philosophical agreements and conclusive scientific evidence.* In fact, the majority of scientific "atheists" base their studies on agreed material of evolution, material that was founded by an eyewitness who is unknown. What is even more unusual is that the majority of Scientology is based on information that has been handed down by atheists who claim their information to be true. But what evidence is that? Now, on the other hand Christianity is not based on handed-down information; it is based on sixty-six Spirit-led scribes, interweaved into one holy Bible from its original source. The point is that this is information you can see. Now if you were to ask a Christian to give you evidence of God, they will plainly say, "You are looking at it." An atheist will then probably try to argue that *the Bible was written by man.* Well, is that a fact? Well, if it is, then now you have your first fact in Christianity! I have to smile when an atheist utters, *God is meaningless*! Well, again if you mean what you are saying, then what you are saying is meaningful. So not everything about God is meaningless. Why is it that atheists say that they need evidence when the majority of atheists base their studies on handed-down information? Again, here is what I mean. The greater part of atheists base their evidence on evolution. Okay, how about taking a poll across America and asking every atheist where water came from, where human life came from, and where insects came from? But wait, before you raise your hand to try and answer that question, I don't want opinions from other people's studies . . . I want fact! How many of you were alive when this process began? You see, with God and how God evolves the human mind, the human life, and the human belief, evolution will occur in your very presence. The problem is that revelation and evolution will not occur until you refer to the information in which God is a verified *fact*! It is humorous when I hear about atheists who say that *God should be eradicated because there is no evidence of Him.* Well, if everything must be based on evidence, then prove that God doesn't exist. *Well, God is not a certain thing.* Are you sure? If you say yes, then what you are saying is certain. Yes, mind-boggling! You cannot have evolution without an origin. You cannot have fact without *your* eye as a witness. You cannot have creation without a Creator! Amusingly enough, atheists will say that *man created God.* So then based on living your life derived from "facts," prove that creation.

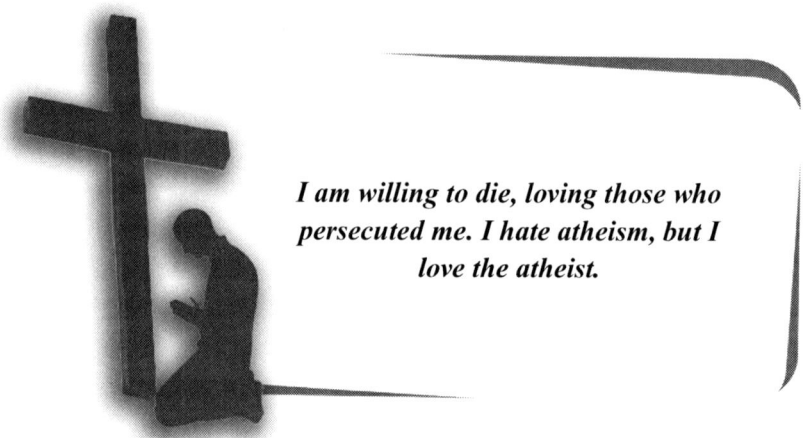

I am willing to die, loving those who persecuted me. I hate atheism, but I love the atheist.

A fun fact given by many atheists of the twentieth century is that when asked about the significance of the holy Bible, all of them concluded that the Bible speaks most accurately to the human condition—the very definition of a rational choice. When asked, *what is Christianity?* They easily stated that in Christianity the perception of life is not merely something to believe in, but more importantly, there is something that undeniably believes in you. Without the question of whether the Bible is infallible or not, it is certain and statistically proven that Christian faith transforms individual lives. Now, in terms of secularism or atheism there is one undeniable truth that has been acknowledged by converted atheists—that atheism is founded on theory that actually sustains uncertainty and weakens personal hope. When asked why Christianity above other religions? *It is the experience of life.* Why the Bible? *Because it gives a choice for living, consistent with the way life works.* When asked why secularists have a hard time with the Bible? One man simply stated that it is secularists' inability to understand the Good News.

DESPERATE FOR GOD

A man explained to me once that his life has been a downward spiral of misfortunes—drugs, divorce, and being financially unsteady. I asked him, *"What have you done to change this?"* He nonchalantly replied, "I don't do drugs *as much* anymore. My wife needs me, and she'll realize. And work has just been slow." I asked him if he knew of God, and he said that he's prayed a few times and it didn't work. It was at that moment I came to understand that many people without God don't know the variation between being sincere and impassive.

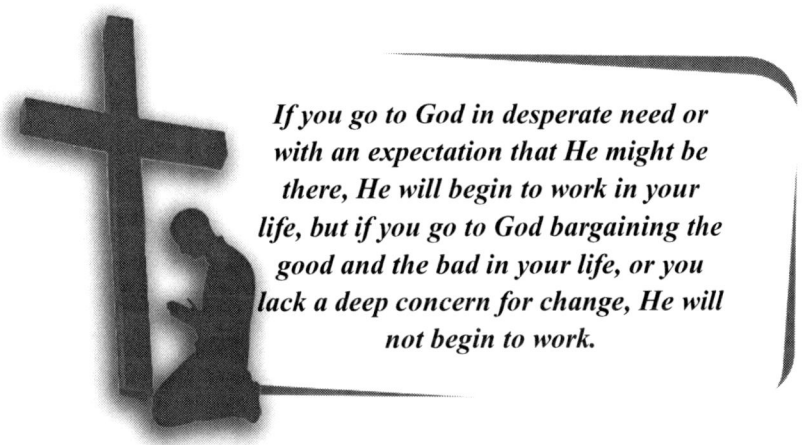

If you go to God in desperate need or with an expectation that He might be there, He will begin to work in your life, but if you go to God bargaining the good and the bad in your life, or you lack a deep concern for change, He will not begin to work.

There is a major difference in emotion between, *"Can I please?"* and *"Give it to me"*! What is the difference? A sincere call out to God is heart-driven and presents an earnest and genuine feeling. It has the value of being open and truthful, and most importantly, it's natural.

An impassive call out to God presents a dead emotion or opinion. It reveals the absence of interest for certain aspects of life, and most importantly, it leaves you in a state of indifference.

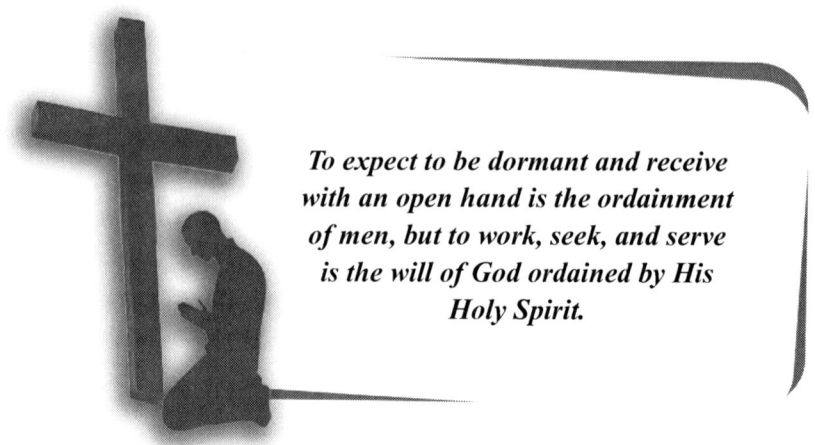

To expect to be dormant and receive with an open hand is the ordainment of men, but to work, seek, and serve is the will of God ordained by His Holy Spirit.

Nobody can ever say that he or she was not given a fair chance at life because we were all born under the death penalty. God gives you an efficient opportunity to have life and to know Him better just by leaving us with His infallible Word in the holy scripture. If you cry out to God sincerely from the depths of your dying heart, He will be there. However, you must understand that everything you want to happen after the point of calling out to Him will only happen according to His Word. Why am I in pain? *Read God's Word*! Why do I feel like my world is falling apart? *Read God's Word*! Why do I feel worse now than I did before calling out to God? *Read God's Word*! Why am I praying and don't see anything happening? *Read God's Word!* Why am I listing a series of questions that indicate pain and not prosperity? The Word of God will present God's truth and not religion's philosophy, where the church is so stuck in tradition and self-power that they are softening up people with prosperity and happiness . . . not for the greatest reward of the inheritance into God's kingdom, but for their own increased church attendance. The most powerful men and women of God are formed as their strength and power is imparted to them from their devotional life.

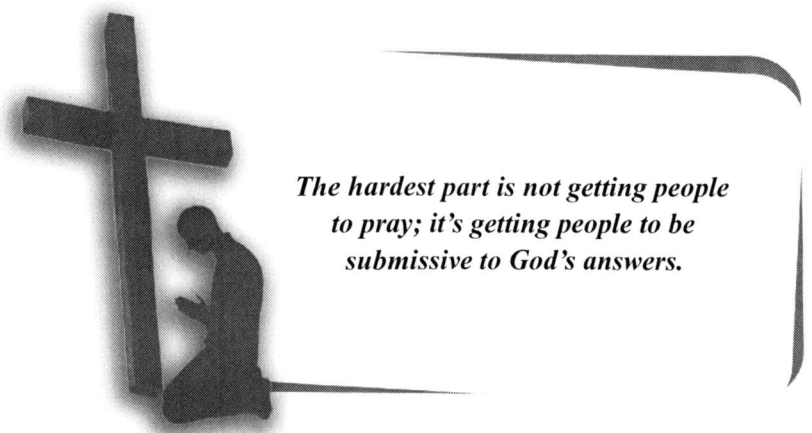

The hardest part is not getting people to pray; it's getting people to be submissive to God's answers.

Does the scriptural word "ask" *mean if you ask God for anything then you shall receive*? First, let's understand this—asking is meant to draw you into prayer, prayer brings you into conversation, and conversation presents clarification of God's will. We are asking God, but not listening to God. It is not that God doesn't answer prayers; the problem is we are waiting for *exactly* what we prayed for. At the same time, God is trying to give you a completely different answer than you're expecting, because it is better for you. Nonetheless, He did indeed answer your prayers. This is why conversation with God is so crucial, because if He were to tell you what is best for you, then you wouldn't mind when God says, "Wait, I have something even better for you!" Unfortunately, we close God off when we don't receive what we want, not realizing that our prayers have already been answered . . . but somehow we didn't involve ourselves in that conversation. *Here is the best example*: You have two people praying a prayer; one person prays to take the other person out of his life, and the other one prays for the person to stay in his life. The question is, how can God answer both their prayers? Easy, God says this person needs to be in your life because you are going to be the one to lead him closer to Me. You are happy with the answer because you now understand the effect. God answers prayers, but understand that most often it is different than what you are expecting. We petition in prayer; we get answers in conversation!

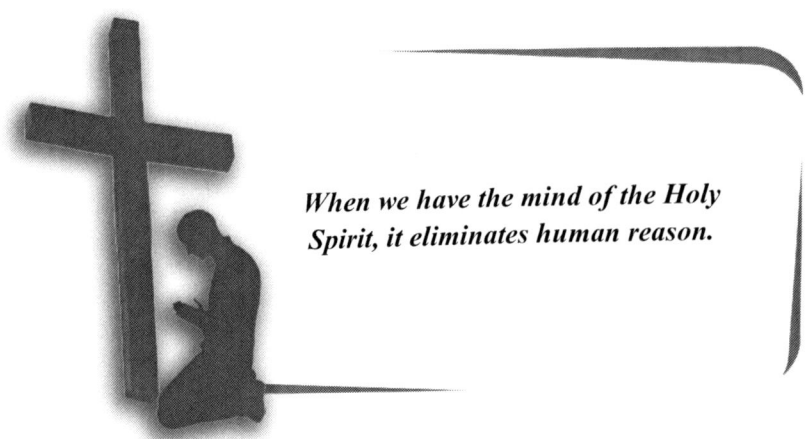

When we have the mind of the Holy Spirit, it eliminates human reason.

What's Behind My Belief

I was speaking with an old friend from school, and when we got into a conversation about God, she quickly said, *"Oh, that's great, I definitely believe in God."* As the conversation changed, her self-assured belief in God became an excitement for her party life. So I asked her, *"Who is God to you and what do you hope for from Him?"* She replied, *"Umm, He's God, and I hope He'll give me a successful future because I believe."* It was at that moment revelation was given to me.

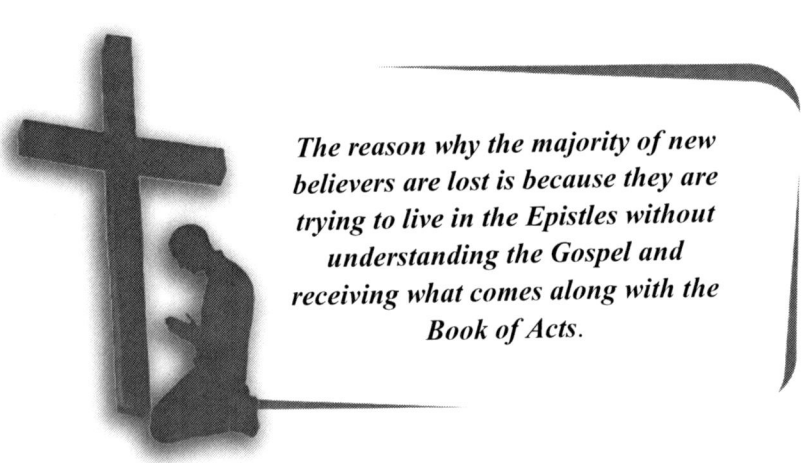

The reason why the majority of new believers are lost is because they are trying to live in the Epistles without understanding the Gospel and receiving what comes along with the Book of Acts.

I devoted time to God and nothing ever happened. So basically you didn't have faith, since faith is the certainty of what you have yet to see. If you do not have faith, then it is obvious that you cannot believe in God, because without faith, what are you believing in? God doesn't need your time; He needs your life!

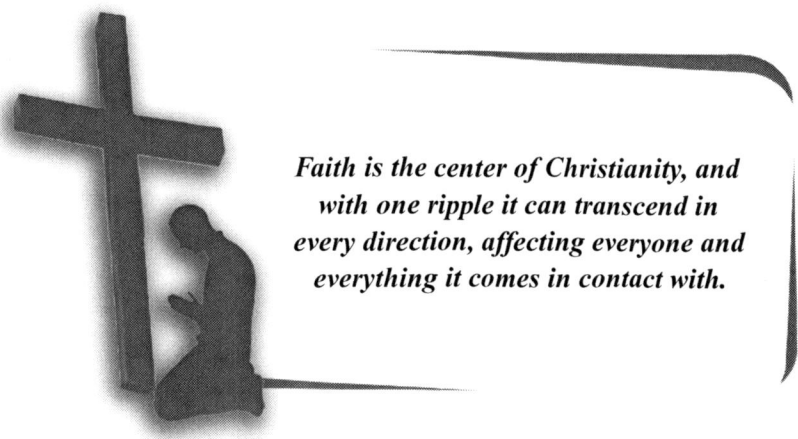

Faith is the center of Christianity, and with one ripple it can transcend in every direction, affecting everyone and everything it comes in contact with.

Hebrews 11:6 states, *"And without faith it is impossible to please God, because anyone who comes to Him must believe that He exists and that He rewards those who earnestly seek Him."* Now, this message is extremely important for the people who say they believe in God but enjoy their nights around the bar and club scene; for those people who say they believe in God, but their high is when they smoke and drink their life away; for those who go to church and say they believe, yet never read God's Word; and for those who say they believe and quote scriptures, yet they don't live by them. The problem today is not with mixed drinks, but with mixed belief. The problem is not with smokers, but with "Gospel-declaring" smokers. The problem is not with sinners, but with "Bible-declaring" sinners. The principle word in Hebrews 11:6 is the word "please." In John 5:30, Jesus says that *He only judges according to what pleases His Father*. Okay, then we must ask ourselves, what pleases God? Read Ezekiel 18:23-24 very closely:

> "Do I take pleasure in the death of the wicked? declares the Sovereign Lord. Rather, am I not pleased when they turn away from their ways and live? But if a righteous man turns away from his righteousness and commits sin and does the same detestable things the wicked man does, will he live? None of the righteous things he has done will be remembered. Because of the unfaithfulness he is guilty *of and because of the sins he has committed, he will die.*"

Oh yes, condemnation is going to fall on a multitude of people today who believe their belief is acceptable. The problem is there is no in-between or "acceptable" with God. It is either hot or cold; there is no lukewarm. It is either condemnation or eternal life; there is no limbo. It is not about the belief; it's about what's behind the belief.

I believe in God, but do I know that behind that belief is a list of laws and commands, character and conduct, honesty and deeds, ways and morals, faith and hope, pleasing and displeasing, wicked men and righteous men, honor and sin, life and death, commitment and dedication, promises and rewards? It's not the belief that's most important, but the understanding and following of what's behind that belief, because that's what allows us to experience the faithful God and the promises that come along with God's Word. The devil believes in God, but it doesn't mean he's going to heaven. For the record, I am not going to heaven because I read the Bible, but because I have built an ever-increasing relationship with the God of the Bible through His Word. Now the question is: Do you *believe* that you live your life according to what *pleases* God? Do you believe? Then comes the most important question of your belief; you may say, yes, I know God, but that is not the question, the question is, does God know you?

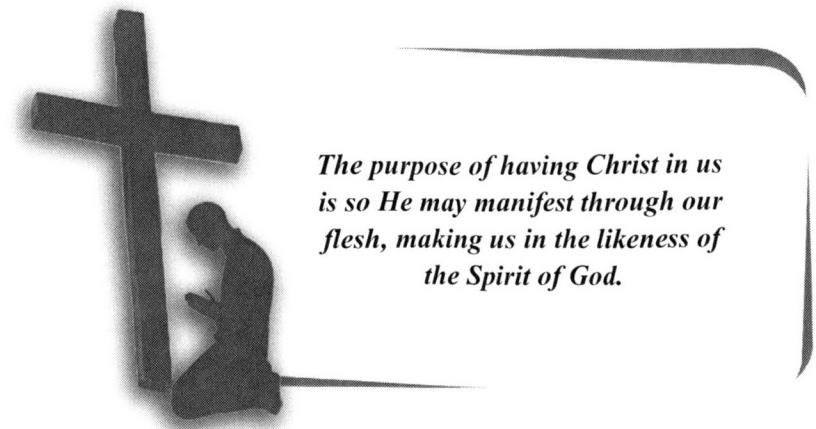

The purpose of having Christ in us is so He may manifest through our flesh, making us in the likeness of the Spirit of God.

I NEED EVIDENCE

You not only need faith to believe there is a God; you need faith for the evidence of God.

There was a particular group of individuals who, when speaking about God, asked me to show evidence of His existence. One man began to explain how Scientology is the true development in the teaching of the body and it requires precise evidence for its belief. In fact, Scientology was created *as a self-help way of life* and an outgrowth of *a self-help system*. It distinguished belief in the power of a person's spirit to wipe itself of prior painful occurrences through self-knowledge and spiritual fulfillment. I am confused, because if testimony is meant to be a solution for other broken hearts, then why would you want to wipe those past occurrences away? If your strength is acknowledged by the persecution you have conquered, why would you want to take away your source of triumph? Scientology was established and formatted for individuals to be encouraged for development of the body by themselves. If this is the case, Scientology is only an arrangement of the mind telling itself it is happy when in fact it's distressing *by self-concept, not self-healing*. Self-concept is the arrangement of current feelings, which is influenced by self-actualizing with no actual intentions of evolving from that state. Self-healing is *the process* of deliverance, which involves a collection of development; assistance, an aid, a *deliverer*, to the core complex of self, which is evidently signified and received in the Gospel of Christ!

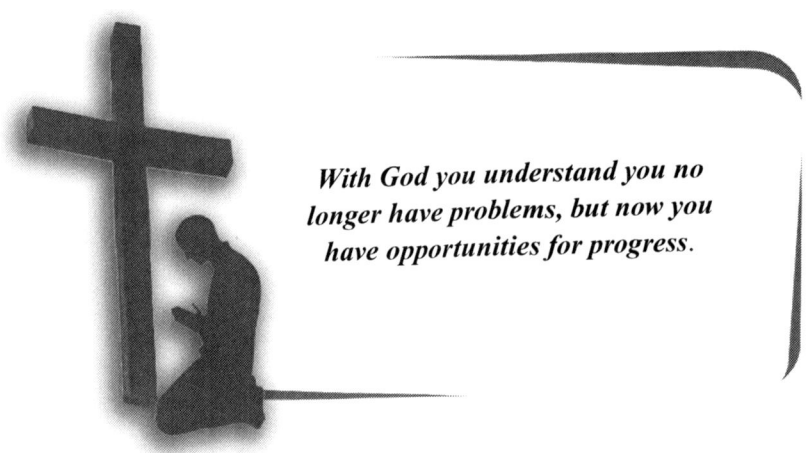

With God you understand you no longer have problems, but now you have opportunities for progress.

God never said you were alone to figure out how to live and be free except when you don't know Him. I am thrown off when people say, "I know, I have everything . . . now all I need is Jesus." No, I hate to break it to you, but you don't need Jesus . . . Jesus is all you have! It is great to build yourself up and position your mind into serenity and expectations of self-completion, but it is God who fills the emptiness and gives spiritual healing. Human reasoning will always interrupt God's position to impart divine power. We must be Spirit-involved, not self-involved. Have you ever lost a loved one and shut the door to remorseful love? Try self-help and see where it takes you. Have you ever fallen into a pit where it seems almost impossible to climb out? Try the self-help system and see where it gets you. It is God who positions the right people in your life. It is God who strengthens. It is God who is your deliverer, and it is God who provides all to those who believe.

The Prayer of My Life

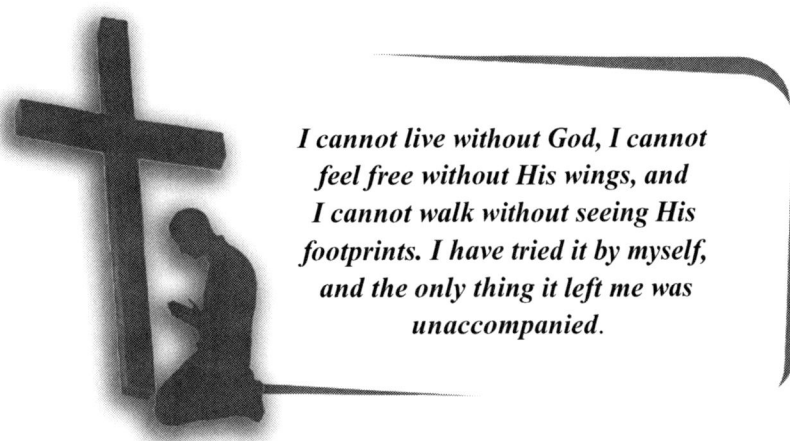

I cannot live without God, I cannot feel free without His wings, and I cannot walk without seeing His footprints. I have tried it by myself, and the only thing it left me was unaccompanied.

For all those atheists who need evidence, the evidence of God not in someone's life is your life. The evidence of God in my life is my life! I cannot explain what God has done for me because it is unexplainable and quite remarkable. He has done something in me and throughout me that I have never experienced. So what do I call it? He has given me revelation I've never received in this world, so how do I clarify it?

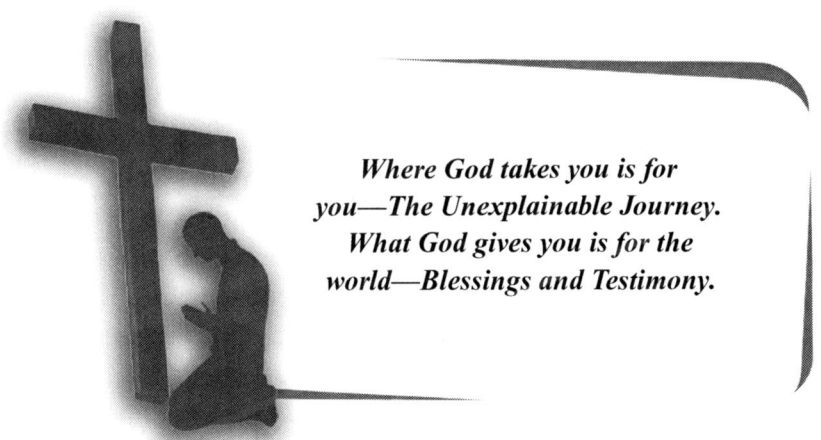

Where God takes you is for you—The Unexplainable Journey. What God gives you is for the world—Blessings and Testimony.

God on My Mind

In another discussion I was involved in was a man who said, "*The belief of God is only in your mind, and the mind can do unbelievable things.*" Yes, the mind can take you on an extraordinary voyage and has the capability of indescribable possibilities. However, the mind does not make a million dollars; it gives the capability to generate a million dollars. The mind does not provide healing; it establishes the process of healing. This was an establishment that was given to you before you were conceived; let's just call it God-given, because it was thought of even before you had the mind to think of. Without God all you will have is capability without tools, a process without a route. Your thoughts come from a channel of brilliant thinking whether you believe it or not. Just as everything on earth must go through Christ to get to the Father, everything that comes from heaven must go through Christ to get to earth. Yes, that includes your visions, dreams, and ideas. The only difference is true Christians are able to see their visions become reality, while nonbelievers pass great ideas on to others.

God is an Illusion

Well, what is an illusion? An illusion is known to be a mistaken mental depiction and an altering of reality which occur more with the human senses than visions.

This is a very funny statement and easily opposed, because those who've carried out an unshakable belief have felt the power of God, not sensed something odd. Those who have had constant faith have witnessed miracles, not fictional phenomena. If those who are demanding that God is an illusion are basing their conclusion on individual studies, they are studying individuals who don't know God. How can you call God an illusion if in reality you've never looked for His promises, the same promises that are provided when earnestly following His Word? If an illusion is solely based on senses, maybe that's why God declared He would give youth visions and old men would dream dreams. (Acts 2:17.) It is common for man to disbelieve in something he knows nothing about. You can say to yourself "I have read the Bible thoroughly," but if you have not committed yourself to righteously pursuing the Word of God, then you have never seen or experienced the marvel and miracles of God. A converted atheist told me that he wanted to know God more, so I handed him the Bible. He explained that he had been given plenty of Bibles and has read the Bible many times. I smiled as I pushed over the Bible and told him that this Bible will be different, because it won't be read with a curiosity of mind, but rather a desperate change of heart. Your knowledge means nothing while your power lies dormant. What is having an understanding of God's Word without any conception of its spiritual power?

How can you call God an illusion, if in fact you've never had any perception of Him and never witnessed any account of Him? How can He be an illusion to you? How can you claim or give name to something you've never seen or had in mind?

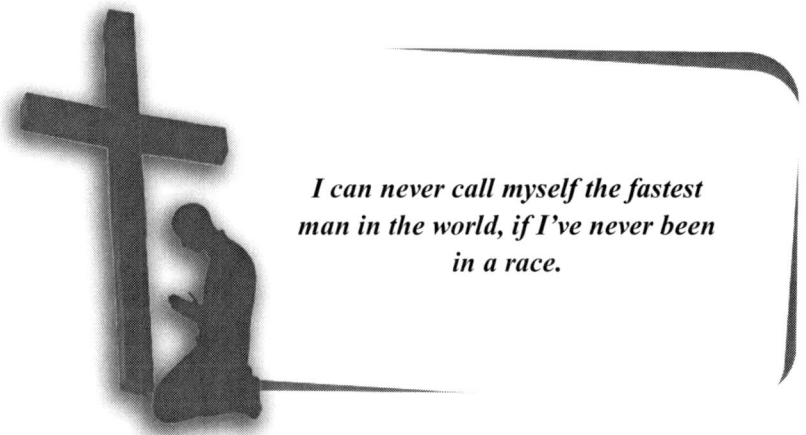

I can never call myself the fastest man in the world, if I've never been in a race.

How can you come up with a definition for a non-existing Word in your life?

It is a work of faith that enables God's "will" to be seen in your life, not a work of trying to prove yourself worthy to see God's will! You don't earn salvation. You don't earn faith . . . you understand it! How, you ask? God's Word! Your faith is a work all by itself . . . learn to maintain your garden of faith and see what is produced because of it! There is no work more essential than that of faith!

GOD IS A DELUSION

Well, what is a delusion? A delusion is resistant in confrontation creating a deceptive or a false belief of unfinished information in perceptions, properly termed as an illusion, a contradiction to proof or evidence.

Resistant in confrontation. Whether you consider God to be real or disbelieve in Him completely, He will remain by your side, but, He will not begin stabilizing your life until *you* confront Him.

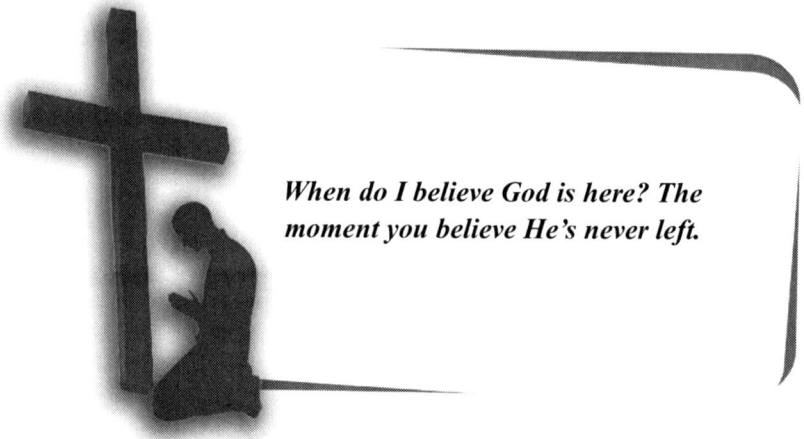

When do I believe God is here? The moment you believe He's never left.

Unfinished information. How can you possibly have complete information on something that has no maximum bounds?

Contradictory to proof or evidence. The proof of God is shown individually, touched individually, and experienced individually, and is only evident to those who wholeheartedly believe and seek what pleases Him and His righteousness. If the proof of God is individual, you might want to ask the individual who has seen God, "*How did God reveal Himself to you?*" They will then explain the only method: live in "The Word" and let "The Word" live in you.

It was God's decree that people shall have their own choice, the choice of what they shall receive from God. Illusion and delusion have been positioned within an equal category. If you have not trusted in God, in no way has He had depended on you. You have to wonder why is it that those who are faithful believers in God choose to look away from ignorance and either choose not to associate with sinners or begin praying for their well-being. So why do nonbelievers or doubters go out of their way to badger or cause affliction to the same people who are searching for a better way, who are living a blissful life, and who choose to pray for others rather than trample upon them? Could it be that these same people who call God a delusion are dissatisfied with Christianity and what God will do for His people? Or is it more than that? Possibly these people who call God a delusion are playing the unfortunate role of what God said would happen if they fell under the rebellious attack of unrighteousness, by becoming the devil's advocate. Salvation is in Christ alone, change is in Christ alone, and deliverance is in Christ alone. He didn't die to give you salvation; He died to become salvation. Which means it will only become an attachment to your life by serving Christ alone.

Nonbelievers are used as an example of blindness. Those who have never witnessed God's glory and promises cannot be persuaded by the blind. They must lean on the understanding of the righteous in order to take proper direction and to fulfill the Word of God. A blind man cannot explain to another blind man where to set off if he's never taken this particular route or has never seen what lies ahead. You can't explain something you haven't seen or felt for yourself. If you cannot identify with the way, you must bond yourself with righteous individuals because those individuals of God will bind up the testimony, which gives reassurance and independence in faith for singly acquiring what some unfortunately assume to be a delusion.

Though you may not see Me, I am near.
Though you may not feel Me, I am here.
Though you may not hear Me, I am there.
Where?
Though you may question, the answers are quite clear.

Jesus said to me, *(People of faith) If you prayed for a financial blessing and received an indefinite check in the mail, what would be the point in stirring up questions if you already believed in the answer?*

The point is, don't overanalyze anything because you will waste your entire life searching for answers that have no intended solution for you.

Don't spend your time debating God; spend your time glorifying God.

Unlike a superstore "two per customer," when Jesus offers a deal and we show up, there is no limit to how many blessings we can collect. Did you know it's easier to create a habit than it is to break a habit? Give yourself a repetitive schedule for God and allow His importance for your life to become a habit. Just as righteousness can become a habit for your life, so can God's blessings. Believe *He is* the truth and He will accurately position your life for greatness. *I just cannot explain what God is doing to me.* God has created the unexplainable in people, simply because it's something they have never experienced. Do not overanalyze the certainty and assurance of miracles, because it will only add uncertainty to belief. By not overanalyzing the truth, it will keep you focused on God's intentions for you, which opens a passage into the presence of greatness, exposing what many people tend to overlook.

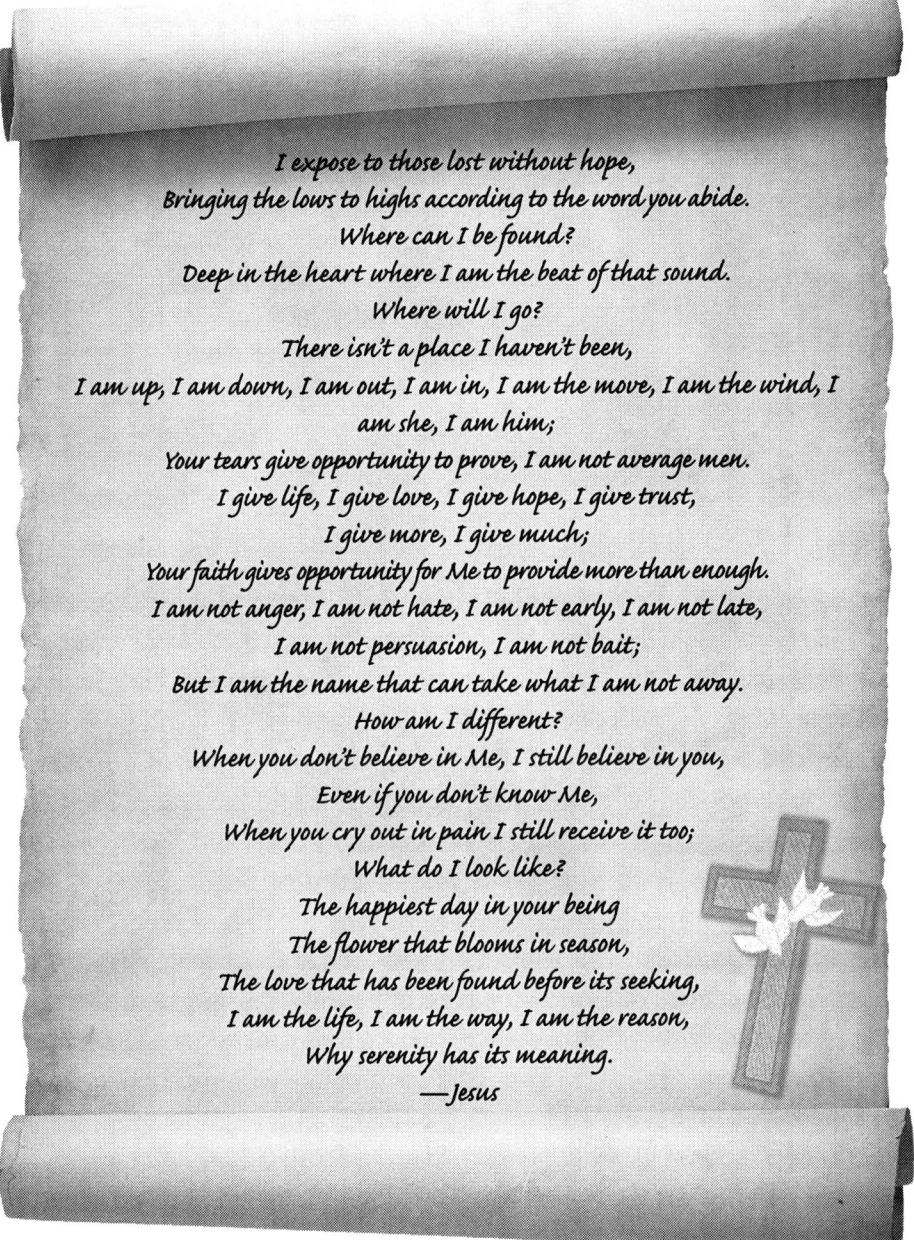

I expose to those lost without hope,
Bringing the lows to highs according to the word you abide.
Where can I be found?
Deep in the heart where I am the beat of that sound.
Where will I go?
There isn't a place I haven't been,
I am up, I am down, I am out, I am in, I am the move, I am the wind, I am she, I am him;
Your tears give opportunity to prove, I am not average men.
I give life, I give love, I give hope, I give trust,
I give more, I give much;
Your faith gives opportunity for Me to provide more than enough.
I am not anger, I am not hate, I am not early, I am not late,
I am not persuasion, I am not bait;
But I am the name that can take what I am not away.
How am I different?
When you don't believe in Me, I still believe in you,
Even if you don't know Me,
When you cry out in pain I still receive it too;
What do I look like?
The happiest day in your being
The flower that blooms in season,
The love that has been found before its seeking,
I am the life, I am the way, I am the reason,
Why serenity has its meaning.
—Jesus

God's grace alone will not be sufficient enough to accomplish the will of God. Imagine getting accepted into an art school. You may have been accepted, but in order to pass, you must show up and do the work.

I Am Saved

Like Jesus, in my passion I grieve when seeing the absence of God in the ungodly man. A sinner's only course of life begins with repentance directed by the words of tender conviction.

I was speaking to a lady about God at a grocery store, and she looked at me as if she never heard the Word of God before. She asked, *"When did you get saved?"* I said, "Ma'am, I'm still in the process of being saved!" She replied, "But you know so much of the Word!" Then I replied, "Yes, and I still have so much of the Word to know." *Well, what was your prayer of salvation?* I eagerly responded with beautiful imagery: it is still being prayed at the altar; you can't miss it. It's lying right next to my heart and tears.

Yes, you may have been saved from a life that displeases God, but what about the commitment for the rest of your life to now do everything that pleases God? *Why are you still in sin?* What about the commitment of keeping the Word of God as the core of your life? *So why is it that you don't know God's Word?* Why do you believe that you are saved? *Because someone told you?* The disarray of God's truth came within a small opinion in American Christianity and Western evangelism where the opinion was "Let's use a method that will get people excited about God." The intention was not initially wrong, but somewhere along the tangling of religion, it all changed! There came a sequence of questions that were followed by a short repetitive prayer that would help people be saved (born again). This is where tradition became established over God's infallible Word, where people became excited at the thought of a new home, a fancy car, and "living at the utmost." What a disappointment when God pulled the ground from underneath these people and they fell straight on their face in shock that a prosperous God could bring so much pain. They were expecting a new car, and instead got a full body detail where God was destroying who they were, to make them into who they were intended to be . . . but they were not aware of this! People began to repeat this short prayer that was only intended to ask God to "take away the old and bring on the new," a process of regeneration. The sinner's prayer was meant to be a process of understanding God's Word for righteousness, which became a family celebration that no matter what happens now, you are going to heaven. Blasphemy! Being born again is a process of God breaking you down and taking away the old to bring in the new—regeneration. You confess after conviction falls over you, and your heart is burdened, which leads you to repentance, because you now recognize your sin and ignorance and lack of knowledge of God's holy scripture. Remember, when you confess to God, you are making a vow to Him that you will never return to your lawless ways. Romans 10:1 says, *"Brothers, my heart's desire and prayer to God for the Israelites is that they may be saved."* Be sure you understand the Bible when it describes being saved. The word "may" is crucial! Our modern-day version of "saved" simply means regeneration, not *eternal life*! The correct word usage should be born again, or regeneration, not saved, because no matter what we confess, plead, or cry out for, we will always be striving toward sanctification. Just as your natural life began with birth, your spiritual life also begins with birth—the regeneration of your old self. The beginning of your salvation requires that you leave your old life behind because God has birthed you into new life and a new way of living. A new birth will always prove itself to serve. As you live your new life in Christ, you must still strive for holiness because living outside of Christ subjects you to God's penalty for sin—wrath. Just as Christ sacrificed His life so that we may receive life, we are to sacrifice our lives to bring Him glory. We are not altogether saved until we are judged before the throne and sealed with glorification. You don't receive the full magnitude of salvation until you are inherited into the kingdom of God. Be careful with the word "saved." Fight for salvation and fight to find yourself favored in God's eyes.

When the devil pushes against you, turn and push him back! Why are we praying for God to save us from the battles, when we should be pleading for God to send us into the battles! Thank God for His peace and all in the same breath tell Him you're ready for war!

Psalms 18:20-21: "The Lord has dealt with me according to my righteousness; according to the cleanness of my hands he has rewarded me, I have kept the ways of the Lord and have not done evil by turning from my God."

A composition of 150 different individual Psalms. It proclaims the work of God's hands, being the longest book in the Bible. (*Refer Ps. 18:2-28.*) (2) The Lord is my rock, my fortress and deliverer; my God is my rock, in whom I take refuge. He is my shield and the horn of my salvation, my stronghold. (3) I call to the Lord, who is worthy of praise, and I am saved from my enemies. (4) The cords of death entangled me; the torrents of destruction overwhelmed me. (5) The cords of the grave coiled around me; the snares of death confronted me. (6) In my distress I called to the Lord; I cried to my God for help. From his temple he heard my voice; my cry came before him, into his ears. He has saved me, because (22) all his laws are before me; I have not turned away from his decrees.

1 Corinthians 12:3: "Brothers do not be ignorant, somehow or other you were influenced and led astray into mute idols. Therefore I tell you that no one curse the spirit or speak about the Holy Spirit except by

God. There are different kinds of gifts but given by one God, there are different kinds of services but given by the same Lord, there are different kinds of working, but the same God works all of them in all men."

The First Epistle of Paul (called to be an apostle of Christ Jesus by the will of God) to the church in Corinth. (*Refer 1 Cor. 12:1-11.*) You can never understand the works of the Spirit without an unshakable faith and a strong belief system. God gives the Spirit as He determines, and will not place the power of knowledge, wisdom, healings, prophesy, distinguishing spirits . . . etc. into the wrong hands or an unruly life.

1 Corinthians 10:13: "No temptation has seized you except what is common to man . . ."

The First Epistle of Paul (called to be an apostle of Christ Jesus by the will of God) to the church in Corinth. (*Refer 1 Cor. 10:1-11.*) God warns his people to watch out and not to follow Israel's footsteps, because it led to their ruins by being disobedient. God warns us not to set our hearts on evil things as they did. Do not test the Lord and begin to grumble. Even if you think that you are standing firm, be careful that you don't fall. Trust in the Lord even in the midst of resistance because God will not let you be tempted beyond what you can bear.

Acts 28:27: "For this people's heart has become calloused; they hardly hear with their ears, and they have closed their eyes. Otherwise they might see with their eyes, hear with their ears, understand with their hearts and turn, and I would heal them."

Written by Luke, the medical doctor. The first Acts of the Apostles after Jesus ascended into heaven after a period of forty days of teaching. (*Refer Acts 28:17-31.*) Paul preaches at Rome, calling together the leaders of the Jews. Paul's own people came against him and tried to have him put to death after giving him over to the Romans. He set up a new meeting with the leaders of the Jews, and it was in a larger assembly than the first time they met. Paul then began speaking about Jesus and the kingdom of God. Some were convinced by what he was saying, but the majority overruled in disbelief. His last statement was said through the prophet Isaiah: Go to this people and say, You will be ever hearing but never understanding.

2 Peter 1:3: "*His divine power has given us everything we need for life and godliness through our knowledge in him who called us by his own glory and goodness.*"

Peter, a servant and an apostle of Jesus Christ, to those who through *righteousness* of our God have received a precious faith. (*Refer 2 Pet. 1:3-4.*) Through Christ we have received every great and precious promise. If you haven't received what the Lord has promised, you may want to ask yourself in you are in-Christ. Find yourself in the Word of God and test yourself to see if you are in the faith. It is not about our modern belief of "*Oh, I believe there is a God*"; it is a belief that becomes certain by the works that God is doing in your life, so that through those *works* you may participate in the divine nature and escape the corruption in the world caused by evil desires.

> *People are trying to move this country in a different direction, but I believe someone in the carpool forgot to pick up Jesus.*

INFLUENCE OF THE WORLD

> ***The teaching of God's Word opens a doorway for the filling of purposeful desire.***
> ***The Word of God was not only created to be read, but to be engraved on the heart and read by God Himself through you.***

Jesus said, *Why is it people of faith can call out my name among other people of faith, but are so timid of glorifying it around those who lack in faith? Christians have the obligation to speak and preserve the lost, but somehow Christians have become lost, because they are preserving their obligation to speak.*

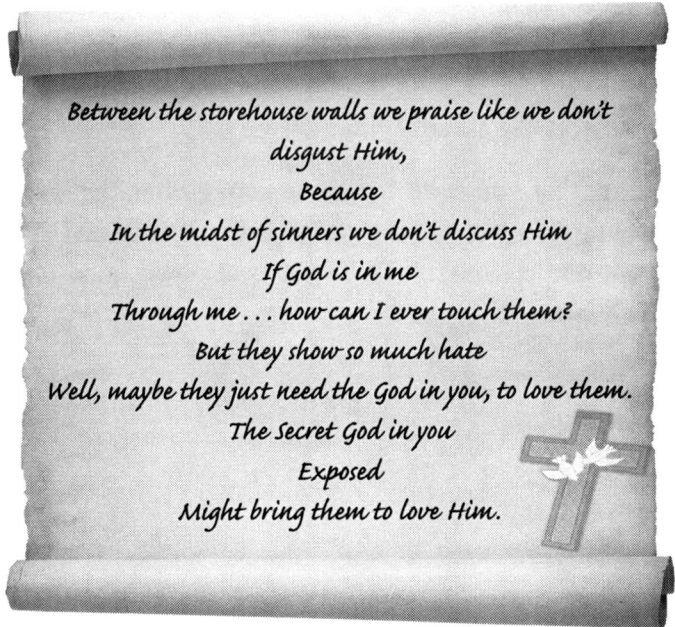

Between the storehouse walls we praise like we don't disgust Him,
Because
In the midst of sinners we don't discuss Him
If God is in me
Through me . . . how can I ever touch them?
But they show so much hate
Well, maybe they just need the God in you, to love them.
The Secret God in you
Exposed
Might bring them to love Him.

Jesus said to me, Your *testimony will be the example of My grace, your life will express My truth, and your words will reflect "The Way," but if you never open your mouth, I will never be heard.* The Bible is a history, made to be able to repeat history, which is God Himself clarifying what I did before I can do it again. If you fear Me, it is impossible to fear the world. You build your life on the Word of God, and how your faith is strengthened will depend on where you stand. At what point do you realize you have an unwavering faith? It's when you no longer have to move the mountains, but because of your faith, the mountains begin to move themselves.

Christians maintain the outlet to impart God's power.

This means that you have the same capabilities that heal, deliver, release, and guide people into and through the visions and principles of the Word, because the Word that is in you is as powerful as the God who works through you.

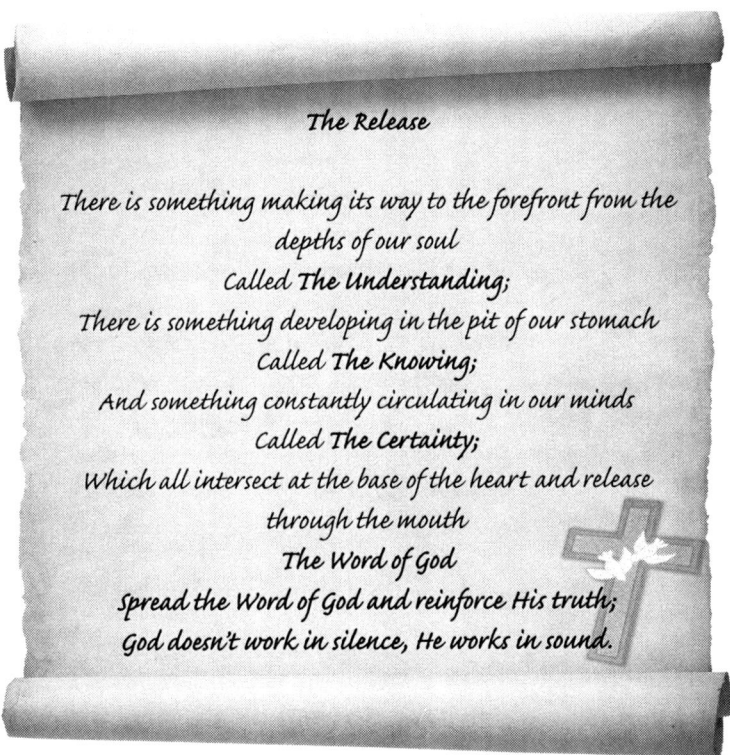

The Release

There is something making its way to the forefront from the depths of our soul
*Called **The Understanding**;*
There is something developing in the pit of our stomach
*Called **The Knowing**;*
And something constantly circulating in our minds
*Called **The Certainty**;*
Which all intersect at the base of the heart and release through the mouth
The Word of God
Spread the Word of God and reinforce His truth;
God doesn't work in silence, He works in sound.

I had a job back when I first started high school, and I can remember clearly two girls having a conversation about God. One of my section managers stopped the girls and said, *"Ladies, this isn't a discussion we have here."* I didn't have any type of relationship with God then, but for me to remember that three-minute conversation means that it had a purpose that I definitely understand now—that Christians are being silenced. Did you know that communists' main reason for atheism is the power it gives them to destroy individual moral sense and independence? This means that a heart without an atheistic covering would never permit an atheist leader to overpower or marionette individuals who have become mindless, subordinate, and inactive in hope. The question is, has America let a state of communism slip in the backdoor, because a communist's way of demanding atheism is *"man's"* power to control *men*?

When the World Says We Can No Longer Speak of God Confidently

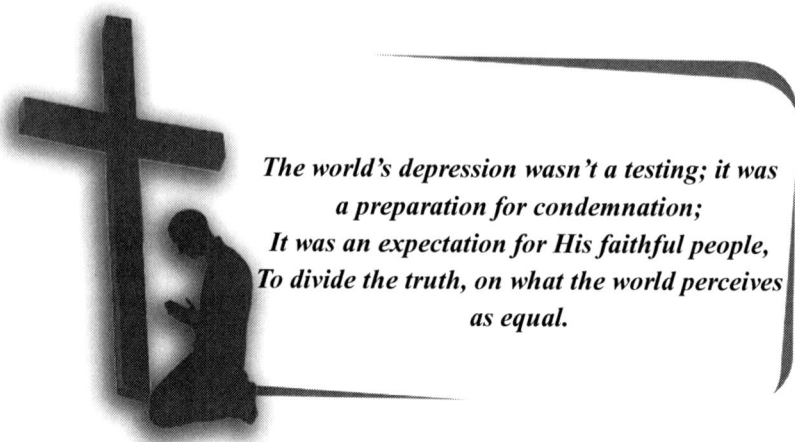

The world's depression wasn't a testing; it was a preparation for condemnation;
It was an expectation for His faithful people,
To divide the truth, on what the world perceives as equal.

When a teacher, manager, or government personnel says that you can no longer speak about religion or Jesus in the workplace, what exactly is he really implying? He is saying it is no longer logical or appropriate to speak about these: The Hope, The Peace, The Salvation, The Moral Excellence, The Concrete Character, The Fact . . . that the Lord is all we need, and undoubtedly all we have. The government has situated Christians into a marionette—categorizing our freedom of expression, our will to live in liberty, and giving us a choice of peace or persecution.

This worldly misfortune was a prepared recession,
in a Godly opportunity for a Kingdom progression.

You can talk about God briefly, but you cannot say the name of Jesus. What this means is you can believe in peace, but you cannot talk about how to receive it. You can believe in life, but you can't know Who it is that will allow you to live. Strangely enough, the conforming world is now saying we cannot say the name of Jesus because it identifies a particular religion, and it shows no equality.

> *Quoting mankind's philosophy pulling the Word of life from the root.*
> *Traditional theology, claiming more condemnation than we know what to do.*
> *Historical studies not bringing certainty but it is a system of dispute.*
> *He who has an ear, let him hear*
> *Social confusion, our thoughts and intentions are screaming out "delude."*
> *Enthusiasts and scholars spiritually dead, no familiarity of the gift that was left by the Father according to the Book of Luke.*
> *Woe to him who follows the blind*
> *Civilized knowledge what a vain deceit, without grace, imagine the wrath when the mercy seat is departing from you.*
> *Human mythology, speaking death into those vulnerable mentalities sitting in the pew.*
> *Brainwashing psychology, not the same cleansing that's brought from Psalms 51:2.*
> *Demonology provoking lawlessness, knowing the time of judgment is soon.*
> *The doctrine of Christ the only regeneration that converts the old into a new.*
> *But you have chosen the world; therefore you'll stay divided from truth.*

What is the common principle of progress? Jesus Christ has paid the price for us to have a chance at eternity. We are in His debt, which simply means we owe Him our life, which is a common principle in the Word of God, because without turning our life over to Him, all we will know is going through the motions of life, and never actually progressing in life. The liberty of human rights is a choice of following or not following the Word of God. Nobody forces you to make that decision. It is a decision that's made with a free will that God Himself has left for you to live in life or to live in death.

Start breaking statistics with choices.

Mr. President, you said that you will keep this nation in your prayers. So will I, but most often we pray to have wisdom and a mind to have life, but in contrast, we should possess the mind of Jesus's death to have knowledge on how it is we're able to have *life*! Mr. President, there is no in-between with Christianity; it is Christlike, not Christ-somewhat. You may not plead among the nations who the only Savior is, you may not address the glory of God among your own nation, but one day I promise you, you will! Whatever you do, never count yourself out on feeling the presence of God. One of two things will happen—you will fall before the Cross or the Cross will fall before you. You will bow before God out of pure love or you will be compelled to bow before Him broken in torment. You will shout the name Jesus because of His grace or you will cry out

His name in hope of mercy. Either way, every tongue will confess and every knee will bow! (Phil. 2:10-11)

I am quite mystified by our president because He continues to exclaim that he is Christlike. So why is it that our president will talk about Christianity in America, talk about the holy Quran in Cairo to the Muslims, and talk about Buddha to the Buddhists? Everywhere he goes he says, "I will only speak the truth." What truth are you speaking about? Mr. President, you said this regarding equality: "Peace . . . to love our God . . . this is the hope of all humanity. *Our failure to meet them will hurt us all.*" I believe someone above is trying to speak to the Christlike image you claim to illustrate so well. Mr. President, how can you be a Christian by going against God's Word? How can you be Christlike without representing any of His characteristics—claiming you are a Christian while standing on foreign soil uttering false scripture of misleading and counterfeit gods? There is one name given to men under heaven. There is one holy scripture that is God breathed! Yet you condemn people by joyful declarations of unity, but keep the name of Jesus a million miles away from their lives. I will pray for you, Mr. President.

You shouted with a smile that America has had the greatest progress the world has ever known. Thank God for that, my friend. Had the Holy Spirit not guided the apostle Paul toward the West, rather than toward the East, then the power of the Gospel and the foundation of God would have never been laid here in America. This country is the only nation in the world that established a covenant with God as "one nation under God." Freedom, prosperity, and privilege are based solely in the hands of God. We as people, we as reserved lands, are meant to live in equality and as an undivided people as nations under God. Wait! But now the vein is being ripped out of the body, and this nation is slowly dying because we have turned our back on God and have become a self-interested nation.

Dear Jesus,

If you are the Savior, why did you allow so many students to die over the last several years through school terrorism? Why has there been bloodshed and over fifty-eight school slayings between 2006-2009 in schools across America?—students being shot, students being stabbed, teachers being killed, teachers committing suicide, faculty and students being wounded, mass homicides occurring right in our very own school hallways, and high school massacres. I thought you were our Deliver and our Redeemer? Why is gun violence in our schools at an all-time high? Why are athletic coaches being shot by their own student-athletes? Why are children under the age of thirteen being murdered in school? Why?

Dear student,

I am no longer allowed in schools.

Dear Jesus,

If you are the Savior, why are there so many people losing their lives at their workplace?—robbers killing store clerks over fifty dollars, thieves stabbing customers over jewelry, multiple homicides in local family grocery stores, armed men opening fire at fast-food chains. Jesus, where are you? So many people are losing their jobs. So many people are unemployed. Jesus, where are you?

Dear employee,

I have been banned from the workforce.

Dear Jesus,

If you are the Savior, then why is our country in such crisis? Why has the stock market become the biggest economic threat and still being ignored? Why is America's financial future at risk? Why are our leaders lacking economic responsibility? Why are our leaders being led astray? Why is our president supporting the unity of world religion? Why is America, one of the most powerful nations in all of history, beginning to plummet?

Dear world,

I am no longer allowed in government ruling.

**I Am Not Ashamed of the Gospel,
For the Gospel is the Power of God!**

Romans 1:16: "I am not ashamed of the Gospel, because it is the power of God for the salvation of everyone who believes . . ."

> The Epistle of Paul (a servant of Christ Jesus, called to be an apostle and set apart for the Gospel of God) to all of Rome. Paul is praying to those in Rome because their faith is beginning to grow and be reported around the world. Paul begins to write to these believers and says, "I hope by the will of God He will allow me to come to you to impart some spiritual gifts to make you strong. Also so we can get together and be encouraged by each other's faith. Now, it is time for me to come to you, because I am obligated to both the wise and the foolish, to the Greeks and non-Greeks . . . The gospel must be spread to everyone, but the belief is up to them!

2 Thessalonians 3:1: "Finally, brothers, pray for us that the message of the Lord may spread rapidly and be honored, just as it was with you."

The First Epistle of Paul—an apostle of Christ—to the church of the Thessalonians. (*Refer 2* Thess. 3:1-14.) The apostles requested the need for prayer for both themselves and the church of the Thessalonians that they may be delivered from wicked and evil men, for not everyone has faith. Praying that the Lord may direct their hearts into God's love and Christ's perseverance. Then commanding to keep away from every brother who is idle and does not live according to the teaching you received from the Word of God. Do not associate with wicked men, in order that he may feel ashamed. Preach the Word to wicked men and do not regard him as an enemy, but warn him as a brother.

Revelation 12:9: *"The great dragon was hurled down—the ancient serpent called the devil, or Satan, who leads the world astray."*

The Revelation of Jesus Christ, which God gave him to show his servants what must soon take place. (*Refer Rev. 12:1-12.*) The accounts of Satan and his angels being cast down out of heaven. Satan who brings the world into ruins and leads men astray will work fast to deceive and manipulate men and he is filled with fury, because he knows that his time is short. The only way for salvation is by the power and the kingdom of our God, and the authority of his Christ.

Proverbs 28:2: *"When a country is rebellious, it has many rulers, but a man of understanding and knowledge maintains order."*

The purpose of the Proverbs of Solomon, the son of David, king of Israel, is to know wisdom and instruction, knowledge and discretion. (*Refer Prov. 28:1-28.*) (1) The wicked man flees though no one pursues, but the righteous are as bold as a lion. (3) A ruler who oppresses the poor is like a driving rain that leaves no crops. (4) Those who forsake the law praise the wicked, but those who keep the law resist them. (5) Evil men do not understand justice, but those who seek the Lord understand it fully. (7) He who keeps the law is a discerning son, but a companion of gluttons disgraces his father. (9) If anyone turns a deaf ear to the law, even his prayers are detestable. (10) He who leads the upright along an evil path will fall into his own trap, but the blameless will receive a good inheritance. (12) When the righteous triumph, there is great elation; but when the wicked rise to power, men go into hiding. (15) Like a roaring lion or a charging bear is a wicked man ruling over a helpless people. (16) A tyrannical ruler lacks judgment, but he who hates ill-gotten gain will enjoy a long life. (25) A greedy man stirs up dissension, but he who trusts in the Lord will prosper. (28) When the wicked rise to power, people go into hiding; but when the wicked perish, the righteous thrive.

Proverbs 26:25: "Though his speech is charming, do not believe him, for seven abominations will fill his heart."

The purpose of the Proverbs of Solomon, the son of David, king of Israel, is to know wisdom and instruction, knowledge and discretion. (*Refer Prov. 26:1-28.*) (4) Do not answer a fool according to his folly, or you will be like him yourself. (6) Like cutting off one's feet or drinking violence is the sending of a message by the hand of a fool. (8) Like tying a stone in a sling is the giving of honor to a fool. (9) As a dog returns to its vomit, so a fool repeats his folly. (12) Do you see a man wise in his own eyes? There is more hope for a fool than for him. (24) A malicious man disguises himself with his lips, but in his heart he harbors deceit. (26) His malice may be concealed by deception, but his wickedness will be exposed in the assembly. (27) If a man digs a pit, he will fall into it; if a man rolls a stone, it will roll back on him.

Conclusion

On My Way Home

*I have seen hell standing in front of me, but something within
me convinced me that my best days were still ahead of me.*

The main cause for God leading me through this book was solely to give insight and revelation to the billions of people who are new believers or are struggling to believe, who sit in church every Sunday and all they hear about is change, prosperity, joy, happiness, peace, and financial freedom. Yet they never experience it. This is because they are never told about or prepared for the difficult struggle that they will face the moment they turn from their everyday living outside of God's will and acknowledge Jesus. Let's not get this misunderstood, because it is an amazing sequence when generation upon generation stand behind the pulpit and deliver God's Word to His people; on the other hand, there are so many people born into ministry preaching about happiness who have never had a firsthand experience of what it is like to never know God, never be in church, and never read God's Word. This is why God is raising up an abnormal generation. Before my happiness, not only did I find myself in the prayer of my life, but I found myself in the battle of my life. You may say, well, the moment you go to God you will be happy. No! The moment you go to God it will be strenuous, but it's His way of demonstrating His love for you with His methods of change, which makes it seem like God is a million miles away from you. If I am out in the middle of the ocean drowning and I yell for a life preserver, I am not happy the moment I receive the life preserver, because I am still in rough waters fighting for my last breath. I am happy once I am in the boat away from the waters that were once trying to take me under. The problem is the majority of churches today are tossing the preserver, but never explaining how it is you will find yourself in the boat. There is an uncomfortable stage that you will go through the moment you call on God to change your life. The reason why you become uncomfortable, feel alone, and feel lost is because God has started a process of removing your comfort zones and your people of comfort, just to make Himself your only comfort. Yes, it takes time! The greatest breakthrough in your life is when you let Jesus break through in your life.

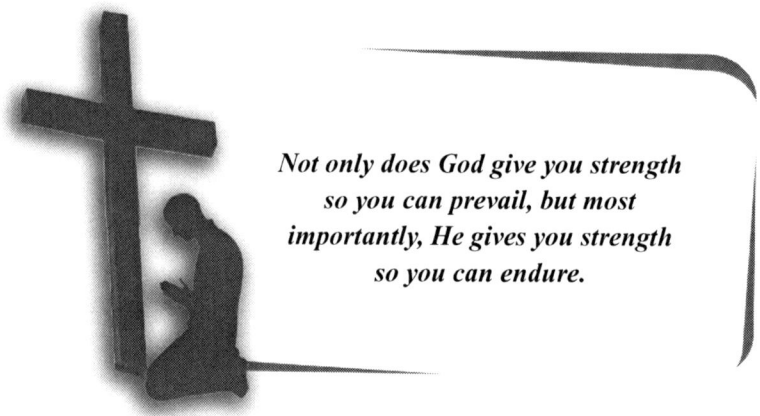

Not only does God give you strength so you can prevail, but most importantly, He gives you strength so you can endure.

I am living with somebody I shouldn't live with, I have so many bills to pay for, I am so lonely, I am depressed, and I am hurting. Understand this: You work God in to be able to work everything out. If you don't trust in Him, you will always be in the position that you are in. You must trust in God even when your entire world is falling. Hebrews 11:1 says this: *"Faith is being sure of what you hope for and certain of what you do not see."* Not only does that mean Jesus, but this also means your day of peace, your togetherness, your perfect love, the solid rock you will stand on. You must have faith in the day you hope for and must fight for that day of hope, which you have put your faith in. Trusting God is going where He tells you to go with no details. The number one cause for giving up on God within a short period of time is the misconception of thinking God is not answering you, or He has not heard your prayer. God will always work in assignments, because not only it allows you to develop as a child of God and grow in faith after the assignment, but it builds trust in Him by you acting according to His Word even when it appears to be illogical. Meaning, if you call on God to do something in your life and you are constantly hearing, "The person who you are with is a hindrance for what God is trying to do for you," then what God is trying to tell you is this: "Detach yourself from the person who is holding you back, and then I will tell you what to do from there."

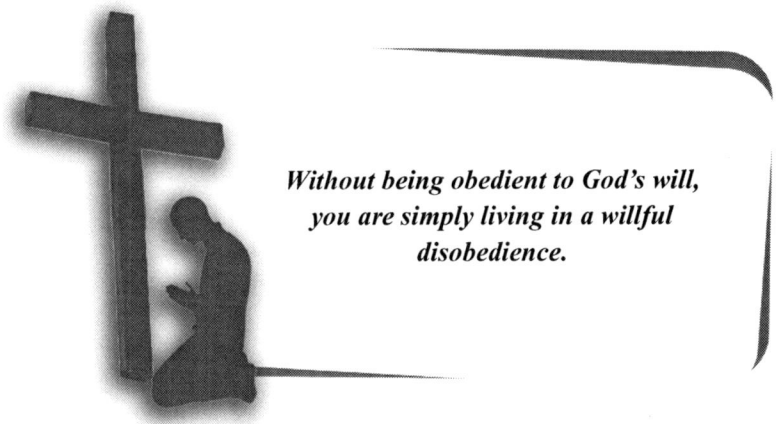

Without being obedient to God's will, you are simply living in a willful disobedience.

If you want to know God, you must know His Word because they are one. How can you do anything that pleases God if you never know what pleases Him? How can you possibly know what God guarantees for your life if you've never read His promises? The problem with people today is that they have so many questions for God, yet never take the time to read His answers. I had a conversation with a man not too long ago who went through a list of questions he had concerning God, and each one started out with "I don't believe." I let him conclude his fallible theory and then I asked him a very short question, "Have you ever read the Bible?" He said, "No." Then I sat there and answered his entire list of questions, and his response to each of my answers was this: "I didn't know that." This is the point that I am getting at: in order for God to become apparent in your life it will all based on your faith and your belief system. We are all dealt a measure of faith; the problem is it lies dormant until it is awakened.

We are all congested with confounded beliefs throughout our life, but in order to reveal what is real, we must get to the core of our belief system. The Word of God will change your belief system because it is revelation. Revelation comes with conviction because it leads you into truth. Once you have the truth you will repent because you will never want to do all the things you've always done. If you don't do what you've always done, you will develop a new characteristic. This characteristic has the character of Christ—being Christlike. How then does God become evident? God becomes evident when your character matches your belief system.

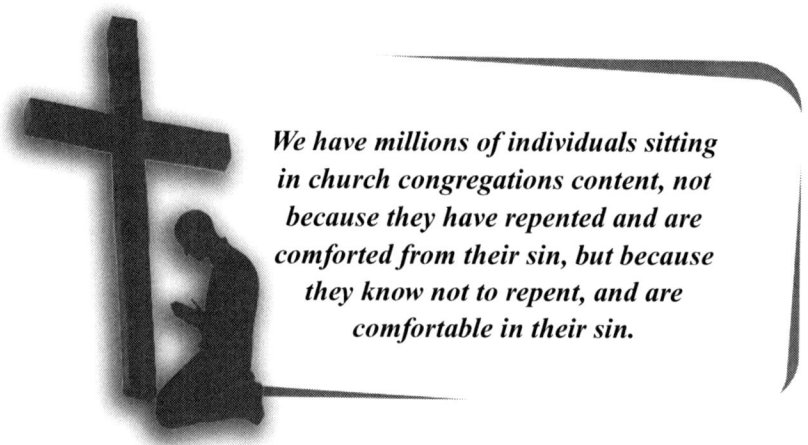

We have millions of individuals sitting in church congregations content, not because they have repented and are comforted from their sin, but because they know not to repent, and are comfortable in their sin.

Do not allow the word "saved" to lead you into condemnation. There are three elements of being "saved," which have absolutely nothing to do with a repetitive prayer you pray. How are we born again of water and of Spirit? Through Jesus—by faith, believing God, loving God, being obedient, and carrying out His commands. (1 Pet. 1:13-25.) Jesus says that no one will enter the kingdom of God unless He is born of water and of the Spirit (John 3). We learn in 1 Peter 3:21 that "Jesus is the baptism," and in 1 John 5 that everyone who believes that Jesus is the Christ *is born* of God. Being born again is taking away the old to bring in the new. It is not a confession where you are forgiven of sins; it is an acknowledgement that you have already been forgiven of your sins. This does not mean that you will enter the kingdom of God; it simply means that now you have a chance to be able to enter the kingdom of God. You have been saved from your old lifestyle and brought into a new way of living, but there is a lot more willful obedience to be understood. The second element of "saved" is living your life according to God's Word. This simply means that you are married to the Word of God and loyal to the Body of Christ. How you find yourself backsliding or outside of being "saved" is when you are in a married life, living single. Everything that we do after the point of calling and crying out to God must be worthy of the Gospel. How do we find ourselves through justification and into sanctification?—by being obedient toward God's commands and by consistently following His Word. The third element of "saved" is when you are sealed with glorification and have entered into the kingdom of God because you have found favor in His eyes. In the words of Bishop Tony Miller, "You were saved, you're being saved, and you will be saved."

We are in a time where we crave information, but are not obedient enough to gain the knowledge.

We will put on our breastplate of righteousness and our helmet of salvation but the majority of us are too scared to pick up our sword! Not only were we made to fight, but never forget . . . we were made to conquer. The kingdom of God is built by those who fight! We are put into a position where either the enemy can profit from our weakness or we can profit from our enemy by strengthening what he exposes as our weakness. Don't be defiled by the word of tradition, but find yourself pleading in hope that your stoned heart can be reconciled to God. I speak about the wrath of God because it is what makes me tremble. I speak about a just God because it is what keeps me cautious. I speak about sin because it is the epitome of hell. Sin is the most appalling act of violence anyone can do before the grace of God. People continue to say how afraid they are of going to hell, not realizing that sin is the substance of God's wrath. Stop saying God will save me from going to hell! Hell is not hell because God isn't there. Hell is hell because God is there! Hell is the dwelling of God's wrath for people because of sin! Yes, God's grace is indescribable, but it is given to you feely as a gift the moment when you become overwhelmed with the fear of being condemned. Fear is what opens up the cloud for grace to fall over your life. Fear will draw conviction and a hatred for everything God hates. You will literally see before your own eyes the darkest parts of your life being poured out along with your tears. The Bible has set something so significant in front of me: the grace of God and the wrath of God; a loving God and a just God; and eternal life and condemnation. Are you beginning to understand the sequence? The Bible is meant to drive a marker of fear in your way of living, which makes you tremble at the thought of a just God who finds you shameful in His eyes. How do you establish God's gift of grace in your life? Easy, when the fear of God's Word abides in you and you refuse to allow the presence of God to get away from you. My firmness comes directly from a place of love standing on the Word of God, whose sacred writing will never be withered away. I can't even begin to explain God's love because I would fall short of describing how much love God has toward His children of faith. God's love is demonstrated throughout our lives on a daily basis, where we are given a merciful chance to turn from sin and find favor in God's eyes.

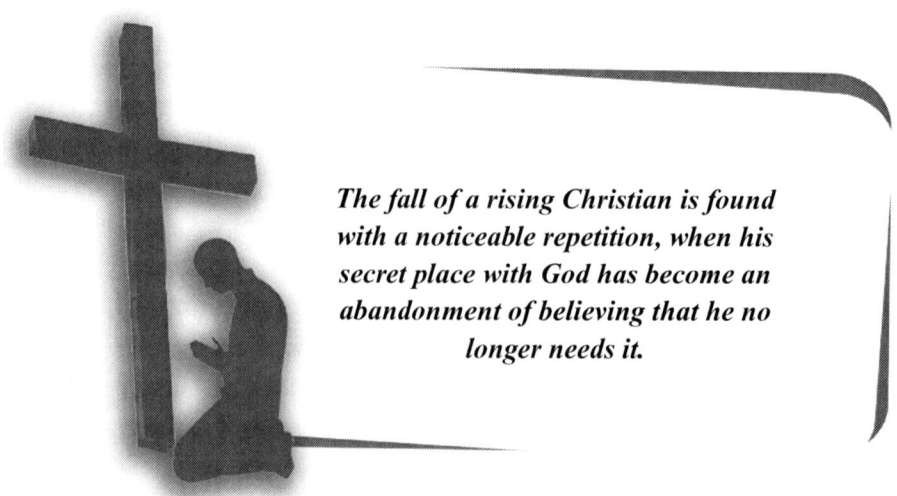

The fall of a rising Christian is found with a noticeable repetition, when his secret place with God has become an abandonment of believing that he no longer needs it.

Why are we crying over pitiless suffering? Do we not know that God raises up warriors, missionaries, and prophets during times of tribulation? Do we not know that it is when we bear the afflictions of Christ that it is God's way of saying *I trust in you*? I labor in prayer. I toil in intercession. I dwell in conviction. I am awakened in repentance. My faith sustains anguish because I am at eye level with the Cross. My belief drives me to my knees. The grace of God brings me to my feet. I am guarded by heaven; this means I am being prepared for war. I bear the afflictions of Christ because I am sponsored by God's trust. How can we as people of faith have such a desire for God—praying men pleading for God to use them, and weeping women falling before the Cross asking God to do something different in their lives? So why is it that when God turns around and places you on the battlefield this strong desire all of a sudden dies? Allow Jesus to be enthroned on your heart, and around your heart allow the Holy Spirit to build the walls of a temple. Then establish a faith that will shoot iron arrows from your mouth at the enemy and a belief system that will protect the name of God from being blasphemed, and the Word of God from exporting heresy. *It is your duty.* You *must* protect your *fortress*!

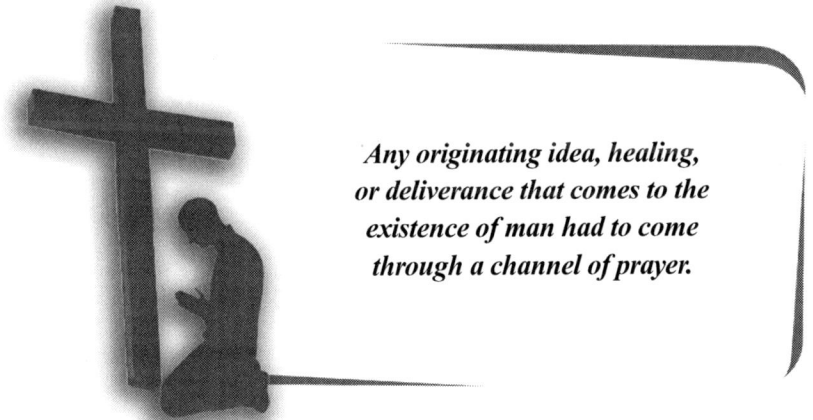

Any originating idea, healing, or deliverance that comes to the existence of man had to come through a channel of prayer.

Sick and tired of life? This world is defined on an individual basis, with individual desires, at an individual rate. The world is enriched by self-request on a wavering scale that is formatted on unstable grounds. This perplexity of sudden changes is an illness without God and prayer we call "the world in motion sickness." Prayer is what becomes the stillness to your life, called

"God above *all* the world in motion." How important is our prayer life? Prayer shouldn't sound rehearsed; it should sound like a dire need, a cry. In all honesty, it's simply conversation. It's not a presentation; it is a cry of pardon until the interceding of the Holy Spirit falls on you to supernaturally assist you. Are you sincere? The Holy Spirit will communicate through your pain. The unveiling of God's answers in our lives has never been within a routine prayer. Prayer is what keeps God close. God never leaves us; without prayer we tend to always drift away from Him. Prayer is what keeps you heavily guarded by heaven and encamped with angels. You can be surrounded by thousands of people, and still without God and prayer you will be standing alone. You can enlighten yourself simply by indulging your faith with requests that are answered by God. With prayer you begin to notice that it is hard to go back when there is so much to look forward to. Prayer is what invited me into the Trinity Church International revival. Yes, a revival starts off with people and children of God who have fallen asleep on their walk of faith that escalates into an awakening. It is a tremendous reign of love, Spirit, and grace where there will also be a conversion of lost souls. Moreover, we do not need an awakening caused by a revival; we need a nightmare of conviction to wake us up and draw us into repentance. *"My fire is dying down and I need a revival."* No! You don't create a revival and a move of God; you are invited into it! Repentance will have you weeping in your sin, which will then have you pleading for a change that will stir up the Spirit of God to fall on you. It will then generate not only a move of God, but a reign and rule over your life. A revival happens when that process becomes a domino effect! Prayer has made me so grateful, praying not for what God is going to do to my life, but in thanks for what He has already done for my life.

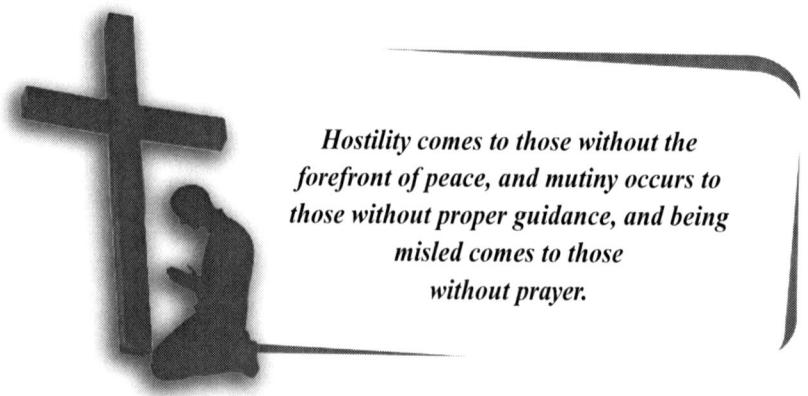

Hostility comes to those without the forefront of peace, and mutiny occurs to those without proper guidance, and being misled comes to those without prayer.

I thank the Lord for continuing to bury me in His baptism, while I'm abounding in faith, standing firm on the rock He is elevating beneath me. My desire is for You, God, and I plead for You to show me mercy for everything that I have ever done to dishonor Your name. Even if I cannot find favor in Your presence, I will still spend the rest of my life serving You because You are worthy of honor and loyalty. You are all I have, Lord. You are all I can call on. I will devote my life to following You. Let me rise, O Lord! Please don't leave me. Lord, You are the greatest thing I have ever been a part of in my entire life. It is unimaginable the journey You have taken me on. It is unthinkable to comprehend why You didn't let me die in the pit of hell I dwelled in. It is unexplainable how such a divine conversion of love can make you whole again. Even if tomorrow were never to come, I would lie down elated with angels on my mind. I am so overwhelmed at the chance of getting to know You, Lord, because it gave me a chance to know myself. At times, concerning my family, I feel as Jesus did when approaching the city of Jerusalem. He began to drown Himself in sorrow, viewing a city that was lacking peace and being overwhelmed by its enemies. He saw what could and should be a powerful city. He saw what no one else could see. In my family I see this invisible power hidden behind massive stones. My only request as I've cried out to you, Lord, is that you would deliver my family . . . and in the midst of my cry, I found myself in the prayer of my life . . . because now the life of my family depends on it.

+

Further Reading

emedicine from WebMD. (2008). Rhabdomyolysis. Retrieved January 22, 2009, from http://emedicine.medscape.com/article/1007814-overview

emedicine from WebMD. (2009). Malnutrition. Retrieved January 20, 2009, from http://emedicine.medscape.com/article/985140-overview

Concrete. (1995). Albert and Loy Morehead (Eds), The New American Webster Handy College Dictionary (3rd ed, p. 148). New York, New York: New American Library.

Valor. (1995). Albert and Loy Morehead (Eds), The New American Webster Handy College Dictionary (3rd ed, p. 718). New York, New York: New American Library.

Lot. (1995). Albert and Loy Morehead (Eds), The New American Webster Handy College Dictionary (3rd ed, p. 405). New York, New York: New American Library.

Illusion. (1995). Albert and Loy Morehead (Eds), The New American Webster Handy College Dictionary (3rd ed, p. 345). New York, New York: New American Library.

Delusion. (1995). Albert and Loy Morehead (Eds), The New American Webster Handy College Dictionary (3rd ed, p. 185). New York, New York: New American Library.

Center for American Progress. (2007). Number of US population below poverty. Retrieved January 20, 2009, from http://www.americanprogress.org/issues/2007/04/poverty_numbers.html

BBC News. (2008). Rwanda genocide. Retrieved January 20, 2009, from http://news.bbc.co.uk/2/hi/africa/1288230.stm

UNICEF. (2008). State of the world's children, 2008—Child survival. Retrieved January 20, 2009, from http://www.unicef.org/sowc08/

UNICEF. (2007). Child protection from violence, exploitation and abuse. Retrieved January 20, 2009, from http://www.unicef.org/protection/index_exploitation.html

Expressindia.com. (2008). 100 mn children forced to live in streets: UN. Retrieved January 20, 2009, from http://www.expressindia.com/latest-news/100-mn-children-forced-to-live-in-streets-UN/287763/

National Incidence Studies of Missing, Abducted, Runaway, and Thrownaway Children (NISMART-2). (October 2002). Retrieved January 20, 2009, from http://www.ncjrs.gov/pdffiles1/ojjdp/196465.pdf.

RAINN. (2007). Statistics. Retrieved July 26, 2009, from http://www.rainn.org/statistics

Child Welfare Information Gateway. (2009). Child abuse and neglect fatalities: Statistics and interventions—Numbers and trends. Retrieved January 20, 2009, from *http://www.childwelfare.gov/pubs/factsheets/fatality.cfm#children*

DrugWarFacts.org. (2000). Annual causes of death in the United States. Retrieved January 20, 2009, from *http://drugwarfacts.org/cms/?q=node/30#item1*

Edgar Snyder & Associates. (2008). Drunk driving accident statistics. Retrieved January 20, 2009, from http://www.edgarsnyder.com/auto-accident/drunk-driving/statistics.html

Guttmacher Institute. (2008). Abortion. Retrieved January 20, 2009, from http://www.guttmacher.org/sections/abortion.php

State of Food Insecurity in the World. (2008). FAO. Food security statistics. Retrieved January 20, 2009, from *www.fao.org/es/ess/faostat/foodsecurity/index_en.htm*

Cozay.com. (2008). Extreme poverty in Africa. Retrieved January 20, 2009, from http://cozay.com/

Education Human Development Resource. (2006). Press briefing: Education for all fast track initiative. Retrieved January 20, 2009, from http://web.worldbank.org/WBSITE/EXTERNAL/TOPICS/EXTEDUCATION/0, contentMDK:20898169~menuPK:282429~pagePK:64020865~piPK:149114~theSitePK:282386,00.html

Psychiatric Nursing. (2007). Assisting nursing faculty through the crisis and resolution of student suicide. Retrieved January 20, 2009, from http://www.psychiatricnursing.org/article/S0883-9417(06)00225-1/abstract

Socyberty. (2009). A child's cry: Abuse and neglect of children. Retrieved January 20, 2009, from *http://socyberty.com/crime/a-child%e2%80%99s-cry-abuse-and-neglect-of-children/*

About.com. (2008). Alcoholism. Retrieved January 20, 2009, from http://adam.about.com/reports/000056_2.htm

Thomas M. Kiley & Associates, LLP. (2008). Drunk driving glossary for Massachusetts (Part A). Retrieved January 20, 2009, from http://www.tomkileylaw.com/library/oui-crash-injury-attorney-boston-personal-injury-lawyer-boston.cfm

Yohannan, K. P. (2004). *Revolution in World Missions*. Texas: GFA Books.

Breinigsville, PA USA
17 March 2011
257900BV00002B/4/P